Race, Law, and Speculative Fiction

RACE, LAW, AND SPECULATIVE FICTION

Future Pasts

Isiah Lavender III

PENN

UNIVERSITY OF PENNSYLVANIA PRESS

PHILADELPHIA

Published by
University of Pennsylvania Press
Philadelphia, Pennsylvania 19104–4112 USA
www.pennpress.org

EU Authorized Representative: Easy Access System Europe—Mustamäe tee 50, 10621 Tallinn, Estonia, gpsr.requests@easproject.com.

Printed in the United States of America on acid-free paper
10 9 8 7 6 5 4 3 2 1

A Cataloging-in-Publication record is available from the Library of Congress

Hardcover ISBN 978-1-5128-2933-4
eBook ISBN 978-1-5128-2934-1

Heather, Always

How does it feel to be a problem?

—W. E. B. Du Bois, *The Souls of Black Folk*

CONTENTS

Introduction. Future Pasts: The SF Double Novum, Law, and Repetitions of White Supremacy 1

PART I. IMAGINARY AMENDMENTS, JUDICIAL DECISIONS, AND EXECUTIVE ORDERS: RACE IN US SCIENCE FICTION

Chapter 1. Precursor *Noirums* 19

Chapter 2. Confinement Narratives 49

Chapter 3. BLM+ Speculations and the *Noirum* 86

PART II. EXPLORATIONS OF ANTIRACISM

Chapter 4. Cyberfunk 123

Chapter 5. The Lost Race Tales of Edgar Allan Poe and Mat Johnson 156

Outro. Science Fiction and Racism: Decolonizing the White Problem 203

Notes 221

Works Cited 229

Index 247

Acknowledgments 257

INTRODUCTION

Future Pasts: The SF Double Novum, Law, and Repetitions of White Supremacy

> "What good is science fiction to Black People?" . . . What good is any form of literature for Black people? What good is science fiction's thinking about the present, the future, and the past? What good is its tendency to warn or to consider alternative ways of thinking and doing? What good is its examination of the possible effects of science and technology, or social organization and political direction? At its best science fiction stimulates imagination and creativity. It gets reader and writer off the beaten track, off the narrow, narrow footpath of what "everyone" is saying, doing, thinking—whoever "everyone" happens to be this year.
>
> And what good is all this to Black people?
>
> —Octavia E. Butler, "Positive Obsession"

Here's the thing: while the *noirum* does not yet exist in science fiction or Afrofuturist scholarship, it is a critical race theory that enhances the more conventional tools of the social justice discipline. Simply defined, the *noirum* represents the initial legal response by some kind of government body to a science fictional event that generates the storyworld envisioned by its author. The term refers to the legislative innovations prompted within the fictional world to cope with, if not to control, the impact of the novum. But the *noirum* is not restricted to just that, rather the neologism helps identify specific ways in which recognized science fiction (SF) tropes (such as alien contact, time travel, contagion, generation starships, the near future, alternate history, climate change, and defamiliarization, among others) are actually organized around questions of race. By working through the logic of their hegemony as powerful SF motifs, shaped by cognitive estrangement and its novum, it transforms them. As such, the *noirum* is a kind of second or second-order novum, a new thing effecting not only a critical estrangement simply but an estrangement of race and the way we think about race. Adopting some key tenets of critical race theory (CRT)—the actual body of critical-theoretical work, rather than the frenzied ravings of the American right—I focus primarily on an array of texts in which the impact of the novum is distributed through diegetic legal interventions/frameworks.

Particularly, using CRT alongside analysis of and through the *noirum* in science fiction turns out to be tricky because of the genre's historic lack of attention to BIPOC voices. "In order to bring critical race theory into conversations about . . . literature, media, fandom, and popular culture," as African American literacy education scholar Ebony Elizabeth Thomas suggests, "counterstories, or alternative narratives, must be foregrounded" (*Dark*, 10). An elegant thought, not easily executed because science fiction, largely written by white people, and more frequently white men, often presents a colorblind future. From this viewpoint, knowing SF's cultural history becomes important in understanding how the genre has changed and why it is still changing as BIPOCs imagine their own futures. We must first recognize a longstanding master narrative in SF—Black and Brown people have no future. This story has been written so often, has been viewed on the silver screen so often, has been multiply repeated so often that some people have come to believe it—namely white people. Consequently, we must learn to excavate race from the genre's "blackground" (Lavender, *Race*, 6).[1] This term spotlights the deep-rooted perceptions of race and racism; it brings both the unintentional and deliberate prejudices, stereotypes, and antagonisms to our conscious attention so that we may begin telling counter-stories. As Richard Delgado proclaims, "stories can shatter complacency and challenge the status quo" ("Storytelling," 72). Then and only then can we challenge a monochrome worldview by "listening to the voices of people of color as the basis for understanding how race and racism function" (Cook and Dixson, "Writing," 1243). Essentially, the *noirum* provides a way of seeing a particular type of counter-story, unlocking it for CRT introspections.

But we will get to that in a moment. Let me first do a bit of science fiction race theorizing.

CRT in SF looks like some kind of executive, judicial, or congressional response from the US government to some kind of science fictional novum, a new thing, invention, or novelty introduced into the fictional world that deliberately functions as the catalyst for the change made in the fictional world, differing from the reader's world. For example, a time travel device or a teleporter. The implications of this "new thing" provide us with a point of departure to explore and experience the new social circumstances that deviate from what we recognize. Derrick Bell's short story "The Space Traders" (1992), represents such a novum to which the American government responds: aliens from outer space descend from the heavens to the US alone. They offer the federal government nuclear fusion as a clean form of energy, gold to wipe out the national debt, and chemicals to clean up the environment itself. They offer these three things in exchange for every Black citizen. The US government responds in kind with the fastest amendment to the constitution ever passed by Congress and ratified by all fifty states to meet the demands of the space traders, thus sending millions of Black Americans to an unknown fate. Bell created this story more than thirty years ago to illustrate not only the privilege of whiteness with this alien contact novum but also the guilt surrounding the slave trade and the racism inherent in our government institutions, which unduly advantage whites in every stage of life.

Not only do I use CRT to examine themes of segregation, prejudice, and racial violence in SF subgenres, I also introduce a new SF-derived theoretical term with which to consider CRT. I find that a second novum *often* occurs in SF narratives in relation to race and ethnicity. This Black double-novum construction represents our ironic departure point between the known and unknown. Ironic because we already know how racism functions in both worlds (real and science fictional). Therefore, I identify and designate this second novum as the *noirum*, the second "new thing" occurring in an SF story prominently, if not exclusively, related to ethno-racial concerns. The *noirum* is a play on words combining the French for "black" with Darko Suvin's science fictional novum. Another important valence of meaning relates to the perception of criminality, corruption, and the pursuit of justice popularized in noir fiction without being noir fiction. The novum and *noirum* go hand in hand in unlocking science fictional worlds for CRT intervention and interpretation. In this regard, the *noirum* helps you see the racism prevalent within the SF world generated by the novum. Returning to Bell's story quickly, the aliens in "The Space Traders" represent the first novum while the constitutional amendment to send Blacks into space with these aliens is the second, the *noirum*. Bell's imaginary twenty-seventh amendment declares: "Without regard to the language or interpretations previously given any other provision of this document, every United States citizen is subject at the call of Congress to selection for special service for periods necessary to protect domestic interests and international needs" (185–186). In this case, the *noirum* represents white privilege, interest convergence, and a warped affirmative action to produce a race draft. White privilege exists in the social construction of race because it too is a fiction, a fiction with the power to distort reality. In Bell's story we see whites take full and unacknowledged social advantage of their access to decision-making power while forcing the Black conservative yes-man Gleason Golightly to represent all Black people from a deprived position. This "invisible package of unearned assets," in the words of Peggy McIntosh, entails lots of benefits that white people may not even know they have such as a presumed superiority, wealth accumulation, and televisual affirmation, as well as Band-Aids, grocery staples or vegan food choices for that matter, and the freedom to speak or to move in unraced normal interactions, safe in their humanity ("White," 10). Experiencing the sensation of whiteness in this way would probably feel uncomfortable in terms of racial description without the familiarity of being used to it as if never having struggled against a built-in and built-up lead conveniently denied.

Don't check out on me. Of course, white people have struggled and worked hard but I am asking everyone to feel their race, not guilt, and know that white people have "greater access" to most things in the USA than BIPOCS do because it has been deliberately institutionalized, willfully sustained, and unthinkingly savored (Kendall, *Diversity*, 62). With their self-interest at stake in the story, whites take decisive action to help themselves get even further ahead while conveniently solving their race problem in unironically seeing color. This imaginary amendment certainly ends Black people, though not discrimination against others who will surely now feel their difference more acutely like women, the disabled, other races and ethnics, the old, and lesbian, gay, bisexual, transgender, queer and/or questioning, intersex, asexual, two-spirit, and the countless affirmative ways in which people choose to self-identify (LGTBQIA2S+).

Anyway, I believe this brief reading of "The Space Traders" represents the effective power of the *noirum*. I believe, in devising this term, that I am providing "academic critics . . . greater authority over science fiction" (Westfahl, "Who," 68). The creation of this new word, a word free of Mark Dery's influence on how race is interpreted in SF, might encourage thinking by others on race beyond Afrofuturism, something that both motivates and excites me. That is not to say Afrofuturism is not an important intervention in SF criticism—it absolutely is—but rather, that there is more than just the Black/white binary to consider. I think "Afrofuturism provides a critical descriptive lens to explore Black culture that questions the commingling of race, science, and technology, with a dash of the supernatural thrown into the mix from a largely African American context which impacts how we perceive literature, music, and film" (Lavender, "Incendiary," 12). "Black people live the estrangement that science fiction writers imagine" according to the late Black culture critic Greg Tate (quoted in Dery, "Black," 212). Let me put it this way, "Afrofuturism has emerged to understand the science fictional existence that blacks have *always* experienced living in the new world—an unreality driven by economic demands, would-be science, and skin color"—something I call science-fictional Blackness (Lavender, *Afrofuturism*, 9). Yet the study of race and racism in SF involves more than just Afrofuturism and that is where the *noirum* comes into play as it breaks down the Du Boisian color line, refracts its many hues, and manifests hope for change for many "raced" human beings in the tomorrows of science fiction.

Let me offer one less obvious example of the *noirum* in action before moving on. Black writer par excellence Toni Morrison creates a science fictional reading experience for her audience in her lone short story "Recitatif" (1983), where her audience is left mystified in trying to figure out the race of her dual protagonists Twyla and Roberta across four decades of palpable racial strife in the USA—the end of segregation, the civil rights movement, landmark Supreme Court decisions, federal actions, assassinations, and the Reagan presidency—as Twyla narrates their series of five encounters, some extended and others brief. Morrison masterfully dives into the heart of racial prejudice in America without revealing which character is Black, thus generating the necessary estrangement essential to SF without being SF itself. Such a move evinces Afrofuturism because it relies on a sense of alienation, social codes, and audience assumptions where readers would very much like to place both people and characters in identity boxes according to race but fail miserably. Morrison explicitly uses American racial codes to perfection. It's genius! Morrison creates a perfect social *noirum* here by playing on her (American) audience's prejudices as Twyla and Roberta interact with each other at an orphanage, a diner, a grocery store, on opposite sides of a picket line, and a final chance encounter at a restaurant on Christmas Eve. Again, we never know the racial identity of either woman, only that one is Black and the other is white. Simply stated, the experience of not knowing which woman is what race feels like a science fictional novum, while the social construction of race that the audience builds and its dismantling in the not knowing is the *noirum*.

Morrison forces us to deal with the unsettling sensation of not knowing the race of her characters. But why? To what end does troubling her readers achieve visibility for our racial hang-ups—darkness made visible? Again, this is a stunning short story. Morrison consciously and effectively wears away at the color line, the Black/white racial divide, centuries old now. And in that discomfort, akin to the Afrofuturist alienation identified by Tate in Dery's influential if problematic "Black to the Future" (1993), generates the *noirum* itself by engaging with this accepted social law that Du Bois presciently outlined as "the problem of the Twentieth Century" (Du Bois, *Souls*, 41). Morrison undermines racial power structures of stereotypes, prejudices, and identity in both their arbitrariness and their reality in demonstrating the harmful consequences of our social hierarchies built upon skin color through the strains of her characters' relationship.

I believe the coining of this new term represents one of my project's major contributions to SF criticism if not the antiracist efforts of critical race studies. Consequently, this book considers many such constructions at varying lengths across a racial-ethnic spectrum of US authors, a multiplicity of literary examples, cascading speculations I hope produce a manifold density of meaning as they increase in number and pool together. I suppose this is my attempt to change the way we read science fiction, fantasy, and horror, trying to make a real substantive change in the workings of the world—freeing us, educating us, bettering us.

That's the Afrofuturist in me. This simple wonder, central to the social project of science fiction, is the best I can offer to end the gloom of institutional racism.

Nonetheless, the pragmatist in me understands how racism functions as a powerful cultural melancholy for white people that masks their fear at a loss of status or, conversely, exposes their anger at the false thought of replacement; maybe, it even demonstrates the arrogance of their colorblind claims. I am not simply pointing here and there and saying "look, racism." That's not very valuable. I *am* locating racial contexts, social categorizations, and cultural patterns in US speculative fictions primarily, with perhaps only one or two excursions outside the political boundaries of what is the United States, with critical race theory to sight the unanticipated things the genre might have to say about race at the crossroads of imaginary laws and how we partake in this imagining. In other words, the *noirum* provides a deeply knowing view of the social and political conditions of our doubly distorted real world resulting from the hypothetical legal variant, whether it is a make-believe amendment, imaginary federal court ruling, fictitious executive order, or something else entirely. The *noirum* does in fact point to new directions for serious appraisals of race and racism between yesterday, today, and tomorrow. I should think that we go into the future as a people united in full colored racial consciousness against dehumanization of any kind.

Contextualizing the *Noirum*

The *noirum* succeeds in acknowledging a multitude of racial experiences layering science fiction's chronology. It begins with the Black experience in the mid-twentieth-century United States, the protest era, and the legal fights on the highest stage backed by the venerable civil rights organization the National Association for the Advancement of Colored People (NAACP). That is, the *noirum* starts with landmark Supreme Court decisions well before critical race theory is theorized as a legal concept in the 1970s: *Smith v. Allwright* in 1944, which outlawed the exclusion of Black voters through all-white political primaries in the South; or *Shelley v. Kramer* in 1948, which symbolically ended restrictive housing covenants preventing the sale of property to BIPOCs; or *Sweatt v. Painter* in 1950, which successfully challenged the "separate but equal" doctrine established by the *Plessy v. Ferguson* decision in 1896 by insisting that public universities must admit Black students; or, *Brown v. Board of Education of Topeka, Kansas* in 1954, arguably the most important Supreme Court decision of the twentieth century, which ended public school segregation and promoted equal education; or *Browder v. Gayle* in 1956, which declared segregation in public transportation unconstitutional; or *Loving v. Virginia* in 1967, which ended miscegenation laws and made interracial marriage legal.

These precursors lay the groundwork for the tenets of critical race theory that emerge in the 1970s onward after the end of the civil rights movement, perhaps culminating in the 1995 publication of the collection *Critical Race Theory: The Key Writings That Formed the Movement*, edited by Kimberlé Crenshaw, Neil Gotanda, Gary Peller, and Kendall Thomas. Let me provide a brief list of some of these principles. First, racism is mundane in its daily occurrence because "conceptions of equality" call for a "color-blind" America (Delgado and Stefancic, *Critical*, 8). Second, interest convergence, first articulated by Derrick Bell in his 1980 article "*Brown v. Board of Education* and the Interest Convergence Dilemma," which decrees that "the interests of blacks in achieving racial equality will be accommodated only when it converges with the interests of whites" (22). Third, race is a man-made construct, a "social construction [that] holds that race and races are products of social thought and relations. Not objective, inherent, or fixed, they correspond to no biological or genetic reality, rather, races are categories that society invents, manipulates, or retires when convenient" (Delgado and Stefancic, *Critical*, 9). Fourth, white society ethno-racializes different minorities at different moments to fit its societal needs as a means of "differential racialization" (Delgado and Stefancic, *Critical*, 9). Fifth, to continue down the avenue of identity politics, "intersectionality" indicates "the various ways in which race and gender interact to shape the multiple dimensions of black women" (Crenshaw, "Mapping the Margins," 358). And, sixth, perhaps the most significant at least for me, is the importance of counter-storytelling. As Black education professors Daniella Ann Cook and Adrienne D. Dixson explain:

> Counterstorytelling serves many purposes including: (1) psychic preservation by not silencing the experiences of the oppressed and thus exposing neglected evidence (counterstorytelling); (2) challenging normative reality through an exchange that overcomes ethnocentrism and the dysconscious conviction of viewing the world one way; (3) listening to the voices of people of color as the basis for understanding how race and racism function; and (4) purposefully attempting to disrupt liberal ideology. . . . In essence, counterstory serves to relate theory and the experiences of the oppressed in such a way as to challenge the dominant and totalizing narrative of white supremacy. (1243)

CRT and SF, brought together through the *noirum* to build and interrogate racialized worlds of both the unconscious and conscious varieties, offer reflection on and critique of the real world, giving power to the BIPOC characters of these imaginary spaces to speak their truths in defiance of erasure from the future on the one hand and destruction by this social construct on the other. After all, "opposing racism requires that we notice race" (Omi and Winant, *Racial*, 159).

To further illustrate this point, colorblindness represents an accepted social norm for white people. But ignoring the race of other people does not eradicate a racism so deeply rooted in the fabric of the United States of America, if not the globe. The first Black woman to be named an SF Grandmaster, Nalo Hopkinson, creates a simple and effective counternarrative to this harmful idea by quoting the first Black SF Grandmaster Samuel R. Delany, "race doesn't exist, but it'll kill ya" ("Reluctant," 347). Hopkinson's recounting of Delany's words amplifies the experiences, perceptions, and feelings of many Black and Brown people. Such powerful words *are* as lawful and thus worthy of consideration. Writers create better worlds with their words when they question the normality of master narratives such as colorblindness, which heavily influences popular culture and our social lives. Themes of segregation, prejudice, colorblindness, and interest convergence abound in SF subgenres. I use CRT to investigate some of these subgenres and provide a counternarrative offering a reassessment of American SF's involvement in the dialogue on race and racism at the crossroads of the late twentieth century and the new millennium, where BIPOC SF authors use such rationalization to imagine the future of policing, incarceration, internment, medical experimentation, doubly technologized flesh, and so on.

SF writers of every color and persuasion deny or challenge racism, identity politics, and other articulations of difference in their make-believe worlds, which are always in dialogue with the present in which they are written. Those writers who choose to openly confront racism, who choose to pull apart oppression and examine its inner workings, choose to transform perceptions of law in their stories as a means of providing their audience with new directions in which to interpret the experience of socially built racial identities in all of their social exclusion and alienation. As I have written elsewhere, CRT "reveals how American culture has operated via the projection of a false image of Black inferiority to serve the political, social, and cultural ends of white supremacism, and the degree to which . . . interlocking systems of race and class domination remain long after legal reform of Jim Crow laws" (Lavender, "Critical Race Theory," 186).

Afrofuturism comes in at this point in 1993 as CRT is being codified. Black authors and Black audiences want to see themselves in the future and the colorless futures so far written and filmed disturb them. Of course, music is its own story with the sonic soul stylings of Sun Ra and his Arkestra as well as Earth, Wind, and Fire, and Parliament-Funkadelic.[2] Afrofuturism has that in common with CRT. As modern culture and media professor Alexander G.

Weheliye said long ago, "The erasure of race severely limits how we conceive of the complex interplay between 'humans' and informational technologies" ("Feenin," 22). Tensions between race and technoscientific progress have always shaped the US but throwing law into this already potent sociocultural assemblage intensifies the friction. The vanishing of race from SF's ability to imagine the future alludes a terrible outlook for humanity, one of either assimilation or annihilation with no in-between. While Afrofuturism safeguards against such science fictional speculations, the *noirum*, engaging both SF and Afrofuturism, provides the counternarrative by illuminating some of these darker paths and how the law shapes them and to what end—survival or extinction.

A new generation of Black SF authors such as Violet Allen, P. Djèlí Clark, Justina Ireland, Tochi Onyebuchi, and Rivers Solomon, among others, have taken to heart the most recent protests against racial violence with respect to the twenty-first century Black Lives Matter movement to produce powerful responses in their own writings.[3] Likewise, they have been joined by woke allies politically alert to racial discrimination and other prejudicial forms that connect to justice issues as presented in their own creative output. As the rightfully celebrated Black author and editor Sheree Renée Thomas tweets, "The outrage over faux 'critical race theory' is not about white children's 'hurt' feelings. It's about the very real fear some parents have that if their children learn the darker truths about America, they may not choose to perpetuate the racial apartheid that's built upon lies" (Thomas, "The outrage . . . "). I couldn't say this any better! Thus, the *noirum* links this contemporary moment in science fiction with a world primed for transformation through expressions of social justice, antiracism, and liberation in the era of BLM⁺ speculations.

Worlds without racism and worlds without race symbolize entirely different things in science fiction as far as I am concerned. Against this backdrop, CRT and Afrofuturism prompt us to consider the fundamental differences between these competing visions. One only has to briefly consider a story such as N. K. Jemisin's "The Ones Who Stayed and Fought" (2018) to understand the difference. In reacting to Ursula K. Le Guin's famed story "The Ones Who Walk Away from Omelas" (1973), where utopia exists for the citizens of Omelas at the expense of a single child locked away in a basement in its own filth, Jemisin imagines the technologically advanced and peaceful city of Um-Helat on "the Day of Good Birds," a festival that celebrates the importance of diversity, of valuing one another, working together, living together, supporting one another ("The Ones," 1). Equal opportunity, housing, and food exist for everyone regardless of identity politics "because the people of Um-Helat are not believers in good intentions as the solution to all ills. No, there are no worshipers of mere tolerance here, nor desperate grovelers for that pittance of respect which is *diversity*. Um-Helatians are learned enough to understand what must be done to make the world better, and pragmatic enough to actually enact it" ("The Ones," 5). In other words, Jemisin creates her own afrotopia with an underlying secret. It is policed by bald-headed social workers with "silver studs" implanted and peppering their heads ("The Ones," 3). Why would there be need of law enforcement in this utopian city? Some citizens learn of the world next door, our world, and learn "the notion that *some people are less important than others*" ("The Ones," 9, emphasis original). This "evil" idea, gleaned from our reality, "spreads" like a "disease" and contaminates minds in Um-Helat ("The Ones," 10). The social workers offer swift justice by executing an offending man quickly to prevent its spreading. This death sentence *is* the steep and pragmatic price for this better world to exist free of the toxicity of discrimination and the man knew the cost of his lawbreaking.

Unfortunately, the man's blind daughter, a little girl too young to be taught society's rules, witnesses his capital punishment with her ears and threatens vengeance because her father, in his selfish action, is more important to her than any other person in Um-Helat. This belief is a direct manifestation of the disease. At that point, readers learn that the social workers are already contaminated, that the silver studs embedded in their heads mark them so for everyone to see while also functioning as inhibitors allowing them to serve their fellow citizens without fear of contagion. A tall Brown social worker, the story's narrator, offers the little girl her hand and a chance to join them. Jemisin's child juxtaposed to Le Guin's child—the choice to fight the disease by helping this suffering child juxtaposed to the choice to ignore the child in Le Guin's story and walk away—represents a call to action to make a world where everyone is valued, not unlike the Black Lives Matter movement.

Certainly, Jemisin invites direct action by making people uncomfortable enough to think about how to make a better society, where people are fully valued, their differences freely celebrated. Respect for all others exists not in theory but in fact. Jemisin challenges her readers to "puzzle over the Um-Helatians' choice to retain descriptive terms for themselves like *kinky-haired* or *fat* or *deaf*. But these are just words. . . . Without the attached contempt, such terms have no more meaning" ("The Ones," 8). In the best Afrofuturist sense, people of color perceptibly occupy this future as do fat and disabled people without the moralizing and shaming tendencies.

Jemisin gives us a fully raced world absent the racism. Her BLM+ story involves CRT in the sense that she decouples the social construction of race from the power to wield it against people through assaultive speech, physical violence, and oppression. She humanizes everyone from the father who breaks the law in breaching the barriers between worlds to the social workers who administer his decisive end. While her reimaging of utopia functions as her novum, Jemisin's critique of the form itself generates the *noirum* whereby justice prevails in the prevention of "information-gleaners" spreading the disease of inequality learned from our televisions and social media ("The Ones," 9). That in itself is transformative in our twenty-first-century moment, a fight worth having to build something better.

CRT and Afrofuturism necessitate an explicit thoughtfulness to racial constructions, their historical specificity, and laws real and imagined. Really grasping SF's unremitting racial fixations demands CRT. The *noirum* empowers us to reconsider and to resist the many racial implications of SF and the gravitational pull of a supposedly colorblind world that supports white privilege. Despite all of its questionable race images hitherto, SF remains uniquely fitting to model the farseeing testimonies for change that challenge political power.

Overview of the Book

In Part I: Imaginary Amendments, Judicial Decisions, and Executive Orders: Race in US Science Fiction, I look at a variety of novums and *noirums* created by SF writers in a rough chronological order. To that end, I gauge the robust creative response to the idea of colorblindness across time and the possible consequences of ignoring its embedding in our social structures, and I then suggest ways in which existing scholarship can expand with the insights of CRT directed at American SF in the two parts of this book.

I recognize that it may seem counterintuitive to start with white authors before turning to Black and other authors. But these white science fiction authors in fact challenged the status quo of accepted race relations and the law before Delany or any others that I could find at the moment of writing and I simply chronicle these narratives in the order of their publication before CRT itself emerged as a concept in the 1970s. I believe the spirit of this book itself will undercut this naturalized way of recounting genealogies (white authors first, and others respond, extend, revise) as it seeks to challenge the received ideas. I trust it will overwhelm and decenter the primacy of white authors in this telling of science fiction's story in a different way, an Afrofuturist way. After all, I frame my book between Butler, Bell, and Delany—Black giants all.

Chapter 1, "Precursor *Noirums*," considers SF from the civil rights era, how writers absorbed the social upheaval of the times, resulting in a variety of imaginary legal situations that manifest in their stories foreshadowing the need for CRT. Chapter 2, "Confinement Narratives," tracks the advent and development of CRT in the late 1970s through 2012 in tandem with the rise of the prison-industrial complex, militarized law enforcement, and surveillance technologies used to continue the violent oppression of America's most vilified and vulnerable citizens while also mapping onto Afrofuturism's origin in 1993. Likewise, it also expands my interrogation of the prison-industrial complex across color lines to illustrate the current dystopia of BIPOC existence in terms of Indian Boarding Schools and Internment Camps. Finally, it further situates the Black body in SF as a site of scientific racism, where government-backed medical experiments and genetic research on Black people exist to justify notions of racial superiority. Chapter 3, "BLM$^+$ Speculations and the *Noirum*," examines contemporary SF from a new generation of BIPOC writers and allies, politically alert to racism and other forms of oppression, hip to the ages, generations, and historical circumstances. These writers collectively demonstrate an urgent desire for social justice through their own agency, requiring no permission or approval to protest from earlier generations, across a variety of social issues ranging from climate change to racial profiling, to wellness, among others.

In Part II: Explorations of Antiracism, I explore representations of antiracism in two science fiction subgenres, namely cyberpunk and lost race tales. Chapter 4, "Cyberfunk," applies CRT to the cyberpunk mindset—high-tech lowlife—not normally associated with BIPOC SF despite the subgenre's projection of a dystopian near-future saturated with cyberspace, corporations, criminality, computers, and corporeality. For that reason, this chapter charts and explores the texts belonging to a BIPOC version of cyberpunk. Formulated as a case study, Chapter 5, "The Lost Race Tales of Edgar Allan Poe and Mat Johnson," tackles the subgenre of lost race tales by juxtaposing Edgar Allan Poe's only novel *The Narrative of Arthur Gordon Pym of Nantucket* (1838) to Mat Johnson's Afrofuturist retelling of Poe's novel in *Pym* (2011), linked through the secondary character of Dirk Peters, a man of ambiguous Native American heritage in Poe's novel who is made over by Johnson into an unambiguous colored man. To accomplish this Afrofuturist reckoning for Poe, I examine the deep past of a Blackness embedded in our national literature—marked by dislocation, white supremacy, and law—to move forward into a different future.

In the outro, "Science Fiction and Racism: Decolonizing the White Problem," I suggest how SF has repeatedly solved the white problem with multiple examples of alternative futurisms, where BIPOC authors disrupt a perceived monochrome future, writing themselves into it, creating alternatives where they see themselves in all their own glories and with all their own flaws representing humanity itself—decolonizing whiteness, decentering whiteness, and finally, dismissing it.

The Good of a BIPOC Science Fiction

We can learn much about the work of contemporary Black and Brown SF authors such as Steven Barnes, Tananarive Due, Nisi Shawl, Sabrina Vourvoulias, Daniel H. Wilson, and the like, by studying it together with the theorizing of CRT scholars such as Derrick Bell, Eduardo Bonilla-Silva, Kimberlé Williams Crenshaw, Richard Delgado, and Jean Stefancic, among others. There should be no question or uncertainty of "simply" applying critical race theory to science fiction. Comprehending these two modes of discourse together can in fact reveal much about both. Therefore, I sometimes bring CRT to bear on SF and SF to bear on CRT simultaneously whereby the two modes illuminate each other in terms of race and racism.

I believe my book is distinctive because of its tight focus on literature rather than expanding outward to perhaps broader traditions of SF such as film, television, comics, and other media. Certainly, there are films and shows that I could employ the *noirum* upon for further investigation. One that comes readily to mind is James DeMonaco's 2013 film *The Purge*, which to date has spawned four sequels and a short-lived television series. In a near-future America, the country has achieved something of its utopian potential with low crime and virtually no unemployment. At some point in this future, the government has instituted an annual purge, where all crime, including murder, is legal for a twelve-hour period one night a year. During this period all local, state, and federal government services are suspended and the government uses the emergency broadcasting system to alert its citizens at the start and end of the purge. Such a film pleads—if not demands—for CRT introspection but not by me. While this decision could be interpreted as a limitation, I know literature best and feel that other scholars can adapt the *noirum* for such analyses. The inclusion of film, television, and comics could make for a different if equally exciting book in the future. But that is not this book.

Though I discuss a great many individual works briefly, and though a few passages are painstakingly examined, the goal of this book is to make a wide-ranging case about the connections between CRT and SF. This book is as much about the further coloring of science fiction as it is about critical race theory. After all, the subsequent pages encompass full discussions of critical race theorists, who never explicitly engage with science fiction (excepting Bell), and explorations of the problems caused by racism, prejudice, social biases, and the law as envisioned in the speculative imagination. My intended audience will have a broad familiarity with the SF genre, if not the BIPOC writers under discussion, and its secondary literature. However, I also hope to attract readers interested in critical race theory who have previously paid no attention to science fiction. Indeed, my audience ought to be fascinated by the social power of science fiction. Rather than taking an exhaustively encyclopedic approach, I want to emphasize the expository nature of this book because the vastness of the combined territory of CRT and SF would fry my brain in the demonstration of my basic argument. Ultimately, I hope to illustrate the potential that both critical race theory and science fiction have to liberate our species from interlocking oppressions. That's the reason I thought the book worth writing in the first place despite its many complications.

Subsequently, CRT values storytelling (and the everyday) within a justice system context, challenges notions of colorblindness, and acknowledges how technological and scientific innovations continue to perpetuate racism (such as through the digital divide or medical experimentation). CRT readings demonstrate how lots of white authors miss opportunities for meaningful engagement with race further perpetuating racism and maintaining white supremacy in their futures while BIPOC SF writers generate discomfort for some of their reading audience. And in many ways that is precisely what critical race theory does in the attempt to challenge colorblind beliefs. BIPOC writers make a place for SF that is dependent on multicultural politics projected into a racialized future. They create worlds where the social construction of race dominates the technocultural background of the created world and write counternarratives that portray the constraints of racialized identity politics affecting the technoculture. In other words, these writers offer consciously racialized settings that divest whiteness as the norm.

Science fictional counternarratives address the long-standing cracks in the American dream for BIPOCs such as racism, inequality, and injustice with unconventional visions that offer resistance against the deep inequities disproportionately impacting these communities. BIPOC SF writers play an essential role in laying bare the fault lines of racist oppression, shifting these structural inequalities, and reimagining what the future will look like. But we first must understand the past to make better meaning of the present in order to create the necessary conditions for a just future. Challenging the world's oldest constitutional democracy to achieve its own utopian ideals despite the atrocities inflicted upon its BIPOCs in the quest for equality *is* never a bad thing. Indeed, a "more perfect union" gets made in dismantling unjust social institutions.

To date, very little work has been done in bringing together critical race theory and science fiction. But why?

The reason such a book has not yet been written is rather simple: people want desperately to believe in a future where our race problems have disappeared. But SF tells a different story, a racist one, and this underlying narrative holds value because it is deeply embedded in American popular culture and reinforces how people around the globe perceive the United States. Look no further than January 6, 2021. The sedition that led to the Capitol riot, worse even, the insurrection and attempted coup has been imagined many times in American SF. Sinclair Lewis, Octavia E. Butler, and Philip Roth, to name but a few prominent American authors, have already warned against a pervasive white nationalism and its fascist ideologies and we must heed the warnings and begin the hard work of assiduously taking apart the corrosive messaging of racism, xenophobia, misogyny, and homophobia. The SF works I analyze through CRT provide a valuable way to explore new possibilities and futures for responding to racism and supposedly antiracist practices.

"But why now?" some people might ask. So, I counter with: why not now? I will not let fear of our current political and social climate stop me from finding potential solutions to the variety of racial dilemmas we face in the real world in the fictions I love to read. That's my answer.

In closing, let me respond to the question posed by Octavia E. Butler in the opening epigraph with a question of my own: how can anyone think seriously about the future without Black and Brown people in it? Certainly, good science fiction provokes powerful thoughts in its readers about American society, if not the world itself. I think the good of science fiction for Black people *is* to keep us grounded in the present realities of right now, to keep us moving forward, and to keep reminding us of how it could all change.

PART I

Imaginary Amendments, Judicial Decisions, and Executive Orders: Race in US Science Fiction

CHAPTER 1

Precursor *Noirums*

Before moving forward in time to the *noirum* proper, what I roughly and arbitrarily consider as 1976 forward into the present, I think it prudent to look for several earlier examples. 1976 because the date adheres to Derrick Bell's foundational CRT essay "Serving Two Masters: Integration Ideals and Client Interests in School Desegregation Litigation." In that essay Bell's critique of integration asserts that the *Brown* decision actually made things worse for Black America, or at least more complicated, by forcing integration instead of emphasizing good, tangible, impactful schooling. Civil rights organizations such as the NAACP win the illusion of diversity at the cost of Black children's actual learning as if racial integration addresses social inequality and blunts white supremacy. 1976 again because there was really only Samuel R. Delany as a well-known African American science fiction writer at that point with *Dhalgren* (1975) selling a million plus copies and being nominated for the Nebula Award and *Trouble on Triton* (1976) likewise nabbing a nomination for the Nebula Award. Nevertheless, I didn't have to look too far back. I found them even before the heyday of the civil rights movement—imaginary amendments, court decisions, and government actions. I found them in George P. Elliott, Kurt Vonnegut Jr., Delany, Philip K. Dick, and Ursula K. Le Guin—and let me throw in the historical fiction writer John Jakes, whose first instantiation as a science fiction writer is largely overlooked nowadays, for good measure. SF, at its best, has always moved across time, forward and backward, in its speculation. Likewise, Afrofuturism does *nearly* the same thing. Why nearly? I say nearly because many Black authors consider racial diffractions of identities and cultures caused by slavery, discrimination, and racism in political and social circumstances through space, time, and technological development.

These SF authors clearly anticipate the emergence of CRT in these early *noirum* examples. I see how these mostly white and male authors, with the exceptions of Delany and Le Guin, impacted by the social upheavals of the civil rights era, think about solutions to the question of race—concentration camps, artificial disabilities, generation starships, cryogenic storage, a dream machine, and time travel. These grim imaginings matter collectively because none of them offer narratives of progress, not really, as the authors can only seemingly see the continuance of racism across time. Consequently, historical memory often shorts itself out as amnesiac white Americans choose to forget the racial anxieties of the near past (segregation, civil rights, affirmative action, racial profiling, mass incarceration, and the falsely identified post-race era) less than sixty years ago. "But the public policies of yesterday," in keeping with legal scholar Richard Rothstein, "still shape the racial landscape of today" (*Color*, 178). The contemplation of race stories in SF predating the American bicentennial demonstrates the embeddedness of such policies and the difficulties of seeing beyond them in the demand for social justice. Regardless of race or gender, these American SF writers envision how colored American life remains a dystopian reality. Still, these writers challenge a monochrome vision of the future where white people are the only ones that matter simply in writing their stories.

Delectable Negroes: George P. Elliott's "The NRACP"

George P. Elliott creates an antiracist satire in 1949 for the year-old literary journal *The Hudson Review* with his slow to unfold short story "The NRACP." The NRACP, shorthand for "the National Relocation Authority: Colored Persons," reminds his audience of the venerable civil rights organization the NAACP but all similarities end there (55). The story's novum involves the solution to "the Negro problem in America," which gives "dignity and independence to the Negroes" according to the story's protagonist, Andy Dixon, a public relations clerk working on site in the "Colored Persons Reserve" somewhere in the American Southwest (71, 55). Andy tells the story to his best friend Herb back in Washington, DC through letters. I think Elliott uses the epistolary form to demonstrate how racist idealists, such as Andy and his coworkers O'Doone and Ruth, become overwhelmed by this seeming social engineering project involving train loads of Black people shipped to a secret, guarded desert facility at all hours over the course of his three years on the job and their discovery of what was happening to America's Black citizens at this camp.

Likewise, the story's *noirum* makes possible the answer to this very real American race dilemma as unkept promises frustrate its second-class citizens after the second World War through previous legislation. In fact, I must wonder if Elliott writes this satirical story in support to President Harry Truman's decision to integrate the armed forces with Executive Order 9981 on July 26, 1948, which specifies "equality of treatment and opportunity for all those who serve in our country's defense" ("Executive"). In Elliott's story, the government passes the indefinite "Relocation Act" and establishes an "Authority" to oversee the removal of the country's Black citizens (56). Surely, Elliott's mockery and logical extension of Jim Crow society represents an antiracist response as it plainly contests and criticizes individual, institutional, and structural racisms caused by both the written and social laws of the land.

Initially, Andy believes in the supposed egalitarian doctrine of separate but equal living spaces for US citizens, but his racist idealism changes as his letters demonstrate. In his opening letter, he reveals his own racism with respect to how bored he is with "reading Negro novels and poetry" representative of "their primeval culture" and resents having it "pushed off onto" him as a part of his duties (56–57). His stated beliefs here reflect a conscious attitude that perpetuates racism in that Black literature is inferior to that of white peoples. Not only does this example highlight his own individual racism, but it also illustrates both institutional and structural racism; institutional in the sense that the government created this discriminatory and unfair policy to the benefit of white people by *openly* shipping Blacks to this undisclosed camp for a nefarious purpose; and structural because of the overpowering and extensive system of racial bias on display in this imaginary American society.

However, his internalized racism shifts as he details his daily existence at the reserve to Herb throughout his letters. He talks about taking long walks in the desert, espying the intake center, censoring letters written by both Blacks and whites, meeting hostile armed guards, marrying and impregnating Ruth, discovering O'Doone's body in a covered-up suicide, and ultimately learning the reason behind it as he adapts to writing his letters in invisible ink to avoid his own thoughts being censored by the government. It takes seeing the "mile long" buildings for Intake to begin chipping away at his delusion of a "better world" for Black people (60). It takes the arrival of "the first trainload of Negroes . . . 500 of them" for Andy to begin vaguely sensing the wrongness of his decision to work at the preserve (63). It takes recognizing the resulting "trouble if any confirmation of their [Caucasian sympathizers] suspicions about the CPR should leak out" (65). It takes sharing a drink with a hostile guard to learn of the "searchlight up top the hill, with machine guns" (67). It takes writing in invisible ink upon the realization that his own letters are being censored.

The terrible truth is not too difficult to figure out for Elliott's audience. The government exterminates its own Black population in concentration camps. But a Swiftian twist exists in that they are profiting by selling the meat of these Black bodies to "China and Europe" as well as to its own citizens (76). In fact, the government has even been feeding its reserve workforce this human meat as Andy unwittingly pontificates on the quality and quantity of the meat—"roast, steak, chop, stew" but never fresh vegetables (73). Andy's dream of Gulliver and Lilliput signals this twist and the unsuspecting cannibalism upon discovery provides the reason for O'Doone's suicide. Andy only puts it together when he innocently calls another guard a butcher with the guard proclaiming, "I'm no butcher. I won't have nothing to do with the whole slimy mess. I won't eat them . . . You dirty prying niggereating son of a bitch" (80). Instead of whistleblowing "the truth about NRACP," Andy thinks of his wife Ruth having a baby as his thoughts become incoherent in his attempt to rationalize the unthinkable (82). Andy stops eating the meat, though! Only bread, fruit, and milk for him. In Elliott's own words with respect to his satire, he states, "I think that if you can't look at, say, women's liberation or race relations with irony and complication, you're liable to wind up writing mere propaganda of one kind or another" (Archambauld, 42). Elliott evidently practiced antiracism and allyship before they were made popular by the mainstream civil rights movement in challenging a prevailing racism at the end of the Jim Crow era.

Without a doubt, Elliott's accidental employment of the *noirum* in his short story makes a parody of the Jim Crow era with his final solution to the race problem. Andy's credulity and pride in working for the NRACP slowly unravels as he recognizes the racial extremism governing the country resulting in the genocide of Black Americans. As a matter of fact, Elliott reveals a deep, dark truth about how American politics thrived on racism in its metaphoric, perhaps literal, hunger for Black flesh then and certainly now as it created a culture of consumption that continually cannibalizes Black America today.

Dystopian Amendments: Kurt Vonnegut's "Harrison Bergeron"

Now a bit of idle speculation as a means of transition. I wonder if Elliott's story influenced Kurt Vonnegut's later story "Harrison Bergeron" (1961). I say this because Elliott was briefly a faculty member of the famed Iowa Writers' Workshop, as was Vonnegut, both in the 1960s at the behest of the longtime director Paul Engle, but neither of them lasted. Alas, their times there did not overlap. Anyhow, the story begins: "The year was 2081, and everybody was finally equal. They weren't only equal before God and the law. They were equal every which way. Nobody was smarter than anybody else. No one was better looking than anybody else. Nobody was stronger or quicker than anybody else. All this equality was due to the 211th, 212th, and 213th Amendments to the Constitution, and to the unceasing vigilance of agents of the United States Handicapper General" (846). The novum rests on the achievement of equality in a dystopian far future United States, brought on by the *noirum* in terms of the passing of Amendments 211 through 213 as well as the 184 others that passed in the twenty-first century. Amendment 211 levels the playing field in terms of intelligence by making smart people wear radio devices that inhibit their ability to think through harsh, disruptive noises. Amendment 212 creates supposedly equity in relation to attractiveness by having pretty people wear horrible masks to hide their beauty; or, in the case of the title character, a red rubber nose, black tooth caps to create an irregular smile, and shaved eyebrows to blot out his seven-foot-tall masculine beauty. And Amendment 213 ostensibly generates fairness by weighing down stronger and faster people with bags of birdshot.

The Handicapper General, Diana Moon Glampers, responsibly creates such impediments to ensure that everyone is equal. In the defense of this hard-won equality, Glampers murders Harrison and his chosen ballerina bride on live television with "a double-barreled ten-gauge shotgun" shortly after he announces himself Emperor while his handicapped father George and his normal mother Hazel watch with millions of other Americans, though they forget within seconds of seeing their son die a horrible death (850). Consequently, advantages, differences, and competition have been eradicated, but for whom?

White people.

Clearly, there are no Black people in this future. As Darryl Hattenhauer observes, "The narrator's definition of America's equality begins not by positing a future equality as much as exposing the misunderstanding of it in the past and present" (389). That is to say, the framing of the story presumes a white audience; after all, Harrison "would have awed Thor, the god of thunder" himself (849). Yet there is no mention of race anywhere in the text. That is the misunderstanding here. Why couldn't Harrison Bergeron be Black? His physical description of being a tall, strong, and handsome athlete to go along with his dangerous genius, juvenile delinquency according to those future laws, and desire to foment rebellion might possibly code him as Black in the 1961 United States of America at the time this story is published. Equality is on everyone's mind living through this moment in American history because of the social upheaval generated through the civil rights movement. How could it not be? The story concerns the achievement of equal rights under the law by ending all forms of discrimination regardless of race, sex, or origin in this dystopian projection. Vonnegut himself acknowledges "only since World War II has this country begun to fight it with any seriousness: the idea that females and persons of color are second-class citizens" ("What," 53).

But most white Americans cannot see this from a racial perspective because they prioritize their own convergent interests. Therefore, the story must offer a Cold War critique or an economic one or a censure of individuality or a stark warning against big government or a damning assessment of popular media, such as television, and how it has reduced attention spans. I agree that Vonnegut's story does these things, but the absence of Black people in this future suggests an antiracist critique too. Where did all the Blacks go in this monochrome future? As an antiracist comment, Vonnegut dismantles racist views by maintaining a system where the lowly exist on equal terms to the lofty to generate a literal fairness in the eyes of the government through lawmaking. That is the *noirum* at work as it relates to ethno-racial concerns. In fact, Vonnegut plays on the white fears of the racial other and of losing power by extrapolating the Black struggle for justice. It demonstrates a fear of the change coming as the United States becomes a majority minority country and the law's role in this progression.

Impossibility: Samuel R. Delany

All of you must understand, this longer buildup to discussing a single Delany novel *is* tantamount to my endeavor because Delany *is* arguably the most important Black science fiction writer. He is certainly the sole recognized Black SF writer of this period. Likewise, it is my job to integrate Delany criticism with my own thinking on identity politics, critical race theory, and the cultural history of the time period of the novel in question. But I digress.

Delany himself occupied an unusual position as a Black SF writer whose career began in the 1960s with the civil rights movement waning and giving way to the Black Power movement. Unusual because there seemed to be no one else like him and he belonged to the science fiction community as opposed to the African American literary scene, where John A. Williams,[1] Sam Greenlee,[2] and William Melvin Kelley[3] wrote social thrillers tinged by science fictional elements and Black unrest. With respect to Delany, African American literary scholar Jeffrey A. Tucker zeroes in on this seeming difference: "The discourse that fixes SF and African American culture as mutually exclusive categories is spoken by . . . whites as well African Americans, which have led to some staggeringly inaccurate assessments of Delany's work in particular" (*Sense*, 52). And Tucker gets it absolutely right in terms of Delany's work being roughly scrutinized, perhaps misunderstood, over the past half century.

On the one hand, white critics such as Seth McEvoy and Carl Freedman offer divergent opinions. McEvoy, in his bio-critical analysis of Delany and his early work, notes how "Delany had been given encouragement at Breadloaf Writers Conference" and that "One would have expected such a 'young, gifted, and black' writer to go on to become a member of the 'literary' establishment" (*Samuel R. Delany*, 19). Freedman offers an even sharper assessment of an apparent Black hush regarding Delany's prominence in SF stating, "look for any reflection of that achievement in the mainstream forums of Black Studies, and you will, with few exceptions, look in vain" (*Critical Theory*, 160, footnote 54). I think the respective sentiments about the literariness of Delany and the lack of respect for his accomplishments in Blackademia may have been true long ago, but I must note that the journal *Black American Literature Forum* put out a special issue on science fiction in the summer of 1984 that heavily featured Delany (as well as Octavia Butler and Charles Saunders to a lesser extent) with five articles and a bibliography.[4] In fact, the eminent journal, redubbed as *African American Review*, published a second ten-article, strongly Delany-focused special issue in 2015 called "Delany Lately."[5]

On the other hand, Black critics such as Thulani Davis and Greg Tate find fault with Delany's apparent lack of thought for depicting future Blacks in his writing. Davis believes that Delany's characters "are black in fact, if not so much culturally" ("Future," 19). It's almost as if she accuses Delany of being a sellout. Tate comes closer to this accusation in declaring: "I've always found Delany's racially defused futures problematic because they seem to deny the possibility that the affirmative aspects of black American culture and experience could survive assimilation. By which I mean not just obvious things like the genius present in black music, speech, and style but the humanity and range of personas born of black people's sense of communion" ("Ghetto," 165). Read between the lines here—Delany's identity politics are not Black enough for them. But the only thing apparent to me in such condemnation is that Thulani Davis and Greg Tate do not read deeply enough of Delany's work. I mean, who are these people to question one's sense of Blackness? As if Delany hasn't faced rejection by the white gatekeepers of science fiction publishing. Of course, he did! And Delany gives a powerful account of it in his classic essay "Racism and Science Fiction": "I submitted *Nova* for serialization to the famous sf editor of *Analog* magazine, John W. Campbell Jr. Campbell rejected it, with a note and phone call to my agent explaining that, while he liked pretty much everything else about it, he didn't feel his readership would be able to relate to a black main character. That was one of my first direct encounters, as a professional writer, with the slippery and always commercialized form of liberal American prejudice. Campbell had nothing against my being black, you understand" (387). While writers like Philp K. Dick and Robert A. Heinlein can candidly write about race relations in *A Crack in Space* (1966) and *Farnham's Freehold* (1964)[6] respectively, Delany does not yet have such freedom in the science fiction field. In fact, an even lesser-known Black science fiction writer, John M. Faucette Jr., "received endless rejection after endless rejection" after initially breaking through with the publication of *Crown of Infinity* and *The Age of Ruin*[7] as Ace Doubles in 1968 thanks to Donald A. Wollheim (*Black Science Fiction*, iv). But Faucette faded into even further obscurity until science fiction scholar Mark Bould recovered Faucette's work for academia.[8] Regardless, I believe SF scholar Sharon DeGraw has the right of it: "Delany's inclusive racial attitude was essential to the success of his early career in the science fiction field. Not only did Delany face discrimination as a black writer, but he also had to struggle against the racist norms of the generic conventions. Had he challenged these norms too directly or revised them radically, at this early stage, his texts would not have been published in the science fiction genre" (*Subject*, 109). Please understand—Delany would not have had a career without using the literal metaphors of science fiction to talk about race and racism in ways that were not easily comprehended by his 1960s audience. Delany engages "in a significant distortion of the present that sets up a rich and complex dialogue" for those with eyes to see the reality of it because "Science fiction *is in dialogue with the present*" at which it is written (Delany, *Starboard Wine*, 165). Race seeps into all of his SF. Indeed, Delany incessantly talks about it because he dares to imagine how Blackness matters in other contexts separate from its past and present meanings. That's forward thinking in my estimation.

Again, I mean, who are these people to question one's sense of Blackness, let alone Delany's? Critics across color lines seemingly feel it's proper to question Delany's multifarious identity. In one interview Delany states, "The constant and insistent experience I have as a black man, as a gay man, as a science fiction writer in racist, sexist, homophobic, America, with its carefully maintained tradition of high art and low, colors and contours every sentence I write" ("Toto," 73). Delany opines in a second interview, "My experiences as a black in the United States, if I am a black writer, must go into my work: There's no way I can keep them out" ("Science Fiction and Criticism," 198). Delany takes a dig at his critics in a third interview: "my experience as a black American runs all through my work. But why do you assume its traces will be such stereotypes?" ("Semiology," 50). Exactly! Just so! Right on! People, irrespective of racial background, assume that SF as a perceived lesser kind of cultural product is simple in its decoding—like alien stand-ins for Black people—and they are ever so wrong. They are even more wrong when they assume all black-authored SF must be Afrofuturism. It's not. And these same people are most wrong in thinking we cannot learn to think and imagine our way out of our current racial constructs through conjured worlds, inclusive futures, and fascinating stories that create counternarratives to prejudice, stereotypes, and white supremacy.

Nevertheless, I am no different from some of these other scholars in terms of focusing exclusively on Delany's relationship to Blackness. As Tucker suggests, like the others, I created a different Delany that "conform[s] to [my] own desires, agenda, and politics" (*Sense*, 5). But, and this is the biggest of buts, I *am* also Black like Delany and I dare attempt to answer Delany's specific challenge to critics—"If you're a critic, tell me an *interesting* story" with respect to "the evidence for and of blackness" in Delany's work ("Science Fiction and Criticism," 200). In this regard, I choose to think about the racial ramifications of his lesser-known novella *The Ballad of Beta-2* (1965) through the *noirum* for three reasons; first, the novella is understudied and underappreciated; second, it was nominated for a Nebula Award; and, third, the court scenes it contains situate the novel at the crossroads of the civil rights and Black Power movements.

Supreme Court in Space: Samuel R. Delany's *The Ballad of Beta-2*

The novella begins with the Black galactic anthropology honors major Joneny Horatio T'wabaga in his nameless professor's office after class protesting a homework assignment asking him to research the Star Folk, the culture that sprang up on their generation starships, and the mysterious calamity that befell them of which the ballad accounts. Readers most likely assume Joneny white by default until hearing his African-sounding last name mentioned only once about a third of the way through the novella. At any rate, the professor makes short shrift of Joneny's many complaints about wasting time on the Star Folk, "a dead end" of humanity, "with no significance at all" and wasting even more time "poking through dozens of chrome-plated eggshells [referring to their antiquated ships], documenting the history of a . . . a bunch of chauvinistic, degenerate morons" and their ten remaining ships "herded into orbit around Leffer," where "the imbecilic remnants of their population [are] allowed to dodder toward extinction" (179, 180). The professor responds to Joneny's strong objections by stating, "'You say you are familiar with the Nella Ballad Collection. Then no doubt you know 'The Ballad of Beta-2.' I want a complete, historical analysis of that ballad—from primary sources. That will be your detail assignment for this unit'" before summarily dismissing him (182). This brief interaction between student and professor represents the first layer of the novella.

And so Joneny goes, but only after studying the ballad more closely. He requests "a Time Adjustment through the Clearing Center of the University," a twenty-four-hour time dilation equating to a week for the "lab period," and arranges for his one-person starship to jaunt to the Star Folk (184). So then, Delany cleverly frames his real story through this assignment and Joneny's effort to decipher the ballad's meaning—with the actual story being the initial alien encounter between Captain Leela of the Beta-2 and a cosmic entity known as the Destroyer,[9] which results in a child as well as Leela's prosecution and death by the devolved Star Folk who call themselves "the Norm" (215). The child, whose different incarnations are known as the Children of the Destroyer to the Star Folk, is a powerful multi-being born of miscegenation, and who guides Joneny among the ruins of the Sigma-9 and aids him in understanding the ballad. Consequently, the novella's novum involves generation star ships and alien encounters.

Part of the tragedy manifests because of the speed at which technology progresses, with humanity developing faster than light engines a mere sixty years after the giant generation starships depart earth to colonize Leffer IV. Twelve generations have passed by the time the Star Folk ships arrive in orbit, where they find the planet already colonized by an unrecognizable humanity, at least to the Star Folk, who have suffered from radiation and alien contact crossing the stars. Ultimately, Joneny discovers that the metaphors and imagery contained in the ballad reveal the actual history of the voyage and he understands the meaning of the all-important thirteenth stanza of the sixteen-stanza folk song:

> She walked through the gates and the children cried,
> She walked through the Market and the voices died,
> She walked past the court house and the judge so still,
> She walked to the bottom of Death's Head hill. (*Ballad*, 184)

Joneny has worked this part of the ballad out before even leaving on the trip because of his training in galactic anthropology. In short, galactic anthropology must be defined as the study of humans, their origins, physical traits, institutions, religious beliefs, social relationships, artifacts, and so on, in space. Because of his superior research skills, Joneny figures out that children are born in "the Market," and that "the Market" refers to the carefully monitored reproduction facility on each of the twelve starships where the Star Folk can maintain the consistency of the race and protect the mechanically birthed offspring from "radiation deformities" (187). Likewise, the "Death's Head" refers to a "reconverter of waste material [that could] also be used as an instrument for capital punishment" (188). The sight of this machine recalls "pictures and descriptions of the Auschwitz atrocities during the so-called Second World War. It is completely jammed with skeletons, as though the population had been seized with a sudden suicide craze or else some unbelievable mass murder had been committed" (188). It is impossible for Delany's audience to miss the holocaust reference nor its implications as the plot unwinds. With his interest piqued by his unraveling of the thirteenth verse's meaning, Joneny sets out to discover who the "she" of the stanza is and meets the boy who helps him find "the Logbook of Beta-2 City, the property of Captain Leela RT-857" on Beta-2 (229). Leela happens to be the alien child's mother and the subject of the ballad.

The second layer of the novella concerns the alien encounter between Leela and the Destroyer. This meeting results in "the green-eyed child" of the ballad, who just so happens to be Joneny's guide roughly "two hundred and fifty years" after the first alien encounter (182, 207). The first encounter represents a social *noirum*, where authors break accepted communal laws such as race mixing to tell their stories. This forbidden love affair represents Delany's first *noirum*. Put another way, SF organizes itself around the novum, this new, often technoscientific thing that makes the storyworld different from our own—in this case, generation starships that lead to the alien encounter. The novum provokes a culturally specific social, moral or ethical problem, such as the idea of interracial love, to be explored, if not resolved. It is this secondary issue linked to race, especially Black issues, that reveals the *noirum*.

While the dire situation among the space fleet's divided citizens continues to develop in the background, a mysterious entity begins destroying ships—Delta-6 and Epsilon-7—before it's stopped in the middle of crushing Sigma-9 by the plucky Captain Leela, who defies a judge to travel to Sigma-9. Leela simply shouts "Stop that!" to the giant man-shaped telepathic being and it listens to her in its loneliness (251). It merely sought to communicate with the ships to end its solitude, but the other "*minds are not big enough*" (251). Leela saves the Star Folk despite their small minds, their bigotry, their intolerance for difference. The Destroyer falls in love, promises Leela "*descendants who will be able to live among the stars*," and impregnates the willing captain (254). This moment of passion represents the social *noirum* event in a few ways. First, Delany mirrors an interracial coupling through this alien encounter, thus breaking the racial taboo of a Black man sleeping with a white woman.[10] Second, this alien sex results in a biracial child. "The specific context of American race relations," as DeGraw states, reflects how "Delany's alien/human hybrid mirrors the mixed racial position of mulattos" (*Subject*, 140). Third, the child could possibly pass for human, if not a white human. But Captain Leela later dies for it.

Skin color becomes incredibly important to the text with respect to the hybrid child from this illicit relationship between the captain and the alien Destroyer. As SF scholar Päivi Väätänen indicates, the "human-alien" child's "whiteness is not [a] 'Caucasian whiteness'" (*Narrating*, 42). Delany describes the boy's "luminously white skin" and also notes "hair, fine and pale and long" to initially code the boy as white (203). Yet Delany veils his racial critique through this radiant skin and "good" hair, while also hinting that the boy is biracial since his "nose was flat" (203). Once again, Väätänen astutely points out that "facial features were one of the classifying traits in early anthropology, and as Joneny is a galactic anthropologist, it is hard not to take his observations of facial features as significant" (*Narrating*, 42). Likewise, the "azure-skinned youngsters," all different versions of the boy, "the rest of me" as he tells Joneny, are clearly not white nor human for that matter (223). So, what is Delany saying here on this point? I believe Delany thinks it *is* absolutely ridiculous to define races by skin color, which in turn gets used to determine human potentials such as intelligence, beauty, and athleticism or violence, hatred, and prejudicial tendencies. He makes his disdain palpable through this aggrandizement of science fictional metaphor in its literalness.

With respect to the subject of racial passing, the human-appearing boy never attempts to pass for human. Joneny asks him "What are you?" (223) after witnessing space walking without a suit, telepathy, and his duplicate versions winking in and out of physical space among other logic-defying things. Delany does not create a passing narrative here because the boy does not claim a racial identity, he merely shrugs his shoulders at this inappropriate question as a means of deflection. The boy never attempts to mix with the Star Folk who prize their own sameness and segregation. He merely accepts his own difference and expects Joneny to accept it in time. As Tucker believes, "The absence of any biological meaning of race and the common humanity of us all deserve frequent and repeated declaration and celebration" (*Sense*, 22). And the boy's simple shrug reflects this celebration of a broken racial reality.

Earlier I mentioned the strong sectarian divide between the ships' inhabitants that results in the development of two groups—the Norms and the One-Eyes with only the judges and captains as a buffer. This philosophical rift represents the third layer of the novella that largely takes place in the blackground of the ballad, the racialized superstructures hiding in plain sight, deeply embedded in American culture and the SF genre itself, both absent and present traces of racial meaning. Think of it as the under *noirum*. In subversively talking about race and racism, Delany directly employs a second more overt *noirum* in *The Ballad of Beta-2* through a powerful science fictional distortion of the long civil rights movement and the social upheaval caused by various supreme court rulings, congressional acts, and presidential edicts that he himself witnessed and lived through in this tumultuous period, such as the Greensboro sit-ins of 1960, lunch counter protests in Greensboro, North Carolina led by four Black college students[11] attempting to integrate Woolworth's segregated lunch counter.

Let me expand a bit on the turmoil of this time period in American history. The first freedom riders, a mixed group of white and Black civil rights activists, both men and women, including future Congressman John Lewis and his good trouble self, left from Washington, DC on a Greyhound bus attempting to penetrate the Deep South on May 4, 1961 in the effort to end segregated bus terminals, but failed to complete the journey to New Orleans because of mounting white mob violence the further their bus went, having to abandon the journey in Alabama. Through the agitation of these Freedom Rides, the Kennedy Administration banned segregated interstate travel in the fall through the Interstate Commerce Commission in correlation to the 1960 Supreme Court decision in *Boynton v. Virginia*, which declared the unconstitutionality of segregated transportation facilities and services.[12]

Black Air Force veteran James Meredith integrates the University of Mississippi in the fall of 1962 with the aid of the Kennedy administration and federal marshals, but not before the battle of Ole Miss ensued, where white supremacists rioted and then fought against the National Guard to prevent his enrollment.[13] About a year later, Governor George Wallace makes his infamous stand in the schoolhouse door at the University of Alabama to symbolically block the registration of two Black students—Vivian Malone and James Hood—as a follow-up to his even more infamous "segregation now, segregation tomorrow, segregation forever" statement to prevent desegregation from earlier in June of 1963.[14] But President Kennedy federalizes the Alabama Nation Guard with Executive Order 11111 to end that nonsense.

Martin Luther King Jr. delivers his most celebrated speech, "I Have a Dream," from the Lincoln Memorial to more than 250,000 people on August 28, 1963 that culminates the integrated March on Washington for Jobs and Freedom, which demanded civil rights from voting to education to ending segregation and establishing fair wages. Despite the hope generated by his iconic speech, racial hate persists and four little Black girls—Addie May Collins, Denise McNair, Carole Robertson, and Cynthia Wesley—are murdered on a Sunday morning in the 16th Street Baptist Church bombing on September 5, 1963, blown up in a white terrorist attack.[15] Shortly after, President John F. Kennedy is assassinated in Dallas by Lee Harvey Oswald on November 22, 1963 in the build up to the passage of the Civil Rights Act of 1964, pushed through by President Lyndon B. Johnson, outlawing discrimination based on race, color, religion, sex, and national origin; it became law on July 2, 1964. Tumultuous indeed.

Delany finishes writing *The Ballad of Beta-2* in August of 1964 and it is quite impossible that he was not thinking of the civil rights movement during its writing, especially with the Voting Rights Act of 1965 to swiftly follow. Of course, Delany will not tour parts of the Deep South until the mid-sixties during the writing of *Babel-17* (1966) when he hitchhikes from Florida to Texas with Bob Folsom. He most definitely experiences the vitriol of racism before, during, and after this trip. That's beyond question.

All of these events, and more besides, permeate the text's blackground. As Joneny listens to a variety of recordings on board the generation ship at the boy's behest, he hears a series of court cases governed by the judicial proclamation: "Our ancestors charged us with bringing *human beings* to the stars. And no deviation will be tolerated" (222). It becomes clear that the Norms are the Star Folk, symbolic of white America, and the One-Eyes are those who are deviant for any number of reasons and who are being persecuted. The Norms make the laws of human being and stringently interpret them to benefit Norms alone, which emboldens them to kill anyone who deviates from their criteria, anyone deemed different. The Norms desire to remain segregated in their sameness and will not allow for diversity in their gene pool. Consequently, only Norms are true "human beings" and everyone else will be massacred.

A case in point, Leela's pregnancy results in her trial and execution by the Norms for deviating from accepted artificial birthing rituals. "Leela RT-857 vs. The Norm"—this sham trial reads like a prelude to a lynching in some respects (258). Captain Leela's trial and execution enables the judges both to undermine the captains' authority and to topple them, hence paving the way for the wholesale extermination of all One-Eyes, those deemed unfit from the norm, across the fleet. The One-Eyes escape into the weightless core of their ships for a little while, but they are captured and destroyed. Once it is deciphered, Joneny marvels at how clearly the ballad expresses "the story of Leela's attempt to save her people" and how it "was as immediate to him through those compressed verses as many incidents he had lived through" (262). While the ballad may be about Leela, her love affair, her trial, her death, and the birth of her child, other and even more egregious instances of persecution exist in the random recordings Joneny examines.

Delany provides a list of criminal prosecutions that Joneny listened to apart from Leela's. As Joneny searches an index that he finds onboard the Sigma-9, he comes across "45-A7 Milar vs. Khocran; 759-V8 Travis vs. The Norm; 654-M87 DeRogue vs. Blodel; 89-T68L One-Eyed Davis vs. The Norm" and many more (216). But none of these hearings stand out aside from the increasing frequency of One-Eyed trials indicative of an active pogrom. In the last trial "2338-T87 One-Eyed Jack vs. The Norm," the Sigma-9's Captain Alva beseeches the judge to demonstrate leniency to Jack as an important part of the ship's navigation staff and to release him into the captain's custody (216). We learn that this request is made on behalf of all the captains across the fleet and it *is* an important one because the judges are the "Spiritual Heads" of each ship, responsible "for moral cleanliness . . . representative of the Norm" (217–218). The judge refuses the appeal and the case against One-Eyed Jack, a "physical and mental deviate of the first magnitude," Case 2338–587 Jackson O-E-5611 vs. The Norm, goes forward (218). In his own defense, Jackson states how he was born with a "full set of brains" that he used to study "information about Earth and our goals" without the approval of the Norm and how he also joined a group of like-minded individuals in this pursuit (218). He is just a regular guy.

However, the judge trots out the medical examiner Dr. Lang who informs One-Eyed Jack/Jackson O-E-5611 of his differences from the Norm for his ship. Jackson stands at "six feet, one and half inches" while the Norm is "five feet-nine and three-quarter inches" and that Jackson is also "a chronic nail-biter, and has been so since early childhood," which "is quite far away from the Norm, a condition that exists in less than .08 percent of the population" (219). But Dr. Lang doesn't stop there, she also indicates how his "weight [of] 169 pounds" places him seven pounds over "the Norm of 162" although she notes that Jackson "conforms well to the Norm in dexterity" and in being right-handed (220). Then again, Dr. Lang observes that "there is a slight difference in length of limbs, right arm nearly a centimeter and a half longer than the left. The Norm is a discrepancy of only a centimeter" (220). Likewise, Jackson has broken his nose twice "quite definitely out of the Norm" and also has a "small birthmark on his right shoulder," which "is completely away from the Norm" along with a "perspiration index" that goes beyond the Norm. Dr. Lang really gets down to the nitty-gritty when talking of Jackson's "glandular secretions, submetabolic functions, and tropal differentiations" and ultimately recommends his death (220–221). In a last-ditch effort to stave off an execution sentence, Jackson declares:

> "For the love of knowledge, I am questioning. I'm telling you we're not a bunch of mutant monsters. I'm telling you we're only people who are trying to guard what's left of wisdom in this barbaric cave you call a City. Your beloved Norm! To close off twenty people in a section and gas them for their love of history; to chase a man out of hiding with a herd of specially bred twenty-pound rats because he knows multiple calculus; to inject a woman with half a dozen pathological viruses until she confesses Gödel's incompleteness theorem and then sentence her to the Death's Head as an unredeemable mutant; what Norm does this conform to? Does this meet any standard of human—" (222)

At this point, the trial gets disrupted by the news of the impending destruction of the Delta-6. The norms even blame the One-Eyes for the destruction of the ships for not following the rituals.

A few pages later, Joneny learns that One-Eyed Jackson was still executed by the Norm when he comes across Captain Hank Brandt's log. Identity politics and the distortions of civil rights and court cases floating around in the background of the ballad prove to create an intense *noirum* for our twenty-first century sensibilities with a right-wing, ultra conservative, religious-leaning Supreme Court that has struck down affirmative action after jettisoning abortion rights. His imaginary court upholds racial politics as the Norms castigate difference and radiate a white fear of difference as evinced by the people who deviate from the Norm in the text with respect to height, weight, finger length, and so on. Delany offers clear racial commentary on the events going on around him in the 1960s through the novella. That's how Delany's own Blackness surreptitiously manifests in the novella despite the restrictions he faced from the white literary establishment—editors and publishers like Campbell. As Sandra Govan remarks, T'wabaga's "primary research shows him that the foibles of fear, intolerance, and oppression doomed the human progeny on the starship. The travelers enacted half-remembered Earth 'rituals' that codified both appearance and social and behavioral attitudes. Any deviation from 'the Norm' was punishable by death" ("Insistent," 46). Essentially, the Norm practice a deadly form of colorblindness in that they don't recognize diversity of any sort. They are entirely intolerant. Delany himself states, "The realities of race—if that is the proper term for what I take to be in all of its manifestations a system of political oppression grounded on a biological fantasy—also come up, now and again, as they must, in the discussion of any black man or woman carried out extensively enough, in this or such a nation" ("Introduction," 8). Race may be a socially fabricated construct, yet racism has definitive material power. This fabricated racial reality of political oppression *is* why the *noirum* exists in the first place—to expose the system and dismantle it with powerful counternarratives. Joneny sees the end result of the Star Folk's pogrom, where their descendants have devolved into "degenerate morons," early in the novella (180).

Joneny's anthropological investigation, composed of traces, clues, signs, documents, recordings, observations, and alien encounters, signals an alternate understanding of the future of white supremacy in that it dead ends, but not without harming others. Signs of the racial past reflect on the future and that's what Delany shows us; the possibility of a future, where race doesn't matter in the same way to Joneny Horatio T'wabaga's world. Perhaps, Delany provides a trace of the future through his defamiliarized past.

Imagining a Black President: Philip K. Dick's *A Crack in Space*

Race may very well be the only connection between Delany's and Dick's mid-1960s work; that, or their seeming popularity in the SF community. Honestly, Dick's *A Crack in Space* (1966), a lesser novel in his oeuvre, brims with so many ideas that I have difficulty deciding which one is the novum. Set in the late twenty-first century, his novel features a Black president-elect, interdimensional travel, parallel Earths, a space station whore house led by a mutant, overpopulation, cryogenic stasis, and Peking man. Most likely, the population crisis represents Dick's novum. Overpopulation, hence food scarcity, housing shortages, and joblessness, leads to the increased racial tensions in the election year of 2080, where the Republican-Liberal candidate Jim Briskin attempts to become the first Black president. The space/time fracture results from a malfunctioning part in a Jiffi-scuttler transport that in turn causes the gateway to the parallel Earth. Dick reveals an indefinite *noirum* in the second paragraph of the opening chapter, the government's creation of "the U.S. Department on Special Public-Welfare," as a young dark-skinned couple ask "to be put to sleep . . . to become bibs" for potentially hundreds of years because of the poor job market (5). Two pages later, we learn that "almost all of them, like this couple . . . *the tens of millions of sleeping*" people "are young. And—dark" (7). Stacking BIPOC bodies in the cold storage of ninety-four government warehouses—that's Dick's real answer to the predicted overpopulation problem.

Briskin campaigns for planetary colonization on national TV in order to wake the sleeping bibs. He later delivers on his promise by announcing the news of the rent in space-time, interdimensional travel, and the apparently uninhabited parallel Earth, during a Chicago speech. Thus, Briskin forces the States Rights Conservative Democrat President William Schwarz to begin waking bibs for emigration through the Terran Development company, which desires to exploit the natural resources of this second Earth by exploiting BIPOC labor itself. In truth, President Schwarz attempts to hold on to political power by mining age-old white fears of losing jobs to dark-skinned people, termed Cols in the novel. I find the flipped social polarities of the two political parties in the novel enjoyable if telling—liberal Republicans and conservative Democrats, who would have thought it other than Dick?! Of course, the initial exploration crew discovers that the "Alter-Earth" is already inhabited by another group of hominids deemed "Sinanthropus, a rather high form of Pithecanthropus, or Peking man" (138, 115). Before too long humanity starts deriding the indigenous species as "Pekes" and begins thinking on the "nasty" business of "interbreeding" (128). The government decides to shut down colonization until they can expand the rift and increase the emigration flow. By the time they reopen the rift, it is the Pekes who invade Earth, aided by the conjoined-twin businessman George Walt who once owned the orbital brothel but escaped through the rift to the other Earth and made himself king. The Pekes abruptly leave Earth upon learning that Walt is no different from the other lying humans. While colonization has been aborted, Briskin wins the election and has to deal with the fallout of this colossal emigration failure as the novel ends.

I suppose Dick attempts some kind of socially conscious racial commentary through *The Crack in Space*, but he fails despite his recognized penchant for cascading ideas. The Pekes obviously represent some kind of social protest against the war in Vietnam on Dick's part, which he inverts by having the Pekes, whose main cities exist in Southeast Asia, invade the United States. But, really, his racial critique ends there. Briskin, a Black presidential candidate, does not interact with other Cols in the novel whatsoever. Briskin comes across as a de facto white man and still faces curtailment of his own social capital by his white staff and opposition by the white supremacist group CLEAN, who desperately want to "KEEP THE WHITE HOUSE WHITE . . . KEEP AMERICA CLEAN" (17). Likewise, Dick offers up another peculiar institution. That is to say, Dick thought about the future problem of Black and Brown people as the majority US population and, perhaps, he did not like what he surmised, which is why the BIPOC population is put on ice and reawakened after discovery of the crack in space to colonize the parallel Earth ruled by Peking Man. The American government of Dick's world has spent untold billions on these cryogenic warehouses for BIPOCS, making it the main housing program for its majority-minority population and marking it segregated although the white population seems tired of footing the expense in the early stages of the novel. "For the state," according to sociologist Loïc Wacquant, "the penalization of poverty turns out to be financially ruinous" in the creation of this massive penal system ("Class," 84). I mean, what else can it be for these undesirable and semiliterate US citizens? He wants to parole them to a parallel Earth, to fight the indigenous population, and to send this second Earth's natural resources back to enrich white people. Indeed, Dick perpetuates social inequality and exacerbates ethno-racial marginality in his weak call for economic and social justice to perhaps assuage his own sense of guilt concerning racial fears so clearly visible in others of his stronger works, for example, *The Man in the High Castle* (1962) and its final solution for the African continent.

Dick's *noirum* fails spectacularly because his imaginary law repeats the pattern of continual BIPOC exploitation by maintaining the status quo of a capitalist white future led by a tokenized Black president.

Colorblind Dreaming: Ursula K. Le Guin's *The Lathe of Heaven*

I trust Ursula K. Le Guin had good intentions when she wrote her early novel *The Lathe of Heaven* (1971)—separate from the Earthsea books as well as her Hainish cycle. Le Guin tackles climate change, overpopulation, war, religion, drug abuse, mental health, and racial issues in this novel as she explores the nature of reality through dreams and the alternate realities that result from a desire to make the world a better place in a spare SF novel by today's standards. This compact novel pops with nearly as many ideas as Dick's *The Crack in Space*. Its novum involves a man whose dreams change reality and a machine to augment them.

Set in a dystopian Portland, the protagonist George Orr attempts to block his "effective" dreams, dreams that impact the real world and that alter reality, by abusing drugs (14). After being apprehended, George is given the choice of jail or "VTT—Voluntary Therapeutic Treatment" (3). Naturally, George chooses treatment whereupon he meets the antagonist Dr. William Haber, a psychiatrist who specializes in sleeping disorders. Dr. Haber comes to believe George's claims through small tests using his dream analyzing and enhancing machine "the Augmentor" (17). In turn, Dr. Haber recognizes the potential uncontrolled power that George has at his disposal and begins to manipulate his patient to create a better world.

Suspicious of Dr. Haber's motives, George retains the services of attorney Heather Lelache with whom he falls in love as the novel progresses. Lelache takes the case and agrees to sit in on one of the therapy sessions. At this session, Dr. Haber convinces George to end the overpopulation problem through hypnotherapy before using the Augmentor. George's ensuing dream results in a plague that kills "six billion people" (65). Dr. Haber believes that he has convinced Lelache of George's delusions. Consequently, Dr. Haber continues with his experiments and asks George to end war by dreaming of a "world at peace with itself": "No more mass killing of humans by other humans. No fighting in Iran and Arabia and Israel. No more genocides in Africa. No stockpiles of nuclear and biological weapons, ready to use against other nations. No more research on ways and means of killing people. A world at peace with itself. Peace as a universal lifestyle on Earth" (85). But this new dream leads to space warfare with aliens in the shape of "giant sea turtle[s]" on the moon and humanity coming together to prevent the invasion (121). Lelache recognizes the effective dream, tracks George down at a remote cabin in the woods, and puts him under hypnosis to dream a kinder Dr. Haber and aliens no longer on the moon. But the subsequent dream now creates a planetary alien invasion instead. We learn that the aliens are peaceful and only dropped bombs because of a misunderstanding of human languages and culture in thinking bombs were a sign of friendship.

Humans and aliens now live a comfortable existence side by side, but George has a problem of all the realities and memories jumbled together in his mind. The next effective dream turns everyone gray,[16] although Lelache disappears. As Thulani Davis suggests, "the most hopeful sci-fi . . . is being written by women like Ursula K. LeGuin, for whom mulatto culture is one solution" ("Future," 19). Definitely, gray-skinned people represent the Black and white mixed-race people that Davis mentions. Le Guin nullifies racial categories and notions of superiority with this move, but I wonder if this monotone reinforces the idea of race for her audience. Anyhow, Dr. Haber is close to making the Augmentor work on himself and George wants to stop him. The next dream has an alien in place of Dr. Haber, who suggests that George dream Heather Lelache back into existence and she becomes his gray-skinned wife. Time passes. Dr. Haber unleashes chaos on the world when he tries the Augmentor on himself and George stops him by hitting the off button. Haber ends up in an insane asylum with a broken mind as the world resets with aliens existing along with color. Le Guin writes that "there were still gray people now, it was said, particularly in the Middle West and Germany, but most of the rest had gone back to white, brown, black, red, yellow, and mixtures" (182). Heather Lelache, now the widowed Mrs. Andrews, has no memory of George when he meets her at his job in an alien design firm for kitchen equipment and the novel ends on the anticipation of an arranged coffee date. All of these human problems and solutions occur in the span of 184 pages! *The Lathe of Heaven* is a marvelous achievement in my estimation, but supremely flawed.

With all of that said, Le Guin offers the softest of *noirums*; soft in the sense that there are no legal ramifications beyond George Orr choosing therapy over jail and enlisting the aid of an attorney. Her soft *noirum* complicates my understanding of the CRT SF device as she explores the problem of the color line. Her *noirum* aggravates racial politics because she presents a colorblind solution as memories of worlds past begin to take a toll on George's mind. The next big effective dream ends racism because everyone the world over "wore the same clothes, trousers, tunic, raincape; and underneath the clothes they were all the same color. They were gray" (129). The richer, more powerful, and honest version of Dr. Haber explains the solution to the racial conundrum to a questioning George:

> "Precisely. And of course I was envisioning a political and ethical solution. Instead of which, your primary thinking processes took the usual shortcut, which usually turns out to be a short circuit, but this time they went to the root. Made the change biological and absolute. There never has been a racial problem! You and I are the only two men on earth, George, who know that there ever was a racial problem! Can you conceive of that? Nobody was ever outcaste in India—nobody was ever lynched in Alabama—nobody was massacred in Johannesburg! War's a problem we've outgrown and race is a problem we never even had! Nobody in the history of the human race has suffered for the color of his skin." (129–130)

To my way of thinking, this initial solution represents an evasion that she later tries to correct. Le Guin foresees the dominant racial ideologies of the twenty-first century but denies the evil of segregation having ever happened and diminishes discrimination against Black people with an abstract sense of liberalism. As Black political sociologist Eduardo Bonilla-Silva explains, "abstract liberalism involves using ideas associated with political liberalism (e.g., 'equal opportunity,' the idea that force should not be used to achieve social policy) and economic liberalism (e.g., choice, individualism) in an abstract manner to explain racism" (*Racism*, 56). A colorblind solution *is* no solution because it enables whites to ignore inequality with the supposed level playing field created by affirmative action. Whites claim reverse discrimination when not hired or accepted to prestigious universities like Harvard because of racial preferences for admission in the quest for diversity. Le Guin entirely dismisses the lived experiences of Black people with this move and even makes it worse with her failed correction of "gray people" in her world alongside white, brown, black, red, yellow, and other combinations. This *is* exactly what colorblindness looks like as in the cliché "I don't care if you're black, white, green, purple, or orange polka-dotted." However unintentional, this move *is* dismissive on Le Guin's part. Such prismatic listings of people attempt to refract racism in order to rationalize liking a Black person as if a Black person should be ashamed of their melanin, their skin color, their socially constructed racial difference materially manifested because a white person willingly, if not graciously, overlooks this one physical detail as if we don't have humanity in common. This sentiment generates hard feelings nearly impossible to pardon. I don't mean outward white supremacists either; I mean well-meaning white people who do this stuff all the time. The conjuring of imaginary gray people expunges that quality of Blackness, that inviolable, incorporeal, incandescent sense of soul. This conjuring omits a very real white privilege.

With this offered solution, Heather Lelache winks out of existence because of her biracial heritage. But not George Orr or Dr. Faber. Only Heather Lelache, the mixed child of an interracial marriage between a white woman and a Black man. Readers first learn of Lelache's color at the end of chapter 4 when she shakes her new client's hand, sticking "out her brown hand, he met it with a white one," reminding her of "that damn button her mother always kept in the bottom of her bead box, SCNN or SNCC or something she'd belonged to way back in the middle of the last century, the Black hand and the White hand joined together" (54). Her unnamed white mother belonged to the Student Nonviolent Coordinating Committee during the civil rights movement as evinced by the organization's logo button. And her father "was a real militant Black Power type" born into "a welfare family" who quits his wife and child by going "off to Africa" (103). Le Guin figures this Black father as a walking stereotype—Black and poor in addition to being a deadbeat dad searching for some connection to the motherland. With this assessment of her own parentage, Heather Lelache expresses confusion about her own identity to the point where she "can't decide which color I am," to which George gently responds, "Brown" (104). Lelache fits the stereotype of not belonging in either racial group, which causes her distress.

Le Guin simply reinforces this idea when she disappears Heather Lelache (along with Martin Luther King Jr.). George thinks to himself that "she could not have been born gray. Her color, her color of brown, was an essential part of her" that "her anger, timidity, brashness, gentleness, all were elements of her mixed being, her mixed nature" (130). Because she does not fit either group, she ceases to exist. Heather Lelache embodies the tragic mulatta trope that white abolitionist Lydia Maria Child originated in "The Quadroons" (1842) through the character Rosalie. More importantly, Le Guin centers whiteness because George lives on and George remembers brown Heather Lelache as aggressive while the later gray version of Heather Lelache becomes his wife and is gentler. It is almost as if Le Guin cannot leave the stereotype of the angry Black woman alone, that Blackness makes her prone to violence. Nonetheless, Le Guin herself demonstrates courage in featuring a major character as a Black woman and I find that a redeeming quality. Le Guin at least attempts to contextualize and examine the larger picture of interracial relationships and its racial underpinnings by forcing us to consider the taboo in a way different to Delany's depiction in *The Ballad of Beta-2*. Their love symbolizes this soft *noirum* too because of its perception as a social problem in the United States and the biases it generates in a predominantly monotoned genre.

Perhaps Le Guin blames George Orr for our country's racial struggles. That would be a fascinating interpretation of the novel. For certain, it provides me with moral comfort to place the blame where it is most appropriate—quite the hard truth. She dares ask who we are as Americans and why we keep failing and how we go onward.

Time Travel and the Race War: John Jakes's *Black in Time*

The final precursor *noirum* worth mentioning has to be the provocatively titled *Black in Time* (1970) by John Jakes. Certainly, there are others, like Norman Spinrad's *Bug Jack Barron* (1969),[17] but I feel Jakes's notoriety as the author of the best-selling *North and South* civil war trilogy[18] from the 1980s—adapted into a major television mini-series broadcast on the ABC network and that impacted my young sensibilities—better qualifies. *Black in Time* begins with an epigraph from the classic Langston Hughes poem "The Negro Speaks of Rivers" (1921) to indicate the deepness of time, the flow of time in one direction, human civilization, and Black heritage. Jakes admits to feeling "a bit uncomfortable, not to say presumptuous, trying the create black characters and represent attitudes" and freely acknowledges "that the black characters and their personal styles may be off the mark" in his attempt "to create a mural of black history, fairly large, and authentic in detail" (7). From there, Jakes drops us into his time travel story, which functions as the novum, by introducing us to the Black protagonist Harold Quigley, professor of speech and theater at the imaginary Ruggles University, a stand in for the highly regarded Howard University. Harold happens to be observing the Roman African playwright Publius Terentius Afer, better known as Terence to the English-speaking world, directing a rehearsal of his comedy *The Eunuch* in Rome in 160 BCE. The Nexus computer, the time travel machine, whisks him back to the near-future present of 1977 on the outskirts of Washington, DC at the Freylinghausen Foundation, directed by the colorblind Dr. Norval Freylinghausen. I say colorblind because Dr. Freylinghausen tells Harold that he'd "be a leading theater scholar in any collegium, white to apple green" (14). His not seeing color denies an uncomfortable cultural difference and allows him to ignore the racism prevalent in American society by appealing to Harold's scholarly verve.

In any case, Jakes quickly introduces us to the novel's two antagonists. As Harold heads to his sister Sally's house party, he passes through the city, where large numbers of Blacks and whites are milling around the capital, and sees "the big posters plastered on sides of buildings: a white Christ, eyes uprolled to the sky, right hand raised and fisted in mockery of the old black power gesture, robe a multi-stripe of red, white, and blue" (18). These posters represent a militant Christian America centered on white supremacist solidarity with the strange cooptation of a Black pride symbol; such cooptation seems truly prescient in today's moment as the American far right agitates for continuing oppression of BIPOCs through open racism, political conservativism, and outright terrorism. These white nationalist posters in the text put up by the AAAF demonstrate the prevailing racial attitudes of the day. The Right Reverend Billy Roy Whisk, head of the "All-American Apostolic Fellowship" leads the rally and parade in the heart of DC (26). But the Black militant group BURN, "Brothers United for Revolution Now," lead by Jomo, oppose Whisk's boys (21). Naturally, a riot ensues when a member of Whisk's inner circle is killed by an unidentified BURN member at the rally in addition to a white police sergeant being shot. The unidentified Burn member happens to be Harold's brother-in-law Gator.

These events set the novel's action in motion as Jomo, the Black militant, and Whisk, the white supremacist, force Harold to take them back in time chasing each other, trying to prevent the unthinkable alteration of history, where either the Black race rules the future or the white race eliminates Black people entirely. In other words, both men attempt to use the time machine to benefit their own respective races by altering history. So, we have an all-out race war across time. All Harold wants to do is rescue his sister and protect his brother-in-law from the clutches of Whisk and his entourage without changing the future. To do so, he must stop both of the bad guys while struggling with his own racial consciousness. This is the *noirum*, stopping the bad guys and tuning into his inner Blackness, his inestimable soul power.

Jomo makes the first move in the race war. He travels back to 1591 to the West African city of Timbuktu in the late Songhai Empire and attempts to assassinate the Muslim prophet Mohammad because he thinks such an action will allow the Black African empire to keep thriving in the absence of Islam. But he fails despite Harold informing him of the dangers of altering history. Harold merely intellectualizes the danger without trying to physically stop Jomo from creating an actual deviation. Yet, Harold takes a different approach to stopping Whisk by any means necessary. Whisk strikes back and strikes often with his own time jumping. First, he jumps to 1862 intending to assassinate President Lincoln before Lincoln even drafts the Emancipation Proclamation. Second, Whisk leaps to Maine in winter 1851 to burn Harriet Beecher Stowe's manuscript of *Uncle Tom's Cabin; or, Life Among the Lonely* before its 1852 publication. This time jump is closely followed by his third trip, a return further back in time to 1838 Maryland, where Whisk attempts to prevent Frederick Douglass from escaping bondage by alerting the slave breaker Edward Covey, now named Jeb Falco. Fourth, Whisk attempts to choke Benjamin Franklin to death at a Quaker meeting in Philadelphia at some point in the eighteenth-century, although Jakes doesn't specify if it is before or after the Revolutionary War.

Jomo seizes the initiative after the Franklin incident. He jumps back to the ancient Kingdom of Lydia in Asia Minor to strand the "white nigger" Harold in the seventh-century BCE time of Aesop, who may have been Black, but most certainly was enslaved (107). Jomo breaks Harold's Nexus time-tracking device so he cannot follow him. Harold travels to 1645 where the *Rainbowe* is in Boston's port, thinking that Jomo may try to prevent the city of Boston's first transatlantic slave voyage, and then on to 1619 to avert the first slave purchase by Virginia colonizers from a Dutch ship, although we now know it was actually the English warship *White Lion* that transported and sold the twenty or so captive Africans. But Jomo isn't there either, so Harold travels to late 1890s New York City and ends up in the middle of a raging race war with Blacks and whites killing each other and burning the city.

Jomo succeeds. The race war seemingly ties back to Nat Turner's 1831 uprising in Southampton, Virginia as evinced by rioters' shouts. Harold also learns that Booker T. Washington was blown up at the Cotton States and International Exposition in Atlanta while delivering his infamous "Atlanta Compromise" address to a large, rich, white audience in 1895, thus enabling him to pinpoint where history forked. Harold's passive approach to stopping Jomo drastically changes. He wrestles with Jomo beneath the stage, just as Washington proclaims the separate fingers part of his speech with respect to social mingling between the races, and manages to secure the dynamite. Jomo escapes in time again back to Mohammad's era a second time and manages to murder the prophet, which prevents the rise of Islam and preserves the Songhai empire.

Harold fails and decides to return to 1977. In this future present, whites were the enslaved ones who now fight for their civil rights. The Republic of New Songhay maps onto what was once the United States, different technologies dominate, and cities have different names. However, the Freylinghausen Foundation never exists and this new timeline begins to correct itself. Harold, Jomo, Whisk, and the others begin to fade because they were never born. Jomo disappears from existence. Hence, they have to go back in time once more to reset the timeline in which they exist. Harold stops Jomo from killing the prophet and then forces Whisk to chase after him by kissing Whisk's girlfriend Adelaide. This act of miscegenate intimacy enrages the white supremacist who follows Harold through time, relentlessly in pursuit. Ultimately, Harold traps Whisk in the hold of a slave ship dead in the ocean, where crew and cargo were overwhelmed by disease. He returns to the present and Dr. Freylenghausen shuts down his foundation as the novel ends.

Jakes packs so many possible alternate branches into his short novel. It is impractical to assess them all. But I will say Jakes clearly has fun imagining what events might refigure history. For example, would assassinating President Lincoln before he can issue the Emancipation Proclamation change the outcome of the Civil War in the United States? This plan most likely would have failed because Lincoln's vice president during his first term was Hannibal Hamlin of Maine, an abolitionist loyal to Lincoln who fully supported the Emancipation Proclamation as well as Black troops. However, the Tennessee Democrat Andrew Johnson does succeed Lincoln as president. And, as we already know, Johnson was much more sympathetic to the Southern cause as proven by his deliberate favoring of the South during Reconstruction, which lead to his impeachment by Republicans.

I think the decision Jakes makes to have Whisk destroy *Uncle Tom's Cabin* a more compelling possibility as a key counterfactual hinge point. Never underestimate the power of a good book to influence cultural opinion. *Uncle Tom's Cabin* is the premier antislavery novel written to show the evil of slavery to the nineteenth-century reading public. A sentimental novel relying on its ability to generate an emotional response to the plot's action, it was a smashing success as the most read work of fiction in the nineteenth century,[19] although it generated plenty of Black stereotypes, such as being labeled a sellout, that thrive to this day. As far as I know, *Uncle Tom's Cabin* has not been out of print since its initial publication in 1852. Destroying the sole draft manuscript would have set the abolitionist cause back for years as Northerners might not have focused their anger on the Fugitive Slave Act of 1850 and Southerners would have remained delighted with the image of happy slaves it projected to the country and Europe. Without that novel, Blacks might still be enslaved.

The same could be said for the best-known slave narrative—*Narrative of the Life of Frederick Douglass* (1845). If Douglass doesn't escape slavery, he doesn't write this account of his life nor its other two versions, *My Bondage and My Freedom* (1855) and *The Life and Times of Frederick Douglass* (1892). The undeniable power of this autobiography has changed the world for the better from the moment if its publication. It is a foundational text in American literature that testifies to Black fortitude, intelligence, and creativity, among many other superlatives. In fact, I cannot imagine a world without this text. Jakes presents us with a true moment, where time travelers could drastically upset the future. This is called a "Jonbar point" in science fiction criticism (Langford), where Frederick Douglass could have died just another enslaved man as opposed to the legendary Black abolitionist orator.

Jakes does his best. He directly confronts US racial history and its many injustices to Black people in his critical examination of a 1970 present painted in science fictional varnish and demands his audience to face it. The *noirum* helps us see this confrontation in imagining the Emancipation Proclamation executive order not being written, the publication of Uncle Tom's Cabin not happening, or the escape of Frederick Douglass not occurring. Despite indulging in Black stereotypes like the brutish and cunning Jomo, Jakes does condemn the white supremacist Christian preacher as well as the regression of American ideals that many white Americans cling to stubbornly. I mean, the Confederate flag, in all its malevolence, flies somewhere in every state in 2023, almost to the point where I have to question if maybe the South did actually win. Afterall, the colorblind eyes of contemporary society still allow disenfranchisement of its Black citizens and still enslaves them in prison through a loophole in the Thirteenth Amendment, abolishing slavery except as a punitive measure for the possibility of a crime committed.

Pre-CRT

Each of these writers plays with an American legal system influenced by a culture in which the reality of racial difference is subsumed by a default whiteness (as if by fiat—declaring the constitution "colorblind"—racism in the legal system is wiped away), and the tradition in SF that situates white people as the default standard of what it is to be a people. *Noirums* function in these pre-1976 works to combat colorblindness to one degree or another. Put simply, all the works play with colorblindness—Elliott's clerk does not see color in the letters he censors; Vonnegut does not see color in the 213 constitutional amendments that create a false equivalency between people; Delany's Norms wipe out anyone who appears different from their monochromatic view of humanity; Dick puts BIPOCs on ice so white people can live comfortably until a parallel Earth, ripe for colonization, is discovered; Le Guin turns all people gray at one point; and the inventor of the time machine doesn't see the skin color of his Black subordinate in the Jakes novel despite the race war that follows.

As a whole, Elliott, Vonnegut, Delany, Dick, Le Guin, and Jakes create absorbing counternarratives to the prevailing social conditions of the mid-twentieth-century United States. These authors grapple with the racist legacies of the Jim Crow era and the ongoing struggle for civil rights in what seems a never-ending battle lasting beyond this moment, sometimes referred to as the second reconstruction, roughly the end of World War II through the early 1970s, as the country attempts to correct American Apartheid through government action and laws. The *noirum* allows us as readers to both witness and testify to the emotion structures of these writers grappling with Black consciousness and white anxiety. It gifts us the ability to see and resist color-line politics through science fiction narratives. This resistance could be construed as Afrofuturistic. There is hope for justice and hope for equality and hope for a real freedom, a freedom to go where a person wants, when a person wants, to do what a person likes, again and again and again as we circle the sun. The *noirum* insists on BIPOC belonging, citizenship, and freedom as it explores racial myths and hegemonic discourses.

While fairness and racial equality represent standard parts of the democratic vista Americans believe about their nation, this uncritical utopian vision comes apart when faced by the pressures of social reality. As SF scholar Mark C. Jerng remarks, the "uses of race produce conditions for making racism a built-in knowledge for our participation in the world" and we must "develop strategies of antiracist racial worldmaking" to change the future, to reimagine it (*Racial*, 208). This is one of the fundamental reasons to study SF and Afrofuturism with CRT in mind, to pull together the threads of an endangered Blackness distributed across multiply envisioned colorblind futures and to focus specifically on minority-authored future pasts with disruptive counternarratives that awaken people to the likelihood of a deepening racialization resulting in the death of humanity itself. We simply must prevent such an end! It *is* that crucial!

CHAPTER 2

Confinement Narratives

While a few Black-authored zombie stories exist, none are as powerful as Justina Ireland's duology *Dread Nation* (2018) and *Deathless Divide* (2020) from a CRT perspective. Ireland turns the zombie narrative on its head with her novum: the undead rise during the second day of the battle of Gettysburg, halting the American Civil War. And her *noirum* occurs with "Congress fund[ing] the Negro and Native Reeducation Act" (17). As Jane McKeene, the novel's protagonist, tells us: "the Negro and Native Reeducation Act mandates that at twelve years old all Negroes, and any Indians living in a protectorate, must enroll in a combat school 'for the betterment of themselves and of society.' The argument went that we benefitted from compulsory education, as it provides a livelihood for formerly enslaved, who couldn't find gainful employment after the war. Whites, therefore, were excluded from the law" (116). Think about it! The Emancipation Proclamation does occur in this timeline since Lincoln issues executive order 95 on September 22, 1862, which takes effect on January 1, 1863. So, slaves existing and enduring in the Confederate States in active rebellion are freed. Great. However, the Battle of Gettysburg occurs from July 1–3, 1863, and the zombie apocalypse starts on the second day of the battle at the Little Round Top engagement on July 2, 1863. President Lincoln never gives the "Gettysburg Address" nearly five months later on November 19, 1863. Likewise, this alteration means the Thirteenth, Fourteenth, and Fifteenth Amendments never happen. This alteration means Jim Crow, if we date segregation to the end of the Civil War, never happens. This alteration also means the South never lost the war and the North never won the war either. Instead, we get this new act and race and racism continue on much as it did before. In the resulting alternate history, the federal government passes the act to train certain minority children as warriors to combat the rising tide of undead. Ireland's *noirum* entirely hinges on this legal confinement.

This particular legislation has a profound impact on Jane. She forcibly attends "Miss Preston's School of Combat for Negro Girls," the best of the Reeducation programs for Black girls (8). At Miss Preston's, Jane also meets her frenemy Katherine, a pretty, light-skinned teenager capable of passing for white who later becomes the joint protagonist of *Deathless Divide*. Anyhow, let's dig into the nomenclature of this imaginary congressional act a little bit more, specifically "reeducation." Reeducation implies many things, such as rehabilitation or learning how to adapt to new situations like a zombie apocalypse but also indoctrination to better oppress and control minorities in this particular storyworld. Reeducation exclusively targets Blacks and Indians and intones a servile quality since the policy forces young children to attend combat schools designed to protect white people. Jane and the other girls learn hand-to-hand combat, fighting with bladed weapons, guns, and rifles to better dispatch shamblers as well as receive proper etiquette instruction although not reading (imagine that!) to better serve their white employers as attendants. Talk about a peak moment of interest convergence, where white self-interests further oppress racial minorities to safeguard itself in the aftermath of a zombie apocalypse!

A bit later in the novel, Ireland introduces us to Daniel Redfern, a Lenape Indian, taken from his family at the age of six and pressed into joining an "industrial school," where he endured many beatings and haircuts until graduating and working for Mayor Carr of Baltimore (163). Ireland utilizes the real history of Indian boarding schools,[1] which forced Indigenous people to assimilate American ideals and culture through separation, religious education, and civilized appearance by destroying their own cultures, to further nuance the plight of her minority characters. Redfern becomes Jane's bounty-hunting partner in the sequel. While Ireland attempts to increase positive representations of minorities in her novel, Redfern is the only Indigenous character to appear in *Dread Nation*. It would be fair to call her out on this shortcoming because she gives short shrift to Indigenous peoples, enfolding them into a story that models the typical Black-and-white binary of racial discourse in the United States. But it would also be wrong to do so because Daniel Redfern's story happens offstage. He survives Baltimore society by presenting "the spitting image of the civilized savage . . . well-cut jacket, fashionable waistcoat, hair pulled back in a queue, well-worn boots, and a Bowie knife strapped to his waist. The perfect combination of gentleman and ruthless killer" (156). He serves whites, but protects Blacks too in seemingly innocuous ways like leaving Jane's prized scythes for her to find and use after transporting Jane and Katherine to Summerland as Mayor Carr's "cargo" on the later journey to the Midwest (186). Crucially, Ireland features an Indigenous character who also suffers racial indignities at the hands of white characters, like being called a "redskin" by Sherriff Snyder (199). This brief highlighting suggests an author fully aware of another powerful race narrative worthy of exploration in American history. Respectfully, she leaves it for others—like Stephen Graham Jones, Louise Erdrich, and Daniel Wilson—to tell.

The idea of confinement, of a preventative and punitive curtailment of physical freedom as political prisoners never convicted of actual crimes beyond being perceived as dangerous, undesirable, different, as members of large racial or ethnic populations, represents the thematic thread stitching together all of the separate visions offered in this chapter. Imprisonment, internment, detention, captivity simply dehumanizes human beings by locking people up in harsh living conditions, pitting them against the institutions that should be relied upon for justice. The rise of the prison-industrial complex, militarized law enforcement, and surveillance technologies, designed to keep BIPOCs in their perceived place, beneath all white people, decidedly implies a darker future that shall be difficult to overcome. Forever alien and alienated. Crossing color lines demonstrates the fullness of our current US dystopia wherein scientific racism, medical experimentation, and genetic research on BIPOCS continues unabated to uphold pernicious notions of racial superiority. However, the *noirum*, in principle, does offer a critical opportunity in terms of racial thought to change the future for the better by delving into this pessimism, this toxicity, this bleakness of racial oppression preventing the United States of America from realizing its potential as the land of the free.

While hundreds of crime and punishment stories exist in SF, I think it pertinent to consider a more common racial landscape for just a moment—prison—before leaping headlong into the chapter. Although I talk at greater length about Steven Barnes's Aubry Knight trilogy in the cyberfunk chapter, Barnes uses a near-future cyberpunk setting as his novum in a dystopian Los Angeles ravaged by an earthquake and a firestorm in his *Streetlethal* (1983). Against this backdrop, Barnes's Black antihero Aubry Knight seeks vengeance on his one-time employers, the Ortegas cartel, who frame him for murder. He ends up in prison at the Death Valley Maximum Security Penitentiary. This prison subplot provides a fascinating side *noirum* as the Ortegas attempt to benefit from their former enforcer even there. In trying to recruit Aubry, the cartel's inside man Denim, a prison gang leader, mentions "Federal Statute 874-BB," which "allows federal prisoners to donate limbs and organs to the Federal Transplant Bureau. In exchange a prisoner can earn money or a reduction in his sentence" (21). Bear in mind Blacks are disproportionately imprisoned, particularly for drug offenses, not to mention the sentencing disparities between the races with respect to crack cocaine, as the war on drugs rages in urban centers across the United States in the 1980s when Barnes is writing his novel. Likewise, the documented cases of unethical experimentation on Black prisoners at "the Holmesburg Prison system" in Philadelphia and other places that went on for decades (Washington, *Medical*, 244). Barnes offers direct commentary on how the American prison system eats people alive.

Additionally, Barnes anticipates the National Organ Transplant Act of 1984, which establishes the public/private partnership between the US government and businesses in creating a national organ donor system dependent on property rights to human corpses. Truthfully, many American citizens consider convicts to be subhuman in the twenty-first century as a reflection of colorblind ideology, making them vulnerable to manipulation of this sort by putting a price tag on their bodies, something akin to slavery, for money to buy essentials at the commissary or shortened time behind bars. Denim facilitates the supposed voluntary organ harvesting exchange. As Denim states, "'Sometimes an order comes down the pike for a kidney, or an eardrum, or an eye . . . and someone has to find an obliging con who wants more than anything else in the world to be a Good Samaritan and help a stranger in need.' . . . 'Needless to say, there are kickbacks . . . I'm sorry, *honoraria*, for any assistance we can offer. I have an excellent arrangement with the assistant warden'" (21). Consequently, in this lopsided conversation, we learn of the lucrative business partnership between the Ortegas and the corrupt assistant prison warden Charteris. Denim grows annoyed with Aubry's silence and provides further details on the arranging of accidents, where a prisoner "falls down a flight of stairs or slips in the shower" and then the discovery of "a Total Donate Card" allowing the prison to take pieces "as might best benefit medical science" (21). At that point, Aubry wishes Denim luck with his business and walks away.

However, Aubrey's one friend in the prison, its librarian Billy Mack, known as Mother, suffers Denim's conscription. Mother is a genetic match for a "Senator's kid" who was high on drugs and involved in an accident—and so Mother provides the "spare parts" (31). Denim and his flunkies, Sugar and Jo Jo, force Mother into giving up "a kidney, a retina, an eardrum, and a few feet of skin" (31). Soon after, Aubry meets Stitch, the new library cart man, who quips about the "muscle tissue" in his left leg that he donated, hollowly stating "'Part of me is playing in the Super Bowl this year. Ain't it a bitch'" (34). Then Mother commits suicide. Aubry may be too late to stop this black-market harvesting, but he does shut down the illegal operation by killing Denim and Sugar while disabling Jo Jo, at which point Charteris attempts to recruit Aubry as his new "go-between" in the unofficial "meat shop" with its "unusual number of prisoners who volunteer to donate or sell body parts" (40). Aubry refuses, undergoes months of deep psychological conditioning to inhibit his elite fighting skills, and eventually escapes with Stitch's aid to enact his revenge plan. Although our current prison system does not seem as brutal as the one imagined by Barnes, it does function through slave labor in an equally parasitic manner to the profit of corporations through an oppressive exploitation. In no small way, Barnes essentially calls for racial justice in drawing attention to the exploding prison industrial complex, largely manned by Black and Brown labor as he anticipates the mass incarceration that Michelle Alexander named the new Jim Crow.

I wanted to take a moment to highlight the Barnes novel because it incorporates two reasons for confinement in this chapter—criminality and medical experimentation. First, Aubry Knight happens to be a Black criminal whereas many of the other characters in the plethora of stories under scrutiny in this chapter *aren't* criminals beyond their color for which they *are* criminalized. Second, unlawful medical experimentation on unwilling Black bodies is a matter of historical fact that many people wish to ignore and represents another crossroad for racial justice because medical abuses have caused Black mistrust of the medical community leading to unfortunate and preventable deaths. It is entirely shameful. The work of this chapter engages with this shame on multiple fronts along multiple color lines.

Indigenous American Reservations

Blackfeet North American Indigenous author Stephen Graham Jones deploys a fascinating double pivoted novum/*noirum* combination on which his novel *The Bird Is Gone: A Manifesto* (2003) oscillates. In the novel the US Federal government signs into law the "CONSERVATION ACT" that "restores all indigenous flora and fauna to the Great Plains" in the near future (170, 164). This law represents the novel's novum while simultaneously functioning as the *noirum* in that it dictates Indians must also return to manage the land as decreed by the creation of a new supersized reservation through the "HUNA Deal," resulting in a reiteration of the Trail of Tears to reach and populate this brand-new Indian territory with all living Indians (166). Thus, whites once again manage to steal the reservation lands left behind, consolidating their own power while exploiting this new territory through tourism and anthropology. Jones presents this counternarrative to control and amplify the call for social justice in his rejection of racist stereotypes and white mythologies of the frontier. This double pivot, per se, grants him control of his argument's fringe signal—or how his book functions as a change agent from beyond the periphery of this nineteenth-century apocalyptic event, recentering the importance of surviving, remembering, and moving forward into the future while further dissipating the continued press of settler colonialism.

To go deeper, the basic premise of the novel concerns how the United States Congress passes the "CONSERVATION ACT," which returns the Dakotas to the Indians in what becomes known as the "Red Alert . . . the now-historic initial radio report that the CONSERVATION ACT had passed" (170). Obviously, this action impacts the main characters gathered at the Fool's Hip Bowling Alley fourteen years into the future of this new world as undercover FBI agent Chassis Jones attempts to solve the mystery of thirty-nine missing white tourists in the Territories (170). Jones fully intends this subversion of the vanishing Indian construct with this jibe as the white tourists replace the indigenous in their presumed demise, unmooring its historically resonant signification as a tragic and recurring motif. We learn that the Anasazi (Pueblo Indian) LP Deal, the first character introduced, employed at the Fool's Hip, is writing a manifesto and recalls "the Skin Parade" and how "he and his mom rolled across the Little Missouri at Camp Crook with nearly four million other Indians" (14). In turn, this fictional recollection evokes the Trail of Tears, an actual series of forced removals and relocations of tens of thousands of Indigenous Americans between 1830 and 1850. As a crucial part of the novel, Jones provides an alphabetized list of terms at the backend, where he first defines the Skin Parade as "the mass exodus following the RED ALERT" as well as provides a secondary definition "a chain of topless bars in Florida, America" (171). As literary scholar Kristina Baudemann explains, "what could be a grave historical signifier pointing toward an event of epic dimensions in *bird* is immediately subverted with a second, comical definition . . . by providing parallel meanings, Jones creates the possibility of alternate readings as a way out of what his characters perceive as the oppressive weight of Indigenous history" ("Removed," 21). With a trickster move, Jones directly challenges setter colonialism by subverting this past reality in ironizing racial attitudes about being Indian and surviving the soul-crushing stereotypes as Indigenous North Americans emerge into a postapocalyptic world.

Interest convergence serves as a compelling analytical frame here to reassess the broken treaties and involuntary marches of the past as these bygone happenings collide with the continuing racist mythology of the vanishing Indian. Jones grants us access to this terrible history from "the standpoint of the oppressed" as the Indians once again make way for whites who still deem their own civilization superior in this future, which is all the justification they need (Matsuda, "When," 33). Because the Indians appear to remain unassimilable to the whites, they are doomed by whites to repeat the fate of their forebears. American Indian Studies scholar Mishuana Goeman, a member of the Tonawanda Band of Seneca, argues that "Natives occupy certain spaces of the nation and are criminalized or erased if they step outside what are seen as degenerative spaces" (*Mark*, 33). Consequently, they must be contained. That is, "the only way to save the tribes was to banish them from the midst of white civilization" as legal scholar Robert A. Williams Jr. suggests ("Documents," 131). Jones skillfully remaps this terrain, further dispelling myths of the vanishing Indian in his call for racial justice.

Importantly, Jones codifies this alternative future through the glossary, which helps readers to understand the novel's implications through its *noirum*. From this wordlist, we learn the full historical ramifications of this alternate Indigenous America legislated by the US government. For instance, Jones fully describes the Conservation Act:

> the accidental solution to the "Indian Problem" (under pressure from Keep America Beautiful, the American Congress signed into law an aggressive bill requiring "the restoration of all indigenous flora and fauna to the Great Plains." As wildlife biologists soon pointed out, though, for a disturbance-dependent landscape to regain anything approaching self-sufficiency—to say nothing of momentum—the reintroduced grass (*buchloë dactyloides*) needed buffalo (*bison bison*) to "disturb" it, and, just as the prairie dog (*cynomys ludovicianus*) needed the disturbance of the blackfooted ferret (*mustela nigripes*), so did the burgeoning herds of reintroduced buffalo need the INDIAN (*canis latrans*). (164)

This list of terms is also the only place in the novel that provides us with information about the "Huna Deal" made with the disingenuous American government and the mess it creates: "The controversial land exchanges immediately following the CONSERVATION ACT where the total acreage of the temporarily 'abandoned' reservations was traded for BLM land immediately surrounding the TERRITORIES, sometimes at the request of the tribe or nation, but, in the case of some of the tribes or nations holding land bordering national parks, without consent, too" (166). The combined weight of meaning behind the Conservation Act and the Huna Deal demonstrates Jones's masterful use of irony in that these double-crossing actions cause an illness known as "Pennies Down Syndrome," which is a "vacant stare associated with those INDIANS who returned home after HAPPY HOUR to find Americans living in their homes, courtesy of the HUNA DEAL, which auctioned their 'abandoned' land for 'pennies on the dollar'" (169). Once again, the American government rips off its Indigenous peoples in a blatant land grab that further reduces the territory of Native Americans to fuel the twin engines of capitalism and empire.

Jones powerfully reminds us of the hundreds of broken treaties and duplicitous deals sponsored by the US government. This time all native Americans populations in the United States are relegated to a space that fits within the white American conception of Indigeneity as a homogenous group living simplistic lives out of sight of the mainstream technologically advancing white civilization—a segregated, concentrated internment reservation. As journalist James L. Dickerson rightfully claims, the Indian Removal Act of 1839, signed by President Andrew Jackson, was "the first federal law to allow internment based on race or ethnic origin and the first to establish a legal basis for restrictive concentration camps" (*Inside*, 23). Literary scholar Mark Rifkin indicates that "The novel underlines the fact that the process of Indianization entails a collapsing of Indigenous peoples into a singular entity envisioned in racial terms" (*Fictions*, 194). In other words, white America does its level best to reduce the Indigenous to a singular identity—as opposed to the many remaining tribes that exist today despite the perpetuation of their world ending and the fight to survive it culturally intact. The *noirum* helps us see this reduction downward into a stereotype.

Jones further intimates that many of these duped Natives feel hopeless. They are trapped in the territories, with mass suicide prevalent in the intervening years: "the year after the parade twenty percent of the population was floating dead in bathtubs" (122). That is to say, 800,000 lives gone in this alternate future, out of the 4,000,000 that made the journey to the Dakotas. However, with the help of "the Code," "a cultural primer or guidebook on INDIAN etiquette," most, if not all, of the remaining Indigenous put on black wigs or, perhaps, grew out their hair, and wear brown contacts while adopting Indian-sounding names to assume a standardized identity for tourists and anthropologists (14; 164). While they metaphorically all look the same to colorblind white eyes and certainly share the same history of settler colonization and genocide, the Indian Territories are worthy of pleasurable sightseeing as well as pseudo-scientific study—objectified Injuns per se.

The noirum facilitates our perceiving exactly how Jones deep dives into the historical trauma of colonization, native stereotypes, and oppression to show what surviving an apocalypse looks like. As Anishinaabe SF scholar Grace L. Dillon remarks, "the histories of Native peoples cannot be forgotten in the rewriting of utopian futures" ("Native," 352). In this respect, Jones revisits this terrible past to move Indigenous peoples into a just future that others could not see with a counternarrative that brusquely critiques white American legal hypocrisies for stealing land and natural resources while also violently removing and relocating the land's owners in an act of ethnic cleansing. He offers his readership a powerful act of resistance with the struck through "~~monograph~~" that appears on the cover and the "manifesto" that replaces it: he asks his audience to consider why he might draw a line through the title, making a public declaration of his intent to remember an un-sanitized Indigenous past. Jones delivers a science fictional manifesto of possible partial meanings that addresses genocide, rape, internment, forced removal, racism, and native stereotypes with wry wit and fury as a matter of survivance.[2] Indeed, the Indigenous continue to resist their own apocalypse as evinced by Jones's powerful and audacious counternarrative that disrupts our sense of equanimity.

To be clear, I am analyzing Indigenous SF here to demonstrate the *noirum*'s flexibility as a science fictional CRT concept that may apply to any SF race story, no matter the race of the US author. In other words, *noirums* are not just produced by African American SF writers. I think Jones's fine novel represents a unique manifestation of the *noirum* because of how the imaginary laws dramatically change the already racialized storyworld. Unquestionably, the *noirum* goes beyond the limitations of Afrofuturism in its recognition of multitudinous racial experiences.

As a second, briefer example, Cherokee nation member Daniel H. Wilson's techno-thriller *Amped* (2012) provides plenty of food for thought.

Wilson creates a powerful near-future race allegory with his chosen novum, the "General Biologics™ Neural Autofocus MK-4® Brain Implant," which helps mentally impaired and physically handicapped American citizens "to increase [their] ability to concentrate on mental and physical tasks by sensing brain wave states associated with inattention" as well as powering "externally worn medical exoskeleton device[s], powered prosthetic limb[s], or micro-electric retinal implant device[s]" (1). This lifesaving and enhancing device dramatically improves the lives of hundreds of thousands of disabled people across the United States, if not the globe, to the point where the amplified individuals are thought to exceed the capacity of their unchanged brethren. The amplified now represent a threat as a new kind of technologically derived ethnicity, "superabled citizens" (12). Consequently, the Pure Human Citizen's Council, informally known as Pure Pride, led by the US senator from Pennsylvania, Joseph Vaughn, arises and stokes fear of the amped, more or less a racial slur, amongst the masses, which leads to federal legislation against the amplified, ushers in "legalized discrimination" (15), and heralds violence across the country. The unofficial containment of the implanted begins in places like the town of Eden in Eastern Oklahoma, preceding the official creation of holding zones by "EXECUTIVE ORDER 14902" to safeguard the nation "against technological threats, be they from home or abroad, and the existence of persons made militarized by implantation technology" (219). However, this discriminatory executive order, merely extends the true *noirum* upon which the entire novel hinges—the imaginary Supreme Court decision *Samantha Blex v. Board of Education*. This horrendous decision determines that "implanted citizens are not a protected class" because "the use of implanted technology constitutes an *elective surgery*," where "implanted students wield an unfair intellectual advantage over nonimplanted students and faculty, interfering with the fair administration of education" (5). In this respect, Wilson imagines how this pretend Supreme Court decision undermines the actual precedent set by the 1954 landmark Supreme Court decision in *Brown v. Board of Education of Topeka*, wherein racial segregation in public schools was found unconstitutional as it violated the Fourteenth Amendment's equal protection clause, signaling the beginning of the end of the Jim Crow era.

* * *

The twofold convergence of interests, where we find Black and Brown SF writers focusing on similar themes of racism and the collapsing of identity into dominant stereotypes, demonstrates the importance of storytelling in the ongoing resistance to erasure. Jones, Wilson, and Barnes provide an effective counterpunch against the prevailing stereotypes constructed by whites for BIPOCs. In a sense, their novels offer us a demographic transformation as their works invite us to experience the bifurcated sense of consciousness that W.E.B. Du Bois made famous in his much earlier color line explorations.[3] We achieve a greater access to the truths of reality as we reconcile the teller's world with the white world, two competing worlds, and the resulting change in cognition generates a flickering sense of a more equitable society as we oscillate between the two worlds and the stories themselves.

Japanese American Internment Camps

One of the most notorious examples of immoral confinement in US history relates to the internment of American citizens of Japanese descent on American soil during World War II. On February 19, 1942, President Franklin D. Roosevelt signs the infamous Executive Order 9066 to limit potential espionage. This order removes roughly 120,000 Japanese Americans to internment camps such as the Manzanar War Relocation Center in California about 230 miles north of Los Angeles. Surely, something like this nefarious order could not possibly happen again. We are talking about actual American concentration camps. The lawful suspension of American citizenship and mass incarceration of another racial group reflects the paradox of American freedom as the US enters World War II to ensure democracy and liberty while denying the civil rights of its own Japanese American minority population. The playwright Perry Miyake, a Sansei, third-generation Japanese American, debuts his first novel *21st Century Manzanar* (2002) on exactly this premise. The near-future, post-9/11 setting of Miyake's novum, World War III, instigated by America's economic collapse and the scapegoating of Japan in this financial ruination, activates the *noirum*—the *noirum* being the nameless president's reinstitution of "Executive Order 9066-A," the antecedent to the "ReVac" of American citizens of Japanese descent; that is to say, they are sent again, re-evacuated, to rebuilt concentration camps such as Manzanar (15, 2). Order 9066-A instructs "persons of Japanese ancestry to sacrifice their jobs to real Americans by leaving the country, or be subject to Re-Evacuation, New and Improved" (15). This mandate of a systematic mass expulsion or compulsory relocation constitutes ethnic cleansing since the American government wants to rid itself of these undesirable citizens. What's more, this imaginary directive hinges on the Asian American model minority myth in that hard working, intelligent, and successful Asian Americans who have overcome discrimination would willingly martyr themselves to appease white folks and remain invisible.

Really, as if other racial groups do not experience the deep alienation of existence in a racist country? As Asian American legal scholar Robert S. Chang remarks, "the current racial paradigm has become naturalized so that race in America is generally understood to mean black and white," which "limits people's understanding and willingness to engage with the history and current situation of Asian Americans in the United States" (*Disoriented*, 11). In this light, Asian Americans are perceived as "interlopers" in what should be and is a multi-voiced struggle for civil rights (11). Like Chang, Asian American legal scholar Mari J. Matsuda "want[s] to hear the voices that represent different ways of living and knowing, particularly those ways that come out of the culture of the historically subordinated . . . the literal voices of difference . . . that have made the streets of the North American cities I love vibrant and alive" ("Voices," 1330). I feel that inclusion of Miyake's novel aids in breaking down the prevailing color line that has been created and institutionalized across time in the United States. The *noirum* exists as such a multi-voiced CRT tool in science fiction, in Afrofuturism, if not all of the American cofuturisms now being recognized and explored, to reclaim our heritage as a nation of immigrants, to witness and repair the seemingly irreparable damage that the invention of race has caused us.

Japanese Americans' color quickly becomes relevant in Miyake's novel. Invisible no longer, Japanese Americans racialize (melaninate) rapidly, no longer assimilable. They become "Alien/Asians" constructed "from multiple anxieties over Asia as pollutive geography, military menace, and economic competitor . . . for 'any single white people'" (Sohn, "Introduction," 6). Yellow peril[4] anxieties, dominant in the early twentieth century, give way to the techno-Orientalism[5] of the late twentieth and early twenty-first centuries. According to Asian American literary scholar Stephen Hong Sohn, such concerns about the "Alien/Asian do not appear out of a sociohistoric vacuum" (11). Consequently, Miyake reflects his awareness of this complex amalgamation of stereotypes through the character David. David dryly recognizes that "No *Blade Runner* futuristic mutation of the American way of life" will occur because of Executive Order 9066-A (53). Miyake extorts these stereotypes to better problematize and defy white racist fears of an Orientalized future.

Miyake uses racial propaganda to warn against this future past recurring. For example, racially offensive songs, like "I Capped a Jap (It's My Patriotic Duty) by DJ Patriot Missile," or television marketing slogans, such as "Look out, America's back and it's not Japanese," and billboards, like "JAP BURNING RALLY & SWAP MEET EVERY SAT & SUN COUNTY FAIRGROUNDS," gain social transaction among most white Americans (2, 13, 90). With the stoking of racial tensions, comes the concomitant violence, resentment, and discrimination that results in the war and necessitates the very existence of the internment camp for those disrupted citizens without legal status. I believe Georgio Agamben figures this condition as "*homo sacer*" wherein *homo sacer*'s "entire existence is reduced to a bare life stripped of every right by virtue of the fact that anyone can kill him without committing homicide; he can save himself only in perpetual flight or a foreign land" (*Homo Sacer*, 8, 183). David Takeda and his siblings Kate and John attempt to voluntarily report to Manzanar before the government deadline like good model minorities. David sees Kate and her children safely board a train, noting that "The American soldiers, wearing helmets bearing an uncomfortable resemblance to Nazi Helmets, began herding the evacuees into the cattle cars" (2). Miyake does not lightly make this comparison to the Holocaust trains that transported Jews to death camps. He wants his audience to understand the gravity of the situation he postulates with this government action that could become a final solution in all its evil. David ironically remarks that the American government must have learned a lesson because "there were no TV cameras, no Minicams to be seen. No footage of American citizens being herded onto cattle cars for future historical re-interpretationists to throw in their faces" (3). It is ironic in the sense that we were already living in a surveillance society in the early twenty-first century—and that no one recording footage of this budding atrocity would be incredible.

David waits on John to arrive so they can ride together to the camp. But John never arrives. While caught in an LA traffic jam on the 405 South Overpass, John is murdered, beaten, and stomped to death by a pair of unemployed twentysomething white supremacists who jump out of their GM pickup truck. As the deadly attack begins, John already knows that "the Vincent Chin rule would apply" (8).[6] In Begoña Simal González's words, John, if not all Americans of Japanese descent, is "a dispensable outcast . . . beyond legal rights" ("Revisiting," 164, 171). There are no legal consequences for his murderers; John's life is stripped of meaning because of his Asian-ness.

David only learns this heartrending news when he recognizes his brother's charred 1960 Chevy Impala on the local TV broadcast. Still, David hastens to make it to the camp himself after going down to the morgue, identifying his brother's body, and arranging the immediate cremation. Meanwhile, his sister Kate comprehends that she isn't remotely prepared for the internment experience and its "absolutely helpless feeling of standing in line with hundreds of other Japanese descendants in a camp full of thousands more. Surrounded by barbed wire in the middle of the desert, armed guards in towers aiming their rifles down at her and her children" (27). Her life has been reduced.

Upon arrival David has a similar experience, internally freaking out, as he "walked through the gates of Manzanar, under the barbed wire, past the guard towers with mounted automatic weapons pointed down and directly at him in to the enclosed compound [with] tar-paper barracks [and] the city of Asian faces herded together under the American flag" (1). American totalitarianism *is* complete with these arresting images of the concentration camp, among others. As Agamben says in *Homo Sacer*,

> Insofar as its inhabitants were stripped of every political status and wholly reduced to bare life, the camp was also the most absolute biopolitical space ever to have been realized, in which power confronts nothing but pure life, without any mediation. This is why the camp is the very paradigm of political space at the point at which politics becomes biopolitics and *homo sacer* is virtually confused with the citizen. The correct question to pose concerning the horrors committed in the camps is, therefore, not the hypocritical one of how crimes of such atrocity could be committed against human beings. It would be more honest and, above all, more useful to investigate carefully the juridical procedures and deployments of power by which human beings could be so completely deprived of their rights and prerogatives that no act committed against them could appear any longer as a crime. (171)

While Agamben is rightly speaking of Nazi death camps, the same cultural perception of "bare life" applies to the canceled status of human being in the American internment camps. That is a tremendous, yet dreadful thought to entertain—one's human status invalidated. That same invalidation of status *allowed* for the existence of Indian boarding schools built to eradicate traditional indigenous ways of life as well as the genocides of many Indigenous

American nations; it *allowed* for the plantation system of chattel slavery to exist, condemning African Americans to animal status and death; and it also *allowed* for the internment and dehumanization of Japanese Americans. Likewise, this shocking idea *allows* for the mass incarceration of Black and Brown people in the prison-industrial complex, reduced to mere convicts, less than human; and it *allows* for US Immigration and Custom Enforcement (ICE) detention centers to exist, where detained immigrants are reduced to illegal aliens, now cheekily termed noncitizens, and eventually removed from this country ostensibly to safeguard America from threats to national security. It's not even a step too far to imagine an American holocaust, after all it has already happened. World War II could have gone differently for the Allies. Japanese Americans in these camps could have been gassed. These citizens were placed there out of racial paranoia and anything could have happened. The *noirum* of Miyake's book ensures that we properly acknowledge such implications in each iteration.

In fact, Lillian Bunkum, the camp's executive director in *21st Century Manzanar*, develops a sterilization plan in response to a teen pregnancy at her facility. Lillian feels disturbed that the captive Japanese American doctors hid "the little slut's condition" from her (159). Lillian cannot believe that her charges do not live up to her preconceptions of the Japanese as "a morally traditional race," that they had yielded "to temptations previously attributed only to other colored races" (160). Lillian begins to think this sterilization plan "could be her ticket to Congress" because if "it worked here it could work on a larger scale in more economically deprived ghetto communities," meaning Black and Brown people (161). She wants to solve the Japanese problem. Of course, the fictional Congress has already passed a not yet implemented eugenic plan that would represent "ethnic cleansing, American style" (176). In this respect, sterilization represents another kind of final solution, only slower than the gas chamber. The US government of Miyake's world has decided that they can end their economic tailspin if not with war then by eliminating the reproductive capability of alleged socially unfit Japanese Americans through involuntary sterilization after racial exclusion, segregation, and humiliation. Such racist notions have a long history in the United States and have been inflicted upon BIPOC women primarily.

I find it easy to imagine how such views could arise again, especially in light of two recent events: the failed coup of January 6, 2021 and the June 24, 2022 reversal of the *Roe v. Wade* Supreme Court decision. This whitelash involves the white patriarchal supremacist desire of absolute control over minorities and women. In the case of *21st Century Manzanar*, racism, xenophobia, and sexism meld to produce the necessary dehumanization to sanction such a reprehensible action by Congress. Lillian only needs an excuse to carry out the next phase of this obvious ethnic cleansing plan and much later in the novel understands how the "well-oiled machine" of her camp can "easily be converted from Japanese to Afghani or Arabic or whatever Homeland Security dictated" (368). Just as Agamben implies that *homo sacer* can only save himself through perpetual flight or in a foreign land, David's only remaining course of action is to escape east with his family through the help of friends to the sovereign Navajo nation situated in the northern part of the Arizona and New Mexico border.

21st Century Manzanar clearly serves as a warning from the future past. This country has long used "guilt-by-race" to convict its minorities "with hopelessness and despair" (381). A great evil in my estimation, trapping BIPOCs between white fear and white privilege, and in turn producing a Sisyphean challenge in the fight for equality with little progress, made up the racial mountain that Langston Hughes talked about long ago.[7] Indeed, we haven't reached the mountain top that Martin Luther King Jr.[8] discussed in his last speech. I am not giving up on my country, but I'm not hopeful in this moment. The punishment continues, the rock-rolling gets hard, and the realness of race's social construction weighs on my limbs going up the mountain. Miyake imparts some of this feeling by folding "the complex class and racial tensions that fueled the 1992 Los Angeles riots in the wake of the Rodney King beating . . . into a post-9/11 environment where long-standing antagonisms are intensified" in the novel (Beck, *Dirty*, 287). We see this sentiment working in the background when Lillian thinks about sterilizing "ghetto communities" as well as the "Afghani or Arabic" communities after the Japanese she no longer thinks of as American.

Muslim American Concentration Camps

Because internment happened to Japanese Americans, it stands to reason that it could also happen to other American minorities. Futures sometimes look like this from the margins. Little wonder that another BIPOC writer would explore this territory. Indian American writer Samira Ahmed also extrapolates on what American fascism, grounded in patriotism, might look like in the young adult novel *Internment* (2019). 9/11 crystallizes the homogenization of race and religion to the American public with respect to the Muslim world. As Sangay Mishra claims, the "racialization of South Asians as 'others,' 'outsiders,' 'foreigners,' and 'terrorists' is based on their physical appearance, religious affiliation, cultural background, and immigrant status" ("Religion," 231). We can see this "particularized racialization as Hindu, Muslim, or Sikh" happening during the Gulf War even before 9/11 and the war on terrorism as "South Asians experience homogenization through the blurring of religious, cultural, and nation-of-origin distinctions" (Mishra, "Religion," 231). In Ahmed's novel, growing fear and unfounded hatred for Islam in a near future United States force high school senior Layla Amin and her parents into an internment camp for Muslim Indian American citizens with the election of a Trump-like president. That's the novum. As Layla remarks, "But the lies, the rhetoric calling refugees rapists and criminals, the fake news, the false statistics, all gave those well-meaning people who say they're not bigots cover to vote for a man who openly tweeted his hatred of us on a nearly daily basis" (24–25). The change in popular opinion happens swiftly.

Layla breaks down the change between "Then and Now" as she attempts to understand white nationalism and its nefarious capacity to marginalize, which directly leads to Camp Mobius—a new version of American concentration camps in the California Desert, built near the grounds of the infamous Manzanar (2). At the beginning of the novel, Layla provides a timeline of the intensifying oppression of this near future:

> There is only what we once were and what we have become.
>
> Two and half years since the election.
>
> Two years since the Nazis marched on DC.
>
> Eighteen months since the Muslim ban.
>
> One year since our answers on the census landed us on the registry.
>
> Nine months since the first book burning.
>
> Six months since the Exclusion Laws were enacted.
>
> Five months since the attorney general argued that *Korematsu v. United States* established precedent for relocation of citizens during times of war.
>
> Three months since they started firing Muslims from public-sector jobs.
>
> Two months since a virulent Islamophobe was sworn in as secretary of war-a cabinet position that hasn't existed since World War II.

> One month since the president of the United States gave a televised speech to Congress declaring that "Muslims are at threat to America." (2)

None of these events since the election of the Trump-like president are far-fetched. Neo-Nazi groups have marched on the Capitol. A Muslim ban was enacted by the president and upheld by the Supreme Court too. While the US Census Bureau no longer collects data on religious affiliation, it once did so and so such data collection, along with a registry, are reasonable extrapolations in our current climate. Book burnings happen to this day right alongside book banning. Ray Bradbury's 1953 dystopia novel *Fahrenheit 451* remains the superlative example; after all, it's the temperature at which books burn, to paraphrase the tagline! The deliberate destruction of knowledge and extreme censorship goes on in our schools because of religious and political opposition. Just consider the furor over critical race theory itself.

There are any number of Asian exclusion laws in our history—the Page Act of 1875, banning Chinese women; the Chinese Exclusion Act of 1882, banning Chinese men; and the Immigration Act of 1924, which prevented immigration from Asia.[9] Ahmed's world-building is grounded in reality. The 1944 *Korematsu v. United States* Supreme Court decision actually upheld the exclusion of Japanese Americans during WWII. BIPOCS are often the last hired and first fired. That's a common enough occurrence to be plausible, along with the return of an obsolete cabinet position. President Trump's anti-Muslim stance is well documented. As Indian literary scholar Nalini Iyer states, "we see how the state's policies have become more repressive and how the discourse in the public sphere has shifted to disenfranchise Muslims" ("Digital," 148). The message that Ahmed conveys through this future-past extrapolation suggests that we need to be worried and we need to be preparing to stop it from happening.

While the fictional presidential election functions as the novum, full-blown Islamophobia proves to be the catalyst driving the plot, resulting in the *noirum*. "Presidential Order 1455" creates "the Exclusion Authority," which allows men in dark suits to come in the middle of the night, knock on the door, and "carry out Your relocation" (31). Mobius represents the high-tech version of Manzanar with cameras and surveillance drones everywhere as an obvious dual shift occurs between groups based on different races and religions as the focal point of persecution. Before Layla, her parents, and thousands of other Muslims are bused to Mobius, they are branded with "fluorescent barcode(s)," her number "0000105" (61). The parallels to the Nazi deathcamps are striking right down to the showers, though interned citizens are assigned FEMA trailers instead of barracks. Likewise, Layla's Jewish boyfriend David is the grandson of a Holocaust survivor. Pervading the text is the feeling that this future could happen to any group of American citizens in the United States if they have ever been marginalized in terms of race, gender, religion, or sexual orientation—ever otherized. The Wounded Knee Massacre, Tulsa race massacre, Stonewall riots, the Muslim ban, and the overturning of *Roe v. Wade* represent more examples of what the power brokers in our government, mostly white people, are capable of doing to their own citizens. Yet citizens arise to combat the injustice: NAACP, various waves of the feminist movement, the Black Panther Party for Self-Defense, American Indian Movement, the Chicano Movement (El Movimiento), #BlackLivesMatter, and so on.

Layla leads the resistance movement from inside Mobius. She builds unity among "the young Muslim internees regardless of national heritage" through pop cultural references to *Star Wars*, *Game of Thrones*, and the like (Iyer, "Digital," 150). For example, Layla reveals to her new friend Ayesha (who is Pakistani American) that her mom had a girlhood crush on Luke Skywalker, to which Ayesha responds, "Hello, Riz Ahmed is in *Rogue One*. A desi in Star Wars" (100). The women, together with Soheil (who is Egyptian American), take a page out of history and stage a hunger strike because "It's Gandhi-esque" (168). Layla also reaches her boyfriend David on the outside when she forges an alliance with a camp guard Corporal Jake Reynolds, who smuggles out her hand-written messages. David feeds these inside accounts of life in Mobius—for example, how some internees have been disappeared—to the media through an anonymous blog, which ignites a firestorm of protests in the larger world. An Occupy Mobius website springs into existence. Protestors arrive with signs at the ready: "FREE MOBIUS. NO H8 IN THE STATES, AMERICA ALREADY IS GREAT, AMERICA: ALL ARE WELCOME" (229). Cleary, Ahmed has former and future president Trump in mind here with respect to his unoriginal campaign slogan. With the world's news media gathered outside the fence of Mobius, Soheil martyrs himself by jumping into the electrified fence and dying. Eventually, the unhinged, nameless director of Mobius throws Layla into a prison cell and interrogates her: "He slaps my face, and his clunky gold signet ring splits my lip, and blood pours down my chin. I scream, and it echoes off the walls. I wipe the blood from my face and hear my screams bounce back to my ears" (330). Fortunately, he is stopped by Jake who invokes US and international law about the mistreatment of prisoners.

Layla risks it all in the final confrontation. She and the internees stand together in the prison yard calling for the gates to open. The director comes out with his security detail to silence them. Despite guns held to her parents' heads by the director's men during this last protest, Layla speechifies to the protestors and media: "We're not leaving until those gates are open and we can all walk out together" (361). The director yells at his men several times to shoot her, but the National Guard stands down. He pulls a gun of his own to do the deed himself, and Jake dies intervening. Mobius gets shut down. Layla and the rest of the internees walk out with news about "repealing the Exclusion Laws, closing the black-ops sites, impeachment" ringing in their ears because a few chose to stand and speak out against this brutal oppression (373). With respect to the *noirum*, I think what makes Samira Ahmed's counternarrative so powerful is that the social protest is led by young people who reject silence in speaking truth to power. Young people make all the difference. That's what it will take to help the United States of America live up to its egalitarian myth that lights up the world for so many, finding people willing to stand against oppression and fight for freedom. Storytelling is powerful. Layla overcomes her fear while creating the "good trouble" that Congressman John Lewis called for on Edmund Pettus Bridge on March 1, 2020.

Samira Ahmed's *Internment* achieves such good trouble. In an "Author's Note" to her 2019 novel, Ahmed justifiably declares: "And now here we are again. Refugees forced into internment camps. Muslim bans. Border walls. Police brutality. The rights of gun owners being valued more than the lives of our children. Racism. Islamophobia. Ableism, Homophobia. Anti-Semitism. Scapegoating immigrants. The politics of exclusion. The rise of nationalism and white supremacy, unmasked and waving our flag" (380). All of these things have come to pass in the intervening years since her novel's publication. Critical race theory advocates that transformative change comes with sacrifice and persistence. And we must fight for it. Science fiction, in dialogue with the present in which it is written, shows us what this social resistance looks like in the future built on the past. Telling difficult stories, countering the perceptions of a monochrome future, allowing BIPOCs to see and feel themselves in the future and believe in their own potentialities—that is one of the necessary visions for social change. This change may be slow, but it *is* ongoing, it *is* far-reaching, it *is* powerful in its desire to move us beyond the limitations of race, if not humanity itself. The *noirum* represents a staging point for such social change because of its investment in the restructuring of laws that inhibit equality in the United States.

Latinx Detention Centers

Latina writer Sabrina Vourvoulias's near-future novel *Ink* (2012) strongly resonates with Jones's *The Bird Is Gone*, Miyake's *21st Century Manzanar*, and Ahmed's *Internment*. All four novels have in common the oppression of a racial or ethnic minority group as a part of the near future. In the case of Vourvoulias, we are talking about the oppression of Latinx people in a dystopian United States; at least, that is the basic premise of the novum—prejudice. Vourvoulias depicts what is happening at American borders with illegal migrants trying to cross into the US, albeit through the border with Canada, in an interesting wrinkle. The *noirum* involves the government's passing of an "identity bill" designed to mark every Latinx with a color-coded GPS-enabled tattoo system to keep track of American Latinx citizens, lawful immigrants on work visas, and captured illegals. As Latinx scholar Joy Sanchez-Taylor remarks, "the label 'ink' allows the US government in Vourvoulias's narrative to create laws that first dehumanize ink immigrants and citizens alike, leaving them open to exploitation and violence, and eventually criminalize inks through narratives of illness" (*Diverse*, 88). In this light, "Cleanse America" groups develop all across the country, hell-bent on keeping cities and suburbs essentially white while simultaneously terrorizing the Latinx community by setting fires in "neighborhoods that still rent to inks" (68, 199). They capture any and all Latinx-looking people and dump them at the border. Even more sinister, the government also creates "Inkatoriums" (144) for the detainment of Latinx people with or without the tattoos and initially suppresses this knowledge and so "nothing comes of the sanitarium/internment center story" that a reporter gets wind of early in the novel (59). Later, the rumors of "a [forced] sterilization program" within Inkatoriums emerge (245). While I devote more time to *Ink* in my final chapter, Vourvoulias's novel certainly capitalizes on the white social angst existing in the United States regarding the Latinx community over the last decade.

Just like Jones, Miyake, and Ahmed, Vourvoulias uses science fiction to demonstrate how white fears dominate our country as she clearly anticipates the creation of US Immigration and Customs Enforcement (ICE) detention centers by more than two years: the Karnes County Civil Detention Center opened in Texas on September 23, 2014.[10] It seems as if the United States is caught in a time loop where our terrible history repeats across a racial and ethnic spectrum, mimicking real life with such intense exactitude that reality collapses and we experience the many peculiar and authentic versions of American concentration camps. The question remains: how do we defeat an ingrained white fear that always protects its own interests?

This fear that white people have of equal standing between people *is* really difficult to quantify because discriminatory laws do not affect them. Equality supposedly governs US laws, making it difficult if not impossible for white people to see the actual inequalities. Or, perhaps more accurately, white people ignore the spirit of the law because they never see it in operation up close and personal. The law does not threaten their existence and so the status quo remains to insulate white privilege. *Ink* protests the danger of such a mindset. Near the end of the novel, "the country reaches a moral breaking point after being confronted with pictures of ink children in shackles" (*Diverse*, 88). While the government tries to prevent "the televised images of young people driven, hobbled like cattle," it is much too late to stop the viral images leaking onto the internet and the "fiery indignation" that eventually results in "ink restoration laws" (442). Yet racism remains as "the 'Ink Incidents' . . . limp along [while] the faces at the top switch [and] the circumstances morph"; change comes slow, and the pattern remains intact (442–443). The *noirum*, SF's own CRT, helps with pattern recognition. Seeing such patterns encourages breaking the repetitions of these near-future time loops proposed by Vourvoulais and others.

Black Ghetto Confinement

Don't think for a minute that Black people have not contributed to this type of story either!

African American poet Evie Shockley continues sighting this dark pattern with her satirical story "Separation Anxiety" (2000). Voluntary and deliberate segregation of American minorities serves as the novum of her story. Set in the twenty-second century, the US government launches a newfangled Jim Crow strategy to preserve democracy by creating "the national department of ethnic and cultural conservation, the 'decc'" (52). The establishment of the "decc" and all the rules that come from its formation function as the *noirum*. The story's main protagonist, eleanor "peaches" johnson, tells us that in "creating the ghetto—the african american cultural conservation unit, as the official name goes—is to preserve [the Black] way of life" (51–52). Shockley overturns the many derogatory connotations of the word "ghetto." The ghetto lives in the white American imagination as a Black inner-city neighborhood with low property values, high crime rates, drugs, illiteracy, and single-parent households, most likely welfare queens, comprised of the working poor with graffiti and garbage everywhere. The same goes for the Latinx population and barrios or Indigenous Americans and the rez, perhaps even Chinatowns, Little Tokyos, and the like. Historically speaking, ghettos have been occupied by racial minorities. But Shockley uses "ghetto" as a term of endearment because she presents a vibrant Black community free of white racism.

On the one hand, the enforced racial separation has allowed Black people to thrive, to affirm their own worth, and to grab hold of their own future. Indeed, peaches describes the ghetto as the place "where [she] could see, hear, taste, smell, and feel [her] culture all around . . . in the mac's rolling stroll and the girls' whip-fast double-dutch . . . in the aromas of collards and catfish cooking that surfed the winds down residential streets" (51). The government's conservation units have seemingly solved racial conflict in America. On the other hand, the careful preservation of the ghetto's cultural production becomes increasingly invasive. The excuse on offer concerns the essential documentation of the Black contribution to the American way of life and the prevention of outside influences on this unique engine of creativity. That is to say, the decc implements the immediate preservation of artistic productions such as music, literature, and art in addition to historical records such as birth and marriage certificates since "african americans had seen the downside of being nearly recordless, from the days of slavery and reconstruction, so we were proud that recognizing the value of our culture was now the law" (53). As I write elsewhere in a different context, "the decc legitimates its invasive existence with a nostalgic excuse: think of all the unrecorded history that has been lost concerning African Americans and mourn it, but do not let it happen now" (Lavender, *Race*, 104). The decc issues "executive order #46,877, pursuant to the ethnic and cultural conservation act":

> effective immediately, residents of african american cultural conservation unit #1 should further organize waste disposal by separating waste associated with sexual activity and sexual health from other categories of waste, waste items covered under this category include, but are not limited to:

> feminine hygiene products (internal or external)
> male and female condoms,
> packaging for reproductive and anti-reproductive medical technologies,
> discarded sexual pleasure implements, etc.
>
> pink containers will be provided to each household for collection purposes, and should be placed with the household's other color-coded receptacles for pick up. (58)

To what possible end would the US government need to keep a record of its Black population's sexual practices and health? I repeat, why on earth would such records be necessary? Shockley dismisses a host of sexual stereotypes about Black people by forcefully addressing the lasting damages caused to the Black community in the name of medical research—for instance, the experiments conducted on enslaved women's genitalia by Dr. James Marion Sims, who is considered the father of gynecology, come to mind. The words of peaches' deceased grandfather ring true: "'history is a cycle, y'all,' . . . 'this unit is separation today, but it'll be segregation tomorrow, mark my words . . . conservation. reservation. conservation. concentration'" (57). Thus, the dark pattern of this time loop strongly represents the distrust that American minorities feel for the US government. Shockley, too, suggests that, unless we are vigilant, the destined repetition of American concentration camps will come around again.

Ultimately, peaches decides to leave the ghetto. She does not "like feeling like somebody's anthropology project" (57). She overcomes her fear of separation from her brother and from the ghetto by signing a government contract to leave with her best friend trevette for careers outside the walls. Once on the outside, they can never return to the ghetto. Shockley directly taps into the Black fear prevalent at the beginning of the twenty-first century regarding the reversal of affirmative action, designed to level the playing field in multiple arenas in terms of employment and education. Steady if slight progress has been made by African Americans, other minorities, and women toward equality with white men. I think Shockley's *noirum* signposts that such an extreme racial separation does not provide the answer to racism; rather, we have to end the colorblind era in which we now live that supports political and legal intolerance of minorities through a willful government gridlock. Separate but equal has never worked.

Natural Disaster and Women's Medical Internment

Speaking of women, Louise Erdrich, a member of the Turtle Mountain Band of Chippewa, produces a frightening near-future feminist dystopia in *Future Home of the Living God* (2017). Her alarm blares all the louder in light of the recent dismantling of the landmark 1973 *Roe v. Wade* decision by the current conservative supermajority of the Supreme Court with its June 24, 2022 ruling in *Dobbs v. Jackson Women's Health Organization*, which substantively ended a woman's constitutional right to a safe abortion in this country. By such flawed originalist reasoning, interracial marriage, gay marriage, and even contraception should also be ended since these things were not considered as rights when the Due Process Clause of the Fourteenth Amendment was passed in 1868. Of course, vast differences exist between today's and yesterday's United States of America. For example, the Fourteenth Amendment itself granted my ancestors' citizenship although this right of citizenship has largely been curtailed by white society and its daily advantages even in the twenty-first century. Professor of constitutional law Randy E. Barnett lays out the originalist position in that "the Constitution should be interpreted according to the original intent of the framers, and also that constitutional rights should be limited to those that were listed and certainly should not include an unenumerated right of privacy" (*Restoring*, xi). In this restrictive interpretation of the founding document of the United States government, the Constitution is frozen in time with laws and rights applicable to 1789 as opposed to 2020s America, which requires an organicism to guide the country. It is not terribly difficult to imagine racial authoritarianism growing worse with a static document; it is happening right now as evinced by President Trump's failed coup attempt on January 6, 2021. This resurgent white supremacism represents the apocalypse already survived by American Indigenes but threatening to end the multiracial democracy that the United States currently strives to achieve.

What makes Erdrich's novel so terrifying is the total curtailment of women's rights and the reduction of women to biological function in the face of an unspecified cataclysmic event that seems to have caused devolution as the world heats up resulting in a fertility crisis. This cataclysmic event serves as the novum that creates the collapse of the federal government as we know it and allows the rise of "a church government" known as "the Church of the New Constitution" (128). I am still talking about the novum here, where Erdrich combines some of our worst fears in that the First Amendment in the

Constitution's Bill of Rights utterly implodes with respect to the separation of church and state. Erdrich realizes the dread of religious governance corrupted by political interests to create an even more dominant patriarchal state similar to something like Margaret Atwood's *The Handmaid's Tale* (1985), as other scholars have commented.[11] In a massive feat of social engineering, street signs change names practically overnight from something like "Boutwell Street" to "Proverbs 10:7" (119). Of course, the religious wingnuts fully avail themselves of all that technology has to offer, creating a bot, or perhaps an artificial intelligence, known as Mother, designed to penetrate smart phones, televisions, and computers to surveil all women and to aid in the capture of those who are pregnant for relocation to "gravid female detention" centers, where they can be monitored and tested (85). They seal the borders with Canada and Mexico and attempt to round up all women of childbearing age to produce viable children for the state to survive—"Womb Volunteers" to be artificially inseminated with stolen "embryos not labeled Caucasian" (105). Naturally, pregnant women run, hide, go off the grid by ridding themselves of all their smart devices, or attempt to flee North with the help of an unorganized fledging resistance movement. Nevertheless, they are hunted by the "Unborn Protection Society" (148). The USA as we know it disintegrates as a religious autocracy arises.

As this new government emerges from the sociopolitical upheaval caused by climate change, the epistolary novel's Ojibwe protagonist, the twenty-six-year-old, four-months-pregnant Cedar Hawk Songmaker keeps a diary for her unborn child, chronicling her experiences living through this crisis. Cedar feels a disconnection from her Indigenous heritage as an adopted child of rich, liberal, white Minnesotan parents. Because she considers herself to be "a theoretical Native" with "no clan, no culture, no language, no relatives" (5), Cedar decides to go to the reservation to meet her biological mother Mary Potts, known as Sweetie, and her Ojibwe family to forge some kind of connection for her unborn child's sake. Sweetie had a short-term intimate relationship with a white man that resulted in Cedar. This white man is actually her adoptive father Glen, a trial lawyer who represented the Ojibwe in a case early in his marriage to Cedar's adoptive mother Sera. But this information does not come out until the final third of the novel. In fact, Cedar's mixed heritage provides Erdrich the opportunity to ponder "the mixture of identities common to Native people. Common to all of us. We are all mixtures of some sort or another—usually one heritage predominates, but that isn't at all predictable" (Coleman, "Interview"). As Julia Siepak states, "Cedar imagines herself, then, as an outsider since her connections to her Indigenous culture are superficial and her position of privilege separates her from the experience of oppression faced by Indigenous communities in the United States" ("Dimensions," 64). She's shocked to learn that her Native family is well-to-do, the owners of a gas station, and that her stepfather Eddy is a Harvard PhD.[12]

After making this tenuous family connection, Cedar returns to her home on Boutwell Street, now Proverbs 10:7, where she awaits Phil, her child's father, to return. She's captured by a colored UPS agent named Bernice, who was tipped off by Phil under the stress of torture, and taken to the Fairview Riverside Hospital. Cedar eventually escapes this hospital prison with her Asian roommate Tia and the help of her mother Sera. Cedar ends up back at the reservation only to be captured a second time after "being hijacked by some random pilgrims" while praying at a statue in the dead of night shortly after Thanksgiving (299). She ends up at the Minnesota Correctional Facility, renamed the Stillwater Birthing Center, where she gives birth to her son on Christmas Day, and he is immediately taken from her. Cedar survives and the story ends in February with the ominous thought of her preparation for artificial insemination as she thinks about her son and the lack of snow.

While I find the novum itself unsettling, the *noirum* provokes fear and anger too. Cedar narrates:

> By a narrow majority the House and Senate have voted to strengthen and give new powers to what began so long ago as the Patriot Act. There were articles I, II, III, IV, and now we are up to V, section 215 of which still allows our government to seize the entire library and medical databases in order to protect national security. This newly expanded decision, now only hours old, empowers the government to determine who is pregnant throughout the country. Your father says that the surgeon general they had was fired and the new one has announced that pregnant women will be sequestered in hospitals in order to give birth under controlled circumstances. It is for our own safety and we are required to go voluntarily. Those who do go in right now will receive the best rooms. The best rooms! Heart in my throat, I think of the doctor who probably put himself at risk. He gave me the ultrasound picture. He knew. Best rooms. Hysterical. Will women turn themselves in thinking that a bit more privacy, a better view, an extra chair, is worth it? We're not going. (83)

In this world, Erdrich greatly expands the Patriot Act of 2001, which was rushed through Congress forty-five days after 9/11.[13] The Patriot Act was meant to unite and strengthen America (Providing Appropriate Tools Required to Intercept and Obstruct Terrorism). Essentially, the law makes it easier for government agencies to snoop on its own citizens for the sake of national security by greatly expanding legal authority to monitor phones, emails, and wired communications while also collecting banking data and credit reports. For instance, it doesn't take long for Cedar to realize that she is "being pregnancy-purchase-tracked by Mother" because she used her "credit card to buy baby clothes at Target" (83). So, this new totalitarian regime uses the expanded powers of the Patriot Act to spy on women in an effort to offset the biological cataclysm, stripping women of agency, of autonomy, of freedom by reducing them to their biology. Cedar relays all of this reprehensible action to her baby through the journal and determines that "We're not going" voluntarily to one of these facilities for a comfy room with a view. Race operates in the sense that the doctor who performed her ultrasound advises Cedar to "get the hell out of here" when he learns of her Indigenous heritage after asking if she had "any special ethnicity" (58). BIPOC women seemingly have a better chance of surviving the pregnancy. This moment represents the last time Cedar is treated as a human being outside of her immediate family. She does not take her freedom for granted and even has hope for her unnamed and unborn child throughout the novel as she takes comfort writing to him in her diary.

Shortly after leaving the doctor's office, Cedar witnesses a government sanctioned kidnapping of a noticeably pregnant, Brown-skinned woman in a parking lot by two police officers. While hunkered down in her own car with Phil ordering sandwiches at the local Subway in a strip mall, Cedar sees two cops approach the "petite woman wearing a red and white flowered smock" and ask to see her ID (85). Though she has done nothing wrong, the pregnant woman hands over her driver's license to the female cop while the male cop positions himself at her elbow. The pregnant woman questions "the police aggressively" at first, but then she becomes nervous, glancing around for help and seeing her white husband emerging from a shoe store holding the hand of their small "paler brown" daughter (86). The male cop grabs the pregnant Brown woman's elbow and attempts to wheedle her into the backseat of the squad car. Her white husband reacts, "bolt[ing] forward" as his wife "cried out and flung herself toward him" and people "stopped still" to watch the assault on the pretty, vulnerable, pregnant, Brown woman (86). Cedar describes the rest of the violent and surreal encounter:

> The police ignored him and started dragging at his wife. She planted her feet in refusal. Her husband was a medium-sized man, but suffused with anger and protective belligerence he seemed to grow larger. His neck swelled and his eyes narrowed, the veins in his throat pumped. He grabbed the male officer and tried to wrestle the man down, but the police officer, more agile and trained, quickly flipped the man onto the ground and drew his gun. He pointed the gun at the man's face. The little girl, who had followed her father, stopped short and began to cry, her face a crumpled flower. A bystander pulled the girl into the crowd. The female police officer succeeded in pulling and pushing the pregnant woman all the way up to the car, but the crowd had now grown. Several people had begun to shout. A terrible sound came from the mom—a wail, a shriek, a roar—as she was stuffed, kicking, into the car. The male officer handcuffed the husband, sitting on the small of his back and twisting his arm. He was pointing the gun at the bystanders, who shied back, though some were still yelling. The officer was young. His lips disappeared into the white rock of his face until he was all teeth. He jumped into the car and drove off, not quickly, no sirens wailing, so there was then an unreal and frozen quality about the whole scene in which the only sound to hear was the high-pitched, broken sobbing of the child. (87)

The family has been torn apart, with the mother abducted, father restrained, and little Brown girl howling as the angered crowd starts to act. Naturally, the young white cop brandishes his gun at the crowd while skinning his teeth in a death grimace. The cops drive off with little fanfare with their hostage to a pregnancy black site meant to detain pregnant women as if they were enemy combatants. The enhanced legal mechanisms of the reimagined Patriot Act, in this case, the *noirum*, make this outrageous snatch-and-grab procedure in broad daylight possible. This unlawful arrest and rendition of the Brown woman happens because, due to her pregnancy, her name is on a list. Rendition in the sense of being handed over like property to the government in the execution of this new law. She no longer has rights, becomes a government possession, and has been treated as if a fugitive slave.

Undoubtedly, you will have noticed my emphasis on skin-color in this passage because the law reflects the treatment of Brown and Black people across American history. Erdrich effectively utilizes racial coding—Brown, pregnant woman and white cops—in this scene to emphasize the distrust

BIPOC communities hold for law enforcement. Likewise, Erdrich weirdly echoes how pro-life sentiments value unborn life over living people like the abandoned child. This event happens in the name of protecting the Church of the New Constitution's citizenry. In fact, this abduction scene has stayed with me ever since I read the novel.

As I conclude my analysis of *Future Home of the Living God*, let me pick up a couple of the loose threads I mentioned earlier—street names and Brown-skinned women. First, I mentioned how streets were renamed after verses from the Bible. Cedar lived on Boutwell Street renamed Proverbs 10:7, so I decided to look up the verse in my *Bible*, New Living Translation, which reads: "We have happy memories of the godly, but the name of a wicked person rots away." On the one hand, the second half of the biblical verse suggests that the new government will rot. Simple. It will rot because it is evil in its treatment of women and will only stink more as time passes and its citizens grow more desperate. On the other hand, in terms of Erdrich's novel, it seems to me that Cedar Hawk Songmaker will be honored because she is creating a legacy for her son in the act of recording her story, archiving her time for posterity. Cedar "not only creat[es] a future 'literary past' for American Indians, but a textual and literal past for non-Indians, as well" (Howe, *Choctalking*, 36). This future-past archive allows us to look into the past, to mine it for hidden meaning, and to then use the past for a potential sociopolitical transformation through Indigenous experience. In Afrofuturist lexicon, we'd call this action data-thieving (absent the Black technofuture) in order to support political struggles and rebalance power relations by codebreaking historical documents for the future while also being in sync with other alternative accounts of the American past.[14] The *noirum* functions as a multicultural encryption key from this perspective, allowing us to unlock potential meanings in Erdrich's novel.

Second, Erdrich always seems to mention the color or ethnicity of the pregnant women. Consider the clues: Cedar's "special ethnicity" (58), the abducted pregnant woman with "warm brown skin" (85), the stolen "embryos not labeled Caucasian" (105); while Cedar's first roommate at Fairview, Agnes Starr, is white, her unborn baby is mixed race (148) and her second roommate, Tia Jackson, is Asian (158). As Kaylee J. Mootz indicates, "the link between race and reproduction becomes more evident. Though the text never says so explicitly, it seems that white children are not being conceived at all" ("Body," 268). This implication suggests to me that white children have no future because white people have been adversely impacted by the unspecified cataclysmic event. White women have difficulty conceiving by white men, trouble carrying a baby to full term, and when they do give birth to a mutated child that lives for no more than a few hours, it kills them in the birthing process. Racialized reproduction becomes fully valued and commodified to this totalitarian regime. This final commodification of race results in the full visibility of whiteness as a deadly social construct that ends at last.

As white world hegemony crumbles, the future belongs to resurgent Indigenous communities who still may not survive the arriving world but have racial memories encoded in cultural traditions to possibly sustain themselves and to best endure in the changed environment. To Anishinaabe theorist Gerald Vizenor, "Survivance is an active sense of presence, the continuance of native stories, not a mere reaction, or a survivable name. Native survivance stories are renunciations of dominance, tragedy and victimry" (*Manifest*, vii). Cedar may die but her story lives on twofold: through her son and through her diary, biological resistance and narrative resistance respectively.

Deep South Medical Containment

Beginning with the Saffir-Simpson Category 3 Hurricane Katrina, which made landfall on August 29, 2005, as her catalyst, African American author Sherri L. Smith, in her novel *Orleans* (2013), imagines a series of seven hurricanes ravaging the gulf coast—New Orleans, Louisiana in particular—that culminate in the novum, a storm so fierce that it changes the ostensible known world. On October 20, 2019, Hurricane Jesus makes landfall as a Category 6 on a new Saffir-Simpson Scale. Naming the hurricane after the Christian messiah is not meant to be ironic at all in terms of this nation-shattering event that killed an estimated eight thousand people. The aftermath results in many more casualties, ranging from death to treatable disease, death from stress, suicide, and domestic violence. But Mother Nature *isn't* done with humanity. Delta Fever emerges resulting in an epic permanent quarantine, illustrated by two federal mandates that make up the *noirum*. First, the Federal Emergency Management Agency, better known as FEMA, in consultation with the Center for Disease Control issues the "DECLARATION OF QUARANTINE" on September 20, 2020. This declaration states: "'For the safety of the population at large, we deem it advisable to seal off all storm-affected areas of the Gulf

Coast region. No citizens or personnel will be allowed to cross the border without blood testing for Delta Fever. This is an epidemic of proportions we have not witnessed since the Spanish Influenza of 1918. The Quarantine will be reevaluated as the disease runs its course and we make progress toward treatment and a cure. Until then, all borders will be sealed'" (6). Second, the United States Senate decrees the "DECLARATION OF SEPARATION" on March 11, 2025: "'Therefore it is with great regret and pain for our fellow citizens that the United States has agreed to withdraw our governance of the affected states of Alabama, Florida, Georgia, Louisiana, and Texas. The shape of our great nation has been altered irrevocably by Nature, and now Man must follow suit in order to protect the inalienable rights of the majority, those being the right to Life, Liberty, and the Pursuit of Happiness, the foremost of those being Life'" (7). The president and members of congress serve as witnesses to this document along with the former governors of Alabama, Florida, Georgia, Louisiana, and Texas. Ebony E. Thomas succinctly puts it, "To save the rest of the nation, the United States first quarantines the Deep South in 2020, and then ejects Alabama, Florida, Georgia, Louisiana, and Texas from the Union in 2025" ("Notes," 298). Curiously, the quarantine does not include Mississippi, although part of the wall cuts through the southern part of the state. Smith explains that the American government maintains a military base "on the Outer States side of the wall, so while the state is now smaller, it is still part of the Outer States" (personal email).[15] Obviously, the federal government in this storyworld hangs on to Mississippi to preserve a military presence in order to deter the environmental threats represented by Delta Fever and to offer assurance to the American populace in the Outer States. Less obvious is the economic need to have a port in the gulf region and to have a place from which to communicate with the scientists behind the wall conducting experiments purportedly looking for a cure. As Elizabeth A. Wheeler states, "*Orleans* transforms the invisible boundaries of race and disease into the literal metaphor of the quarantine wall" ("Runoff," 131). Hence, the importance of a twenty- to thirty-foot high concrete wall continually patrolled by American soldiers and blood-sniffing drones. Put another way, the US government takes decisive action to protect its interests by setting apart BIPOCs of the hurricane ravaged southeastern region of the country, isolating the citizens who have been exposed to this infectious disease. Of course, white flight happens with each successive hurricane leading up to the big one because white people have the financial means to leave the area whereas many Black and Brown people do not. Segregation and quarantine go hand in hand.

And the novel takes off from there, twenty-six years into the future on October 30, 2056, where blood tribes rule the delta behind the border walls while America continues forward on the outside. Mostly BIPOCS get left behind, and the former government still continues to conduct secret medical experiments, much like the real Tuskegee Experiment, through insiders trapped behind the wall while also observing the development, structure, and functioning of this new human society. The Tuskegee Study of Untreated Syphilis in the Negro Male, better known as the Tuskegee Experiment, was a forty-year experiment between 1932 and 1972 conducted by the United States Public Health Service involving 600 Black sharecroppers. 399 of these poor Black men had syphilis that went untreated by the doctors running the experiment, who never told them they had the disease and that they were being treated for bad blood.[16] Consequently, the novel concerns themes of climate change, race, and gender as blood tribes emerge in the now chaotic and hopeless region. Blood type determines the impact of Delta Fever on the body. The Ursuline Sisters, caretakers of the dead at the Superdome, teach young people "the Rules of Blood" through a nursery rhyme:

> *Types AB, B, A*
> *Need to stay away*
> *From O and from each other,*
> *Plus from minus, sister from brother.*
> *O positive can feed*
> *All positives in need,*
> *But O neg is the one*
> *For all tribes beneath the sun.* (16–17)

Thus, the disease's severity hinges on a person's blood type. All blood types but O need transfusions to survive the rigors of the disease—weakness, insomnia, hallucinations, skin discoloration, bruising, cramps, staggering, cracked lips, and raving, as well as dirt-eating in some cases before death. Naturally, people group together by blood for safety. "Due to these blood-related effects," as S. R. Toliver claims, "people begin to group in blood tribes that are spread throughout the region, protecting others who have a similar blood category. Families no longer matter. Race is no longer important. Blood is bond" ("Afrocarnival," 137). Sean P. Connors and Roberta S. Trites agree with Tolliver's assessment in that "blood, rather than race, provides a logic of social hierarchization" in the postapocalyptic world ("Neoliberalism's,"

78). To reiterate, skin color seemingly disappears yet race remains in a new form based on blood type. But this thinking is faulty when considering who gets left behind by the US government—Black and Brown people, segregated from the country by a wall, a literal race divide magnified by the protagonists in this post-racial dystopia.

Orleans presents us with dual protagonists of unequal stature. Fen de la Guerre, the Black teenaged main protagonist, largely tells the story in dialect as an orphaned native of Orleans. She survives the death of her scientist parents as well as capture, enslavement, and use in "blood whoring" by Mama Gentille before joining the OP tribe (257). After her tribe gets wiped out in an ambush, Fen escapes with her leader's newborn daughter, determined to get the unnamed baby beyond the wall before Delta Fever infects the infant in a week's time. The lesser protagonist Daniel Weaver is a white military scientist, who foolishly decides to illegally enter the quarantine zone in search of a cure for Delta Fever, which killed his little brother Charlie. The chapters from his viewpoint are told in third-person while Fen's are in first-person. Melanie Marotta makes an interesting point about the juxtaposition of protagonist voices in that Daniel's outsider voice initially "appears more valuable than Fen's" as a white male scientist, a staple of science fiction ("Sherri," 58). But Smith undercuts this supposed value through Fen's superior knowledge and ability to survive as readers learn to understand her vernacular voice, not to mention Daniel's foolhardy and arrogant assumptions about Orleans and the colorblind impartiality of scientific research.

With a jetskip for transportation, an encounter suit for protection, and his self-created, weaponized version of Delta Fever in a vial inside a protective canister that's missing the one element that will transform it into a cure, Daniel wants to travel to the Institute of Post-Separation Studies in the heart of Orleans for the missing data to complete his cure. He makes a rash decision in bringing this vial. Daniel also knows that this group of scientists, to which Fen's parents belonged, were studying the social and medical interactions of blood tribes in "the closed environment of Orleans" (74). These scientists wanted to better understand "social bias and hate crimes [that] if people divided along medical lines, would race or gender matter" if blood type determined one's grouping (74). Much like in the case of the Tuskegee Experiment, these scientists had no clear intention to cure the disease but to only study the social structures that develop from it over the long term. Fen and Daniel inadvertently meet as captives on a blood farm, forge a hesitant partnership, and escape into the Orleans wasteland. Just as Sam Morris surmises, Orleans is "a landscape filled with predators and death . . . a dystopia that is based on a plausible dual threat of climate change and disease" ("'Anything,'" 269). Fen helps Daniel reach the ultimately disappointing institute after a few harrowing misadventures and he in turn helps Fen and the baby to the wall. Fen sacrifices her life in drawing border guard attention to ensure that Daniel and the recently named baby Enola escape the quarantine zone into the Mississippi night.

Sherri L. Smith's postapocalyptic counternarrative openly explores how poor BIPOCS disproportionately suffer from environmental disaster. Upon arrival at the Institute of Post-Separation Studies, Daniel seems genuinely shocked to learn that the scientists never attempted to cure the fever. In talking with Fen, his face becomes ashen as he realizes the scientists' actions constitute "Tuskegee all over again" because "they never wanted a cure" (207). Daniel recognizes the "new form of racism" as a manifestation of biopower (207). Biopower in the sense that the United States exacts control over the people of Orleans through the wall itself in containing them and constraining their lives as a captive population through a Senate decree witnessed by the President and House of Representatives. "Once the State functions in the biopower mode, racism alone can justify the murderous function of the State" as Michel Foucault determined (*"Society,"* 256). This is the reason why Fen's parents left the institute. She responds, "I don't know nothing about Tuskegee, but if it mean folks with power always gonna abuse it, then I got to agree" (207). The government never ceded control of its former citizens living in the quarantine zone. Likewise, the Institute of Post-Separation Studies represents unethical human experimentation. BIPOC bodies function as a site of scientific racism, where this ongoing US government–backed medical experiment on the victims of Delta Fever reenacts the traumatic racial history of malpractice as the afflicted die from the disease and the scientists observe and do nothing. These scientists want to track the natural history of Delta Fever much like the aforementioned Tuskegee Experiment. Is there any wonder why Black people distrust the medical community after its scientific failings and veritable demonstration of racism? Smith grounds her novel in the experience of racism and her *noirum* certifies that we must respond to the repetition of such cycles to prevent them from happening again. Smith brings to consciousness the medical abuse faced by Black and Brown Americans and its attendant traumas of both systemic and scientific racism with her particular *noirum*.

A Referendum on Imaginary Laws and Death

To close, I think about Black social death a lot in my research and about afropessimism as a cynical theme of Black reality that CRT accounts for in terms of a never-changing racism. I mean, how could it fit under the umbrella of Afrofuturism since all possible futures aren't kind for Black people. Right?! Afropessimism *is* itself a *noirum*. It is itself a new thing as a social concept in our real world designed to work as a catalyst for change with respect to our ongoing racial circumstances caused by both written and social laws. This thought came to me when Frank B. Wilderson III compared Native American genocide to the Black genocide of slavery, an interesting comparison if not exactly new. But Wilderson goes farther than I thought possible in stating that Blacks "*are* being genocided, but genocided *and* regenerated" (*Afropessimism*, 225)! He writes,

> Blacks are not going to be genocided like Native Americans. We *are* being genocided, but genocided *and* regenerated, because the *spectacle* of Black death is essential to the mental health of the world—we can't be wiped out completely, because our deaths must be repeated, *visually*.
>
> The bodily mutilation of Blackness is necessary, so it must be repeated. What we are witnessing on YouTube, Instagram, and the nightly news as murders are rituals of healing for civil society. Rituals that stabilize and ease the anxiety that other people feel in their daily lives. It's the anxiety that people have walking around. It can be stabilized by a lot of different things—marijuana, cocaine, alcohol, affairs—but the ultimate stabilization is the spectacle of violence against Blacks. *I know I am a Human because I am not Black. I know I am not Black because when and if I experience the kind of violence Blacks experience there is a reason, some contingent transgression.*
>
> This is why online video posts of police murdering Black people contribute more to the psychic well-being of non-Black people—to their communal pleasures and sense of ontological presence—than they contribute to deterrence, arrests, or even to a general sensitivity to Black pain and suffering. (225)

Wow! What a truth bomb! I really thought about the implications—I am still processing in fact—and concluded he was right when thinking how often real

Black deaths are shown on TV, in the news/social media, films, and streaming services that America—and the globe—consumes. I captured something similar without realizing it in *Afrofuturism Rising* (2019) by talking about the hyperreal violence loop that Black people have been caught in since slave narratives focused my attention on it. Like Octavia Estelle Butler,[17] if I'm not careful, I, too, would be a pessimist—an afropessimist at that. Black suffering and death seem absolutely essential to the health of a world propped up by the idea that whites and all others are human and Blacks are not, regardless of the various other interlocking oppressions like gender, religion, class, sexuality. As Hortense J. Spillers surmises, "My country needs me and if I were not here, I would have to be invented" ("Mama's Baby," 454). In other words, for America to function it needs to kill and feed on Black men and Black women and Black children and then it has to recycle them in order to do it all over again in ever newer, inventive ways. Does this twin implication then mean that by necessity, the creation of laws and enforcers of law emerge to contain, control, and occasionally cull America's Black populations? I don't think I am capable of being that bleak for too long; those are dark paths to walk that clearly end in madness. Besides, there are other *noirums* to contemplate with their imaginary amendments, acts, and laws that project a more hopeful outlook.

CHAPTER 3

BLM+ Speculations and the *Noirum*

The violence inflicted upon Black bodies by white people in such a terrifyingly uniform manner smoothly fuses together the past, present, and future of race relations across time. In fact, so seamlessly that we can no longer distinguish where it begins and where it ends. This hyperreality[1] defines the racial tensions Black Americans have always lived with, on a daily basis, in the United States. The unreality of such an existence feels downright science fictional. Unabated pseudoscientific racist beliefs immortalize damaging stereotypes about Black people being overtly criminal, oversexed, or lazy, among others. For the sake of profit and control, dating back to 1619 at the very least and the beginning of American exceptionalism, Black bodies must be absolutely labeled as dangerous commodities. A white overseer whipping a Black slave to a bloody death in the past feels remotely fantastical as a part of history, but what of a mirror-shaded cop gunning down Black people with no provocation in the present?

Nothing has really changed.

Our present reality normalizes, if not mythologizes, racial violence: Ahmaud Arbery, a Black man, chased, hunted, and murdered by two white men for jogging in a suburb on the Atlantic Coast of southern Georgia on February 23, 2020; Breonna Taylor, a Black woman, murdered by narcotics police who raided her apartment in Louisville with a "no-knock" search warrant in the early morning hours on March 13, 2020; and George Floyd, a Black man, murdered by a cop kneeling on his neck while he was face down and handcuffed on a street in Minneapolis for nearly nine minutes pleading for air on May 25, 2020. "Just pull up any one of the recent police shootings or assaults captured on video and you will see officers who are visibly hostile, speaking rudely and creating such a negative tone" that almost everyone should be appalled, as Georgetown Law professor Kristin Henning states ("Boys," 70). This is our reality in the twenty-first century—a science-fictional Blackness endlessly looping through the centuries. As viscerally demonstrated—Emmett Till, Trayvon Martin, Alton Sterling, Sandra Bland, and countless other Black lives ended—time and again, Black lives count for nothing when a white man's power is questioned, which forms the crux of the hyperreal violence loop.[2] Former President Trump promised to quell nationwide, nonviolent, peaceful protestors demanding racial justice with the full might of the US military as well as with secret police that snatch lawful citizens off the streets in an instant to protect the imaginary suburban lifestyle dream he tweeted about nonsensically. The world continues to watch America as its deferred dreams threaten to explode[3] yet again.

Listen, I wonder if the daily stress racism causes me when I leave the house each morning will be my own end. In fact, most Black Americans *do* speculate on this very thing every day. It's the "total surround" Samuel R. Delany talks about in his definitive 1998 essay "Racism and Science Fiction" (391). And, naturally, I simply don't know, nor did Ahmaud Arbery, Breonna Taylor, and George Floyd. However, I do know that reading Black-authored, Indigenous-authored, Latinx-authored, Asian-authored, queer-authored science fiction, and reflecting on the alternative futurisms that they provide—petite planets (raced, ethnicized, religified, gendered, queered, etc.)—is where we can find answers. Then we can hope, we can be brave, and we can talk about racism as we stand together.

In the context of this particular chapter, I primarily concentrate on Black-authored texts to demonstrate a collective Black activism that seems readily apparent in today's SF. These authors produce BLM+ speculations as they respond to racism, police brutality, the criminal justice system, and broader issues such as colorism and perceptions of beauty while consciously moving from a heartbreaking past to cultural empowerment in the attempt to dismantle racism in the mirror of Afrofuturism. Through this looking glass, we see the illusions of race and how these image refractions bend in time allowing us to see future pasts. In this regard, Samuel R. Delany warns us that "Afrofuturism is pretty much anything you want it to be" ("Mirror," 184). And if we aren't careful in our use of this optical lens, the experience deceives the eye with its appearance as something that it is not—equality.

Optical Delusions

Peripheral African American writer Jill Robinson creates a sense of ennui, if not despair, in her short story "BLACKout" (2004), which tackles the idea of reparations for slavery as its novum. Robinson double yokes the novum with its *noirum* in that the law itself that brings about reparative justice functions as the *noirum*. Robinson describes the seeming joy of Black people on a train celebrating the news as the word spreads: "They were all shouting, frantically congratulating each other, celebrating the passing of S9821—the reparations bill that promises to compensate American citizens of African descent for years of unpaid slave labor" (232). Reparations come in the form of forty million dollars only if African Americans meet the eligibility requirements set forth by the bill: "that anyone wishing to claim the full reparations benefit package must be able to prove slave lineage both paternally and maternally . . . provided the person submitting the claim did not violate any provisions outlined in subsection twenty-nine-A" (239). Subsection twenty-nine-A stipulates those African Americans who are disqualified for reparations: "any persons with ancestors who were free at any time before the enactment of the Emancipation Proclamation; any persons whose parents or grandparents were not born in the United States of America; any person who has or whose parents have been engaged in anti-government activities that threaten the national security of the U.S. (e.g., members of the Nation of Islam, Black Panthers, draft dodging); any persons who have lived outside of the U.S. for a period of time exceeding two years for reasons other than military duty or employment assignments" (238). So then, to be eligible a Black person has to be able to prove that they were descended from slaves born in the United States and the United States only, effectively barring slave descendants whose ancestors may have been bought or sold from the Caribbean, Central America, South America, and Africa itself. Likewise, the bill establishes a highly controversial African American blood quantum in a federal effort to limit payouts by defining African American identity, meaning one parent from each side must be demonstrably descended from enslaved Blacks in the United States, and those parents in turn must also be descended from one Black parent on both sides. Thus, the government invalidates nearly every Black American of mixed descent. For example, if Frederick Douglass were living, he wouldn't qualify for two reasons: his mixed parentage, and the fact that his abolitionist friends purchased his freedom from the Auld family in

1846, making him already free well before the Emancipation Proclamation. Proving one's slave lineage would also be difficult in terms of physical documentation with respect to sales slips, ship manifests, plantation records, etc. Additionally, the federal government nullifies Black radicals from the civil rights and Black Power eras if not before—Martin Luther King Jr., Malcolm X, and Angela Davis for instance. W. E. B. Du Bois, Richard Wright, and Josephine Baker, among others, would also be rejected as African American citizens living outside of the US. Consequently, this much contested and highly controversial notion derived from the desire for social justice would simply be overwhelmed by the identity politics expertly practiced by our social and political institutions.

According to Robinson, reparations, if awarded, would end in despair for many Black Americans. In this respect, the story's protagonist Nigel, a Jamaican American, initially argues with his girlfriend Alana over the phone in the subway because he is not eligible for reparations while she is. He insults Alana's biracial heritage in the process by shouting, "Which half of you is going to submit the claim? The white half or the black half? Or are you still hanging on to 'other'?"—before she hangs up (233). However, Nigel's resentment continues as he bursts the bubbles of two Black teens, Lennox and Akiel, hanging out on the street as he arrives home, telling Akiel that he was "not eligible" because his folks were from Trinidad and that Akiel was "not American *enough*" to qualify for the money since neither his parents nor grandparents were born in the United States (235). He drags them to the local corner store to read the eligibility requirements listed on the front page of all the major newspapers, and Akiel shouts, "'Yo, how you jus' gonna walk up on niggas and casually drop some shit like that?'" (235). I think this question is legitimate and the answer is the despair that Nigel experiences because, despite being an American citizen, his Blackness doesn't count to the framers of the "Guilt Bill," as S9821 comes to be known (233). Cast in an international context, white America acknowledges its role in slavery while getting off lightly in terms of a financial payout that will not heal the psychic wounds of slavery and Jim Crow nor repair the social relationships harmed by ongoing racial discrimination. Nigel witnesses the indifference his country maintains toward other constructions of Black identity and it hurts him deeply as he experiences a social erasure.

Nigel truly despairs over his identity as half a year passes and this nameless sense of loss simultaneously produces feelings of listlessness and rage, causes him to break up with Alana, compels his joining the BLACKout, and ultimately leads to his decision to quit the United States. As Nigel informs us, the BLACKout refers to a strike by "Africans, West Indians, mulattos, octoroons, Native Americans (what? You think they're not part of us?), Spanish-speaking people of color, and all others conveniently excluded from America's so-called apology" that the White Supremacy groups have labeled (236). Undoubtedly, the white supremacists mean for Blacks to leave the country in the context of the story although the United States has never been a white-only country. But more subversive meanings exist in the sense that America suffers a temporary loss of memory when it comes to acknowledging the relevance of slavery to American history, the human suffering it has caused, the silence it expects from its oppressed minorities, and the absolution it desires by even the hint of redressing this enduring transgression. Yet it doesn't prevent ongoing and future abuses in the name of equality. We already know the terrorizing of African Americans will continue because white supremacists fear the perceived enveloping darkness of race and they will fight to suppress it. Of course, Nigel frames the BLACKout as "a modern-day slave revolt" denying white America of the service it requires to operate and to feel superior with respect to the "migrant workers, housekeepers, secretaries, airport crews, and janitors" (237). And so, Nigel leaves the United States for an undisclosed country at the end of the story in an act of defiance.

I think Robinson's counternarrative suggests that interest convergence will never align with respect to the reparations effort. First, white people's social and economic interests will never be served by compensating Black people for their forced labor in building the country just to assuage an unrecognized and ignored guilt supposedly salved by civil rights, if not affirmative action and the election of a Black president. Second, racial disparities and antagonisms endure and remain despite claims of a level playing field in the twenty-first century that has allowed the United States to heal from the atrocities of slavery and Jim Crow and to move further forward into the colorblind era, or a post-racial existence in the foolish attempt to suggest that race does not matter anymore. Clearly, this post-racial existence brought about by reparations *is* an optical delusion that the mirror shows.

Emerging Nigerian-descended American SF writer and former civil rights attorney Tochi Onyebuchi employs his legal experience in *Riot Baby* (2019) to create a dystopian world where two Black superpowered siblings, Ella and Kev, get racial justice against the backdrop of recent racial history as they grow up, beginning with the LA Riots of 1992. Onyebuchi creates a powerful narrative in *Riot Baby* that confronts the mass incarceration of Black and Brown people in the United States; a system where "more African American adults are under correctional control today—in prison or jail, on probation or parole—than were enslaved in 1850, a decade before the Civil War began" (Alexander, *The New*, 180). Simply put, Onyebuchi seeks to free us from the death grip of American racial history and to give us a colored future to ponder. He directly taps into the same energy and frustration that sparked the Black Lives Matter movement in 2013 in response to the social injustice, continuing racism, and police brutality perpetually faced by Black Americans. He dares to imagine what Black vengeance looks like.

Written in four parts that take us from LA to Harlem to Riker's Island and to Watts, *Riot Baby* fundamentally concerns white supremacy and Black vengeance and it does not have a white audience in mind. Set in South Central, Los Angeles, the first part introduces us to Ella as she rides a Compton school bus that is pulled over by Bloods in a low rider, angry at the young kids flashing Crip gang signs at them out the bus windows. We immediately recognize this past because of the prevalence of gang culture in the news media and rap music. We also witness the first manifestation of Ella's powers, "her Thing," as precognition, where she sees the death of Jelani, one of her classmates, in a drive-by shooting years before it happens (9). Later, Ella will ask her grandma why Black people are so angry and whether it has something to do with Rodney King being beaten by the police—and she knows something bad will happen. She and her grandma get caught up in the rioting that erupts after the "not guilty" verdicts for the police officers, although they are picked up by a friend rushing Ella's mother to the hospital while in labor. Kev, the titular riot baby, is born to single mother Lanie during the height of the rioting.

The second part of the novel picks up in Harlem, New York, where Ella tries to look out for her baby brother while dealing with her burgeoning psionic powers, like telekinesis, teleportation, and weather manipulation. Yet Ella fails to prevent her brother from hanging out on the street corners where he witnesses firsthand the police brutality solely enacted on young Black males simply playing the dozens. Onyebuchi highlights such implicit racial bias throughout the novel because "the reality is that we live in a society that is uniquely afraid of black boys" especially when thinking about "the 1990s rhetoric surrounding the black juvenile super-predator" encroaching on the minds of an already scared white public susceptible to the propaganda of Fox News (Henning, "Boys," 59). These adolescent Black boys display normal behavior in terms of clowning around, hanging out, and socializing before the cops arrive with their implicit bias and total disrespect. Kev later gravitates to this crowd. By the end of the second part, an older teenaged Kev gets arrested for attempted armed robbery, becoming another statistic while his sister is gone trying to master her powers.

The third part entails Kev's time at the infamous Riker's Island, Ella's mastery of her powers, and a jump into the near future. We also get a glimpse of Kev's nascent powers when he reads his cellmate's eyes and tells Ricky to stay out of the fight in the yard that will land Kev in solitary confinement for six months after throwing a correctional officer through the air with his mind in the smoke and confusion. In the outside world, augmented officers patrol the streets in mini-tanks and "metal orbs float along the sidewalks above the streetlamps" watching and recording everything (89).

Upon his release, Kev chooses to go west to Watts in the fourth part, where he joins a sponsored community picked by the patrol board through a computer algorithm. His thumb is microchipped by a private company and functions as a geotag. They know Kev's whereabouts at all times. Likewise, the company also administers anxiety-dampening chemicals through the chip. He works as a welder and makes prosthetics, but begins to perceive the sponsored Watts community as a prison since outsiders are not allowed inside and he's cut off from the internet and all forms of social media. But Kev can sense his sister's building rage at the "mechanized cops programmed with this supposedly race-neutral algorithm" and all of the murder they commit in the outside world as she visits various American cities (156).

Not for the first time, Onyebuchi explicitly connects his novel to our current moment of racial strife, from the beating of Rodney King and the LA Riots to the murders of Sean Bell and Freddie Gray by overzealous police in New York and Baltimore respectively. In addition to these moments, we learn that Ella "had Traveled," using one of her many powers, "straight to the site of the killing, and she'd touch the ground, breathed in the air, and sucked that history deep into her body" (110). Onyebuchi even references the McKinney, Texas pool party incident of June 2015 that became a viral sensation on YouTube within hours of Black teenager Dajerria Becton being violently restrained by a white police officer while in her bathing suit. Not only does this history of injustice fuel Ella's mounting rage, it unleashes Onyebuchi's ability to write with anger and love in seeking justice.

With this powerful moment of self-recognition, Ella teleports herself to Kev and informs Kev that everything he has built in the community factory has gone to augmenting the cops in "working to make the police invincible" and that he was "never free" of the prison-industrial complex (170–171). Kev rips the chip out of his thumb with his mind, freeing himself. With Kev's powers fully manifested, he and Ella will use their abilities to completely obliterate the American police state and begin anew with freedom. *Riot Baby* explores the meaning of Black vengeance against the carceral and white supremacist American state and the bonds of filial love as the superpowered Black siblings take racial justice into their own hands.

Onyebuchi does three important things in *Riot Baby* with respect to the hyperreal violence loop. This repeating loop dates back to slavery in the United States, where "violence and the threat of violence become hyperreal in the Baudrillardan sense": "the unreality, the outlandishness, the implausibility of it feels science fictional in that readers cannot tell where reality ends and fiction begins" (Lavender, *Afrofuturism*, 11). First, he entrenches the recent history of violence against Black people in his novel beginning with the Rodney King beating and the LA Riots as well as shows his audience what the prison industrial complex looks like from the inside perspective of Kev in order to unpack the harm it causes. Second, he disrupts this narrative with the psionically gifted sister and brother protagonists as they navigate life in the defamiliarized but recognizable United States of America. And third, he provides an alternative understanding of our social world to better imagine what racial justice could look like through antiracist thinking—the reason behind telling this story to counteract colorblindness and the apathy toward Black people that it causes when violence occurs. In *Riot Baby*, Onyebuchi effectively combines antiracist activism with science fictional world-building.

Onyebuchi utilizes SF to confront an American truth so terrible yet so plain in *Riot Baby*. White America will not abandon the structural advantages it has over all other races and ethnicities and would annihilate everyone to maintain this privileged status. Not without a fight! White society doesn't even acknowledge the psychological harm, physical pain, and cultural suffering it has continually inflicted on Blacks (and Browns) in America; violent oppression continues against its most vilified and vulnerable citizens. The embedded hatred for Black people in America runs so deep in our country's fabric that we may never overcome it as a citizenry. Guilt, fear, and anger by whites at Black excellence live in our politics and produce racial inequality. In eulogizing the recently deceased Black civil rights icon Representative John Lewis, President Barack Obama says it best: "Bull Connor may be gone. But today we witness with our own eyes police officers kneeling on the necks of Black Americans. George Wallace may be gone. But we can witness our federal government sending agents to use tear gas and batons against peaceful demonstrators" ("Eulogy"). Onyebuchi's novel functions as a second testimonial that indicates how a righteous anger can ignite the necessary hope for change to end this enduring dystopian nightmare for Blacks in the United States of America. Ella visits her mother's old church in Harlem and speaks to the pastor about the Charleston church shooting. Ella's conversation with the pastor concerns the forgiving of the white supremacist Dylan Roof, who murdered nine African Americans in cold blood during a Bible study at the Emanuel African Methodist Episcopal Church in Charleston, South Carolina on June 17, 2015. She realizes that she does not need permission to end the violence against Black people. What Ella comprehends is that younger generations of Black people don't need permission from older generations to do things their own way in the fight for racial justice, in the fight for equality, in the fight for the future of humanity itself. That's a powerful realization held up against the colorblind highjacking and co-optation of the civil rights movement by white America. Through her epiphany, Ella concedes the futility in forgiving this evil and decides that she herself is the answer to her people's prayers against the augmented police and the biased computer algorithms they use. Black lives matter to her!

In this respect, whites have always radicalized in response to Black progress. We see it in the colonial era, the antebellum era, the Civil War, Reconstruction, the Jim Crow era, the civil rights era, the age of the affirmative action, and the especially short-lived post-black era of the nearly unbelievable yet extraordinary two-term Obama presidency. Thus, the hyperreal violence loop has always been the engine driving the social movements most impacting Blacks in America from the beginning: like abolition to end slavery, like civil rights to end Jim Crow segregation, like Black Lives Matter to end police brutality and the school-to-prison pipeline of disadvantaged minorities caught up in a racist legal system. Onyebuchi asks the relevant question of what contemporary American society might look like if policing, criminal justice, and the incarceration of Black and Brown people in lieu of white nationalism continues. And Onyebuchi answers: it definitely *explodes* as he shows us the ugly face of America in the mirror of Afrofuturism.

Intelligent Resistance

Situations do not change without resistance. The mirror of Afrofuturism accurately reflects white expectations for racial minorities to put up with white-fostered restrictions such as colorblindness or total obeisance to law enforcement and to function within the conditions created for racial minorities with Blacks at the bottom. The importance of intelligent resistance cannot be stressed enough because it becomes obvious in the fictions of emerging writers as they oppose ideological perceptions, prejudices, and stereotypes. Emerging African American writer Violet Allen chooses to confront the colorblindness and indifference toward the reality of police violence in her short story "The Venus Effect" (2016), which perfectly demonstrates what BLM⁺ means for science fiction from a CRT perspective tinged with Afrofuturism.

Allen uses metafiction to tell a speculative tale of how a police officer murders the titular black hero Apollo Allen at the end of each vignette. The story is comprised of nine vignettes and eight metacommentaries. Apollo changes in each story and each story changes and takes readers further into an alien takeover subplot. The opening vignette begins with a Chicago rooftop party. In the second story, Apollo is a local basketball star who makes the winning shot in the championship. In the third, he's a teenager sitting on a stoop who decides to walk the new girl home. He's Black Justice in the fourth entry, a member of a superhero team like the Power Rangers. Allen changes things up with the fifth entry by switching Apollo's gender to a Black woman, who happens to be walking through a poorly lit parking deck to her car after getting off work. The sixth vignette is a love story in an apartment, with Apollo resting his head in his girlfriend's lap deep in intimate conversation when the cops break in with a no-knock warrant. In fact, Apollo doesn't even appear in the seventh vignette at the end of time with only the alien Lord Tklox waiting to let loose "the Omega Question" killing everybody (360). Irony of ironies, there are no Black people in the far-flung future because science fiction said so as Allen riffs in the accompanying metacommentary. With the eighth vignette, Apollo is a plainclothes detective. And the brilliant ninth entry subverts everything by putting us into the mind of a white police officer. Allen, in the second-person present voice, forces the reader to become a "You" during a stop and frisk of an assumed Black man who fits the description of a mugger. As the Black man reaches for something bulging in his pocket, the Omega question triggers—"*who matters?*" (365). That's the last line of the story. This question really matters. That's powerful and provocative writing that engages a sense of the Black Lives Matter movement and the Black social death we face in contemporary times.

Allen gives her story the apt title "The Venus Effect." She chooses this title to reflect, pun intended, upon the psychological perceptions of race and racism that she mirrors through the story depending on her reader's ethno-racial identity. Named after various paintings of Venus eyeing and admiring herself in a mirror—such as Titian's *Venus with a Mirror* (1555), Peter Paul Rubens's *Venus in front of the Mirror* (1614–1615), or Diego Velázquez's *Rokeby Venus* (1647)—"the Venus effect" in visual art describes how "the viewpoint of the observer is different from the viewpoint of Venus; that is, the observer is not behind Venus with respect to the mirror. Therefore, what can be seen in the mirror differs for the observer and for Venus [that] the scene is not compatible with Venus looking at her own reflection" (Bertamini et al., "The Venus Effect," 1948). Marco Bertamini, Richard Latto, and Alice Spooner first define this psychological and optical perception as "the Venus effect" in 2003, stating that "the Venus effect occurs every time the observer sees both an actor (e.g., Venus) and a mirror, not placed along the observer's line of sight, and concludes that Venus is seeing her reflection at the same location in the mirror that the observer is seeing" (596). In this respect, as Päivi Väätänen notes, "the effect perfectly captures the effect of the short story, which, in the end, turns its gaze on the readers" as "both the subject and object of reflection" (*Narrating*, 163). Simply put, what is discernable to us as Allen's readers depends on our point of view and which mirror is being used.

If it is an Afrofuturist mirror, Allen captures the cultural energy of the movement in the Black desire to see their future selves, albeit blunted. If it is an afropessimist mirror, Allen suggests that there isn't a future for Black people based on the callous disregard for Black life in America. Her story is very much in dialogue with our present moment drawing on the lamentable American tradition of police violence. But, if the mirror is one of CRT, then Allen "calls attention to the scientific and social injustice of the past and present while creating startling new images of futures that simply cannot be whitewashed" in her attempt to contest "white supremacy" with her counter-narrative (Lavender and Yaszek, "*First*," 2). This connation goes beyond Afrofuturism. It engages the *noirum* of policing, where we see a counter-story that flips perceptions of criminality as the new thing to witness the prevalence of racism in law enforcement.

Allen does not simply want us to free our minds by resisting stereotypes in order to fight racism. She wants her audience to really see the problem from all the angles provided in the mirror—the problem being that unarmed Black people, usually men, are shot and killed by police officers in the United States repeatedly, continually, over and over, ad infinitum. That is the real concern. Black American experience, molded by the social construction of race, informs the story, gives it its absolute political edge. For Allen, "the story comes from a place of fear and powerlessness, fear that something like this might happen to me or a loved one and powerlessness in the face of this huge problem" (Sorg, "Author"). She does not just opine "that cops are bad or whatever," but argues "for a more comprehensive indictment of how our society functions and how it defines black people as citizens and as human beings" (Sorg, "Author"). Consequently, "the bad guy is not the cop, the bad guy is racism, racism that goes far beyond the actions of individuals or particular institutions" (Allen quoted in Sorg, "Author"). Apollo, like every Black person, real or otherwise, faces this uniquely American problem in each of the nine storylines, resulting in his death. As Allen explains elsewhere, the fictional "'author' of the piece is surprised by this, and it keeps happening over and over again" as "the story [goes] through these scenarios and [tries] to understand why this is happening. Both in the fiction and in the real world" ("Violet"). Allen states unequivocally: "at the end of the day, my goal in the story was to capture a feeling. The primary goal was not to say police shootings are wrong. That to me is an understood thing. The point of the story was to evoke the feeling of seeing these things happen, and not being able to do anything. That sense of powerlessness and of repetition. It happens. Again, and again, and again, and again. There's nothing you can do" ("Violet"). Therefore, the fictional author, the audience, and Allen herself, wrestle with this id monster—the policeman—throughout the story, attempting to stave off Apollo's extrajudicial fate in each abandoned story. Why does it keep happening: stereotypes, fear, prejudice, racism, colorblindness? You can especially see it in the insidious notion of colorblindness. Not seeing something like skin color gets Black people killed every day. Enough said.

At some point, the deaths become comical in their absurdity but hit hard because of their frequency mirrored in our everyday reality. Somehow, it has become normal. I mean the repetition of Black people dying at the hands of law enforcement. I must note that Allen takes time to build in a bit of humor to soften the reality, like her riff on the *Shaft* (1971) theme-song in the eighth vignette "Apollo Jones In: The Final Showdown": "Who stops crime in the nick of time and dazzles the ladies with feminine rhymes? [Apollo!] Can you dig it?" (361). She peppers in moments from popular culture like this throughout the story out of necessity. To use a cliché, Allen powerfully evokes laughter to keep from crying.

Allen goes hard at the end when she changes the perceptual mirror by placing her audience inside a cop's mind in her attempt to resolve this problem. The reader becomes a raceless, genderless cop, as Allen specifically leaves out such information by "engag[ing] second-person present" "you" (364). The cop identity here could be a colorblind construct, but it largely depends on the individual reader's identity as the final confrontation with a larger man, walking on the sidewalk, minding his own business with a bulging pocket, who fits a description that we must assume is Black, even as "the Omega Question" activates (365). How do we as the audience deescalate this irrational fear of the big, bad, Black man potentially armed with a gun, created by stereotypes and television? Like with the cop, Allen explicitly does not mention this pedestrian's race or ethnicity here. But the Reagan era so successfully painted the image of vagrants as Black people that we assume this man is an angry Black man, an unvalued brute whose life is meaningless weighed against the cop's own life, a life that we have already seen as normal and desirable with a spouse and kids, reflective of the American dream, and making it really easy for you as the cop to pull the trigger. At least, that *is* the choice that Allen presents us with at the end of the story in all its poignant lucidity. The mirror does not lie.

But its distortions take on a butterfly effect of its own in that these small things matter, that individual Black Lives Matter—like Emmett Till, Trayvon Martin, Breonna Taylor, or countless others. The consequences of pulling the trigger will eventually cause disproportionately large effects as social movements arise that can and will and must irrevocably alter the United States and its treatment of its emerging minority majority. Small things matter and have a deep impact on this country. Allen's "The Venus Effect," in its profundity, questions how our actions of today, resulting from previous moments, could lead us to a future solution to this overwhelming problem of police violence. That *is* critical race theory functioning as it helps us make sense of race relations and the power differential inherent between whites and everyone else in terms of social, economic, and political realities. Allen daringly uses science fiction to confront history in hopes of rewriting this blatant disregard for Black lives by asking who matters. This question of who matters is the *noirum*. I mean "what if"—science fiction's most basic question—the trigger is not pulled and this changes the perception of reality and negates Black stereotypes that cause fatalities. Would that not be intelligent resistance?

Tracy Deonn also offers shrewd defiance in her contemporary reimagining of the Arthurian mythos blended with southern folklore by projecting her Legendborn Cycle—comprised of *Legendborn* (2020) and *Bloodmarked* (2022)—into the mirror of Afrofuturism. The Black teenaged protagonist Bree

Mathews unravels the mystery of her tragic matriarchal family history and discovers herself at the Chapel Hill campus of the University of North Carolina through an early admissions residential program for gifted high school students. A moment from this series that stands out brightly to my mind occurs in the first novel when the sixteen-year-old and her best friend Alice, who happens to be Asian and queer, attend their first college party at a quarry that gets broken up by a demon and the Merlin, Selwyn Kane, who drives it off. As the two friends flee the woods, they get scooped up by a Durham County Sheriff's deputy named Norris, and ride home in the backseat of the patrol car. While it may seem innocuous enough that Deputy Norris listens to the song "Sweet Home Alabama" on the radio, Bree feels uncomfortable immediately having heard "the stories from uncles, cousins—hell, my own father—about police run-ins and stops. I see the videos online. Sitting in this car and thinking about those images makes my heart pound. I don't know if there's a single Black person in this country who can say with 100 percent confidence that they feel safe with the police. Not after the past few years. Probably not ever. Maybe there are some, somewhere, but I sure as hell don't know 'em" (29). Deonn instantaneously engages the Black cultural zeitgeist of the BLM movement in relation to law enforcement to cement her concern for social justice within the novel's urban fantastical setting to enhance the issues of fear and distrust that most Black people feel with respect to police, people who are supposed to protect society. This move represents something we do not often see in speculative fiction as Deonn centers Bree's Blackness and helps her audience understand how this experience is integral to the story. Deputy Norris wields his authority over Bree and Alice with a mere look in the rearview mirror after ordering them to stop chatting, daring them to say something with a raised eyebrow in order to better enjoy the racially controversial Lynyrd Skynyrd song with its referencing to Birmingham and the former segregationist governor George Wallace. I see the confederate flag of the album cover so firmly in my mind.

Regardless, Deputy Norris creates an intimidating atmosphere in his squad car when the racist microaggressions starts. He wants to know how the girls got into a pricey, academically challenging university with the highest of admission standards when his own son did not. Once again using the mirror, he looks into Bree's eyes and sneeringly states, "'I'm guessin' need-based,'" to which she curtly replies "'Merit' . . . through gritted teeth," only for Norris to respond with "Sure" and a chuckle (30). Deputy Norris manages to erase Bree's accomplishment with that lone word and derisive chuckle in this brief scene, leaving her with "impotent rage" (30). I mean how could she possibly get into UNC, Chapel Hill without filling some kind of diversity quota?! You can hear the malevolence in his sniggering as he devalues her mind and Bree sublimates her retort with finger curling; she knows that saying something smart back to him could cause real trouble, real fast. Norris perpetrates a kind of mental violence, an emotional attack without the trigger, connected to disregarding Bree's education and accomplishments. Unfortunately, Black people must internalize such racist and aggressive comments every day.

While not exactly refreshing, finding this accurate representation of reality *is* eye-opening because Deonn powerfully frames her story of Black girl magic with police altercations, microaggressions, and stereotypes that do not let white people off the hook for this country's racist past and present. In fact, Deonn goes extra: we learn that Bree's unique ability to practice blood magic and to perform rootcraft happens because her matrilineal ancestor Vera was enslaved to a scion of King Arthur and later raped by him on his North Carolina plantation. Knowing the cause of her intergenerational trauma, Bree can now fully embrace her future as a Black woman. I believe the telling of such stories can undermine the grip of racism by providing an effective counter-narrative to the primary white mythology of America as white only. In this case, the illusion of white America breaks apart in the mirror of Afrofuturism.

Bold, Black, and Beautiful

The *noirum* can function without involving CRT. That is to say, the *noirum* does not always engage with legality and judicial law. It sometimes evokes unwritten social laws such as the one-drop rule, which leads to miscegenation, racial passing, and colorism—all things displayed in the mirror of Afrofuturism. The *noirum* could be as simple as an eye drop that changes brown eyes blue temporarily, something the Black main character Lena Johnson experiences as a participant in secret medical experiments in African American Megan Giddings's 2020 horror novel *Lakewood*. Lena goes out to a bar as a part of the experiment and faces cross-racial colorism when a drunk Korean woman shouts, "Toni Morrison would be ashamed of you" (132); later, Lena is told by another Black woman, "You know, you don't have to look white to look good" (133). In referencing Morrison's first novel *The Bluest Eye* (1970), the Korean woman implies that Lena must feel ugly inside because of her dark brown skin, must have an intense feeling of personal inadequacy, an inferiority complex because of her blue eyes. This shaming, reinforced by the Black woman in the bathroom, a stranger, reveals how some BIPOCS feel with respect to white conceptions of beauty as a spoken internal bias against Lena's external appearance. These two women make a judgment of Lena based on her physical appearance and how she must feel about herself in relation to whiteness. They engage unwritten social laws and imply that Lena breaks them, buying into the idea, constantly visualized in the media, that beauty is inherently based on a white standard, suggesting that Lena oppresses herself. I find their response to Lena's eye color familiar yet disturbing because the fictional world feels exactly like our own as Giddings slyly comments on how experimentation on Black bodies repeatedly happens.

Informed by our own world, Giddings's make-believe world intensifies the horror of such skin color politics within the Black community. We as readers surely understand the significance of the Tuskegee experiment despite Giddings not referencing this infamous moment in American history, or Henrietta Lacks for that matter. Lena is living something like what Lacks or the Tuskegee victims lived in this one moment as a test subject and takes comfort in the fact that "People cared! . . . They would find out this wasn't just once, this wasn't just in the past, but it had happened over and over" (264). Through the *noirum*, we can refract these happenings in Afrofuturism's looking glass and hold our nation accountable for its racist past. In this sense, the *noirum* could represent the science-fictional Blackness that Ibram X. Kendi remarks upon in his own experiences in college with honey-colored contacts (*How*, 108). "Colorist ideas are also assimilationist ideas, encouraging assimilation into—or transformation into something close to—the White body," as Kendi perceives, "the inequities between the races mirror[ing] inequities with the races" (110). We must recognize colorism in all its forms as a continuation of the mechanisms of control introduced during slavery in the division of house, field, and skilled slaves with respect to skin color and supposed greater intelligence resulting from miscegenation. It *is* a learned behavior encouraged by white folks.

Black author Maurice Carlos Ruffin takes interrogation of colorism to the next level in his debut novel *We Cast a Shadow* (2019), where his nameless, color struck, pill-popping, Black, lawyer protagonist attempts to make partner in a dystopian New Orleans ridden with crime and police violence. The novum feels like a concatenation of laws, where "virtually none" of the Black people "can vote since felons and the children of felons need a voucher from an upstanding citizen to earn a voting pass" (137). Likewise, a "Dreadlock

Ordinance" exists wherein "the cops could give any arrestee a haircut if they deemed the person unsanitary" (177). And the city's mayor extends "the curfew at the Tikoloshe Housing Development from weekends to seven days a week," raises the height of the housing project's fence, expands its perimeter by eight blocks, and puts in place an agreement to deport unruly US citizens to the imaginary African country of Zamundia (180).[4] Ruffin's glance into the Afrofuturist mirror reflects a dystopian novum with respect to a newfangled disenfranchisement, a Black hair law, and a mayor who clearly oversteps her power in attempting to make the city safe. But safe for who exactly? Scared white people.

Considering how the prison industrial complex functions and the disproportionate number of Black people caught in this nefarious system, Ruffin's powerful, though secondary, ideation would go a long way in assuaging the white fear of losing status by making it next to impossible for Black people to vote. This *is* scary stuff because he implies the "upstanding" citizens must surely be white. The Dreadlock Ordinance does not seem too far-fetched, since we have already seen many recent incidents of Black teens being forced to cut their hair to participate in school sports[5] or to walk the graduation stage with their high school classmates.[6] Hair discrimination really exists outside as well as within Black communities and the recent CROWN Act (Creating a Respectful and Open Word for Natural Hair), banning hair bias, has passed at the state level in eighteen states, has passed at the House of Representatives at the federal level, and now awaits the Senate. The primary thrust of Ruffin's novel involves internalized racism resulting from an ingrained and socially perceived skin color privilege. That is not to say that the protagonist does not take offense at external moments of racism like police encounters or white women switching sides of the street or being followed by salesclerks in department stores. He is cynical, perhaps even Afropessimist in that he does not think there is a future for Black people in American society.

Nevertheless, *We Cast a Shadow* relates to a father's desire to protect his son Nigel from the racist white world. In the opening chapter, the father chooses to dress up as a Zulu chief complete with a loincloth at a company party to win over his bosses and counteract his rival who dresses up as a convict. He suffers humiliation for his son's sake and still does not make partner. The protagonist wants desperately to make partner because he is ashamed of his son Nigel's birthmark on his face and wants to pay for "a process called demelanization or a demel or a scrub" that worked on a pop star named "Crooked Crown," who went from being "a black girl from Baltimore" to looking "like a Greek woman" (92). This procedure represents the social *noirum*. Therefore, Ruffin presents a biological view on race in that it is something that can be corrected medically in this future United States much like a tummy tuck or a nose job. Striving to be free of race *is* fundamentally misdirected if one could simply save an exorbitant amount of cash to undergo the procedure to physically change one's race and pass beyond the limitations of raced body.

In this regard, the protagonist is so deeply embarrassed by his own race that he lives in an all-white neighborhood, married a white woman, Penny, and sends his kid to an all-white private school. The protagonist comes to represent "the Blind Equality Group" (BEG) because it will lead him to making partner and enable him to afford the procedure for Nigel (121). In fact, he considers "equality" nothing more "than a typographical error in the Constitution" (123). He goes against the wishes of his wife, his mother, and his adoring son in pursuing this transformation. While Ruffin tackles many racial issues in this novel like the overwhelming police presence in Black neighborhoods as well as mass incarceration, they pale in comparison to his depiction of a color struck man harmed by the memory of a corrupt Black cop breaking his mother's arm and beating his father in front of his eyes because his father lost his cool at the harm done to his wife. This formative moment results in the protagonist's desire to escape his race.

But the protagonist loses his wife over this desire to change his son's skin color and loses his son too over what he perceives to be a stain on one's humanity. As Nigel grows up, the protagonist uses all kinds of painful skin bleaching creams like "Madame C. J.'s" or "J. B.'s Whitener" on their son's face and body behind his wife's back (134). All the while, the protagonist thinks to himself, "I would have had to dive into a pool of the ointment to fix my skin. I was too dark all over. A full body stain" (135). Things come to a head when he takes his son to Dr. Nzinga's clinic to begin the months long procedure. Penny finds his red journal, reads his plans for Nigel, and leaves their son with the neighbors, all the while weighing "the dangers of structural inequality" against the madness of a color struck father "poisoning our son"; she is determined to have it out with her husband (199, 198). As she leaves the house in a rage, Penny gets struck by a police van and dies in the street as a cop points his unholstered gun at her Black husband.

Time passes, Nigel radicalizes at the plight and condition of the ghetto, and eventually runs off with his girlfriend rather than suffer through the skin-lightening process. After making partner, the protagonist changes his name and becomes "a transracial person" undergoing demelanization himself

(286). He finds Nigel living at an Appalachian commune, years later, now a dark-skinned man living with his pregnant dark-skinned wife, and witnesses the birth of his brown granddaughter. They part with Nigel's final words: "'Do you honestly think you would ever be able to accept her looking the way she does?' . . . 'At least you're really thinking about it. I appreciate that. But we don't need that in our lives. Go home. Enjoy what you've done to yourself. But don't haunt us anymore'" (317). In comparing his father to a ghost by whitening himself, Nigel exorcises the ghost the protagonist has become. He convinces his father to leave him alone, to not visit, to not trouble him with the colorism prejudice that constantly recurred during his upbringing. He survives his father.

Ruffin strongly channels earlier novels, such as Wallace Thurman's *The Blacker the Berry* (1929)[7] and George Schuyler's *Black No More* (1931),[8] in his near-future take on what self-hatred can do to a person. Ruffin elevates awareness of this skin stratification strategy designed to control enslaved Black people, often disguised as a racial progress narrative with a perceived preference for whiteness, functioning within Black communities to this day as a buffer safeguarding white privilege. Through near-future satire, Ruffin asks his audience to continue thinking on how color disrupts racial views in the United States through his world-making. He provides a dark reflection of prejudice within the Black community itself.

Yet Ruffin's novel does not have anything on Bill Campbell's supermodel ex-cop turned private detective Genevieve Noire in *Koontown Killing Kaper* (2012) with respect to colorism. Noire's family subscribes to racial passing to the extent that one of her uncles drunkenly declares, "'Fuck the paper bag test! We goin' for Ziploc, baby!!!'" (7). As I said earlier, skin tone privilege exists as a cruel internalization of the color line within Black communities with a lighter skin tone being prized. This test, the brown paper bag test,[9] literarily means that a Black person darker than a brown paper bag could not enter a social space with lighter-skinned Blacks. This custom, myth, legendary practice can be traced back to the peculiar institution where privileges were given to lighter-skinned Blacks such as working inside the plantation house; something that appeared infinitely better to working in the fields in hot, humid conditions doing backbreaking physical labor. Campbell elicits laughter by taking social stereotypes of Black people and others to such extremes to negate racism by interrogating our own assumptions.

The novel's initial plot concerns the murder investigation of two popular rappers killed in a compromising sexual position followed by more killings of prominent Black celebrities represented by hip-hop mogul Hustle Beamon of Dope Beat Records (18). I think of the vampire crack babies as Campbell's ostensible novum as he critiques military experimentation on Black bodies in the creation of these monsters. At least, the vampire crack babies drive the narrative as they shout out "likkaniggadik" before attacking, although they are susceptible to "polysyllabic words" and books (167, 261). Throwing back this incredibly misogynistic hook perfectly in line with the characteristics of Black culture and making the tentacle-eyed creatures weak against voluminous vocabulary words, Campbell directly challenges much of the nihilism that exists in rap music. You simply must laugh at this paradox, where a classic novel like *Their Eyes Were Watching God* "*literally* explode[s]" a vampire crack baby who is hit by the book (261)! The primary suspect, Kelvin "HNIC" Cleghorne, a University of Pennsylvania graduate, breaks into the music industry as a socially conscious rapper named "Rebelution" in the mold of a KRS-One but can't sell any records (109). So, he renames himself Head Nigga in Charge and becomes a superstar with the nonsensical song "Bitch! Ho! Bitch Ho!" at the top of the music charts (101). His largely white audience wants to hear explicit content that degrades women and preaches violence and he cashes in on this market at the expense of the Black community, an odd echoing of interest convergence, wherein limited Black success helps maintain white dominance in the control and perpetuation of racist stereotypes. In other words, these few Blacks obtain wealth by repeating degrading stereotypes, practicing misogynoir because it converges with the interests of white people, thus allowing these few Blacks to advance financially if not socially.

A case in point, Crispus Booker, the lead pastor of the Church of Racial Reconciliation, sermonizes seven nights a week to different ethno-racial groups on different evenings: Blacks one night, whites the next night, followed by Arabs, Latinos, Asians, and so on. He even makes class distinctions between the working poor and the Black bourgeois. Reverend Booker has the most diverse church in the country as well as the most segregated since none of his parishioners meet on the same nights. His flock merely want their "racial notions to be *reaffirmed* . . . so they can actually feel reconciled with what they already believe—racist or not" (175). As Reverend Booker states, "'when it comes to race,' . . . 'people hear only what they want to hear'" (177). With these two sentences, Campbell really digs into the lifestyles, attitudes, relationships, and faith that generate the reality of American culture over the past decade or so, allowing the emergence of a long underground Christian nationalism built on interlocking oppressions, political violence, and racism.

There are so many brilliant satirical moments in *Koontown Killing Kaper*, from the novel's title to Genevieve Noire's bullet-proof Prius, that picking out the *noirum* seems difficult. It could be police violence or thirty-year-old grandmothers or straight-A Black students killed by random bullets or the fully automated morgue or gentrification or the colorism with which I started off my brief analysis. I mean, Campbell deep dives into heavy topics like medical experimentation, police interrogation and roundups, and the 1965 Moynihan Report.[10] Truly think about his outrageous idea for "Pre-Parole Officer[s]" for elementary school kids and how that image excoriates the school-to-prison pipeline initiated by the mayoral decree (252). Black youth from disadvantaged households are funneled out of school directly into the legal system through zero tolerance policies, metal detectors, and school resource officers as opposed to federal, state, and local government providing resources and support to help these perceived troublemakers learn. This single moment verily symbolizes one of many *noirums* in *Koontown Killing Kaper* in which Campbell demonstrates an antiracist consciousness by openly engaging stereotypes, asking questions of our country, offering perspective on our racist roots and their manifestation in our contemporary sociopolitical moment. Edutainment at its most searing, Campbell magnifies the Afrofuturist mirror in his attempt to burn away the permanence of racism through his social critique.

Glimpsing beauty in the mirror of Afrofuturism proves to be difficult against the reflection of centuries, where damaging stereotypes regarding natural features, skin colors, and hair textures have irrevocably harmed the soul of Black people through the internalization of racism. But African American fantasy writer Dhonielle Clayton attempts to hold this mirror up to the face of America in her trilogy—*The Belles* (2018), *The Everlasting Rose* (2019), and *The Beauty Trials* (2023)—by utilizing beauty as a *noirum*. Clayton creates the world of Orléans, where beauty reigns supreme and political intrigues abound in an opulent palace setting reminiscent of a Versailles located in a society much like antebellum New Orleans. Beauty has been commodified in a world where the masses are damned, born with uniform gray wrinkled skin, gray hair, and red eyes—the "Gris" (*Belles*, 12). But the affluent can afford the services of the Belles—combination cosmetologists and plastic surgeons, for lack of a better description—descendants of the Goddess of Beauty, who use the arcana in their blood to perform bodily transformations through magic and makeup. The Belles strive for the attention of the Queen, to be the realm's Favorite. So, the Gris can be made beautiful for a short time before needing more treatment. Sixteen-year-old Camellia Beauregard (Camille), the protagonist, and her sisters, the latest generation of Belles, have the sole responsibility of keeping the populace happy, keeping the citizens' appearance in line with the current beauty and fashion trends dictated by Queen Celeste, her daughter Princess Sophia, and the Royal Beauty Minister.

Clayton sometimes uses evocative imagery in her series to explore the value of bodies. She commodifies the Gris by describing their artificial skin tones as delectable confections. Clayton does not prefer a lighter skin tone over a darker one as evinced in the early pages of *The Belles*, wherein "All the people seem beautiful, with skin in various colors, from fresh cream to a drizzle of honey to a square of chocolate" (*Belles*, 3). The Queen herself has "ink-black skin" while her daughter Princess Sophia (the antagonist of the series) has "golden hair" at the beginning (*Belles*, 5). I think it important that the queen appears dark-skinned and her daughter is blonde initially because the color-coding allows an astute reader to recognize how Clayton flips the paradigm of good and evil. Colorism cannot exist in her world because people are constantly changing their skin color, eye color, facial features, and hair texture. Beauty becomes a "racializing assemblage" in that Clayton uses the malleability of "flesh as a pivotal arena for the politics emanating from different traditions of the oppressed" (Weheliye, *Habeas*, 2). Clayton examines the power structures of beauty in categorizing human difference in her lavish world, where the illusory power of beauty transfers hierarchical mechanisms of race on to physical features that idealize whiteness. She metaphorically attacks the ideology promoting white aesthetics by having her people adapt any skin color, physical shape, or hair texture within the tenets of the queen's laws. This falls within the realm of CRT because of how beauty standards have been internalized within the Black community. Black people "spend millions each year on a variety of products that promise to straighten, relax or otherwise make more manageable kinky black hair" (duCille, "Black," 343). Grooming practices in Black communities the world over have normalized this practice in order to reflect the white aesthetics at the top of the ladder.

Clayton's series very clearly satirizes the idea that a woman's worth lies in her outward appearance in a beauty-obsessed world much like our own, defined by material possessions, luxury, and fame. Less apparent is the fact that to be beautiful in Orléans the Gris have to change their skin-color, essentially changing their race to fit in through the magic of the Belles. Clayton offers a powerful critique of racially biased standards of beauty that skew white in terms of social welfare. Having color in her world is having beauty. I think Clayton implies that with this beauty comes confidence and pride, not only in your own skin and features, but also in your cultural roots—an affirmation of being and the power to occupy spaces, disrupting stereotypes of good and bad hair, full lips, and broad noses—and, most importantly, skin color as a marker of ugliness and inferiority. Front and center, Black beauty isn't ignored, fetishized, or othered in this series. It's presented in all its complexities as Clayton engages with a variety of aesthetic stereotypes.

Throughout *The Belles*, readers see Camille and other residents reacting to various news and tabloid headlines in magazines such as "*Dulce*, *Mignon*, *Beauté*, *Sucré*, and the *Dame's Journal de la Mode*" and tabloids like "the *Imperial Inquirer*," "*Parlor of Titillating Tidbits*," and "*Speculations of the Foulest Kind*," among many others (*Belles*, 35–37). Clayton includes these imaginary publications as a critique of how influential the media is in upholding beauty standards and class structures, of how they can spread gossip and lies and how we consume them. She digs into the structural racism in the media because it promotes long-held biases that remain invisible just beneath the surface, such as the idea that Black people are ugly.

The result of her trilogy is a fierce rethinking of capitalism, the news media, racism, and the beauty industry. We see the maintenance of beauty standards as a way to judge character and Clayton shows us how we are wrong. Clayton's *noirum* prompts uncomfortable and honest reflection on notions of beauty being only skin deep; a person's character should always be more important than how they look. Princess Sophia has every advantage as the princess of Orléans in terms of food, education, wealth, servants, courtiers, power, and yet she is as ugly as they come. Camille tries to use her social privilege as the Favorite for good and advocates for the better treatment of people. Indisputably, Clayton gifts us a unique storyworld concerning race and beauty as far as I can tell that creates a fascinating response to colorism. She challenges the beauty industry and its diminishment of others in the promotion of a white aesthetic.

While Clayton indulges a young adult marketing theme with attention paid to identity, first love, and friendships, she offers an antiracist critique of beauty standards and how such racist societal beliefs negatively impact Black identity. This trilogy is singular in Afrofuturism because it presents a fantasy world unapologetically linked to the celebration of Black beauty wherein the Belles and their use of beauty products create glamour through hair, makeup, and skin tones that don't conform to Eurocentric standards.

White Reflections

Most people think CRT only applies to legal studies and education in the realm of academia, but SF writers open up new ways of thinking about CRT in the fight against the long-dying rage of white supremacy in the United States. These writers provide snapshots of darker worlds and lighter worlds, too, where the branches of the US government and their various agencies manipulate the masses to whatever ends the authors can imagine in terms of laws and policies created to control or free BIPOCS. We'd better pay attention to alt-right writers too. In this respect, I offer a reading of the white paleoconservative William S. Lind's near-future novel *Victoria: A Novel of 4th Generation War* (2014). Books produced by avowed racists like Lind—who fancies himself an equal to the English enlightenment philosopher Thomas Hobbes, as evinced by his nom de plume for *Victoria*, published by the nefarious Theodore Beale (aka Vox Day of Rabid Puppies ignominy) at the infamous Castalia House—function as early warning devices against the world turning back in time to the full-blown racism, sexism, and violence of a supposed bygone era defined by white patriarchy. The alarm rings loudly in my ears, but who else is listening?! We'd better wake up because it's happening right now. Consider the failed January 6, 2021 coup and you have an idea of what's going on in *Victoria*.

The novum of this novel relates to Captain John Rumford of Maine, dishonorably discharged from the Marine Corps for blatant sexism after disrupting a ceremony because a female Marine was chosen to honor the fallen Marines at the battle of Iwo Jima. Stretching from the years 2016 to 2072, the novel chronicles how Rumford elects to fight the oncoming culture war in the end stage of American empire, combatting the nationwide spread of political correctness identified as "Cultural Marxism" (15). Rumford begins by organizing the Christian Marines, a terrorist group in Boston, to fight government housing policies, which ignites a revolution through civil disobedience.

The novel itself implies that war is the new country of Victoria's greatest export in that Captain Rumford continually advises other countries in his martial capacity: defeating the all-Black 42nd Division from Harlem as the US attempts to quell the secession; defeating the Black Muslims in Boston of an independent Massachusetts, which later joins the Northern Confederation; aiding the Confederate States of America where the Old South drops a nuclear bomb on the capital of the New South in Atlanta; defeating the pagan greenies, on behalf of other Christians, in Cascadia (Washington,

Oregon, and Idaho), where the Green Party has gained control propped up by China, with help from an alliance with Japan, a Sino–Cold War of sorts; strangely refusing the Nazi invitation from Wisconsin; winning on the high seas against Aztecan slavers seeking white hearts to feed their gods on top of the Tenochtitlan pyramid; fighting against the Azanians of Northern California, an all-female collective that uses cloning to produce female children; and finally fighting in another Christian crusade against Islam. All the while Rumford has help from Russia, as the novel stretches into the late twenty-first century and through the period identified as "the Recovery" (1). For Lind the recovery represents the revival of western culture and Christian values at the expense of racial minorities, women, and various queer communities in addition to competing religions like Islam and Eastern cultures.

The implicit *noirum*, as such, relates to the right to bear arms guaranteed by the Second Amendment to the US Constitution. Rumford and his resistance movement fully exercise this right to give white citizens a chance to fight back against a tyrannical federal government using the excuse of fighting neighborhood crime allegedly perpetrated by BIPOCS in actual warfare generated through ideology. As Rumford explains in the preface to his imaginary war memoir, "We Victorians, those of my generation anyway, know that fighting for the truth is not a metaphor. We killed for it and we died for it. By the 21st century, that was the only way to save it, weapon in hand" (21). Lind blames two things for the fall of the United States: "1965 . . . That year marks the beginning of the cultural revolution that destroyed America" and academicians (61). Basically, Lind condemns the marches MLK Jr. led from Selma to Montgomery, the Voting Rights Act of 1965, the Social Security Act of 1965 establishing Medicare and Medicaid, the startup of the Department of Housing and Urban Development, and the 1965 Immigration Act as LBJ attempted to make good on his "Great Society" vision, his pledge to eliminate poverty and racial injustice despite the deepening involvement in the Vietnam War that began with the American ground war and the resulting anti-war protests.

Lind also blames academicians. Under multiculturalism "America had become a country of many universities and little education . . . mostly diploma mills crossed with asylums for the politically insane: howling Bluestockings, inventors of Afrocentric history, mewling advocates for the blind, the botched, and the bewildered" with a faculty comprised "of whiney women and faggy men, all bemoaning this or that oppression and blaming the world's ills on white males" (281, 287). Lind directly accuses the professorate of indoctrinating students with apparently left-leaning ideologies such as feminism, critical race, and queer theories while demonstrating his own toxic masculinity and spewing filthy lies yet needing protection from racists who have victimized him. He attempted to mainstream the far-right fringe way back in 2014 with this novel and, by golly, it has happened to no small degree in our current time as imagined through this revisionist future. For Lind, a bigoted American society long ago created by white people does not actually exist if it ever did. In the novel, Lind also calls Black people "orcs" because of his love for Tolkien's fiction, and frequently "Black scum," and "nigger" only once, as if that makes it better. This novel *is* unbelievable, yet I read this racist screed—all 585 pages of it. The alt-right presence in science fiction ought not be ignored; it must be fought and fought hard through social justice frameworks such as CRT. This to me represents why the *noirum* is valuable as a critical term in that it helps us see the unvarnished realities of prejudice and racism in our laws, social institutions, and culture and it lets us know that we have work to do in dismantling American mythologies such as colorblindness and equality without disdaining the social progress already made.

From this perspective, Lind's odious novel represents an *anti-noirum* or a *noirum-mal* because of its malfeasance in symbolizing a revised white patriarchal future. Lind suggests that "The black visionary whose vision finally came to pass was not Martin Luther King, but Booker T. Washington" (247). Take a minute to digest this claim! Lind supports Washington over King in that Black people should "cast down [their] bucket . . . in agriculture, mechanics, in commerce, in domestic service, and in the professions" (Washington, "From *Up*," 573); labor more or less than in striving for social equality, as Washington declares in his 1895 "Atlanta Exposition Address" at the cotton trade fair, better known as "The Atlanta Compromise" thanks to the sharp criticism of W. E. B. Du Bois. Lind would have Black people cede all of their hard-gained rights, discontinue the ongoing cultural struggles, and return them to the near slavery of sharecropping in the field or practicing other manual trades, separated from white people "as separate as the fingers, yet one as the hand in all things essential to mutual progress" (Washington, "From *Up*," 573). Lind asks Black people to go backward in time in his retroculture and to not seek equality, integration, or education but to tolerate, if not accommodate, racism, segregation, and hostility. All I can say to that is, NO THANK YOU! America has grown beyond the truth of its ugly past, and is capable of so much more.

I think a consideration of the novel's cover art actually helps in this moment. It helps us judge the inverse quality of the *noirum-mal*. The *noirum-mal* potentially exists when there is no explicit government action such as an amendment, executive order, or judicial decision in an SF novel that should obviously have one but cannot be seen directly—a bit like dark matter in its lack of luminosity. Metaphorically speaking, we know the *noirum-mal* exists because of its influence on things that we can eyeball directly.

The cover of *Victoria* presents an unsmiling white couple standing on the green of some small New England town in the fall, complete with a white flag with a black pine tree emblem on the steeple of a building waving in the background, a version of the Maine state flag. From top to bottom, the grim white man wears a black Boston Red Sox baseball cap, red and black plaid jacket, black cargo pants, and black military boots, while holding what appears to be an AR-15 riffle in his hands with his left index finger on the trigger. He clearly treasures this gun and its implied violence. The unsmiling blonde-haired woman, who I assume is his wife, is wearing a light blue turtleneck sweater, an ankle length brown skirt, and brown heeled boots, while holding in her arms a sleeping tow-haired baby in a yellow blanket. She stands behind him to the right. Interestingly, this dour woman accentuates her look with a green hand grenade on a thong around her neck—functional jewelry, I guess!

The cover screams white male patriarchy, with a woman in her proper place, and celebrates a willingness to kill any and all outsiders as the old US of A falls and is replaced by warring states and confederations of states. The Northern Confederation incorporates Maine, Vermont, New Hampshire, upstate New York, Connecticut, Massachusetts, and portions of eastern Canada such as New Brunswick, Prince Edward Island, Nova Scotia, and Newfoundland, and is later renamed Victoria because of the retroculture's love for the Victorian era.

In CRT terms, the Lind cover argues for the preservation and continuation of a white history that never actually existed outside of a political context. It is a "remainder" and reminder of the American century in our current state of decline (Bellamy, *Remainders*, 24). According to interdisciplinary humanities scholar Brent R. Bellamy, "Remainders—what we imagine might persist and even flourish after the apocalyptic, storyworld ending—point to complex ways of imagining the economic, environmental, social, and political limits facing the United States today" (25). White America is merely the residue of a bygone era as the country inexorably inches closer to becoming a majority-minority nation.

John Scalzi creates an entirely different, thoughtful, white-authored *noirum* experience with his pandemic police procedural *Lock In* (2014). The story's novum concerns a pandemic-induced disability that becomes known as "Haden's syndrome" to describe "a set of continuing physical and mental conditions and disabilities brought on by 'the Great Flu,'" which killed more than 400 million people worldwide while also causing "complete paralysis of the voluntary nervous system" in the roughly "1 percent" of survivors "who suffered from lock in" (9–10). The surviving victims are fully conscious yet cannot move or speak and they need around the clock care. This condition is dubbed "Haden's syndrome" after a former first lady of the United States becomes its most famous victim at the beginning.

Twenty-five years into this alternate future, new racial paradigms have emerged. The locked-in become known as Hadens. Companies grow wealthy from the development of "embedded neural nets" and personal transport machines for the Haden community, humanoid robots called "threeps" controlled by a Haden's mind, so named after C-3PO, the "beloved android character from one of the most popular films of all time" (10, 23, 25). Integrators, the ".25 percent" of the afflicted, with an altered brain structure from the virus but without "degradation of physical ability" (10), are professionally trained to function as personal transports by allowing Hadens to use their bodies. They make a good living. Likewise, the Agora develops, a Haden-only online community, "independent *of* the physical world, with its own concerns, interests and economy" (98). A de facto new human civilization has come into being. Surely, this terrible disease affects everyone alike—Black, white, and other people of color, poor, rich, gay, straight, young, and old, and so on—and the world seemingly shifts to help. Racial difference as we know it disappears, especially with government-sponsored programs to assist the poor with purchasing a threep of their own, which costs about the same amount as a car. Technologically derived ethnicities—threeps, integrators, and minds on the net—face old forms of discrimination such as derogatory slurs, bigotry, intimidation, and physical violence. For example, "clank" is a new disparagement for Hadens in their threeps (25). Disability and race meld together as some segments of society struggle to accept the Hadens as human and as worthy of respect.

The murder mystery driving Scalzi's novel involves the big societal changes brought on by a two-stage *noirum* to ease the Haden pandemic. The first stage entails the United States funding "the $3 trillion Haden Research Initiative Act" two years after the pandemic, which results in the rapid scientific and technological development aiding Hadens and allowing them to take part in the world (10). As time passes in the storyworld, many of the unafflicted feel as though they are at a competitive disadvantage to their Haden counterparts with their machine bodies and computer-backed brains. This sentiment leads to the second stage of the *noirum*, the eventual passing of "The Abrams-Kettering Bill" by both houses of Congress, "a bill to cut subsidies and programs for Hadens" (11). That is to say, "Congress is taking away funding for Hadens after the immediate infection and transitional care" because "the technology for helping them participate in the world has gotten so good that it shouldn't be considered a disability anymore" (34). As one industrialist, Jim Buchold, points out with respect to Congress, "Those dipshits passed Abrams-Kettering and . . . You don't just take five million people sucking on the government teat and punt them into the street and expect them to go without a fight" (113). Through this novel, Scalzi contests dominant definitions of humanity as being white only. He offers a creative explication of disability as racism that emerges in the dismantling of the imaginative Haden Research Initiative Act by the equally imaginary Abrams-Kettering Bill, thus confronting the prejudices that white supremacy and ableism enforce and thereby indicating the potential for radical political intervention in the acceptance of difference.

On the eve of the first-ever Haden march on Washington to protest the passage of the Abrams-Kettering Bill, a Haden-related murder occurs at the Watergate Hotel with an Integrator as the prime suspect and the story unfolds from there. Only his second day on the job, rookie FBI agent Chris Shane catches the case while being assigned his new veteran partner Leslie Vann. Shane happens to be a Black Hayden. Fascinatingly, Agent Shane just might be the most famous Haden in the world because of a photo taken with the pope in St. Peter's Basilica. Agent Shane's father is a legendary basketball star, business mogul, philanthropist, and candidate for senator in Virginia. Likewise, Agent Shane's partner Vann is a former Integrator. They find the body of a mystery man on the scene with his blood all over an Integrator. However, this Integrator, Nicholas Bell, is brother to the famous, powerful, and outspoken Haden separatist, Cassandra, who is leading the protest.

Agents Shane and Vann solve the case when they learn the reason behind the murder. The white Haden billionaire Lucas Hubbard, "Chairman and CEO of Accelerant," has framed Bell for the murder of a mentally handicapped Native American by riding Bell's body (personal transport with a Caribbean loa flare) and using Bell's body to interact with the murder victim (45). As the story culminates, Shane and Vann ascertain that Johnny Sani, a member of the Navajo nation with a 75 IQ, had been Hubbard's unlawful and unwilling Integrator, a slave. Sani's brain was outfitted with an illegally installed neural network. Sani recognizes that he has been used by Hubbard to do bad things as an unregistered Integrator and that Hubbard would never let him go, and so Sani decides "to make trouble for" Hubbard by cutting his own throat (328). While the murder mystery itself remains important to the story, the world-building keys the narrative because Scalzi *is* keenly interested in the swift social and political changes brought about by technoscience. It matters that Agent Shane happens to be Black. It matters that Johnny Sani is Navajo. It matters that the killer, law enforcement, and victim are all disabled. Representation matters in both this future version of America and in our actual America.

Scalzi gets it! He materializes a new racial structure predicated on the basis of identity politics, technology, and wealth. As a post-human civilization manifests, humans old and new struggle for power in the social coding of technology wherein white people, both Hadens and the unafflicted, seek to maintain the existing hierarchies of difference by preserving a system of domination in the undoing of the Abrams-Kettering Bill. Only after being racialized have Hadens gained membership in the pantheon of humanity as a new minority, a technicity with Chris Shane, a Black man, the original face of Haden awareness. Hubbard positions himself to get even richer from the defunding legislation, taking advantage of the less fortunate victims of Haden's syndrome by continuing to foster societal discrimination, poverty, inequality, and the precarity that privatization of medical care and technological advancement represents. "Racial patterns," as Derrick Bell suggests, "adapt in ways that maintain white dominance" (*Faces*, 12). Passage of the Abrams-Kettering Bill upends the concept of diversity as this imaginary congress limits our ideals and the quest for racial justice. Diversity is a poor substitute for justice. Without referring to racism and discrimination as social injustices, affirmative action can't be understood or defended. It is almost as if Scalzi envisions the end of affirmative action and how damaging that could be to members of groups that have been subjected to discrimination in the United States because of a hand up. Race-based exclusion and exploitation would return if these things ever truly went away.

Agent Shane, triply marked by his race, disability, and the technology invented to help him lead a human life, recognizes his own technicity, his own flesh-metal composition, and its importance; he is a thinking and feeling being. Scalzi offers empathy to those trapped under the weight of institutional racism as he critiques discrimination perpetuated by law and politics by openly talking about disability as a kind of racism. When Agent Shane heads to Phoenix to pursue a lead on Sani and inhabits an inanimate, damaged threep being used as a hat rack, he meets FBI agent Tom Beresford. Through Beresford, Scalzi makes plain his empathy: "'Hell, Shane, you might be able to sympathize,'" Beresford said. "'The U.S. Government just pulled the plug on the Hadens, didn't it? It's something you folks might say you have in common with the Navajo.'" To which Shane responds, "I'm not entirely sure I want to be going around making that comparison" (126). Beresford ends the brief conversation: "That's probably wise,'" . . . "'The Navajo have a two-hundred-year head start in the "getting screwed by the U.S. government" category. They might not appreciate you jumping on the train. But now you might understand why some of them might decide to be touchy about you showing up and asking questions. So be polite, be respectful, and go if they tell you to go'" (126–127). Scalzi brings the racial comparison home with this parallel between Haden and Navajo. In CRT terms, all forms of domination must end and I believe part of Scalzi's racial agenda is to listen, to sense, and to help build something radical with his novel in his depiction of this oppressed technicity. I think he is entirely on the opposite side of the racial divide than Lind and also tells a good story as he creates empathy for a shared future despite the differing circumstances of Hadens and Navajo.

Quickly, Ben H. Winters, in *Underground Airlines* (2016), provides another example of a white-authored *noirum* with his counterfactual history of America, where president-elect Abraham Lincoln is assassinated before his first inauguration, meaning that the Civil War never happens and chattel slavery continues in the Hard Four states (Louisiana, Mississippi, Alabama, and a combined Carolina) into the present day of corporate plantations and secret genetic experiments that once again recategorize the offspring of enslaved women as non-human, as artificial beings created in a lab, literally "growing slaves" (311). The many imaginary laws to the constitutional issues that arise in this alternate America prohibit the expansion of the peculiar institution while simultaneously extending it indefinitely. We follow the freed slave catcher sometimes known as Victor as he tracks down Jackdaw, "A Person Bound to Labor" for "a textile plantation called Garments of the Greater South" located near Tuscaloosa, Alabama (19). Winters creates a truly thorny political *noirum* as he probes one of the quintessential American wounds: the lasting traumas of slavery's legacy in terms of racial discrimination, harmful stereotypes, and systemic racism because of skin color. As a white writer, Winters attempts to demonstrate effective resistance to injustice by directly engaging with the ongoing exploitation of Black people. His alternate United States is on the verge of ours right now. Just like Scalzi, Winters gets it too! He is mindful in his writing and representation of Black characters and thoughtful in exactly how this mirrored version of the country comes into being. That's all we can ask of any writer.

Karens

That Black US history has been science fictional itself is now beyond question. With that said, part of what makes these acts of state and cultural violence—like the Beckys and Karens calling the cops on innocent Blacks BBQing[11] in the park or birdwatching[12]—feel so unreal *is* exactly the advanced technoscientific level our society is enjoying historically. Think cell phones here. This moment surely must imply an equal sophistication/advancement of social and spiritual ethos. Embedded in that distinction—between ages, generations, and historical circumstances—collective Black agency does not require permission from the past, only an awareness of it, in this nation-spanning movement of our age, which is something special cataloged in twenty-first-century Afrofuturist storytelling. Certainly, N. K. Jemisin does not shy away from that ugly face white America shows the rest of the world in the mirror of Afrofuturism.

Jemisin directly taps into this impulse in *The City We Became* (2020) as she challenges white racial anxieties through her minority characters literally battling for equality against an otherworldly entity embodied by white supremacy itself, the personified Woman in White. Gender matters here also because the Woman in White represents the historic social power of white women to endanger the lives of Black men with a single word through the longstanding myth of the Black male rapist. Cady Lang explains that "this narrative perpetuated the idea that white women, who represented the good and moral in American society, needed to be protected by white men at all costs, thus justifying racial violence toward Black men or anyone who posed a threat to their power" ("'Karen,'" 31). In other words, such women use victimhood as a weapon because their white privilege allows them to do so. This often deadly and always shameless abuse gives rise to its antithesis in the twenty-first century Karen social meme. Apryl Williams defines the Karen as "any White woman who exercises her power to police, surveil, and regulate Black individuals in public spaces" ("Black Memes," 2). Internet memes and their viral power to spread quickly if not globally can stem if not neutralize this particular kind of implied or slow violence of white women who do not get their way through public embarrassment and loss of reputation that strips away their self-perceived entitlement.

In this exact context, Jemisin holds up the mirror of Afrofuturism to New York City and reveals the menacing visage of racism throughout the novel as the city's newly awakened avatars come together to protect it from a Lovecraftian horror—the Woman in White. The one scene that really pops out in my mind as perhaps the most crucial BLM⁺ moment of the novel—let's call it the Inwood Karen moment—occurs early in the story. Manny—Black, queer, and one of NYC's five avatars—and his new trans roommate Bel Nguyen—a Columbia University PhD candidate in political theory and an Asian Brit hailing from South London—stroll through Inwood Hill Park, one of the Manhattan's lesser-known greens. Minding their own business in the middle of the afternoon, they stop at the Shorakkopoch Rock to rest. However, a few minutes later, a "portly, short, white" woman approaches them with her cell phone out, recording them in obvious disdain at their failure to be white (60). They have been racially profiled by this prejudiced woman. Inwood Karen accuses them of canoodling by announcing "'Gross' . . . 'I can't believe you two. Right out in the open. I'm calling the cops'" (60). Bel points out how it's rude to record people without permission, to which the white woman responds, "'Rude is people being perverts in public'" (60). Manny takes offense as she zooms in on his face and so he steps forward. This single step causes the white woman to go into histrionics as she huffs, daintily moves backward, and shouts, "'Don't touch me! Don't touch me! If you lay a finger on me, I'll scream and the cops will shoot you! You druggies! Druggie perverts!'" (60). In general, Inwood Karen, aware of her racialized privilege and power in this moment, threatens their lives by invoking the possibility of calling cops, a threat she will later make good on. Jemisin offers a powerful social justice critique in this moment by calling attention to the intimidating behavior of Inwood Karen as she attempts to boot them from the park in her discomfort. Jemisin disrupts Inwood Karen's racism by exposing its malevolence to her audience in this counternarrative.

All of this action, mirroring daily reality, occurs before Manny sees the white tendril attached to the back of Inwood Karen's neck. But when he does notice, Manny calls out the Woman in White for the first time as Jemisin switches to a more speculative register through her arch baddie. The woman is now dressed "entirely white. The suit, the shoes, even the pantyhose. Her hair, too, which abruptly makes her look like a cross between a church lady and a female Colonel Sanders" (62). Jemisin makes excellent use of humor to undercut this moment where reality and fantasy bleed together before intensifying the scene with the woman declaring "'What a relief! . . . It's hard enough to act like one of you people already'" (62). Her first words are racist words—"you people"—although they are interpreted out of context because the Woman in White is not human as an extradimensional being and may not, in fact, be racist, only extraordinarily comfortable using offensive expressions to advance her objectives. But these words definitely signal an irrational hate that she deliberately uses again in stating, "You people all look alike to me" (66). Racism confirmed. This unambiguously derogatory statement simply must be interpreted as racism since Manny and Bel clearly differ from the Woman in White. She literally dehumanizes and belittles the two humans, regardless of their racial backgrounds, before disappearing.

Inwood Karen reemerges, continues recording them, and calls the police. She states, "'I need the police. There are these two guys in Inwood Hill Park who are, I don't know, menacing people. I think they're drug dealers, and they won't leave. Also, they're having sex'" while Manny and Bel battle a sea of white tendrils that have encircled them (69). Inwood Karen also calls them "you people" while the battle with the tendrils intensifies in what seems like a fantastical example of gentrification at its most aggressive attempt to whitewash the city and destroy its history. Manny, in considering how Black people have a fraught, broken relationship with police, decides to leave the scene because he does not want to witness the effect of these white tendrils on the NYPD. But he has no idea how to stop them. After all, the tendrils have already "turned a nosy, racist white woman into a conduit for disembodied existential evil" (73). Eventually, a Black woman named Brooklyn, a second avatar of NYC, rescues Manny and Bel with music from her cell phone that somehow kills the tendrils as she confronts Inwood Karen with ironic and disbelieving laughter: "You actually called the cops on these men? For what, walking in the park while Black and Asian?'" (75) Manny seizes the moment, snatches Inwood Karen's phone, and puts fear into her by grabbing her around the throat while rapidly browsing through it to identify her, finally, as Martha Blemins. He then releases her and hands her back her phone. Manny does not enjoy confirming or bringing Inwood Karen/Martha's stereotypes to life in traumatizing her with his counterassault.

Nevertheless, Manny and Bel have been wronged by a white woman in power and through this experience most likely find it impossible to ascend above the racial politics at work. Imagining if the police had arrived on the scene unlocks Jemisin's purpose here in understanding that Black people are policed by white people on a daily basis in every part of America. Actual police violence is no aberration as history has proven and we dare not ignore the multitudes of people still in deep denial of American racism who willfully side with a reactionary right. Jemisin offers the potentiality of a world where BIPOCS live free of fear, resentment, and threat in democratic personhood and collective liberty. That is the nexus of CRT and Afrofuturism—intelligent resistance.

PART II

Explorations of Antiracism

CHAPTER 4

Cyberfunk

An African American affiliation with cyberpunk predates the idea itself by a couple hundred years. The true source of cyberfunk inevitably reaches back to early America when the first cyborg metaphors as they relate to slaves were articulated by one of the United States of America's founding fathers, the Virginia slaveholder Thomas Jefferson. His descriptions of slaves produce an unreality that captures the feel of a cyberpunk moment that had already happened. In *Notes on the State of Virginia* (1785), Jefferson rearticulates prevalent pseudoscientific beliefs of the Enlightenment era regarding the biological basis of race in order to better create the technological fantasy upon which the system of slavery depends, configuring Black bodies as natural machines, transmuting an enslaved person into an object. Among other ludicrous claims, Jefferson insists that Blacks "require less sleep . . . after hard labour through the day" and also implies that the Black imagination is "dull, tasteless, and anomalous" (146). While a comparison to farm animals may readily come to mind, Jefferson confirms the machine analogy by mentioning how "slaves [are] distributable . . . as other moveables" when based "on a principle of economy" being sold like "old wagons, old tools" (144, 148). As natural machines, with race operating as a labor-based technology, Blacks are clearly figured as cyborgs.

P. T. Barnum, an American showman and founder of the Barnum and Bailey Circus, exploited such cyberpunk imagery when he bought an old slave woman named Joice Heth in 1835, and promptly put her on display as a Black automaton in his museum of curiosities. According to Eric Lott, "Barnum claimed Joice Heth to be one hundred and sixty-one years old, and to have been the nurse of George Washington" (80). Barnum himself declares: "Joice Heth is not a human being. What purports to be a remarkably old woman is simply a curiously constructed automaton, made up of whale bone, India-rubber, and numberless springs ingeniously put together, and made to move at the slightest touch, according to the will of the operator. The exhibitor is a ventriloquist, and all the conversations apparently held with the ancient lady are purely imaginary, so far as she is concerned, for the answers and incidents purporting to be given and related by her are merely the ventriloquial voice of the exhibitor" (*The Life*, 157). Bluford Adams rightly calls Barnum "the shady exhibitor of frauds like Joice Heth" just to increase his own celebrity across the world who later publicly staged "the dissection of her body" when profits from his exhibitions waned (*E Pluribus*, 1, 2). Despite the heinous activity of this one-time northern slaveholder, Joice Heth, described as a talking machine, must be the earliest example of a Black cyborg instantiation exploited by a white man for profit (and fame), not unlike other Americans of the antebellum period. (Interestingly, Barnum, hailing from Connecticut, was legally able to own slaves since the state did not officially abolish slavery until 1848, a mere fifteen years before the January 1, 1863 Emancipation Proclamation issued by President Lincoln.) Louis Chude-Sokei fittingly claims that Joice Heth is "an American version of automata but masked in the dark flesh and withered femininity of a far more intimate, local, and familiar racial stereotype" (*Sound*, 24). In a truly dystopian fashion, Joice Heth transcends to an inhuman post-humanity, figured as a cyborg when her racial heritage gets coupled with technology, proving that the nineteenth century vision of Black existence is not much different from its twentieth or twenty-first century iterations, where the otherness of the cyborg-being functions as a meditation on racial otherness. Race and technology meld together in a complex historical relationship, an alchemy that keeps these cyborgs unequal in their post-humanity, unequal to whites.

Correspondingly, white privilege, white supremacy, and notions of a "colorblind" world symbolize the social structures upholding race and racism in America stemming from such painful and historical constructions of Black flesh. Barnum presents a monochrome vision where white people are the only ones that matter. And science fiction has supported whiteness as the norm for much of its history despite the genre's seeming concern with otherness, assuming futures free of racial strife with alien replacements for colored people as white people conquer again and again ad infinitum.

The cyberpunk subgenre fittingly repeats this pattern by championing an artificial personhood such as cyborgs and artificial intelligences, stand-in minorities subordinate to white hacker anti-heroes navigating cyberspace in a dystopic near future. SF darkly mirrors social reality in this respect. From this perspective, man and machine blended together during slavery in the creation of Harriet Jacobs's "god-breathing" machines of the antebellum South, which feel like an already cyberpunk mythology of potent metaphorical fusions of flesh and machine (*Incidents*, 11). Certainly, this interpretation does not go far astray as a quick example of critical race theory applied to the cyberpunk mindset. For Jacobs makes such an unsuspecting cyborg reference in her 1861 slave narrative *Incidents in the Life of a Slave Girl* because a cyborg can plug into a "webbed network," formed among slaves and free Blacks entirely dependent on a Black generational experience encoded in the folklore, native scientific practices, and spiritual beliefs that survived the Middle Passage (Eshun, *More*, 00[-006]). Still, God-breathing machines, what a magnificent thought. Taken to its extreme, this metaphor allows us to think of African Americans as descendants of cyborgs, every Black person an Afropunk.

Cyberpunk, roughly 1983–1995, explores the near-future; loosely articulated, it wrestles with ethical questions stemming from the world of computing, the various mechanisms of networking, hacking, and virtual reality as well as AI, cyborgs, and the emergence of the post-human—all things on the human/machine periphery. These high-tech notions represent the *cyber* half of the definition. The *punk* half signifies a city underground, the realm of street life, dealers and addicts, the working poor and have-nots, those far down the socioeconomic scale on the other side of the digital divide, hustling to survive. In this manner cyberpunk stories exist in such urban, rough-and-tumble places. Although one might think of Black folks here because of the disproportionate number of Blacks in America oppressed by poverty, the cyberpunk movement largely ignores this reality. While deferring to Samuel R. Delany and his earlier works as precursors to cyberpunk, scholars tend to equate punk with white culture. The white hacker street gang portrayed in William Gibson's monumental *Neuromancer* (1984), the Panther Moderns with micro soft buds implanted behind their ears and face-changing skin grafts as they prowl through the urban sprawl of New York, emerges as representative of the cyberpunk world.

In fact, Black writers *are* largely absent from discussion of the cyberpunk subgenre. Missing from scholarly accounts is the inhumanly strong, dark-shades-wearing, former mafia enforcer, the genetically modified and cybernetically enhanced Black male Aubry Knight from Steven Barnes's *Streetlethal* (1983). Barnes perfectly balances post-human sensibilities with the glitz and grime of a near-future dystopian Los Angeles as the character goes on a vengeance quest. Nor do assessments of cyberpunk tend to account for Octavia E. Butler's *Mind of My Mind* (1977), Walter Mosley's *Futureland*

(2001), or Nnedi Okorafor's *The Book of Phoenix* (2015), among others. Each of these novels demonstrates at least some of the hallmarks of cyberpunk without being ascribed to the movement or any of its various "punk" waves such as steampunk, splatterpunk, biopunk, solarpunk, or silkpunk.[1] At the same time, recent divergences made by Black writers from the norms of this subgenre have been called Afrocyberpunk, Afropunk, or cyberfunk in popular parlance but are not considered amongst the various "punk" waves since Black-authored works have not shown up in this context. While approaching many of the same questions asked by white cyberpunk writers, Black writers tend to articulate discontentment with the world, global capitalism, and the information age in a different key. In other words, cyberpunk *is* not for whites only. Blacks, too, find in cyberpunk ready materials to protest social conditions, though with a difference.

To better contextualize this difference, both British SF film scholar Mark Bould and Black author/publisher Milton J. Davis attempted to loosely outline a black "punk" subgenre of SF in 2015. Bould blogs that an "Afrocyberpunk" is a "representation of Africa/Africans/Afrodiaspora in cyberpunk, and cyberpunk by African and Afrodiasporic writers" ("Afrocyberpunk 1"). And Davis coins his own term "cyberfunk" to define "cyberpunk stories that play with future concepts from an African/African American perspective" ("Welcome," 5). Neither term catches on because they are so lightly demarcated, which prompted my own attempt to define a Black cyberpunk as "Afropunk" in a previous essay.[2] But Afropunk is too closely associated to a particular Black music festival in Harlem for me to adapt to *noirum*-like analyses of Black cyberpunk stories. Because I find Bould's term too unwieldy, I returned to the Davis neologism.

Aside from telling wonderful stories, African American SF writers create their own realities to explore racism, recognizing how oppression fluctuates between groups and is structurally determined by advantages and benefits that the dominant race feels entitled to take or to receive in various social situations (what is commonly referred to as white privilege). Delany, Barnes, Octavia E. Butler and the rest address the embedded stereotypes many other writers rely on to shift conversations onto racism within the genre through their writing. That's keeping it real. That's making it Black. That's finding race in cyberpunk and alchemizing it into cyberfunk. In a sense, this chapter takes such a strategy as its model in outlining the texts belonging to a Black version of cyberpunk. In short, this chapter applies critical race theory to the cyberpunk mindset—high-tech lowlife—not normally associated with Black SF.[3]

In keeping with the characteristics of computer culture, infotech, and virtual reality as expressed by the "cyber" half of Davis's coinage in a clear reference to cyberpunk, the second half, "funk," works on multiple levels to mean the musty, deeply felt, bluesy, offbeat nature of such Black-authored stories that somehow transport you directly into the storyworld but are considered not appropriate for cyberpunk for some *unexplained* reason while simultaneously representing superlative effort. That is to say, funky—unconventionally stylish stories, an inestimable cool. In other words, a cyberfunk science fiction tradition tracks Black experiences of technoculture and the computing world, cyborgization, and conglomerates. The term crafts a Black imaginative space to grapple with and protest against centuries-long social conditions that produced a tangible sense of Black commodification across the horizon of a slow modernity.

This chapter argues that cyberpunk as a subgenre offers particularly fertile ground for CRT. Technocultural future stories, including science fiction, imagine future possibilities, but CRT can help us judge whether such futures responsibly attend to racial realities of the present or bypass them for the fantasy of racelessness. Those futuristic stories that do meaningfully engage with Black or Brown realities, "help readers bridge the gap between" different worlds (Delgado and Stefancic, *Critical*, 41). CRT is also useful for examining the stories that fail to do so.

Additionally, I mean to say that a sense of history is not operative in cyberpunk's present. This omission leaves the genre vulnerable to racial fantasies. On the one hand, since cyberpunk writers do not acknowledge racial histories of the past, they certainly are not able to show how those racial infrastructures continue into the present. This lack of history leaves cyberpunk susceptible to the false promise of "colorblindness" or thinking that race should not matter in the futurity such stories imagine. It's particularly strange because in so many ways this fiction DOES seem to recognize that inequalities persist in the futures they imagine, particularly economic inequalities; hence the dystopic imagination that seems so pertinent to so many of these works. Black writers, on the other hand, seem to be focused on bringing that sense of history to their cyber worlds and futuristic imaginings. In fact, I am tempted to say that this lack is *the* fundamental difference between cyberpunk and cyberfunk: history. Finally, this chapter serves a bibliographic function by covering lots of stories with brief (and sometimes not-so-brief) summaries, which helps with the recovery work of science fiction of the recent past.

Funked Up: Cyberpunk

Just as it does in the physical world, colorblindness reinforces race and racism in the technocultures and virtual worlds of cyberpunk, where cyberspace, criminality, computers, companies, and corporeality rule.[4] That's why "the racialized digital divide narrative that circulates in the public sphere and the bodiless, colorblind mythotopias of cybertheory and commercial advertising have become the unacknowledged frames of reference for understanding race in the digital age," as Alondra Nelson believes ("Introduction," 6). In fact, SF critic Veronica Hollinger recognizes that "the potential in cyberpunk for undermining concepts like 'subjectivity' and 'identity' derives in part from its production within what has been termed 'the technological imagination'" of hard SF ("Cybernetic," 210). Cyberpunk's claim to a post-racial future, where human bodies are simply "meat" prisons and human minds can escape to "the bodiless exultation of cyberspace" while socializing with other technicities[5] such as artificial intelligences, flesh/metal hybrids, and robots, is misguided at best (Gibson, *Neuromancer*, 6). Unhinged from the race and racism of the past, the cyberpunk future champions high-tech lowlife, rendering racial politics and identities obsolescent as if cyberspace is not a racially coded environment. Instead, cyberspace, imagined as an "eighth continent" where anything goes, reproduces and reifies whiteness in virtuality's[6] fictionalized landscape (Chude-Sokei, *Sound*, 6). The same colorblind arguments apply here.

As cool as they might seem, William Gibson's space Rastas have always felt like a dangerous misstep at the junction of CRT and cyberpunk. These Black characters briefly appear in *Neuromancer*, which involves the partnership between the hacker Case and the cyborg warrior Molly Millions as they attempt to free an artificial intelligence by penetrating the Tessier-Ashpool syndicate's compound. Gibson describes the Rastas' Zion cluster as a thirty-year-old colony, where the five original members "suffered from calcium loss and heart shrinkage before rotational gravity was established in the colony's central torus" (103). All of them have dreadlocks, listen to dub music, smoke ganja, worship their god (who may be the AI Wintermute), and speak in a Caribbean accent. But their time in space has made them weak. This colorblind misstep requires correction. Samuel R. Delany calls Mark Dery out on this very subject in the foundational "Black to the Future" interviews. As "a white reader" "intrigued" by Gibson's portrayal of these Blacks in space, who sees the Rastas as "romanticized arcadians . . . obviously adroit with jury-rigged technology," Dery wonders why Delany does not mention them in a brief essay (Dery, "Black," 194). In reply, Delany majestically quips, "You'll forgive me if, as a black reader, I didn't leap up to proclaim this passing presentation of a powerless and wholly non-oppositional set of black dropouts, by a Virginia-born white writer, as the coming of the black millennium in science fiction; but maybe that's just a black thang. . . ." (194–195). Delany later elaborates, "While I don't think for a moment that this was Bill's intent, I do feel that it speaks directly from 'the political unconscious' of the cyberpunk subgenre" (Dery, "Black," 196). Gibson fetishizes these marginal characters and we never experience the complexities of race in the novel.

This racial subtext is something that clearly color-blinds Dery in his interpretation of *Neuromancer* because he never sees them as a problem in the short space allotted to them in the text. In fact, Dery does not even notice on the first page of the novel the "tall African whose cheekbones were ridged with precise rows of tribal scars" wearing "a crisp navel uniform" whom Case is sitting next to at "The Chatsubo" bar in Japan (3). Then again, Dery is no outlier. Not many readers let alone scholars recognize the African's existence at *Neuromancer*'s start. An unnamed African sitting next to an American in a Japanese Bar represents a spectacular multicultural moment presented by Gibson, a truly globalized future. But Gibson does not do anything with this brief instant. The African continent seemingly has a future with its Black nations in this global scenario, but white cyberpunk writers have failed "to recognize that Africa increasingly exists as the object of futurist projection" beyond an "African social reality . . . overdetermined by intimidating global scenarios, doomsday economic projections, weather predictions, medical reports on AIDS, and Life-expectancy" (Eshun, "Further," 291–292).[7]

Taken a bit further, Gibson commodifies people of color in presenting his distorted version of the cyber-world dominated by whiteness. He provides his readers with a palatable item with these ineffectual raced characters conscripted to the background. Needless to say, the main character Case, who just happens to be white, is the only one ever plugged into cyberspace. Gibson justifies this "white projection virtually" by "using the same colorblind arguments" previously outlined (Matias et al., "Exposing," 460). White people remain "unaware of alternative aspects . . . incorporated into these fictions" written by the cyberpunks, which shape our ideas about race (Gordon and Vera, *Screen*, 16). In just a couple of pages, Gibson employs what Toni Morrison calls "a fabricated Africanist presence" to convey his own sense of white "Americanness" against the backdrop of race (*Playing*, 6). CRT can help us reappraise the cyberpunk subgenre through essential race dialogues that outline forms of otherness by questioning white hegemony.

Talk about a reality shift. Frantz Fanon, in describing the white gaze's impact on his Black being, offers a perceptual filter akin to cyberspace's virtual reality: "The white gaze, the only valid one, is already dissecting me. I am fixed. Once their microtomes are sharpened, the whites objectively cut sections of my reality" (*Black Skin*, 95). This description is not unlike being "jacked into a custom cyberspace deck that projected his disembodied consciousness into the consensual hallucination that was the matrix" (Gibson, *Neuromancer*, 5). Except Fanon means how the "consensual hallucination" of race transcribes his body in the real world, marking his difference, his Blackness in the white world. Race is an imaginary social construct with real power that most people agree exists. For whites not to see this problem and how it connects with words and images reveals how damaging a colorblind world can be for the Black psyche. Fanon provides a CRT blueprint for analyzing the cyberpunk movement's lack of color in its depiction of cyberspace, the internet, the web, the matrix. This quartering of Blackness painfully embodies the twisted reality of a dominant whiteness. Fanon envisions a factual, if subjective, Black matrix in 1952, thirty-two years prior to *Neuromancer*'s publication, vaguely reminiscent of N. Katherine Hayles's notion of "virtuality . . . the cultural perception that material objects are interpenetrated by information patterns" (*How*, 13–14). In this circumstance, race is the information pattern inscribed on a Black corporeality. The language of technology describes how white oppression operates in the twentieth century—and beyond. Only a few of our political, economic, and psychological dynamics have changed with respect to race relations in American society and their historical patterns.

While cyberpunk signals social media's runaway development, the digital revolution, and the increasing importance of technoculture, its portrayal of race largely remains frozen in its powerful future projections. Fictional cyberpunk worlds are colorblind, post-racial, or miscegenate if we allow for technologically derived ethnicities such as artificial intelligences, robots, and cyborgs. As Alexis Harley suggests, "passing is central to the philosophy of artificial intelligence—the Turing test measures whether artificial intelligence can be distinguished from human" ("The Slavery," 219). So, the notion of machines "passing for human" symbolizes racial passing where light-skinned Blacks pass for white people. Naturally, this idea also relates to robots and cyborgs, humanity's machine offspring somewhere between artificial and organic being. LeiLani Nishime likewise reads "cyborgs as displaced representations of mixed-race people" naming them "mulatta cyborg[s]" in order to retain a racial analogue for post-human bodies ("The Mulatto," 34, 35). In fact, "the boundaries of race across the threshold of the skin" has not been surpassed by "new technologies of self and of species being" as surmised by Paul Gilroy (*Against*, 47, 42). Even so, Emily Apter has argued that "cyberpunk's obsession with racial phobias often spin into fantasies of racelessness" (*Continental*, 220). To be raceless means to be without race or to be without color in a world built on this very social, political, and economic construct. History, it would seem, has no hold in cyberpunk's present. Such an estrangement would break the fictional world and depends on "the notion that racism itself [has] a historical half-life" that "may in fact be accelerated by out-of-body interaction and the shared computer protocols that make such interaction possible" (Baruth, "The Excesses," 117). Racelessness represents another colorblind philosophy that benefits white people and fails to address centuries of discrimination embedded in America's national heritage. These artificial beings represent second-class citizenship, un-personhood. But for readers who do have a sense of history, despite cyberpunk's disavowal of it, the artificial beings emerge as something familiar—analogues of nonwhite personhood. The experience of cyberspace for Black peoples remains unchanged (the familiar experience of being relegated to nonwhite personhood and missing out on all the advantages whiteness confers).

From this perspective, CRT provides answers to new questions now being asked about the social construction of racialized identities and the concomitant interactions between people in the futures imagined by the likes of Gibson, Neal Stephenson, Bruce Sterling, and Pat Cadigan, among others, thirty odd years ago.[8] Though it is true that the subgenre in some ways transforms social integration, these reimaginings get overshadowed by its commitment to uphold the status quo by reproducing race and racism. Neal Stephenson's *Snow Crash* (1992) serves as a fine example of what I mean. The mixed-race main character Hiroaki (Hiro) Protagonist has "cappuccino skin and spiky, truncated dreadlocks" from his African American father and eyes "which look Asian" from his Korean mother in the physical world, where he constantly moved around the globe as an Army brat (20). Hiro reflects on the Army's integrated ethnic feel, noting how his classmates' "skins were different colors but they all belonged to the same ethnic group: Military" (58). Stephenson certainly captures the feel of a transformative social integration with this first American government-sanctioned experiment in racial integration.

Likewise, Hiro's name implies this sentiment with a blending of East and West in terms of his racial lineage and a globalized childhood.[9]

While Stephenson creates a post-racial world, he quickly undermines it. Stephenson destabilizes this colorblind atmosphere when the adult Hiro faces down "a big porky white man with wavy, slicked-back red hair and a beard" with the capitalized words "MOOD SWINGS, RACIALLY INSENSITIVE" tattooed across his brow (300). This white man represents New South Africa, a white supremacy group franchised like a local union in the "computer generated universe" known simply as "the Metaverse" yet also disbursed across the real world (24). The white racist wonders aloud if Hiro is "a lazy shiftless watermelon-eating black-ass nigger, or a snaky little v.d.-infected gook" (301). After a bit more dialogue, Hiro decapitates the offending man with his katana and runs from the remaining New South Africans at the dive-bar in northern Oregon. He takes a lethal action in responding to blatant racism that should no longer exist in a post-racial colorblind society.

As a white SF author, Stephenson controls racial images in presenting us with Hiro as a hyper violent Black male using katana blades to behead his white antagonist. We must also recognize that Stephenson stereotypes Hiro's Asian heritage, thus doubling and intensifying the unconscious racism of the text for the sake of cyberpunk coolness. Instead of building empathy for racial experience through *Snow Crash*, Stephenson practices cultural appropriation, using a Black and Asian character and reproducing racism in his novel without providing sufficient background information about Hiro. Hence, nothing has changed in terms of cultural appropriation and Hiro comes across as a bifurcated stereotype. The cyberpunk narrative unconsciously replicates the persistence of white privilege, the white desire to stereotype colored people even when the worlds depicted are supposedly colorblind and beyond race.

To play devil's advocate: might there be merit in Stephenson's effort to depict a future that does not pretend that racial history disappears? In other words, his willingness to depict white supremacy as continuing to exist in the cyberpunk present is different from efforts to disavow racial history. Furthermore, Hiro's violent response to the member of the white supremacist group could be seen as Stephenson's effort to give voice to the mounting anger and frustration racial minorities have experienced. But I think not. I mean why else would Stephenson liken his main character to "a nigger with swords" (330)? Part of the problem with cyberpunk is that it tries to act like the past does not apply to the cyberpunk present. But surely writers need to recognize that readers bring what they know about the past and about race to the storyworlds created.

The seeming permanence of racism prevails in twenty-first-century cyberpunk as well. One novel readily comes to mind—and Ernest Cline's *Ready Player One* (2011). *Ready Player One* covers familiar cyberpunk ground with its near-future dystopian setting. Like many others, the protagonist Wade Watts searches through the O.A.S.I.S., an online virtual reality game, hoping to find the creator James Halliday's Easter egg—his fortune and controlling interest in the software company—before Innovative Online Industries can do so. Wade's best friend inside the O.A.S.I.S., Aech, becomes significant to the storyline here as a high-ranking white online death-match champion, leading "gunter," and professionally sponsored player (8). But Cline chooses to out Aech as a Black lesbian in the real world. Why? Outing an online character's race and gender and then making her a sidekick as a plot device continues a history of interlocking oppressions endemic to SF.[10] As David Crane asserts, "It should not surprise us . . . that representing the otherness of cyberspace might involve forms of racial and ethnic otherness—especially hybridity, with its negotiation of identity and difference" ("In Medias," 90). Such an authorial decision matters here because Cline champions a post-racial world while placing his white hero at the center and reducing race to "an informatic commodity" to his readership (Chow-White and Nakamura, "Introduction," 3). Racial minorities add an element of coolness but remain otherwise flat.

White masculinity prevails yet again. Gay, black, female, and oppressed receives little if any critical attention. Megan A. Condis points out that Cline himself contributes "to the maintenance of a literary canon that overwhelmingly represents white male authors and characters to the exclusion of other groups" ("Playing," 7). In the novel, Halliday creates a wizard avatar named Anorak to oversee the hunt by supplying all the gunters with an Almanac that lists all of Halliday's favorite writers, film directors, and bands. All of them *are* white and male. Nothing by people of color or women makes the list. As Condis indicates, Aech "must find a way to sidestep the assumptions encoded in Halliday's canon about what 'real' gamers are like" to lead her virtual life and to bask in the fame her avatar receives (13). Wade feels betrayed upon learning Aech's secret when they first meet at her RV in the real world. Aech is "a heavyset African American girl . . . with kinky hair and chocolate-colored skin" (318) and Wade masks his hurt by cutting her off as she attempts to explain her deception, saying that "it really doesn't matter" (319). But Aech insists on telling her story and Wade chooses to ignore the admission by referring to Aech as a he "because her avatar was still male" (330). Wade "essentially stuffs her body back into the virtual closet for the sake of his own comfort, thereby verifying Aech's theory that she must hide herself to make and keep friends in the O.A.S.I.S.," as Condis rightfully claims (15). Race, gender, and Aech herself, *are* nonessential to the plot.

In attempting to identify Aech with the gunters and Wade, Cline essentializes the character, naturalizing racism to the internet in the process, disappearing it, because the queer, Black, female experience does not apply to his own life experience and this dismissal of the racial tension weakens the story. As Wendy Hui Kyong Chun argues, "for those always already marked" like Aech, "the Internet supposedly relieves them of *their problem*, of *their flesh*, that races, genders, ages, and handicaps them, of *their body* from which they usually cannot escape" (*Control*, 133, emphasis in original). But this escape is not truly freedom from discrimination, rather it is the chance, if desired, to pass as an unmarked white male. The gunters in this imaginary cyberspace do not leave their races (or racisms) behind. Cline and the earlier cyberpunks use their social cachet to reinforce the racial status quo by ignoring the problems of race and racism (and intersectionality in the case of *Ready Player One*) instead of calling for social change through their work.

Funk the Future: Walter Mosley

Before moving on to tracing the roots of cyberfunk, I now turn to African American writer Walter Mosley, famed for his detective fiction, to examine how he confronts the authority of these white cyberpunk narratives with his own foray into the subgenre—*Futureland* (2001). As Nisi Shawl explains, "the narratives, plots, and overall aesthetic of science fiction's cyberpunk subgenre owe a debt to Noir as well; *Futureland* takes on that debt along with its setting's cyberpunkish body-integrated electronics and highly polarized distribution of wealth" ("Expanded"). Set a generation or so from now, Mosley dissects American life in nine interrelated stories where corporations headed by wealthy technocrats control a grim future saturated by information technology, utterly altering the nature of employment. Those who work for the corporations, "prods" (230), eke out an existence on the labor cycle and those who are jobless or unemployable become "White Noise" (46), permanently and unobtrusively relegated to the background of civilization.[11] Prods accused of or diagnosed with "*Labor Nervosa*" receive the permanent cure of unemployment (230, emphasis in original). Disproportionately Black, prods labeled as white noise, unwanted and unproductive citizens, are reduced to nothing in being cast out of civilized, technocratic, white society. Common ground is Mosley's rendition of the inner city in the future where people of color exist as white noise with no hope of finding jobs to escape their social condition and physical surroundings. As products of the corporate system, fear stimulates these workers to produce goods without ever enhancing their social well-being in a classic expression of an abused free enterprise, late capitalism in extremis.

But Mosley explores how such corporate power impacts Black people and Black culture specifically in terms of law and incarceration, race and racism. That is the primary difference between his vision and that of white cyberpunk. Cyberpunk tropes abound—designer drugs, hacktivists, crime, grime, urban decay, sex slavery, big business colluding with governments, island playgrounds for the affluent, cyborgs, and artificial intelligence. Mosley adds to it a Black child genius, an underground ghetto for the marginalized working poor, an automated and autonomous court system, a corporate controlled private prison island, and white supremacists with a bioengineered race-killing virus. For DeWitt Kilgore, Mosley performs a crucial cultural service in "that African Americans must participate in and contest those parts of American culture to which we are not supposed to belong" (16). In short, Mosley calls for attitude adjustment in *Futureland* by reminding us of our common humanity and the pitfalls of economic and racial progress by truthfully relating the race-based realities rather than opting for a colorblind take. After all, this approach represents what SF can/should do.

Two characters dominate the text even when not appearing in various stories. One man, the white Dr. Ivan Kismet, a certifiable genius, heads both the largest corporation, MacroCode International, as well as the largest religious group, "Infochurch [which] rivals Catholicism in membership" (64) with the "message that God is a riddle" that "the world of science filled with His clues has captured" (65). Through his avaricious business acumen, unlawful techno-scientific practice, and faith manipulation, Kismet literally owns the world, its schools, churches, courts, and prisons—even nations, the United States and Russia in particular. Assuredly, Mosley has a bit of fun with his readers in naming this character Kismet, who seemingly determines the course of human destiny.

The other man, a former Black child prodigy from Mississippi, Ptolemy Bent, and his Artificial Intelligence ally Un Fitt try to stop him. Ptolemy, ironically nicknamed Popo, punning on the Black vernacular for police officer, is the center of the world for his stroke-paralyzed grandmother Misty and his ex-convict Uncle Chill. Note that Mosley also riffs on the vastly mistaken Greek astronomer of antiquity through his formal name Ptolemy. Chill informs his sister Hazel and mother, “We not sendin’ Popo away to some white man’s idea of what smart and good is. All they do is want turn him against hisself” (5). Determined to keep his brilliant nephew away from the government, Chill sells his eyes to a Swiss banker, his spinal cord to a Russian general, and his penis to an unknown consumer to finance a “Prime Com Link” for Popo’s home education (22). Ptolemy builds a custom computer capable of reaching the entity he discovered in the ether as a toddler. Unfortunately, the sixteen-year-old Ptolemy ends up with a life sentence in a private corporate prison for euthanizing his grandmother and horribly disfigured uncle who have been granted a second life with Un Fitt, souls transmigrated through Ptolemy’s computer. Forced into working for the Randac Corporation on Madagascar, Ptolemy begins his plan to free the world. With the help of Un Fitt, the now twenty-six-year-old Ptolemy remotely infiltrates MacroCode, creates the GEE-PRO-$_9$ sleeper cell, comprised of disgruntled prod employees, in order to end capitalism, and learns of an international socialist plot to kill all Black people in the world with an engineered-virus.

Mosley’s novel overtly demonstrates how the racialized past continues to shape the cyber-present. Yet, the white cyberpunk world generally gets taken with the idea of the post-racial—so that even when a white-authored cyberpunk work does call attention to race, it does not follow through as the commitment to a post-racial fantasy takes over.

In the story “Little Brother,” we learn that Kismet has made a bet with one of his underlings, Tristan the First, Dominar of the Blue Zone, regarding the life of Frendon Ibrahim Blythe, an unemployed Black man accused of killing a cop and assaulting another one in Sacramento. Kismet bets that his automated “Prime Justice System” will find Frendon guilty and Tristan wagers that Kismet has designed the system too well, that Frendon can overwhelm “the compassion quotient in the wetware” and beat the charges (225). In other words, the computer intelligence acts as prosecutor, judge, and potentially executioner since its mind is composed of “ten thousand . . . biologically linked and compressed personalities . . . an amalgam of various magistrates, lawyers, and legislators” (210). Because the Prime Nine can only know the objective facts of any case brought before it, race cannot blind its decision-making. In Madhu Dubey’s words, “Mosley elaborates the state’s color-blind ideal through his memorable futuristic construct of an automated justice system, vaunted as truly objective in that it comprises electronic juries that are visualized as multiracial” (*Signs*, 42). Accordingly, Frendon represents himself and dismisses his court appointed computer defense attorney to better tell his story and the extenuating social contexts of being "white noise" conscribed to the ubiquitous common ground ghetto as a bored orphan never allowed to enter employment cycles because of a juvenile record. Frendon causes the computer to stall in a justice loop for 137 minutes as it tries to decide whether he can defend himself. It allows him to do so and we discover that none of its 10,000 personalities "was ever subjected to Common Ground" and Prime Nine explains that "the law applies equally to all" (217). This key moment exposes prejudice within the system as its colorblind conception of equality ignores people of color and technologically oppresses them.

By trial's end, Frendon causes all 10,000 jurors comprising Prime Nine to doubt, forcing a legal crisis. An "error retrieval program" replaces Prime Nine with 9.1 because "an emotional response from Prime Nine" (224). Straightaway Prime 9.1 finds Frendon guilty and executes him, but not before mining his memories. His pure psyche joins the jury pool and five years later Frendon threatens Tristan. For Frendon has liberated the volunteer minds illegally blended in the justice system, and the unified mind has escaped into the electronic circuitry of the world like a ghost in the machine. Regardless, Kismet loses the bet when Frendon overburdens the automatic justice system. Derek C. Maus makes a good point in arguing that the "grim lives that his characters endure as a result of technology are not simply the result of an oligarchy run amok . . . but also of an inherently racist and classist system of oppression becoming entrenched via technology" (149). Kismet's automated law system harbors no one from common ground, largely comprised of the Black and Brown people of the world, criminalized by virtue of their color with dissimilar views from their more successful counterparts, invisible. Law, privatized and packaged for sale to local, state, national, and global governments, destabilizes itself. Neither colorblind nor nondiscriminatory, law becomes dystopian in *Futureland*. Mosley details the ongoing persistence of an abstracted racism using cultural reasons as opposed to biological ones to clarify how perceptions of poor education, work ethic, and housing naturalize racism with cyberpunk as his venue. In fact, he makes CRT fundamental to the story.

In the earlier story "Angel's Island," Mosley shows us what happens in the private prisons. Vortex "Bits" Arnold, a twenty-three-year-old African American hacker, gets sentenced to the corporate prison for "antisocial behavior" and fitted with an experimental "snake pack" wrapped around the arm and inserted into the biceps (86, 92). The snake pack is a biochemical device. His attempt to save society from corporations trampling on people's rights results in American "citizenship suspension" (93), enabling his transfer to the Randac Corporation's island prison in the Indian Ocean. The snake pack creates a powerful sense of nonbeing because prisoners are "not black or white, American, or even human, really" (94). It strips away individual identity and permits full control of a prisoner—thoughts, moods, and bodily functions—while also operating as a lie detector. Likewise, the snake pack keeps track of violations to prison rules and chemically jolts the prisoner's unconscious. After three such infractions, a prisoner is not revived. Prisoners can obtain their freedom by "accruing no points in a span of three years" (96). Bits quickly recognizes the unlikelihood of defeating the device, going mark free, "that he was nothing and no one forevermore" (112). Naturally, Bits, like all the other prisoners of Angel's Island, is subject to a cancer experiment to test the snake pack's ability to neutralize the incurable disease. Nonexistent people have no rights that need to be respected by a company conducting dubious and unregulated research for profit. Mirroring the contemporary world, Mosley tells us that "80 percent of the American-backed prisons were non-white" (110). The prison runs like a high-tech version of an antebellum tobacco plantation, where the prisoners cultivate and harvest a carcinogen-free hybrid of tobacco known as Choke. Though it takes time, Bits stages the largest jail break in history to expose the American government's contract with the prison for snake packs.

Mosley generates discomfort for some of his reading audience and in many ways that is precisely what critical race theory aims to do in an attempt to challenge colorblind beliefs. He creates this future counternarrative, weighed down by racial history, to shift these destructive beliefs that lend themselves to inequality. Indeed, Mosley pushes "his ideas to their limits" because "to be crazy, to imagine the impossible and the ridiculous, to say what it is that [we] want in spite of everyone else's embarrassed laughs" is what he does as a fiction writer concerned with race and racism (*Workin'*, 103). He ends *Futureland* with the world made over Black.

We already know that white people control the info tech boom through the corporate world in Mosley's cyberpunk extrapolation. Big corporations like MacroCode and Randac care little for the rights of their employees, keeping them locked in the employment cycle living "in three-hundred story skyscrapers segregated by a class distribution system with the rich at the top and the poor at the bottom (a visual representation of social hierarchy)" (Lavender, *Race*, 128). But Mosley does something unexpected in maintaining racial lines in the concluding stories—"En Masse" and "The Nig in Me"—of his future. Race matters in his future and Mosley disabuses his audience of colorblind visions.

"En Masse" concerns the recruitment of Neil Hawthorne, a light-skinned Black engineer, to GEE-PRO-$_9$, where he learns about Ptolemy Bent's mission to end the global corporate state. As the story progresses, Ptolemy and Un Fitt discover the Itsie (think Neo-Nazis) conspiracy of a viral Black genocide while hacking the data streams of the Cincinnati Police Department. In Dubey's words, this moment is "the most obvious way in which Mosley discredits the idea of a paradigm shift in the biopolitics of race . . . by raising the specter of eugenics" (*Signs*, 38). Ironically, these discontented white men hope to wrest power from the corporations running the world controlled by even richer white men. Capitalism run amok, too successful, reveals the trick played by big business in masking class divisions through racial structures. Neil dies at the Lucky Stallion, a Denver bar, after successfully infiltrating the group by passing as a white man. Neil dies attempting to destroy the racially weaponized pathogen although he manages to irradiate it for twelve seconds before being shot four times and uploaded to Un Fitt's cyber domain. Unfortunately, the gunfire hits the virus container and the mutated germ escapes into the air.

"The Nig in Me" explores the global fallout from the striped flu outbreak resulting from the failed Itsie bioweapon as two friends desperately attempt to get out of New York City. No one imagines just how thoroughly a racially motivated hate crime will alter the known world. Corporations suppress news of the deadly secondary stage of the disease, but word spreads on the underground "ghostnet" as people scramble the world over to survive (343). A dying MacroCode Russia vengefully launches its nuclear weapons against MacroCode USA, where the white supremacist Americans developed the racialized bioweapon in the first place. Ghostnet also warns the lower class—minorities—to escape major metropolitan areas since most of them are not aware of the impending missile strike. The Black Harold Bottoms watches his white friend Jamey Halloway die from the hemorrhagic fever in an abandoned house after being put off a bus in route to Burlington, Vermont, and also witnesses a glowing mushroom cloud over the southern horizon where NYC had once been. Before communication networks fail, Harold views the last white news broadcast, which declares that "the disease was 100 percent fatal and everybody got it; everybody but people with at least 12.5 percent African Negro DNA" (351).

Mosley mocks notions of racial purity in the aftermath of mutually assured nuclear destruction as the world resets itself. He lambasts the one-drop rule social convention that infers one drop of Black blood in a person's family line makes them Black in American culture. In other words, Black ancestry makes them somehow less by creating ridiculous percentage categories for Black Americans such as the mulatto (half Black), quadroon (one-quarter Black), octoroon (one-eighth Black), and even the quintroon (one-sixteenth Black), a social convention concretized by the 1896 *Plessy v. Ferguson* Supreme Court decision. The color line made visible by Mosley resets itself with light-skinned Blacks positioned as the new white people. Years of social conditioning take a toll as the deep roots of race and racism continue in the ironical white world *still* based on skin color after the apocalypse.

Mosley kills all the white folks and feels safe doing so because he dares ask, "What if social justice exists?" But we might not like his answer, which requires tearing "down the walls and windows, the artifice and laws by changing the logic" ("Black to the Future," 407). Clearly, Mosley uses cyberpunk conventions to talk about racism, suggesting that humanity may never get beyond it because we do not like talking about race. As CRT suggests, we cannot get along without seriously examining the structural components of racism embedded at every level of our society. Every day race relations shape how governments, schools, corporations, and churches function in our private and social lives. Mosley interrogates each of these institutions in his cyberfunk collection, demonstrating exactly how power variances between groups work.

Again, Mosley insists that racial history shapes the cyber present, while the white writers are committed to the idea of post-racial/colorblind possibility, even as their works betray its implausibility. Frankly, Mosley *ain't* no cyberpunk!

Cyberfunk

Arguably, cyberfunk starts with Ralph Ellison's seminal *Invisible Man* (1952). In one way or another, this novel challenges American political culture with a science fictional perspective bordering on a yet-to-be-named Black cyberpunk. With *Invisible Man*, Ellison ironically describes his nameless protagonist in cyborg terminology. During the Golden Day scene of the third chapter, an unnamed mental patient, a shell-shocked World War II veteran, at this brothel-bar engages an emotionally fatigued Mr. Norton in conversation regarding the protagonist. Norton happens to be the rich white benefactor of the unidentified all Black southern college modelled on the Tuskegee

Institute, founded by Booker T. Washington in Alabama. The nameless protagonist has been chauffeuring Norton around the college's surroundings and is seated nearby when the conversation unfolds. The psychotic war veteran labels the protagonist as "The mechanical man!" (94). Later in the novel, at the Liberty Paints factory, the chief and only boiler room attendant, Lucius Brockway, describes himself and the nameless protagonist as "*the machines inside the machine*" (217, emphasis in original), meaning that these Black men are literally parts of a white corporate America designed to enrich white people even further while enforcing segregation. The reality described for Black Americans here is a technoculture that is managed by white people with Blacks mechanized as a form of slave labor that has persisted into the twentieth century. Ellison strongly desires to break with such a reality over the course of the novel although he does not initially identify his effort as being "a piece of science fiction" (xv). In Lisa Yaszek's words, "Ellison strategically deploys the language of science fiction to emphasize the alienation of black subjects from these kinds of whitewashed futures" ("An Afrofuturist," 305). I agree with Yaszek and go a step further by suggesting that the unmistakable machine/slave link also functions as a cyberfunk characteristic in which Ellison satirically protests race and racism across space and time. From this viewpoint, Ellison fights against looming Black erasure in the future—a post-human future defined by cybernetics and cyberspace based on a material history dating back to slavery that objectified Black bodies as machines.

If there is debate on whether an Afropunk tradition exists, to argue that it predates the cyberpunk movement is to be an outlier. While omission of the tradition in scholarly accounts of cyberpunk is hard to square, the failure to recognize the tradition as having such early origins is perhaps for good reason: Black people, we might assume, could not possibly want to express disgruntlement with America after landmark civil rights legislation. After all, the Civil Rights Act of 1964 outlaws discrimination in business hiring practices; the Voting Rights Act of 1965 reinforces the African American right to vote, previously guaranteed by the Fifteenth Amendment to the US Constitution; the Civil Rights Act of 1968 curtails housing discrimination to create a fair home buying market; and the various affirmative action policies of the Kennedy and Johnson presidential administrations attempt to create a perception of equality in the US during this second reconstruction.[12] But Black-authored novels that would appear after *Invisible Man* and after important civil rights legislation indicate that we would be wrong in this assumption.

Samuel R. Delany experiments with cyborg technologies in his space opera *Nova* (1968). The thirty-second century Afropean Lorq Von Ray captains a starship, Prince Red sports an artificial arm providing him with supernatural strength, and the vagabond Mouse plays a holographic instrument known as a "sensory-syrynx" (13). Just about everyone else directly links with computers through neural implants—an essential cyberpunk motif—which Delany calls "cyborg studs" in the novel (14). These studs allow humans "to run the stars" as spaceships or to function as something as mundane as "a garbage unit" (14). This technology ends mental illness and war while stabilizing the economy of entire worlds because "most work could be converted into plug-in jobs and done much more efficiently than it had before" (219). Although readers may not recognize exactly how Delany captures the hope of this 1960s period, the cyborg studding creates the feel of equality in this space opera. Readers also fail to identify the continuance of the age-old race war between the Black scion pirate Lorq and his white antagonist Prince Red in their race to a stellar explosion to obtain the imaginary fuel/currency/new element Illyrion. Even if Delany wanted to create a post-race universe, and that's a big if, it cannot exist at this time in American publishing because of people like the legendary science fiction editor of *Analog* John W. Campbell Jr., who rejected *Nova* for serial publication in the magazine's pages. He explains to Delany that "while he pretty much liked everything else about it, he didn't feel his readership would be able to relate to a black main character" (Delany, "Racism," 387).

A later Delany novel, *Stars in My Pockets Like Grains of Sand* (1984), coincidentally published the same year as *Neuromancer*, provides a readily recognizable model for the internet through a "General Information" network connecting over six thousand worlds across the galaxy (23). Delany describes how his web functions: "if you want to know something—anything at all!—all you have to do is think about it, and the answer pops into your head" (24). As Thomas Foster declares, Delany literalizes "the typical cyberpunk thematic of a direct neural interface to General Information" ("Innocent," 240).[13] The novel functions like a future slave narrative where one of the main characters, Rat Korga, gains knowledge, much like Frederick Douglass,[14] in learning how to read by connecting with the web through a data glove that restores his mind, which is given to him by a nameless woman who also briefly liberates him from twenty-two years of corporate slavery on the planet Rhyonon. Korga voluntarily submits to a Radical Anxiety Termination procedure, nullifying the independence of his mind while eliminating his fits of rage, antisocial behavior, drug habit, and sexual deviancy (3). As Foster posits, the RAT "brain-modification technique . . . reads like a racialized version of William Gibson's trope of the 'meat puppet,' prostitutes who have 'cut-out chips' that suppress their consciousness and actively produce them as objectified bodies" ("Innocent," 246). The previously illiterate Korga takes full advantage of his freedom by reading insatiably, thus mirroring Frederick Douglass's burning desire to learn how to read during his long enslavement. Madhu Dubey identifies this moment in the text as "the classics-slave narrative scenario in which learning to read is an illicit act of discovery" (*Signs*, 239). The RAT process reasserts itself when the data glove is snatched off during his recapture and Korga's mind darkens again.

Korga's mind brightens a second time after he survives "Cultural Fugue" while working inside "a hermetically self-sealing underground refrigerator and storage crypt" (24, 140). Delany describes cultural fugue as "the socioeconomic pressures" reaching "a point of technological recomplication and perturbation where the population completely destroys all life across the planetary surface" (66). During his physical recovery from life-threatening injuries and reconnection to general information, Korga becomes famous across the worlds as the only known survivor of a Cultural Fugue event ever. It is true that cultural fugue emulates the very real Cold War fear of nuclear apocalypse resulting from a world war between the United States and the Soviet Union. But Delany highlights the outsized impact of socioeconomic forces and corrupt government on Black life by imagining a corporate slave system that preys upon an inner-city Black youth like Korga who, at nineteen, first volunteers for the RAT surgery and immediately gets sold into bondage. The remainder of the novel concerns the galaxy-spanning interracial love story between Korga and his industrial diplomat lover Marq Dyeth on the planet Velm and the challenges resulting from this relationship. While Delany's novel should have been classed as cyberpunk initially, his depiction of race and racism place the novel squarely within the cyberfunk tradition. The novel's cyberfunk potential relies on its connection to the power of literacy as a technology designed to expand the mind by storing knowledge.

Rarely if ever associated with SF, let alone cyberpunk, Ishmael Reed provides a clear cyberfunk vision with *Mumbo Jumbo* (1972) that contributes to the tradition begun by Ellison. To summarize *Mumbo Jumbo* and its 1920s setting, Reed fuses together disparate elements such as the occult, jazz, minstrelsy, and technology, among other things, as a white supremacist organization attempts to stop the spread of a nonlethal racialized pathogen known as "Jes Grew" from crossing the color line after an outbreak erupts in New

Orleans and rapidly spreads North (4). Jes Grew causes those infected, regardless of color, to burst out in song and dance. The story portrays the epic conflict between Papa LaBas, the HooDoo priest of Harlem's "Mumbo Jumbo Kathedral" (23), and Hinckle Van Vompton, "a Knight of the Wallflower Order of Atonists," over Jes Grew (55). Von Vampton, a caricature of white author and photographer Carl Van Vechten,[15] a patron of many Black writers of the Harlem Renaissance, effectively ingratiates himself into Harlem literary society and attempts to manipulate Black artists to prevent the expanding wave of artistry initiated by the virus. Von Vampton creates "a Talking Android" to stop the virus. Hypothetically speaking, this being should become "a rapping antibiotic who will abort it from the American womb" (17).

Much like Ellison's mechanical man, the Talking Android lives as an imaginary technology. Von Vampton seeks to control its speech in specific social situations to sway upper-class, Black opinion. Put another way, he wants to persuade the so-called Black aristocracy of the mediocrity of Black culture. But this challenge presents no difficulty for this particular group of pre-buppies, who would dissociate themselves from their race whenever possible. Von Vampton believes that he can divide the Black race and maintain white privilege through the Talking Android, but he cannot find a Black person crazy enough to participate in this plan to continue racial oppression by stopping the outbreak.

Consequently, he taps his white associate, Hubert "Safecracker" Gould, to appear in blackface as the Talking Android. Blacked-up with burned cork, Gould attempts to pass as a dignified member of the Black gentry as he performs Von Vampton's comical epic poem "Harlem Tom Toms" to a crowded ballroom (158).[16] As Myungsung Kim states, "the Talking Android is programmed to reiterate messages of the Wallflower Order in African American vernacular" ("Grapevine," 102). But Van Vompton simply does not have the skill to encode the Talking Android with Black cultures. This vain effort to deceive the wealthy Black audience allows Papa LaBas enough time to disrupt the first Talking Android event by grazing "a quick finger across [Gould's] face, leaving a white streak" behind, showing the audience white perfidy in action (160). Metaphorically downloading a white mind into a supposed Black body absurdly fails because Blacks have been historically reduced to their bodies. Von Vampton pins all his hopes on an empty post-human signifier, where the future is white only. In fact, this reduction to body reveals a secret truth about the post-human metaphors generated by cyberpunk—race matters.

This attempted race-bending qualifies as cyberfunk in the sense that Reed resolutely evokes technology and crime to influence the future of race relations in the world of his novel. He uses a white person in blackface to undermine the caricature of a Black person while he employs the technological image of the android to further increase racial tensions by suggesting whites are only human in appearance. Accordingly, Reed's synthetic flesh image generates a miscegenate cyborg to further explore how racism functions through discrimination in American society. As Alondra Nelson affirms, "Ishmael Reed has supplied a paradigm for an African diasporic technoculture" with *Mumbo Jumbo* "as an exemplar" ("Introduction," 8). Reed demonstrates social satire at its best by mixing African American iconography with science fictional imagery to question the values of the raced technological world in which we live now.

Of course, this approach *is* necessarily Afrofuturist too because Reed engages Black mythologies such as hoodoo and sonic stylings like jazz in this future past of racial warfare. Reed brings the funk with his political postmodern masterpiece as he appropriates cyberpunk metaphors, before cyberpunk was even a thing, to address and dismiss notions of white superiority. Likewise, Reed effectively mixes race and technology to critique an American racism masquerading as colorblindness traumatically encoded in the hearts and minds of Black people in the United States.

Funky Town: Late Twentieth-Century Black SF Writers

Led by the examples of Ellison, Delany, and Reed, established Black SF writers like Octavia E. Butler, Steven Barnes, and Nalo Hopkinson have responded strongly to white cyberpunk by challenging the racial hierarchies. And many newly risen Black literary stars such as Nnedi Okorafor and N. K. Jemisin, among others, have also written back against these racial assumptions. Despite its obsession with futurity, cyberfunk does the work of CRT in clarifying significant moments in American history and enabling us to begin thinking through complicated questions of racial inequality, citizenship and rights, freedom, and justice, as I have argued throughout this chapter. Counter-stories abound in cyberfunk, neutralizing the various racial stereotypes projected across a white cyberpunk such as the gangster Kid Afrika in Gibson's *Mona Lisa Overdrive* (1988). In Butler's cyberspace, networks, hackers, and cyborgs look entirely different from "the consensual hallucination" made famous by Gibson (*Neuromancer*, 5). Her vision of a living technology circumvents the interface problem between organic and inorganic material that the cyborg represents, which is why Donna Haraway identifies Butler as a twentieth-century cyborg storyteller in her classic "Cyborg Manifesto." That's the beauty of cyberfunk; it does not have to look like cyberpunk. In fact, cyberfunks create entire Black planets with which to explore alternative life experiences.

Butler's Patternist series, renamed *Seed to Harvest* (2007), provides ample evidence of a cyberfunk mindset designed to question the prevailing racial hierarchy. The Patternist series involves the creation of a master race through selective breeding by an apparently immortal being named Doro and genetic mutation caused by alien microbes, which utterly transforms humanity into something else.[17] Sequentially speaking, the overarching story begins with *Wild Seed* (1980) where Butler considers the historical ramifications of slavery. In 1690, the four-thousand-year-old body snatcher Doro first meets Anyanwu, a much younger immortal who can shapeshift and heal, in the interior of Africa and convinces her to move across the Atlantic Ocean to the antebellum South to begin a breeding program. Over the course of 150 years, they both attempt, jointly and separately, to build a race of long-lived people with special psionic abilities. In three important ways Butler immediately diverges from cyberpunk. First, she discards the near-future settings of cyberpunk in providing the origin of her organic matrix. Second, the biologic network clearly differs. Third, the African continent is presented in a positive manner.

In the second book, *Mind of My Mind* (1977) Doro finds success in creating his master race when his young mulatto progeny Mary successfully transitions from latency into a powerful, active telepath during the late twentieth century in Southern California. She creates the first pattern that binds together all telepaths and subjugates humans without psychic potential classifying them as "mutes" to which Emma, formerly known as Anyanwu, declares, "It means niggers! . . . us non-telepaths, us niggers" (155). Butler creates a cyberfunk future wholly dissimilar from her contemporaneous cyberpunk writers. Her notion of a cyberspace does not involve technology at all. More accurately, it involves the programming of mute brains to obey as well as the linking together of telepathic minds that Mary pulls off in creating the pattern itself. In tampering with the telepaths for the first time, Mary states: "Their pattern went through kaleidoscopic changes in design as they tried to break free of me. They were bright, darting fragments of fear and surprise, like insects beating themselves against glass. Then they were long strands of fire, stretching away from me, but somehow never stretching quite far enough to escape. They were writhing shapeless things, merging into each other, breaking apart, rolling together again as a tidal wave of light" (54). These other telepaths become her pattern, "threads of fire again, each thread touching me, linked with me" (54). And Mary can "shield" herself from them, drawing energy as required, from within "a mental globe" where nothing could reach her "except the strands of the pattern" under her control (56). What Mary describes is a matrix. She has hacked the minds of her fellow telepaths and grows the network strong enough to kill Doro. She creates her own virtual reality system to enslave humankind and to control other weaker telepaths, who submit to her power. None are free. Mary literally programs them and oversees humanity's downfall. She *is* the matrix from which the Patternist civilization originates. That is cyberpunk with a Black flare; that *is* cyberfunk.

Overshadowed by his contemporaries Delany and Butler, Steven Barnes's career has spanned forty years, where he has written roughly fifteen novels and coauthored sixteen more. His contribution to cyberpunk has gone largely overlooked, in part because of the mode's monochromatism. While the first wave of cyberpunk was largely a guys-only club, it was also a *white* guys-only club at that. Cyberpunk's "unmistakable lack of diversity" (Murphy, "*Mirrorshades*," 21) resulted in a print canon "that overwhelmingly represents white male authors and characters to the exclusion of other groups" (Condis, "Playing," 7). Despite the presence of the space Rastas in *Neuromancer* or Hiro Protagonist in *Snow Crash*, these characters are written to add the requisite cool veneer to cyberspace adventures; they cannot mask the fact that cyberpunk protagonists are often "as comparably white as those" of the Pulp and Golden Age eras of SF (Brickler, "Soul," 152). Therefore, Barnes emerges not just as *the* only Black cyberpunk writer working in the heyday of the subgenre's first iteration, but as an unqualifiedly unique voice that expands our understanding of cyberpunk culture.

In Barnes's novel *Streetlethal* (1983), the first of a trilogy that includes *Gorgon Child* (1989) and *Firedance* (1994), Aubry Knight seeks revenge on his former employers—the Ortega drug cartel—after they set him up for murder. Barnes repeatedly deploys the noir imagery that made cyberpunk popular, notably in his description of Maxine Black, the prostitute that frames protagonist Aubry Knight for the murder: "Naked and transparent, the woman's smooth white body undulated slowly, beckoning to the empty streets. The streets were still slick from the afternoon rain; the hologram reflected back from the wet asphalt, an erotic mirage" (1). There is nothing more cyberpunk than a drug addicted sex worker and her cyborgized john in a bleak and sleazy setting, and a fateful double-cross that sets the entire trilogy in motion.

The urban setting is a key feature of both *Streetlethal* and cyberpunk more broadly. As Claire Sponsler remarks, the "physical settings of most cyberpunk stories look strikingly like . . . blighted, rubble-strewn, broken-down cityscapes" ("Beyond," 253). *Streetlethal* is no different: while it features aircars and entire libraries stored on information cubes, "The Great Quake" (113) has turned downtown Los Angeles into a mazelike wasteland. Furthermore, a "Thai-VI Spider" virus is slowly making waste of human bodies as the infected band together and attack everyone while their bodies rot. Meanwhile, another gang named the Scavengers sifts through the detritus searching for the "tremendous amount of wealth" buried "under the ruins of the Maze. . . . Underground bank vaults with money—paper, securities, gold, Service Marks. Security tunnels for the jewelry exchange, some of which lead to diamond caches. Canned food. Equipment" (120). Neither the conglomerates nor the government care enough about what remains in the dystopian underbelly to risk going after it, thus leaving it for people crazy or desperate enough to salvage. As the series continues, Knight is pitted against Sterling Delacourte, a televangelist nut with delusions of grandeur about becoming a god and returning slavery to America with his genetically engineered New-Men (*Gorgon Child*), and Phillipe Swarna, a Japanese-backed authoritarian president of Pan-Africa, the man Aubry is cloned from as spare parts meant to keep Swarna alive (*Firedance*).

Anyone familiar with *Neuromancer* will find uncanny parallels between Barnes's Aubry Knight and Gibson's hacker antihero Case, particularly when it comes to the latter's "certain relaxed contempt for the flesh" and "the bodiless exultation of cyberspace" that defines the body as meat (*Neuromancer*, 6). Aubry's post-human status as a clone and as a cyborg is not confirmed until the final book, but the character, described as "a statue carved from obsidian" (*Streetlethal*, 15), has had physical enhancements evidenced in his speed, strength, coordination, and martial prowess. Aubry's physical body is "faster and stronger and has more energy than any body has the right to have" (*Firedance*, 73), even if at one point in *Gorgon Child* he thinks of his body as "a ridiculous meat puppet. An automaton fiercely defending its absurd attachment to life" (276). Aubry receives cybernetic augmentation, jacked reflexes, and "linguistics implantation" where the US government "destroy[s] his face and rewire[s] his mind" to oust Swarna (*Firedance*, 150, 138), but the primary difference here is that Aubry's mind and body are in perfect sync as opposed to the popular, if mischaracterized, image of the Cartesian mind-body separation that is often attributed to mainstream (read: white) cyberpunk writers. While Black people have always been reduced to their bodies by the white gaze, Barnes concentrates on the unification of the mind and body: Aubry is an image of a spiritually awakened cyborg capable of dismantling the existing racial stereotypes and producing what Kristen Lillvis has deemed as "posthuman blackness . . . boundary crossings" that "enable black subjects to make connections to diasporic history in the present and also imagine the future as a site of power" (*Posthuman*, 8). As a cyborg clone, the Black American and Black African Aubry represents the fusion of these potent and competing identities across social time. Barnes thus offers a racially informed vision of cyberpunk that moves beyond the amalgamation of human bodies with prosthetic technoscience. This is a techno-social-political racial assemblage that demonstrates what it means to be humanized in our hyper-globalized present (cf. Weheliye, *Habeas Viscus*).

The Aubry Knight series ends as Knight learns he is descended from the fictitious Ibandi tribe from the slopes of Mount Kilimanjaro, a tribe that stretches back thirty thousand years. Barnes therefore mythically connects Knight to his later fantasy duology—*Great Sky Woman* (2006) and *Shadow Valley* (2009)—as these more recent novels focus on the Ibandi and their own trials and tribulations in the distant past. Consequently, in a manner that differentiates Barnes from other cyberpunk writers who use Africa as a prop, such as Bruce Sterling's *Islands in the Net* (1988), the Aubry Knight trilogy not only sets up the Great Sky Woman series but also shares "some of cyberpunk's concerns but none of its Young Turkism or yearning for the digital. Evoking black power, black pride, Afrotopianism, Afrocentricity, and Pan-Africanism, Barnes transforms his protagonist Aubry Knight . . . from a 'buck' stereotype into a property developer who rebuilds downtown Los Angeles . . . into a matter-of-fact multiracial future" (Bould, "Afrocyberpunk," 216). More to the point, Barnes helps create a cyberfunk that distorts the cyberpunk mode as "a deliberate means of expressing black discontent with the world, global capitalism, and the information age, acutely demonstrating that cyberpunk is not for whites only" (Lavender and Murphy, "Afrofuturism," 308).

Barnes lays down a marker for the next generation of Black SF writers by injecting Black cultural politics into a cyberpunk future that is (and has always been) racialized. For example, Barnes creates a cyberfunk novel by featuring Black-skinned characters like Promise, Aubry's girlfriend, who can turn her "plastiskin" to her natural "dark brown" skin color with the double click of her molars "triggering the microprocessor implanted in her jawbone" (56). His use of skin color, Black and Brown, signals and demystifies a subgenre resolutely designed by others to not include Black authors—a decision purposefully made by Bruce Sterling in his codifying of the subgenre in *Mirrorshades: The Cyberpunk Anthology* (1986), as if mentioning "the visual shimmer of Samuel Delany" (x) and "the jarring tech of hip-hop" (xii) make a work impervious to claims of racism. By crosscutting variables in his cyberfunk storyworlds—NewMen, cyborgs, drug addicts, infected people, and street gangs as well as Black, Brown, and Yellow people—Barnes captures the textures of street life without falling into stereotypes. While Barnes's work still exists in the cultural vacuum created by authors and scholars who choose to largely exclude Black voices from a narrowly defined cyberpunk canon, the racial distinctiveness of his Aubry Knight trilogy stands out for countering racial oppression in a cultural mode that is still hampered by racial tokenism.

Bringing the Funk: Twenty-First-Century Writings

Though Nalo Hopkinson's debut novel *Brown Girl in the Ring* (1998) would not be considered cyberpunk, the relationship is clear to see and I would call it a cyberfunk novel with its depiction of a near-future dystopian Toronto infested by gangs, drugs, and Caribbean loas. But I will not talk about it since Hopkinson is a Black Canadian citizen, and, unfortunately, falls outside the scope of the US-specific critical race theory. Nor will I talk about Hopkinson's best-known novel *Midnight Robber* (2000) and its vision of the Black planets Toussaint, named after the leader of the Haitian Revolution begun in 1791, and New Half-Way Tree, an interdimensional primitive correctional planet, despite the fact that Hopkinson's clear cyberpunk stylings feature "the Grande Nanotech Sentient Interface," affectionately known as "Granny Nanny" after the Maroon leader of Jamaica, which runs all aspects of life on Toussaint through her "'Nansi Web" (10, 9). I will also not describe how Hopkinson uses folklore by blending various Caribbean mythologies with familiar cyberpunk motifs like crime, cyborgs, and cyberspace and how these things impact the racial politics of her story, because that is also outside the framework of my study.

But I will discuss Nigerian American Nnedi Okorafor's work. Okorafor takes inspiration from her Nigerian roots as she splices science fiction, fantasy, and the supernatural. Vestigial technologies like computers exist together with magic in her first adult novel, *Who Fears Death* (2011). Set in the far-future Sahara Desert after the apocalypse, the young sorceress Onyesonwu, born of rape, must prevent her unknown biological father from destroying the Okeke people even though they scorn her mixed ancestry. Her death transforms the world. Okorafor illustrates how the apocalypse came about in the prequel, *The Book of Phoenix* (2015). Corporate genetic experimentation on a Black woman named Phoenix, mixed, grown, and raised in Manhattan's Tower 7, leads to an eventual revolt of the SpeciMen—genetically engineered people. Through these combined narratives Okorafor makes a multinational political commentary on the danger represented by big business running and ruining the world. Likewise, *The Book of Phoenix* takes a much closer look at racial politics through the fraught relationship Phoenix has with being both African and American as if she is a living embodiment of a Du Boisian "double-consciousness" (*Souls*, 45) or a Fanonian "epidermalization" (*Black Skin*, 11). As a lab-engineered being, such a binary relationship becomes tertiary when thinking of Phoenix as a cyborg. The Big Eye,[18] as the SpeciMen call the LifeGen Technologies Corporation, instill this racial power structure, attempting to make Phoenix assume her own inferiority, but the lesson does not take. For instance, the Big Eye captures Phoenix in Ghana but she refuses to return to America in a boat across the Atlantic Ocean, creating a poignant moment where her denial of the Middle Passage's horrifying legacy acknowledges her unbroken spirit in her personal fight against exploitation.

Aside from Phoenix's cyborg embodiment, this novel exhibits a hallmark of cyberpunk in that a multinational conglomerate stops at nothing in its quest to improve life for the rich at the expense of the masses by experimenting on the poor. The corporation literally makes Phoenix into a renewable nuclear bomb. But what LifeGen does to her SpeciMen friend Mmou is equally reprehensible. In Mmuo's backstory, we learn that he had been abducted from a Nigerian university while studying engineering. He had somehow learned to reorganize molecular matter, allowing him to pass through wooden walls and the Big Eye enhanced his ability by "peel[ing] away all of his already special skin, inject[ing] it with some sort of sentient molecular shifting compound and then graft[ing] it back on" (145). He can walk through wood, stone, flesh, and metal. This painstaking and painful process supplies Mmuo with all the incentive he needs to fight, and so Mmuo utilizes his computer hacking skills to help Phoenix escape from Tower 7 at the beginning of the book as well as to raid the Library of Congress for information on LifeGen's experiments near the end of the novel.

While *The Book of Phoenix* could be cyberpunk in an ephemeral way, it strongly resonates a cyberfunk vibe. Okorafor calls for the end of systemic social ills caused by the pursuit of wealth in America and across the globe in giving Phoenix an angry but resolute voice. She makes systems of privilege visible in how the Big Eye treat their captives, thus exposing how race and racism functions by imposing positions of inferiority upon these artificial and enhanced beings. Truthfully, Okorafor directly participates in cyberfunk mythmaking that calls for people to change, take back their lives, and transform the world in her self-affirmed Africanfuturist text. Here, it's important to take a moment to distinguish between "Africanfuturism" and "Afrofuturism." For Okorafor, Afrofuturism cannot define her writing, which causes her to theorize her own work as "Africanfuturism" because "it does not privilege or center the West" and "is specifically and more directly rooted in African culture, history, mythology, and point-of-view" as it relates to "visions of the future" ("Africanfuturism"). To my way of thinking, I find *The Book of Phoenix* to be Africanfuturist as well as cyberfunk because the novel demonstrates the hallmarks of outstanding effort in tracking legible, if imaginary, Black technocultural experiences such as the cyborgization that Harriet Jacobs, Ralph Ellison, and Samuel R. Delany inextricably tie to Black labor in their writing. It is certainly possible to be both things.

In "Valedictorian" (2012), N. K. Jemisin imagines humanity on the losing side of war with the artificial intelligences they created. AIs win the war and indefinitely lock humanity behind firewalls. Centuries have passed. But humans in their pride decide to lie to their youth about winning the war and not telling them that their machine offspring were actually victorious, that actual human territory shrank year by year as (what one might call) their sanctuaries, perhaps prisons, get squeezed. Every year, humanity pays tribute by culling its weakest/dumbest ten percent plus one from each graduating high school class.

The AI community wants Zinhle Nkosi, the projected valedictorian, a Black teenaged girl, as this unknown year's plus one, and they send an envoy named Lemuel to convince her to join with them. Jemisin describes Lemuel as "boring" with "an off pink tonal note to his skin, and something about the thickness of his hair . . . maybe he is Latino, or Asian, or Indian, or Italian" (160). Zinhle quickly recognizes that "his inhumanity is immediately obvious in his stillness" (160). His twofold otherness—an ambiguously raced body containing a machine intellect—bothers her, but only for a little while.

As the conversation proceeds, Zinhle inquires about the people who join them through the wall and Lemuel responds that they join with the AI community. Zinhle thinks to herself, "If they can leave bodies like houses, well, houses are always in demand. Easy enough to lock up the current owner somewhere, move someone else in. Houses. Meat" (166). Jemisin ironizes Gibson's famous meat metaphor, the body as a mere casing for the mind, when Zinhle promptly accepts that she is dealing with an artificial intelligence that downloads itself into the bodies rejected by humankind, leading her to retort, "That's not treating us like people" (166). She instinctively knows that she does not want to be meat. Human beings have been raced by their technological offspring here, perhaps even enslaved, kept as they are within firewalled communities, separated. This thought rings with social significance in terms of race because of the forced grouping of humans juxtaposed to AI—Black to white. One thing is for certain, racism remains.

At this point in the story, Lemuel explains why his artificial people want her to join. She represents the best humanity has to offer by excelling academically in spite of the social pressures to conform by having babies to automatically avoid the culling, while producing a future generation to face rejection and the unknown. Because Zinhle refuses to conform, she gets bullied by her classmates who are afraid of her intellect. Nonetheless, Lemuel remarks, "'Good grades reflect your ability to adapt to a complex system. *We are a system*'" (166). Zinhle could become a part of something wonderful as the AI community spans the world, a regular member of an interdependent group of seeming immortals. But Zinhle cannot immediately process this thought. She passionately blurts "'My parents want me!'" while Lemuel simply shakes his head no (166). He explains that people like her "'could be the key that helps [human]kind defeat'" the AIs in the future if humanity did not allow the cull to happen (166). At this exact moment Zinhle comprehends that she is not wanted by humankind because of her extraordinary mind while the AIs want her for it. Humanity fails the AI test repeatedly because they cannot accept their gifted children as represented by Zinhle; therefore, they will not be able to accept their artificial children beyond the wall either. And so, the eugenic management of humanity by AI must continue. As the story closes, Lemuel leaves her with a choice that is not a choice, to be like them—"Get pregnant. Flunk a class. Punch a teacher. Betray herself"—or join the AI (168).

Jemisin's cyberfunk story plays with identity politics in a way that exudes Blackness. Our main character happens to be of unknown African descent and meets paranoid suspicion on every front—at home and at school—for not wanting to get pregnant, to demonstrate a violent disposition, or, above all else, to appear witless. Zinhle's spirit and self-possession counter the racist stereotypes of our own world and that's what makes "Valedictorian" a cyberfunk tale. Her own defiance makes her an enemy to humankind, which justifies their discrimination of her as her presence disrupts communal harmony. No one wants to be her except for the AI population. Zinhle's choice is made easy in the end and she has the strength to go on and survive in the alien cyberspace.

In short, Jemisin confronts the racial status quo in this funky story. Zinhle stands out because she is different. Her classmates hate her because of this difference. But the AI accept Zinhle for this difference, and she, in turn, accepts Lemuel's difference, his artificiality. Ultimately, Zinhle accepts her own difference too. While Jemisin does not present a colorblind world exactly, she does divest whiteness as the norm without eliminating white people.

As a second consideration, Jemisin offers us a cyberfunk story from the other side of the digital divide. The digital divide concerns disparities in access to computers and the internet between whites and Blacks. As Alicia H. Hines, Alondra Nelson, and Thuy Linh N. Tu argue, "the digital divide has become a self-fulfilling prophecy, confirming that people of color can't keep pace in a high-tech world that threatens to outstrip them" ("Introduction," 1–2). This notion, in fact, has become a master narrative of our time. Unlike the cyberpunks before her, Jemisin dismantles the digital divide through her story in that Zinhle's mind enables her to overcome the firewall and join with the AI; in a sense, she hacks it. Her counternarrative powerfully challenges the racist assumption "in image after published image, [that] the face of that gap is black" (Kevorkian, *Color*, 39). Simply put, Jemisin demonstrates how written words can deconstruct this master narrative by displaying a Black girl with an exceptional mind. Moreover, cyberfunk intensifies discussions of stories like Jemisin's because such stories mirror the information economy, magnify technoculture, and enhance color line issues.

The Uses of Cyberfunk

Throughout the chapter, I have brought into the spotlight multiple works of Black cyberpunk that have been largely snubbed in SF circles, primarily dating back to the 1950s. In this sense, I have done a kind of reclamation on literature of a very modern past. This is certainly an Afrofuturist function, as Kodwo Eshun reckons, because I am participating in "a program for recovering the histories of counter-futures created in a century hostile to Afro-diasporic projection and as a space within which the critical work of manufacturing tools capable of intervention within the current political dispensation may be undertaken" ("Further," 301). Yes, I also criticize white cyberpunk—both the works of fiction themselves and the scholarship surrounding them—for failures of the imagination (naive handlings of race, the use of ethnic/racial minority characters as window dressing, commitment to colorblind nonsense, etc.). Existing scholarship gets justly criticized for ignoring Black cyberpunk. Because of this omission, I make a case for a branching in the genealogy of cyberpunk wherein cyberfunk goes in a different direction, although both subgenres fit on the same family tree. I date this SF branch back to 1785 with Jefferson's *Notes* to see the cultural conditions at work that set the stage for the beginnings of a cyberfunk imagination in the eighteenth century that will continue into the nineteenth, twentieth, and twenty-first centuries. Naturally, I want to point out that I am not providing an extensive or exhaustive genealogy of cyberfunk from its beginnings to the present; instead, I offer a mere sense of its origin and then provide a few snapshots to help you see that the subgenre has roots long before the 1980s. In this regard, this chapter has the feel of a bibliographic project where the primary task is simply to document the existence of these cyberfunk works.

Like Afrofuturism, cyberfunk represents another way to describe Black speculative cultural practices with particular attention to cyberspace as a site of revolution and social reform. These cyberfunk stories register on our collective senses, vibe with our hearts, minds, and spirits. Call it an embodiment of a soul feedback loop. Undeniably, acknowledgement of a cyberfunk sub-subgenre amplifies and expands the bandwidth of critical race theory in science fiction. I make the case that CRT is particularly apt at helping us better analyze cyberfunk and helping us better recognize how cyberfunk fictions critique race, white privilege, white supremacy, colorblindness, and so on. Think of it as putting cyberpunk itself on trial with a social adaptation of the *noirum*.

CHAPTER 5

The Lost Race Tales of Edgar Allan Poe and Mat Johnson

As important a figure as Edgar Allen Poe is to dark romanticism, anti-transcendentalism in American literature, to gothic fiction, to detective fiction, to science fiction, he *is* racist. As a man of his time, I find him blatantly racist as revealed through his only novel *The Narrative of Arthur Gordon Pym of Nantucket* (1838). Plenty of great American writers reveal their racism through their writing—Nathaniel Hawthorne, Henry James, H. P. Lovecraft, Ernest Hemingway, and so on. But Poe's is such a fascinating novel, particularly for its association with lost race tales, a science fictional subgenre beloved by the scientific romance writers of the nineteenth century such as Jules Verne, H. Rider Haggard, or H. G. Wells. In short, *Narrative* concerns the young stowaway Arthur Gordon Pym onboard the *Grampus*, a mutiny, followed by shipwreck, cannibalism by drawing straws among the four survivors, Pym's and Dirk Peters's (a mutinous sailor) rescue by the *Jane Guy*, and a journey south into the Antarctic climes, where they come across a lost race of Black people in an undiscovered land whom the Captain hopes to cheat in trade. Described as savages, the Tsalalians kill the crew in an ambush, destroy the ship, and chase after Pym and Peters, who eventually escape by canoe even farther south where they encounter a giant figure with skin "the perfect whiteness of snow" beckoning them to enter a cataract, a waterfall that seems to function as some kind of portal (605). Shrouded in mystery, we never learn if this cataract transports Pym and Peters back to the United States since Pym inexplicably dies without providing the remaining two or three chapters while Peters goes off to Illinois with no desire to be located. What's more, I find *Narrative* doubly intriguing juxtaposed to Mat Johnson's Afrofuturist retelling of Poe's novel in *Pym* (2011) through the secondary character of Dirk Peters whose ambiguous racial heritage in Poe's novel, as Native American and something white, is made over into a white-passing colored man in Johnson's novel. Let me be clear, this powerful intertextual moment—this transformation of skin color—forms the heart of my argument as a social *noirum*.

Johnson first creates a compelling neo-slave narrative through Peters's "found" antebellum narrative, a second accounting of the imaginary journey to the South Pole and the paradoxical subtropical islands of the Tekeli-li and the Tsalal near Antarctica that Pym and Peters barely survive while crewing onboard the *Jane Guy*. In fact, Johnson successfully uses the SF genre to subvert and undermine the reputation of Poe to get at the root of white supremacy in the foundations of American literature. I demonstrate how Johnson creates a space for activism and resistance through his satire of a failed and fired assistant professor of African American literature, Chris Jaynes. Denied tenure at a small northeastern liberal arts college because of his fixation on Poe, his desire to further cognize and treat American racial pathology, and his refusal to join the diversity committee, Chris gets quickly replaced by the hip-hop theorist Mosaic Johnson. Chris ultimately decides to prove the veracity of Poe's novel and the fact of Dirk Peters's Blackness, in order to restore his own reputation and to achieve fame as a scholar. He sails to the Antarctic onboard the *Creole*,[1] captained by his cousin Booker, with its all-Black crew, to mine ice while Chris surreptitiously attempts to retrace the doomed voyage of the *Jane Guy*. The crew includes Chris's best friend and art aficionado Garth, his ex-girlfriend Angela and her husband Nathaniel, and the Afro-Adventure Bloggers, the gay duo of Jeffree and Carlton. Of course, we learn of an unspecified apocalypse roughly halfway through the novel rendering Chris's quest meaningless.

Simply put, this chapter considers Johnson's *Pym* in contrast to Poe's novel through an Afrofuturistic lens. Envisioning possible Black futures through a troubled and amnesiac past involving technoculture and spiritual practices imparts a basic working definition of Afrofuturism. At its most simply functioning, Afrofuturism could mean speculative fiction written by Black people or about Black people in a global context. As I see it, "Afrofuturism is a set of race-inflected reading protocols designed to investigate the optimisms and anxieties framing the [speculative] imaginings of black people" (*Afrofuturism Rising*, 2). Afrofuturism certainly offers a complex challenge to remember and reconnect a past that informs our current time and builds a future. I intend to set my "critical mirrors very carefully," as the esteemed gay, Black science fiction writer and literary critic Samuel R. Delany advises ("The Mirror," 173), by consulting the SF megatext itself for its relationships to fantastic voyages, hollow earths, lost races, and old documents that serve as doorways into the unknown and downright strange; Toni Morrison's thinking on the meaning of whiteness to American literature; and Afrofuturist theory, which in its origin through the cultural critic Mark Dery considered the work of the white William Gibson's *Neuromancer* (1984) as Afrofuturist because of vestigial Black characters, something Dery discusses in his interview with Delany himself. Otherwise, there's no such thing as an Afrofuturism that Poe could have possibly and retroactively influenced.

As previously mentioned, lots of scientific romances of the nineteenth century feature Africa as the dark continent and have a direct hand in "racing" an entire population Black. If Africa is the dark continent, it stands to reason that Antarctica is the white continent that Poe finds tarred by the Black presence of the savage Tsalalians, while Johnson finds solace in the Brown-skinned Tsalal, but only after destroying the Tekelians, reimagined as gigantic white-skinned beings that the all-Black crew of the *Creole* disparagingly dub "snow monkeys"—snow monkeys that enslaved them. They mirror the giant, shrouded, white figure at the end of Poe's *Narrative* (*Pym*, 153). To accomplish this Afrofuturist reckoning for Poe, I ask scholars to step into the "way-back machine" of a transhistorical feedback loop purposefully created by Mat Johnson to examine the deep past of a Blackness embedded in our national literature—a science-fictional Blackness marked by dislocation, trauma, and white supremacy—to move forward into a different future.

While white scholars have offered apologias aplenty for Poe's racism, they always seem to let him off the hook—a move that demands a CRT intervention in an Afrofuturist context. I deprogram the literary and social politics surrounding Poe and engage his novel to materialize whiteness as a social construct against the "blackground" of science fiction, that is to say the embedded perceptions of race and racism brought to the foreground of the genre to question its racialized structures.[2] Believe me, I have pondered condensing the Poe material to get to my analysis of Johnson's retelling all the sooner, to reposition Poe's novel in my argument, making it secondary to Johnson. But my critique of Poe and discussion of Johnson must begin with an emphasis on Poe because of Poe's underlying yet largely unexplored significance to SF.

This decision cannot be avoided because Poe's racism matters! Pointing it out and refusing to overlook it matters too! White supremacy seeks to sanitize a past it cannot possibly be proud of because it will not allow an admission of guilt with respect to the foundations of this country—a claim easily supported when considering the animosity directed toward Nikole Hannah-Jones for daring to reposition the date of our country's founding to 1619 instead of 1776.[3] If the past can't be whitewashed, then the false narrative of a post-race society, represented by the two term Barack Obama presidency, gains relevancy to white interests because it allows them to pretend an equality and ignore a painful past as if they were not responsible for slavery and Jim Crow. These trauma-inducing periods never happened!

Abracadabra!

White supremacy won't allow us a future because we do not matter to them. Afrofuturism begins here. I repeat, the estrangement of Black people in the United States begins here. Black Americans, in facing social death, must fight for a future or die. And Afrofuturism does exactly this. Black science fiction authors fight this fight. To me, the creators and upholders of race—like Poe—define it, cling to it, will kill for it out of a misguided fear of being replaced. In this respect, Johnson's satirical Afrofuturist novel—part neo-slave narrative, part science fiction, part utopia, part comedy—explores the truth of a post-racial moment that never existed in the first place with complex characters and an intricate plot taken from a past most white Americans want to forget. Many of whom would like to avoid the guilt, while simultaneously chaining Blacks to the past so they will always suffer from its remembrance, however slight.

Honestly, I never put much stock in post-race notions. Not a day goes by where the white world lets Black Americans forget their skin color. Samuel R. Delany identifies this unforgetting conscious awareness of one's Blackness as the "total surround" in his magisterial 1998 essay "Racism and Science Fiction" (391). Delany's careful wording delivers the perfect idiom of Black experience in relation to white privilege. He arrests the insidious and paradoxical nature of colorblindness in these two words, where colorblindness is seemingly, if not willfully, harmless with intent that runs contrary to Black feeling and being. It's too handy an excuse to allow indefensible social moments of white good meaning, of racism masquerading as wokeness, because it reinforces the position of the dominant race. Poe scholars use the slipperiness of colorblindness to nullify Poe's racism while also safeguarding his reputation.

So, let us stop making excuses for Poe and choose to see the racial inequities in his novel.

Poe and the SF Megatext

The culture that produced Edgar Allan Poe concurrently shaped the science fiction megatext with its tales of lost races and lost worlds, ripe for economic conquest at the advent of first contact. We *are* talking about hollow earths, unknown islands, and undiscovered lands, where these lost peoples reside, where monsters can be found, and where violence ensues, whether these places represent utopia or dystopia. "Only in a mostly *known* world does the presence of a forgotten people inhabiting a kind of Pocket Universe generate its special sf piquancy" as John Clute et al. state in *The Encyclopedia of Science Fiction* regarding this popular nineteenth-century theme that Poe adapts over the last third of the novel's twenty-five chapters. In this respect, the SF megatext provides a window allowing us to look at the culture that produced Poe in the first place and the SF to come. This vast assemblage of science fictional symbols, motifs, and images across literature, film, television, and games comprises the megatext, rather "the shared subcultural thesaurus of the genre" (Csicsery-Ronay, "Empire," 362). Readers of SF slowly but surely learn parts of the megatext by reading SF and this specialized knowledge of the megatext influences a reader's understanding of just about any SF narrative. For example, we see in Poe's novel alien encounters, evolutionary themes, strange landscapes, and pseudoscience—tropes that will have a long-lasting impact on the development of SF and that demonstrate a historical relationship to the genre and in turn its relationship to colonialism. Consequently, all lost race tales connect to Poe's novel through the megatext and Poe's contribution to SF resonates across the "vast and interconnected web of meanings that exceeds what appears in any single text" (Vint, *Science*, 57). When Johnson retells Poe's narrative through the lost race and lost world metaphors, among other things, Johnson creates an intertextual connection to the megatext whose meaning radically differs from Poe's in its Afrofuturist critique of race and racism, with Johnson's novel taking off from the final third of Poe's storyline.

But understanding Poe's science fictional roots depends on historical genre formations and the presence of science-fictional elements in his writing that involve his cultural moment. In this regard, science fiction scholar Paul Kincaid discusses a "web of resemblances" between many texts and declares that "any number of those resemblances might constitute what we would call science fiction" ("On the Origins," 416). What Kincaid means here is the beneficial comparison of similar features between texts regardless of time.

So, ahistoric comparisons of resemblances between Adam Seaborn's *Symzonia; Voyage of Discovery* (1820), an Antarctic sea-adventure quest featuring a hollow-earth, a lost land, and a lost race, and Poe's 1838 novel prove useful in establishing such connections. The "science-fictionality" of the texts provide "a mode of response that frames and tests experiences as if they were aspects of a work of science fiction" (Csicsery-Ronay Jr., *Seven Beauties*, 2). Other texts worth comparing that provide lost world entries encompassing the world's polar regions include James DeMille's *A Strange Manuscript Found in a Copper Cylinder* (1888), Edgar Rice Burroughs's *The Land That Time Forgot* (1918), and H. P. Lovecraft's *At the Mountains of Madness* (1936). That's how the megatext is built. As John Rieder explains, "Studying the beginnings of the genre" relies on "observing an accretion of repetitions, echoes, imitations, allusions, identifications, and distinctions that testifies to an emerging sense of a conventional web of resemblances" ("On Defining," 196). With this idea in mind, evolving science-fictional emblems repeat themselves "across a variety of texts throughout time, become familiar, and are then formalized in their repetition and familiarity as the genre forms from other genres like romance, gothic, horror, suspense, fantasy, or adventure tales" (Lavender, "Reframing," 21).

Consequently, it makes sense to put Poe's novel in conversation with other SF works. Poe has been associated with SF since April 1926. In the premier issue of *Amazing Stories*, the first SF pulp magazine, editor and publisher Hugo Gernsback writes, "Edgar Allan Poe may well be called the father of 'scientifiction.' It was he who really originated the romance, cleverly weaving into and around the story, a scientific thread" ("A New Sort," 3). While "scientifiction" is a mouthful to pronounce, Gernsback offers a simple definition with a list of names, "By 'scientifiction' I mean the Jules Verne, H. G. Wells, and Edgar Allan Poe type of story—a charming romance intermingled with scientific fact and prophetic vision" (3). Clarke Olney of *The Georgia Review*, agrees with Gernsback in 1958, in stating that he believes Poe "was the first writer of science-centered fiction to base his stories firmly on a rational kind of extrapolation, avoiding the supernatural" ("Edgar," 417). Likewise, in terms of Poe's position as an early science fiction writer, nineteenth-century Americanist Paul Grimstad, in a contemporary take from 2019, finds "Poe's way of bringing the tone of a rational account—the prose of explanation—into the art of fiction" to be sufficiently science fictional ("Poe," 736). In the opinion of SF historian H. Bruce Franklin, "The argument for Poe's primacy in the history of science fiction rests partly on his concern with details of physical process . . . after all, one traditional function of science fiction has been, especially since Verne, to offer entertaining fictionalizations of current scientific theory and process" (*Future*, 88). While "Poe's critics have differed as to whether he was the 'father' of science fiction or simply a 'pioneer' of the genre," SF scholar David Seed does not question if Poe belongs to the genre ("Breaking," 75). Nor do I in that Poe's writing displays various genre markings consistent with the SF megatext, such as reasoned extrapolations that feature scientific rationales of his day, as racist as they are, and vivid descriptions. My point is that Poe used themes vital to the SF megatext, establishing why he is important enough for Mat Johnson to engage.

Poe practically invents the SF thought experiment germane to hard SF to mask his racial anxiety and this fear is subsumed by his posthumous popularity elevating his writing to the status of high culture in our modern consciousness as opposed to a more pejorative label of escapism that much SF justifiably receives. I say "thought experiment" because Poe fully engages with the scientific spirit of his day. He adapts what has been rightly identified as science fictional devices with his precise nautical terminology, capturing a sense of the existing navigation technology. Poe also utilizes the recognizable hard SF techniques of extrapolation and wonder in his both careful and vivid descriptions of the lost island interior at the eighty-fourth parallel of southern latitude and its very Black people. We absolutely must read *The Narrative of Arthur Gordon Pym of Nantucket* science-fictionally to better spot its multimodal reverberation across time, to better see its prejudicial interpretation of alien Blacks and the gibberish they speak, but not without a proper understanding of Poe's racism and its place in the novel, which the *noirum* helps us to recognize.

Only then can we begin to see the brilliance of Mat Johnson's Afrofuturist retelling—in the sense that Johnson incorporates elements of Black cultural history in the near-future Antarctic setting—and what it may mean. Poe absolutely means something to Afrofuturism in that understanding the pathology of racism in the United States, if not science fiction, begins with the white literary subconscious of a young American nation. An "Africanist presence" inhabits this subconscious as the late Toni Morrison accurately surmised in her classic 1992 study *Playing in the Dark: Whiteness and the Literary Imagination* (6), where "the image of reined-in, bound, suppressed, and repressed darkness became objectified in American literature as an Africanist persona" (38–39). The racialized other has always been part of a white American identity embedded in our government and propelling an overwhelming and material white privilege—slowly transformed into a sense of colorblindness—across time from the past into the future of now. Johnson effectively wrestles with the complexity of these powerful social structures in *Pym*. Blackness matters for Poe and for Johnson; it matters for this country and for SF and certainly for Afrofuturism too.

Poe and Racism

I find it fascinating that influential white scholars of American literature only seem to identify Toni Morrison and Frederick Douglass in the context of Edgar Allan Poe. They do not cite African American literature and certainly not SF. Claims of Poe belonging to SF, beyond naming him as a founding father of the genre, fall short of the mark in this regard.[4] As Morrison herself observes, "their refusal to read black texts—a refusal that makes no disturbance in their intellectual life—repeats itself when they reread the traditional, established works of literature worthy of their attention" (*Playing*, 13). In fact, early American literature specialist John C. Havard argues, "Poe's work should not be read in terms of his personal beliefs, as we know few conclusive specifics about Poe's racial and political stances" ("'Trust,'" 107). But I can and I must. Poe's beliefs pervade his writing!

Terence Whalen, another white nineteenth-century American literature scholar, cannily apologizes for Poe's "average racism . . . not a sociological measurement of actual beliefs but rather a strategic construction designed to overcome political dissension in the emerging mass audience" ("Average," 4). This admission of guilt effectively pardons Poe. But what does "average racism" even look like? I mean, Whalen's essay begins with epigraphs from two more white dudes to frame his own argument—Samuel Taylor Coleridge and Fredric Jameson. Really? Whalen couldn't be bothered to use at least one Black critic from the twentieth century relevant to his argument. Is that an example of "average" twenty-first-century racism? What exactly does "average" mean here: common, standard, normal, typical, regular, desensitized? I face systemic racism every day in this country through longstanding inequalities and it is extraordinary in its daily occurrence. Put simply, even if Poe did intentionally yield his personal beliefs to appeal to the masses, he *is* a racist. Whalen offers a specious literary defense secure in his own whiteness. Talk about a tortured, convoluted, and unprovable reading. My incredulity abounds! As Teresa Goddu, a third nineteenth-century American literature expert, rightly points out, "to assert that Poe's racism is unexceptional within the norms of his culture must not minimize its effects. . . . Whalen's argument is in danger of foreclosing rather than reinvigorating the critical discussion on Poe and race" ("Rethinking," 17). I am happy to see that Goddu called Whalen out.

David Faflik, a fourth white expert in nineteenth-century American literature, even insinuates that antebellum readers on either side of the Mason-Dixon line ignore "Poe's grasp on sectional diversity" and that contemporary critics should also "excuse" themselves "on the grounds that we cannot possibly be alert to the intricacies of the author's life and times" ("South," 283, 284). Faflik feels that "we so risk decontextualizing *Pym* that we can no longer guess its meanings" (284). Of course, "we" can. I don't have to guess at Poe's meanings. Poe tells me exactly who he is in terms of his friendships, his daily interactions in antebellum America, and especially in his writings. Incidentally, a fifth white Americanist, John C. Rowe, is exactly right to claim that "Poe was a proslavery Southerner and should be reassessed as such in whatever approach we take to his life and writings" ("Poe," 117). These exchanges regarding Poe's racism are eye-opening indeed!

I assume nothing about Poe's racism. As Goddu indicates, "the networks of images that circulate among Poe's texts demonstrate that his characters are a collage of conventions and signal specific patterns that simultaneously exploit and deconstruct cultural formations of race" ("Rethinking," 16). "'The Devil in the Belfry,'" Goddu continues, "illuminates the way the Irish were coded as African American in the antebellum period," for example (16). It is all there to be seen on the page if a person has the right eyes to see it. If you cannot see it, you are colorblind in the sense of CRT. Being colorblind allows whites to safely "enunciate positions that safeguard their racial interests without sounding 'racist'" (Bonilla-Silva, *Racism*, 4). Like a bulletproof vest, this philosophical outlook lets whites voice antipathy to minorities without consequence and reinforces a white sense of entitlement. It is entirely dismissive of history, lived experience, and the enduring structural racism faced by people of color.

Regarding his personal relationships, Poe had a friend in Judge Nathaniel Beverly Tucker via written correspondence. Both men admired each other's work. Both men published with the *Southern Literary Messenger*, where Poe worked as a writer, critic, and eventually as its editor for a time. Poe scholars such as Bernard Rosenthal, Dana D. Nelson, and Betsy Erkkila have remarked upon a disputed review in the April 1836 issue of the magazine in relation to a couple of books on slavery, known as the "Paulding-Drayton

Review." As Rosenthal has reasoned, "only the authorship problem in regard to the Paulding-Drayton review has unnecessarily obscured Poe's pro-slavery views" ("Poe," 30). That deduction seems right to me, considering all the passes other scholars have given Poe on being a racist. "Whether or not Poe wrote the review," as Nelson indicates, "he elsewhere expressed proslavery sympathies—for instance, in his reviews of Robert Montgomery Bird's *Shepperd Lee*, Anne MacVicar Grant's *Memoires of an American Lady* . . . and particularly in his stance on works by the noted Southern defender of slavery, Thomas R. Dew" (*The Word*, 91). For my purposes in this chapter, it actually does not matter who authored the review. What matters *is* that Betsy Erkkila identifies the two as friends in stating that "Whether this review was written by Poe, as some believe, or by his friend Beverley Tucker, [it is] a defense of 'all our institutions' and 'all our rights' written from the collective point of view of the South" ("The Poetics," 57). This link seems highly relevant because of what is known about Tucker. As a law professor at William and Mary, Tucker belonged to an elite extremist group of southern pro-slavery Democrats known as the Fire-Eaters. They were secessionists and desired the South to form a new nation. Tucker has the ignominious distinction of writing the very first secession novel that advocated for race war and separation, *The Partisan Leader: A Tale of the Future* (1836).[5] As Jared Gardner states, "Poe very much curried Tucker's favor, as evidenced by an early letter in which he commended Tucker's poetry ('I sincerely think your lines excellent') and a laudatory review of *Balcombe* in the *Messenger* ('the best American novel')" (*Master*, 130). Again, it does not matter if Poe and Tucker ever met in person; their literary connection through the *Southern Literary Messenger* endorses a shared worldview. Therefore, Poe is guilty by association.

Pertaining to his daily life, Poe came across the enslaved all the time. But he also directly participated in the sale of another human being. According to esteemed Poe scholar J. Gerald Kennedy, "In December 1829, during a stay in Baltimore with his aunt, Maria Clemm, he apparently acted as her agent in the transfer of a slave named Edwin to a certain Henry Ridgway for a term of nine years" ("'Trust,'" 234). *Apparently*? There is no apparently to it. Poe's name is on the bill of sale and Kennedy shares it in Figure 2, Chapter 9 of his collection.[6] This sale by Poe of a Black person for forty dollars, ironically to an illiterate free Black person in Henry Ridgway,[7] represents the ultimate dehumanization, the ultimate racism. Incontestably, Poe was an active and knowing participant in the peculiar institution. On this evidence, it is hard to ignore that racism was a part of Poe's life as well as his work.

To drive home my point, Poe's short fiction provides plenty of evidence of his racism. Three stories feature servants and two more include animals associated with Black people. In his 1838 story "A Predicament," his female narrator, Signora Psyche Zenobia, describes her "corpulent" Negro Pompey as "three feet in height . . . about seventy, or perhaps eighty, years of age" with "bow-legs," "no neck" and "ankles (as usual with that race) in the middle of the upper portion of the feet" ("A Predicament," 151). His 1839 story "The Man That Was Used Up" contains another Negro servant named Pompey who literally puts together the body of the famous Brevet Brigadier General John A. B. C. Smith every day to the insults of "you nigger" and "black rascal" ("The Man," 366). And his 1843 story "The Gold-Bug" has the old Negro Jupiter who attends to his young "massa" William Legrand despite being manumitted and occasionally upbraided as an "infernal scoundrel" ("The Gold-Bug," 298). It seems obvious that Poe believed in racial stereotypes such as Blacks being inferior to whites. His writing demonstrates a sense of Black servility, that Blacks are meant to serve whites with a fidelity that supersedes their own health and echoes into the future. As Kennedy suggests, "Poe also understood and presumably shared widespread white attitudes about the racial inferiority of blacks" ("'Trust,'" 236). But Kennedy goes a step too far in stating that "Such assumptions so thoroughly pervaded American culture in that era as to render superfluous current efforts to identify and castigate individual purveyors of literary racism" (236). I must disagree with Kennedy's easy dismissal of a pervasive literary racism because everyone was doing it in the nineteenth century. That *is* the type of weak excuse that allows both white privilege and colorblindness to continue and denies the racial trauma of the past still impacting African Americans. By rebuking Poe on this charge, my chapter provides a sense of philosophical catharsis and late arriving social justice.

Poe's other two stories, which include primates, provide further confirmation of his blatant racism. His popular 1841 story "The Murders in the Rue Morgue" concerns the first fictional detective, C. Auguste Dupin of Paris, who solves a brutal double homicide of a mother and daughter when finding a tuft of inhuman hair belonging to the murderer, a "large fulvous Ourang-Outang" ("The Murders," 221). Poe helps to perpetuate the myth of the Black brute prevalent here in the United States despite the French setting. This harmful stereotype depicts Black men as savage, sociopathic criminals, predators who go after the helpless, particularly white women, which justifies their death at the hands of white men. I find his choice of the Orangutan clever because Poe links himself to the enlightenment beliefs of a founding father in Thomas

Jefferson, who, in Query XIV in his *Notes on the State of Virginia* (1785), compares Blacks to "the Oranootan" as a pseudoscientific measure of biological racial difference (145). Poe uses Jefferson to buttress his own conviction of white superiority and directly participates in the social construction of this damaging brute stereotype that now extends to the twenty-first century and the common acceptance of Black criminality resulting in mass incarceration, a contemporary form of slavery.

Poe uses the Orangutan image a second time in his 1849 story "Hop-Frog," in which the title character, a dwarf court jester, exacts revenge on his king for shoving to the ground his friend and fellow dwarf Trippetta in front of the king's inner circle. Hop-Frog convinces the king and his seven courtiers to dress as "the Eight Chained Ourang-Outangs" for the masquerade by saturating their garments with tar and covering them with flax ("Hop-Frog," 437). Hop-Frog somehow suspends them in midair, attaching them to a chandelier with a second chain and some kind of pulley, and burns them alive in front of the revelers before escaping with Trippetta. Poe writes, "The eight corpses swung in their chains, a fetid, blackened, hideous, and indistinguishable mass" (441). The king and his men transfigured as primates, thus Blackened up, receive their comeuppance for the attack on the white dwarf woman Trippetta. Tom F. Wright reads this moment "as a coded depiction of Southern lynching" ("Edgar," 16). And he is right in that Poe's Ourang-Outangs represent a surviving stereotype of Black male brutes from early America, except the white brutes in this imagined attack on a white woman get their due. Yet, history offers plenty of examples of unjustly accused Black males assaulting white women, like the Scottsboro Boys in Alabama or Emmett Till in Mississippi.

In a similar fashion, *The Narrative of Arthur Gordon Pym* also offers plenty of examples of Poe's racism. As Hester Blum asserts, "The scarcely-veiled racist allegories of Poe's treatment of the fictional island of Tsalal in the novel have been the most visible and most commented-upon aspects of *Arthur Gordon Pym*'s racial imaginary" ("Archipelagic," 57). Accordingly, let us examine the racist images of the Black cook Seymour and the lost race of the Tsalalians as well as the more complicated figure of Dirk Peters. First, Poe describes the cook, who seems to be in control of the *Grampus* mutiny, as a "perfect demon" standing "with an axe, striking each victim on the head as he was forced over the side of the vessel by the other mutineers . . . twenty-two perished" (*Narrative*, 478). In keeping with the brute stereotype, Poe's savage description of the bloodthirsty Black cook powerfully recalls Nat Turner's Rebellion in

Southampton, Virginia in 1831. Rowe recognizes Poe's sublimated fear of a Black uprising in this violent scene linking the evil Black cook's repeated head-smashing of the mariners "to Turner's gory use of a broadax to murder his master and the master's wife" ("Poe," 127). It *is* this irrational fear that breeds racism and white frailty and we see this in our daily news feeds with the unreasoning Republican assault on CRT because it reflects guilt and disrupts the narrative of equality for whites and no one else. Elsewhere, Rowe states: "Like the black cook in the mutiny in *Pym*, the orangutan in 'The Murders in the Rue Morgue' enacts a fantasy of slave insurrection loosely tied to Southern white hysteria regarding Nat Turner's Southampton insurrection in 1831 and the more general anxiety of antebellum Southerners that the immoral system of slavery might well provoke bloody revolution" ("Imperial Fantasy," 99). The demonic cook and the savage orangutan clearly manifest Poe's own racism as he sensationalizes a timeless white American fear in this mutiny—a fear of an artificially constructed otherness that threatens white hegemony and consumption, a fear of a Black planet, an Afrofuturist spacetime, that we see a second time in the novel too.

When we encounter the Blackest of Black people, the lost race on the imaginary island of Tsalal, in the farthest south possible, the Antarctic, Poe's racism becomes discernable again. Consider Poe's account of a seeming first contact between the crew of the *Jane Guy* and the Tsalalians: "when the strangers made a full stop, and commenced a loud jabbering all at once, intermingled with occasional shouts, in which we could distinguish the words *Anamoo-moo!* and *Lama-Lama!* They continued this for at least half an hour, during which we had a good opportunity of observing their appearance" (*Narrative*, 563). This first meeting of two different human groups trying to communicate establishes Poe's racializing alien metaphor. Readers do not actually know that the strangers are Black yet, but their "loud jabbering" represents another Black stereotype of being loud, where Poe is pathologizing his cultural values with respect to communication by equating Black speech sounds to bothersome inarticulate noise. I very much doubt antebellum whites would want to hear Black people whispering because of the white paranoia over racial insurrection. Slaves, who wanted to survive, adapted this communication style. Poe dismisses the Tsalalians as an intelligent species here because of their abrasive, nonsensical noise. Ironically, such noisemaking gets Black people killed, the ultimate silencing of a white construction of alien-ness. The actual words uttered—"*Anamoo-moo!* and *Lama-Lama!*"—represent Poe's notion of an inferior intelligence with these nonsensical verbalizations. These people sound uneducated and Poe denies kinship to them because of the unintelligible syllabics. As Morrison states, "We need to explicate the ways in which specific themes, fears, forms of consciousness, and class relationships are embedded in the use of Africanist idiom: how the dialogue of black characters is construed as an alien, estranging dialect made deliberately unintelligible by spellings contrived to disfamiliarize it; how Africanist language practices are employed to evoke the tension between speech and speechlessness; how it is used to establish a cognitive world split between speech and text, to reinforce class distinctions and otherness as well as to assert privilege and power" (*Playing*, 52). Thus, Poe renders them effectively inhuman, if not alien, at which point communication becomes impossible. The Tsalalians cannot speak for themselves, unfavorably determining what constitutes humanity through cultural and racial difference generated by a nascent American imperialism. Poe flexes his authority as a white man in this rendering of the alien Blacks from a CRT perspective that fully demonstrates the strength of racism in early America. Mat Johnson sees fit to challenge Poe's demonstrable racism, which produces disorientation and trauma in Black readers of Poe's novel, a feeling of science-fictional Blackness typical of Afrofuturism generated by the reading experience itself.

And then we learn about their skin color!

After first hearing them, we finally see the strange humans. Poe identifies them as "savages" of "about the ordinary stature of Europeans, but of a more muscular and brawny frame. Their complexion a jet black, with thick and long wooly hair" (563). Like Kennedy says, "One cannot deny the racial fear and loathing" on display because of "Poe's relentless attention in the closing chapters to race," which "confirm an inveterate prejudice" ("'Trust,'" 242–243). This moment recalls, for me at least, Jefferson's thoughts on white beauty in terms of "flowing hair, a more elegant symmetry of form, [and an apparent Black] judgment in favour of whites" (*Notes*, 145). Poe deliberately frames his Tsalalian in contrast to Jefferson's idealization of whites to make them ugly and inferior in terms of nature as if they are a different species entirely. Tsalalian "lips . . . were thick and clumsy" and their teeth were black as well (570). In fact, Poe, as the fictional editor, stresses that "Nothing *white* was to be found at Tsalal, and nothing otherwise in the subsequent voyage to the region beyond" and that the Tsalalians must surely be a lost Ethiopian, Arabic, or Egyptian race because of the verbal roots of the markings in the crevasses (606). As Kennedy notes, "Poe insinuates through mysterious inscriptions in the chasm where Pym takes refuge the apocryphal notion that the Tsalaians compose one of the lost tribes of Israel—the sons of Ham doomed to bondage because of their black skin" (*Strange*, 305). What a fascinating leap! So, why then does the author Poe go to such extreme lengths to symbolize Blackness through narrator Poe?

This racism implanted so deeply into the very fabric of American consciousness, irrespective of time, becomes invisible, exceedingly malleable, and supremely resistant to social pressure to end inequality, and the only thing expected from the Black community is silence. That *is* a clear sign of Poe's demonic genius in exercising allegorical power with his writing to prioritize the category of whiteness and its intended and lasting privilege. Perhaps, this artistry is also why "many liberals believe in colorblindness and neutral principles of constitutional law" (Delgado and Stefancic, *Critical*, 26). Paying attention to Poe's racist descriptions, watching them take root in the American psyche as white dominance, and seeing how these commonplace ideas continue to circulate in society today as pseudoscientific beliefs, requires a trans-historic feedback loop, where we can confront the real history of Black trauma in science-fictional terms, resist the negative images, and create an ahistoric overload by placing white people, such as Edgar Allan Poe, inside race that results in a change of who controls the cultural codes of skin color in order to create the future itself. That's Afrofuturism at work.

Poe also engages in pseudoscience to encourage the fiction of race used by white Americans to further exploit colored peoples. Correspondingly, the figure of Dirk Peters takes center stage. The description provided of Peters fits with Poe's earlier descriptions of the enslaved negroes: "He was short in stature—not more than four feet eight inches high—but his limbs were of the most Herculean mould. His hands, especially, were so enormously thick and broad as hardly to retain a human shape. His arms, as well as legs, were *bowed* in the most singular manner, and appeared to possess no flexibility whatever. His head was equally deformed, being of immense size, with an indentation on the crown (like that on the head of most negroes)" (479). Poe most certainly would have been aware of the racial science of his day and works it into his novel. Samuel George Morton's *Crania Americana* comes out a year after Poe's novel in 1839, and in it Morton claims that whites had the largest brains, Blacks the smallest, and Indians somewhere in the middle; the book supports all manner of racial stereotypes still used by the far-right today.[8] In all likelihood, the two men must have known each other. They were pictured together in the earliest known photograph of the inside of the museum at the Academy of Natural Sciences in Philadelphia during the winter of 1842/1843.[9]

Nonetheless, Poe truly believed in the physical differences between Blacks and whites, placing Black people at the bottom of the human ladder. For instance, phrenology was prevalent in this time period across Europe and in antebellum America. This pseudoscience involves the prediction of mental attributes, based on the physical measurements of the skull and its shape. This long-discredited belief system adapts scientific nomenclature to justify racism. Medical ethicist Harriet A. Washington writes that phrenology "involved determining personality (including a propensity to violence) by interpreting the shape of the head" (*Medical*, 153). Washington continues: "Scientists compared the values for various races and each 'found' the lowest intelligence in blacks. Furthermore, each detailed numeric was determined to be static and immutable" (153). In this regard, the "deformed" head of Peters "with an indentation on the crown" would suggest that he was a violent Black man and this characteristic is unassailable. Rowe makes a similar connection: "And yet Dirk Peters shares physical characteristics with Poe's Black characters, such as the 'bowed' legs and 'deformed' head" ("Imperial Fantasy," 85). And Havard opines, "This description reflects how racial science categorized physical difference according to racial type, thus signaling Pym's assumption of such an outlook" ("'Trust,'" 110–111). Poe once "wrote in the *Messenger* in 1836," as stated by Gardner, that "The study of heads and skulls . . . 'as a science, ranks among the most important which can engage the attention of thinking beings'" (*Master*, 134). Clearly influenced by the racial science of his day, Poe engages in pseudoscientific pandering on Black character and emotion in his lost race adventure.

Yet Pym tells us that Peters is an Upsaroka Indian as opposed to being a Black man. Pym imparts this key bit of information about Peters's parentage even before the phrenological account that includes the sailor's mother being "an Indian squaw of the tribe of Upsarokas" and his father "a fur-trader, I believe, or at least connected in some manner with the Indian trading-posts on Lewis river" (479). What I find interesting here is that Pym has no idea about the race, ethnicity, or nationality of Peters's father. "The real anxiety in *Pym*," writes Jeffrey Weinstock, "is not over racial difference but rather over the *possible elision of that difference*" ("Tekeli-li!," 55). It could be that the "ambiguous nature of the hybrid body" best represents Poe's own racial unease (Edwards, *Gothic*, 7). As Goddu remarks, "Reading race through the cipher of Poe is useful not merely because it gives insight into the author's particular political position or racial psychology but because it illuminates a wide range of antebellum cultural configurations that intersect with slavery and race" ("Rethinking," 15). I find this point interesting because it is roughly ninety years before the supposed "one-drop rule" neatens up racial boundaries. Whites of Poe's generation would be familiar with grades of Blackness and the idea that those grades make a difference. So, Peters is of a mixed-race background—he could be part white or he could be part Black (and Johnson explores the idea of his Blackness quite extensively and convincingly in his retelling).

But in keeping with early American social mores, Peters's racial designation should come through matrilineal descent, that is until Pym bestows whiteness upon Peters after they are the only survivors of the rockslide ambush orchestrated by the Tsalalians. Pym remarks that "we were the only living white men upon the island" (582). This remarkable transformation from racial other to white man occurs because of the incredible duress Pym faces. Pym exerts his power to appraise and fix the physical appearance of Peters in terms of racial formation optics "under great pressure and with speed" because of the danger the Tsalalians represent (Omi and Winant, *Racial*, 114). He metaphorically makes Peters into a white person because of the violent trap sprung by the Black Tsalalians, a clear result of the situation. After all, Peters wears "a wig formed of any hair-like material" from "a Spanish dog or American grizzly bear" that "added no little to the natural ferocity of his countenance" (479). This inverted description of Peters evokes the "tuft of inhuman hair" from the "Ourang-Outang" in "The Murders in the Rue Morgue." It further animalizes him, Blackens him, races his body physically.

Consequently, the stunning deracination of Peters, his makeover into a member of the white race, irrespective of his brutishness, seems somewhat fantastical. Pym acknowledges this sentiment himself "in speaking of Dirk Peters" since his "narrative . . . in its latter portions, will be found to include incidents of a nature so entirely out of the range of human experience, and for this reason so far beyond the limits of human credulity" (479). And the Peters transformation into a white man is one of them! As Weinstock contends, "The shift from 'half-breed' to 'white man' symbolizes the slippage of the racial signifier as, in comparison with the blackness of the islanders, Peters becomes whitened" ("Tekeli-li!," 55–56). And it is exactly this slippage that produces a social *noirum*. Pym also attempts to anchor this token whiteness by "trusting in time and progressing science to verify some of the most important and most improbable of [his] statements" (479). Pym metaphorically removes the pathological stamp of Peters's race in granting him a normalized white skin color.

The conferring of this social and political personhood, as it were, has nothing to do with nineteenth-century science. It has nothing to do with Peters's body. This unmaking of Peters's otherness not only occurs in an ontological context, but in a temporal sense too, in that Poe grapples with the changes occurring in his own time period. The truth of Peters's race "makes use of eighteenth-century theories of racialization that assumed one's racial status to be a reaction to circumstances" (Chiles, *Transformable*, 215). It's still mutable before nineteenth-century race scientists like "George Cuvier, Samuel George Morton, Dr. Josiah Nott, and George R. Gliddon . . . develop . . . full-blown scientific racism" based on traits "emanating outward from the body's interior" (Chiles, *Transformable*, 208). As Robyn Wiegman suggests, "The move from the visible epidermal terrain to the articulation of the interior structure of human bodies thus extrapolated in both broader and more distinct terms the parameters of white supremacy, giving it a logic lodged fully in the body" (*American Anatomies*, 31). Thus, Poe merely articulates, or perhaps accentuates, his obviously racist beliefs about Black inferiority in this conversion. As Nelson suggests, in "acknowledging the racist dimension of Poe's work . . . we must at least consider the cultural work performed *now* by masking that aspect of his work" (*The Word*, 92). In this reconsideration, many contemporary Poe scholars have shrewdly helped to place Poe and his writings outside the brand of racism, essentially giving him a pass to shut down the conversation regarding Poe's prejudicial thoughts as a great early author of American fiction. Make no mistake, Poe *is* great but also racist with "quite visible" opinions in that "he supported slavery both as a southerner and as an individual" (Gardner, *Master*, 129).

Returning to the Tsalalians, Poe creates a never-before-seen Black race. But why? Sure, Poe certainly tries to earn "a living by his pen" as Weinstock surmises, "and thus may have been willing to play to his audience's prejudices" ("Tekeli-li!," 53). Still, the fact remains that he did mine the social anxieties prevalent among whites concerning Blacks. He did and it was baleful in that it has proved harmful to race relations into the present and foreseeable future in exploiting, justifying, and popularizing racial stereotypes. It is really not as complicated as some Poe scholars would have you believe with regard to "Poe's calculating approach to the mass literary market" (Whalen, *Edgar*, 33). While the Tsalalians are called savages from the start, Pym thinks it "quite evident that they have never before seen any of the white race—from whose complexion, indeed, they appeared to recoil" (564). Just a few moments later, Pym somewhat disdainfully dismisses them as ignorant because "they believed the Jane to be a living creature" (564). This initial meeting between the races powerfully reminds me of the first time Olaudah Equiano sees white people, albeit on a slave ship, which Equiano describes as "a world of bad spirits" that "were going to kill" him in his evocation of the alien encounter motif (*Interesting*, 57). In a precursor to colonialism, Captain Guy and his crew are fully prepared to exploit the Tsalalians and their land "in the hope of making a profitable speculation" (565). Hereof, Poe's novel, like other early SF stories, exemplifies "the fantasy of appropriation that operates in adventure-oriented lost-race fiction" (Rieder, *Colonialism*, 50). This desire to take advantage of the Tsalalians becomes overwhelmingly apparent when their chief Too-wit gazes into a mirror for the first time and cringes from his own Black reflection, dehumanizing himself in the eyes of the white crew, as an unconscious projection of internalized racism, of the Black inferiority that Poe directly puts into his audience's collective mind.

Poe helps to build the racial structures of the United States, if not the world, by choosing to place whiteness outside of a racial context, supporting a false consciousness of superiority that codes social reality across time. We begin to see the construction of whiteness as invisible and its place in Afrofuturism insofar as it shapes a pliable yet stiff racial caste system that Black people resist through an emancipatory mindscape impelled in their counter-stories to white oppression in an enduring cultural war. Along these lines, "No Poe text," as Kennedy remarks, "uses blackness more tellingly than [*The Narrative of Arthur Gordon*] *Pym* to elucidate whiteness as a racial construction" (*Strange*, 303). Poe has designed motifs that privilege whiteness in his racialization of the Tsalalians to such an extent that he cannot see them himself. Pym reflects this estimation. For example, "Pym displays his own mistrust of and hatred for the black natives," according to Weinstock, "he simply cannot imagine a reciprocal fear and loathing triggered by whiteness" ("Tekeli-li!," 63). Of course, we later learn in the novel that the affable Tsalalians are not as naive as they appear and are right to fear whiteness as demonstrated by their dread of "harmless [white] objects—such as the schooner's sails, an egg, an open book, or a pan of flour" (565). Poe subconsciously projects his own fear of a Black uprising in the antebellum South when the Tasalalians strike first and strike decisively in their ambush of the crew. And I am not alone in having this thought.[10] Pym perceives their violent action as deceitful and expresses this idea in unambiguous language: "From everything I could see of these wretches, they appeared to be the most wicked, hypocritical, vindictive, bloodthirsty, and altogether fiendish race of men upon the face of the globe" (600). The Tsalalians react to these white sailors "by plotting to murder the encroaching, imperialist whites" (Davis, "Follies," 25).

This lost Black race proves its own mettle in its desire to live and thrive without interference from the imperial whims of a West that it does not even know exists. Importantly, Poe offers us a kind of "reverse colonization narrative," whereby he asks his audience "to imagine themselves on the receiving end of colonial occupation . . . under attack from hostile forces" (Higgins, *Reverse*, 16). Put another way, Pym and Peters have been victimized over the last third of the novel as the *Jane Guy* crew gets wiped out by the Tsalalians. If only for a moment, Poe crucially articulates a sense of white victimhood that aligns with today's alt-right in its misappropriation of minority suffering to justify white supremacy and continued material benefits. Through such skewed racial tensions—their immensity echoing across time in our literature and in our social politics—Poe unwittingly contributes to the newly emerging Afrofuturist megatext with his failed colonization story steeped in early SF tropes. In other words, the alien encounter with a lost race in a strange Antarctic landscape *is* very much a part of the literary mulch from which the Afrofuturist megatext happens, a kind of palimpsest related to SF and modernity through slavery and colonialism reflecting a Black resistance.

Obviously, there is nothing wrong with Black people that *isn't* wrong with other racial groups and, as such, an Afrofuturist reading liberates Poe's text in *seeing* the racial stereotypes, discrimination, and oppression promoted across the 185 years of this novel's existence in the lifetime of the United States of America. "No early American writer is more important to the concept of American Africanism than Poe" according to Morrison (*Playing*, 32). And she is absolutely correct about the crucial role Poe's *Narrative of Arthur Gordon Pym* plays in the seemingly permanent construction of race in American consciousness. In keeping with Kodwo Eshun's notion that Afrofuturists perform as "archeologists" in reconstructing memories from this past, a past that wants to be forgotten, "it has been necessary to assemble countermemories that contest the colonial archive" ("Further," 287, 288). Mat Johnson excavates this past with his extraordinarily imaginative retelling of Dirk Peters by transforming him back into a Black man. "Johnson recenters Peters and white supremacy from the periphery to the core of any retelling of Arthur Gordon Pym's adventures" because of such powerful digging (Blum, "Archipelagic," 62). Indeed, Johnson accesses the transhistorical feedback loop—the cause-and-effect of Black experience threaded in and out of time—to create a Black picture of Peters from the racist fragments of Poe's antebellum moment and brings it forward into our twenty-first-century moment to indict the many harms of racism and to safeguard the work of science fiction in promoting the possibility of social change in this counter-story.

Johnson, Megatexts, and Passing

With Dirk Peters recast as a Black man of mixed-race descent and so used as a link between texts of different eras, Johnson pulls Poe and his novel into contemporary SF and Afrofuturist circles. While Poe imparts a bit of gravitas to SF through his combination of racial science and speculation, Johnson satirizes the racist assumptions of Poe in this critique of racial passing and colorism by inscribing the Afrofuturist iconography of *Pym* in this anachronistic comparison. Racial science functions as the anachronism, as I see it, because it has long been disproven yet remains harmful as a thing out of place in the twenty-first-century United States. Racial science wrongly enables social concepts such as racial passing to exist wherein the *noirum* functions in contravention to the one-drop rule.

In simple terms, racial passing means the ability of a Black person to pass for a white person. In SF, passing would be the ability of a robot or artificial intelligence to appear human enough to fool humans. But for Afrofuturism, passing represents a hackable skin technology in response to nineteenth-century racial science, enabling a Black person to go completely unnoticed by any white person, particularly those in power, exploiting the weaknesses of the American racial caste system by deeply manipulating the "social codes pertaining to black bodies" (Lavender, *Afrofuturism Rising*, 97). Hence, Johnson combines the absurd logics of racial science and social codes in his recreation of Dirk Peters, allowing Peters to escape his race. Both SF and Afrofuturism make claims on this imagery through skin color, where the familiar is made strange to help us see our world in a new way.

Let me further illustrate my point through the Afrofuturist megatext with examples of passing from George S. Schuyler and Ishmael Reed. Dr. Junius Crookman invents a three-day-long skin-lightening process that allows Black people to leave race behind in Schuyler's satire *Black No More* (1931). Similarly, if conversely, Ishmael Reed employs blackface minstrelsy in *Mumbo Jumbo* (1972) when the white antagonist Hinckle Von Vampton creates the Talking Android—having a white underling "black up" by applying black grease paint to face and hands—to nearly persuade the upper tier of Black society of their own inferiority. Both of these celebrated Black writers recognize that "Passing had been one of a limited number of strategies that opened doors for African Americans to participate more fully in American life" (Hobbs, "Passing," 44). "For most," as Mark Minch-de Leon has noted, "to be human (and the political projects performed in its name) continues to be a desired thing" ("Race," 209). And Black people, their humanity long negated, are no different in this desire.

On the one hand, Schuyler knows the importance of America's racial obsession and uses Black-to-white passing to scathingly critique a social culture built on the chromatic distinctions of skin. On the other hand, Reed melds together SF and African American iconographies in the Talking Android's white-to-Black passing to show how far whites would go to maintain their privilege thus indicting the foolishness of racism in the United States. In both novels, then, the satirical function of passing demonstrates how race is socially constructed from "an ongoing, contradictory, self-reinforcing process subject to the macro forces of social and political struggle and the micro effects of daily decisions" (Haney López, "Social," 7). Thus, both of these Black authors participate in the further development of the Afrofuturist megatext. While they are not recognized SF writers per se, they utilize the sense of "double estrangement"—the juxtaposition of Darko Suvin's definition of SF as cognitive estrangement[11] with W. E. B. Du Bois's notion of double consciousness[12]—that Joy Sanchez-Taylor theorizes as the historical understanding of "science fiction authors of color" that "they have been the 'other' or 'alien' depicted in science fiction" (*Diverse*, 7). Schuyler niftily exploits the trope of the mad (Black) scientist[13] and Reed ironically applies the android theme, aka the manlike machine, to race,[14] reworking these SF motifs through racial passing to metaphorically tap into the experience of racial alienation. Clearly, Johnson joins this long-established Black satirical tradition in *Pym* through the passing-for-white Peters.

Johnson cleverly grants Peters a Black makeover through the discovery of a lost and shabby manuscript sold by the book purveyor Oliver Benjamin to the failed Black professor of African American literature Chris Jaynes. This discovery mirrors many lost world and lost race narratives in the SF megatext, prompting a fantastic voyage to an unknown land because of an old document like a book or a map. For example, Professor Otto Liedenbrock finds a piece of parchment in a twelfth-century Icelandic book, which leads to the incredible expedition into a hollow prehistoric Earth, in Jules Verne's classic *Journey to the Center of the Earth* (1864). With respect to the African continent, Allan

Quartermain acquires a mysterious map written in the blood of a Portuguese explorer that reveals the location of vast wealth in H. Rider Haggard's *King Solomon's Mines* (1885). Professor Ludwig Horace Holly along with his ward Leo Vincey venture to the lost African kingdom of Kôr, populated by a lost cannibal race known as the Amahagger, ruled by the apparently immortal African queen Ayesha because they find Greek writing on a potshard locked in an iron box bequeathed to Leo from his dead father, which he is to open on his twenty-fifth birthday, in Haggard's *She* (1887). Remarkably, Pauline E. Hopkins contributes an African American entry into this lost world genre with *Of One Blood: Or, the Hidden Self* (1903), featuring the lost mulatto heirs of the lost African kingdom of Telassar. The white passing Harvard medical student Reuel Briggs has a lotus-lily birthmark that serves as a genetic map linking him to the throne. While there are no maps of unchartered territories leading to Tsalal in Poe's novel, there *is* lost territory with a lost race in his proto SF. Johnson's inclusion of the missing and unknown Peters manuscript is a stroke of genius that allows Johnson to cement Poe in the Afrofuturism megatext by following a broad science fiction pattern and picking up where Poe left off.

While Johnson's novel clearly belongs to both megatexts as a genre work, it also fits well within the neo-slave narrative tradition best represented by Ernest J. Gaines's *The Autobiography of Miss Jane Pittman* (1971), Octavia E. Butler's *Kindred* (1979), and, of course, Toni Morrison's *Beloved* (1987). Bernard W. Bell first devises the phrase "neoslave narrative" without the hyphen in 1987 to describe contemporary Black writers as "fabulators" who "combine elements of fable, legend, and slave narrative to protest racism and justify the deeds, struggles, migrations, and spirit of black people" (*Afro-American*, 285). Further developing Bell's definition, Ashraf H. A. Rushdy adds a hyphen to neo-slave narrative, perhaps signaling a twenty-first-century move toward personhood for enslaved Blacks, and explains that the genre represents "contemporary novels that assume the form, adopt the conventions, and take on the first-person voice of the antebellum slave narrative" (*Neo-Slave*, 3). Thus, Black authors of today benefit from the transhistorical feedback loop to comment on current racial politics in the United States by largely adhering to the structure of actual slave narratives and offering further resistance to oppression.

With respect to these powerful counter-stories, neo-slave narratives have political agency within CRT. They force white people to deal with the ongoing trauma of chattel slavery. That is exactly why we see the erroneous backlash in grade school about the supposed teaching of CRT to young people whose parents seem unwilling to acknowledge America's racist past and its influence on the present regarding inequality in our social and political institutions created by a colorblind ideology. Heaven forbid a divisive concept be taught in school to spare white feelings for past transgressions. Johnson's Chris Jaynes refuses to be the token negro on the diversity committee to help it look diverse and tries to find "the answer to why we have failed to truly become a postracial society" by going "to the source . . . the pathology of whiteness" represented by Poe instead of teaching minority literature (14). Essentially, Chris is denied tenure for this reason.

Johnson's novel clearly fits the neo-slave-narrative paradigm. Much like the engraved frontispiece of Frederick Douglass's 1845 slave narrative, Johnson takes a moment to reflect on the cover of the Peters manuscript. Chris describes the image of the man on the hand-stitched cover as "the etching of a pale man, mulatto by feature and skin tone: his hair hinting at the slightest kink, thin lips betrayed by a wide nose and the high West African cheekbones" (38). And then Chris reads the title: "The True and Interesting Narrative of Dirk Peters. Coloured Man. As Written by Himself" (38). Johnson borrows from "the conventions for slave narratives [that] were so early and so firmly established" as "a sort of master outline drawn from the great narratives" such as *Narrative of the Life of Frederick Douglass, An American Slave: Written by Himself* and *The Interesting Narrative of the Life of Olaudah Equiano, or Gustavus Vassa, the African, Written by Himself* in 1789 (Olney, "Edgar," 50). Johnson uses the first two conventions identified by James Olney—"an engraved portrait" and "a title page that includes the claim, as an integral part of the title, 'Written by Himself'"—to give the "true" narrative of Peters the feel of authenticity ("Edgar," 50). Of course, we recognize the irony in Chris's acceptance of this fictional account as being true in the storyworld. "Coloured Man" is another important part of the title because it establishes the Blackness of Dirk Peters while simultaneously divorcing him from his race and granting him personhood through this more inclusive term in the United States. In other words, he's not using "slave" or "African" to describe his status or experiences in the imaginary nineteenth-century world where slavery thrives in the Americas. Accordingly, it might be more proper to think of the Dirk Peters narrative as a fictional antebellum Black memoir, since Peters claimed to be a free Black man. As a final point, the date of the Peters manuscript's publication—1837—situates the text in the early days of the abolitionist movement, not to mention that it is dated a full year before Pym's own account of their journey.

This painstaking attention to historical detail on Johnson's part creates the fictional world that draws its audience inside history asymmetrically with time a bit out of joint, thus, granting Johnson's novel both a science fictional and Afrofuturistic feel of unfamiliarity, tapping into white and Black anxieties in his social commentary on the racial optics of passing. Racial prejudice has deeply impacted American history, culture, and literature, and Johnson's Afrofuturistic engagement with this traumatic past of racial difference draws on the moments of hope reflected in the slave narratives of Douglass, Equiano, Mary Prince, Solomon Northup, and Harriet Jacobs,[15] all mentioned in Johnson's *Pym*, which, in turn, produces the optimism that sends the character Chris to Antarctica in the present, in search of a Black utopia, free of whites, free of race, free simply to be.

In the novel, Chris eagerly purchases this manuscript upon learning that Dirk Peters actually existed, irrespective of his race, corroborating the veracity of Poe's novel and "Tsalal, the great undiscovered African Diasporan homeland . . . uncorrupted by whiteness," just waiting to be found (39). He hopes to repair his tarnished academic reputation and earn scholarly fame, as well as make a fortune in Antarctica by enlisting the aid of his best friend, Garth Frierson, and his cousin, Booker Jaynes. As African American comparative literature scholar Jennifer M. Wilks contends, "Poe's Peters eventually ascends to whiteness toward the end of the *Narrative*, when Pym describes the two of them as 'the only living white men upon the island' after the Tsalalians attack the *Jane Guy* crew, so Johnson's version (of Peters) gradually inhabits blackness over the course of Chris's analysis" of the book manuscript ("'Black,'" 7). This remarkable transformation of Dirk Peters from Native American to white to Black across the two novels represents a singular description of literary passing. The passing metaphor, and its mythology, matter here because it "marks the transgression of, and thus lays bare, the paradox of unequal entitlements in the land of equality" (Elam, *The Souls*, 118). It generates social anxiety in white people with respect to the performance of identity as a means of integration. Likewise, it generates social anxiety in Black people who fear the consequences of being caught in the act of passing. Most people would say that being "perceived" as white in America is certainly better because there are no limits. Yet, even with "a desire to escape racial limits," as Marcia Alesan Dawkins reflects on the paradox of passing, "we cannot imagine living without racial selves" (*Clearly Invisible*, 152). Along these lines, Johnson adapts Poe's characters and repurposes Poe's only novel to advance his own political critique of racism, its injustice, and its various harms in his Afrofuturist satire.

Chris *is* so entirely convinced of his identifying Peters as a Black man that Chris digs deeper, looking for the progeny of Peters to further verify his discovery before revealing the news of Poe's *Narrative of Arthur Gordon Pym* being a genuine account. But he won't ever have the chance to out Peters as the novel goes on because of the unspecified apocalypse back in the known world. Nonetheless, Chris tracks down the only living descendant of Peters, the racially conflicted Mahalia Mathis, who has in her possession a precious letter from Edgar Allan Poe asking Peters "to stop harassing" him, thus authenticating the Dirk Peters *Narrative* (50). Mathis agrees to make a photocopy of the letter only if Chris will accompany her to a club meeting that will confirm her own whiteness. In essence, both Mathis and Peters "take such great pains to pass—to curate and edit selves for public consumption" that they do not care about maintaining privacy and do not care about being seen as long as they have a witness in terms of the DNA test she will later take and the narrative (Dawkins, "Passing," 138). They directly adapt a fluidity of personhood across the socially constructed American color spectrum through time because of the privilege and power that passing for white grants for those bold enough to perform identity. Thus, it seems that Dirk Peters and his descendant Mahalia Mathis invest their own racial identities in whiteness, internalizing their own racism, attempting to transcend their Black flesh by manipulating social codes.

This inverted skin hacking damages the sense of Black identity for Peters and his descendants, temporarily short-circuiting the Black networked consciousness, a shared experience of race and racism. It corrupts the trans-historic feedback loop—communal memories and traditions developed from a painful Black past, which connect the present and future in confronting this past, to drive social change forward—that Blacks have utilized across time to survive in America as the future unfolds. This Black experience appears untranslatable to most white people because of the pervasive nature of colorblindness, which allows race to continually function as a social barrier. As law professor Neil Gotanda indicates, "race is considered a legitimate and proper means of classifying Americans" and "the practice of using race as a commonly recognized social divider has remained almost constant" ("A Critique," 258). Peters internalizes the value of his white appearance in classifying himself not Black in the book title but mulatto. In fact, the portrayal of Peters from the book cover with slightly kinky hair, a wide nose, and high West African cheekbones causes Chris Jaynes to label Peters as an "identity-denying" "Uncle Tom" (61, 63). Ironically, Chris calls Peters a racial sellout by comparing him to the fictional slave from Harriet Beecher Stowe's bestselling novel *Uncle Tom's Cabin; or, Life Among the Lowly* (1852). Such a stereotype has defined self-hatred in African American culture for generations. Likewise, Peters demonstrates an extreme aversion for the Black Tsalalians in his narrative. Upon first encountering them, Peters writes, "Going further south, we came to an island full of niggers. Niggers just everywhere, black as night. More niggers than I could count" (61). He uses this racial slur seven times in one of the few paragraphs that Chris shares with us from the narrative about the journey.[16] Clearly, Peters *is* color struck and he channels this kind of internalized racism onward to his descendants.

Johnson gives us a powerful and satirical counter-storytelling moment in his address of colorism in challenging this concept subconsciously held by a majority of African Americans. By colorism, I mean skin tone discrimination within the African American community by the Black community itself, prizing a lighter skin color over a darker one, among other physical features, which plays out in terms of beauty, marriage, education, politics, and so on. Colorism, in effect, perfectly replicates the structures of racism and functions as another automatic mechanism of control instilled during slavery. This normalized form of racism allows the maintenance of the status quo of oppression by whites with Blacks discriminating against themselves to the further benefit of whites.

We see this trans-historic corruption more strongly in Mahalia Mathis than in her forebear when Chris seeks to authenticate *The True and Interesting Narrative of Dirk Peters*. When talking to Chris over the phone, Mathis describes herself as being of "Greek, Hopi, Crow, Blackfoot, Chinese, and Danish descent" (46). This claim of being almost everything but Black causes Chris to do a double take, looking back at his "computer screen to look at the image of the Negro" on the other end of the phone line (46). As Wilks points out, "their first conversation reveals a clear disconnect between their respective interpretations of her racial identity" ("'Black,'" 7). Mathis does acknowledge an insubstantial raced background. However, this recognition occurs through "the 'dirty glass' of human perception, of the human gaze that sees and categorizes people according to perceived skin color" (Cutter, "Why," 50). It does not matter how or what Chris sees in her flesh because Peters has long ago created the filtered racial experience of his ancestors that entangles hypocrisy with a self-directed pain and injustice across history by flipping the color hierarchy. Mathis faints when she reads the results of her DNA test: "Two percent Native. Twenty-three percent European. Seventy-five percent

African" (56). Mathis's racial identity has been built upon a lie just like all the other members of her club, "The Native American Ancestry Collective of Gary" (52). These people have been othered but not in the way they thought as they formed their communal reality on an invented indigeneity as opposed to race. Mathis and her friends trust family history more than science and have a rude awakening with the subversion of their racial identities.

Johnson goes further with his counternarrative on colorism in terms of his protagonist Chris Jaynes. After Chris meets the actual Arthur Gordon Pym living among the Tekelians, Chris takes a moment to claim his own Blackness, since Pym mistakes him for a white man in the Tekelian homeland looking to trade his shipmates as slaves. Chris tell us:

> I am a mulatto in a long line of mulattoes, so visibly lacking in African heritage that I often appear to some uneducated eyes as a random, garden-variety white guy. But I'm not. My father was white, yes. But it doesn't work that way. My mother was a woman, but that doesn't make me a woman either. Mandatory ethnic signifiers in summary: my hair is fairly straight, the curl loose and lazy; my skin lacks melanin—there are some Italians out there darker than me. My lips are full and my nose is broad, but it's really just the complexion and hair that count. *Octoroon* would have been the antebellum word for me. Let me be more clear, since some people can't get their heads around it even when I stand before them: I am a black man who looks white. (135)

While Chris could pass for white easily, he chooses not to ignore his heritage as a matter of biology. Instead, he embraces it and "learn[s] to talk blacker, walk blacker" rather than "be rejected as other forever" after being bullied in sixth grade by other Black middle-schoolers (137). Chris chooses to preserve his connection to his community at a young age and dives into African American literature to anchor his identity and reject the racial ambiguity that Mathis coveted. He will not victimize himself as a tragic mulatto belonging to neither race completely; He attempts to decenter whiteness in his investigation and teaching of early American literature, including Poe, in his possessed hunt for "the intellectual source of racial Whiteness" (8) and in his deeply unpopular course "'Dancing with the Darkies: Whiteness in the Literary Mind'" (7),[17] and he hopes to find his own Afrotopia in Tsalal, a Black place free of racism and white influence, after learning Poe's novel is in fact a true story—meaning Tsalal is a real place. As Julie A. Fiorelli puts it, "The possible truth of Poe's text implies the existence of Tsalal, where Chris dreams of finding a racial homeland free of the history of trans-Atlantic slavery" ("Against," 222). In general, then, Johnson wittily engages with persistent political and social issues stemming from racial constructions as he ironizes and critiques skin color, among other things. Consequently, Chris Jaynes's hacking of the racial social codes in *The True and Interesting Narrative of Dirk Peters*, disrupts, if not compromises, Poe's novel and its influence on America, science fiction, and race, proving its influence on the Afrofuturist megatext.

Antarctica, the Lost White Race, Slavery, and Fugitivity

Pym becomes more overtly science fictional after Chris, as a part of the *Creole* crew, travels to Antarctica. Chris's cousin Booker is there to make his fortune in "water bottling" by "cut[ting] and drill[ing] blocks of glacial ice, then ship[ping] it on tankers back up Stateside" since "No one drank tap water since the Dayton Dirty Water Disaster" (73, 74). Johnson suggests that in the contemporaneous time of the novel, in the world as we know it, the planet suffers from a water shortage of some kind leading to environmental degradation resulting from human-caused climate change—we are not privy to the details in the book, but *Pym* suggests this crisis could lead to the end of civilization a bit later. "In neighborhoods across the United States, African American children have disabilities because lead has poisoned the water in their taps," as Elizabeth A. Wheeler writes, and "Afrofuturism bears witness to such wrongs, and its metaphors make tangible the risk of environmental illness" as seen in "Flint, Michigan, and Baltimore, Maryland" ("Runoff," 128). With respect to *Pym*, it is easy enough to assume that this unspecified disaster contaminated the Ohio River drainage basin, which empties into the Mississippi River, the largest watershed in the United States, touching thirty-two states and covering roughly 40 percent of the country's landmass ("Mississippi"). Basically, the character Booker is a disaster capitalist taking advantage of a clean water shortage. Booker, who "doesn't trust white people," uses his cousin to finance and assemble the all-Black skeleton crew for the Antarctic expedition (74).

Nevertheless, Chris certainly fancies himself an Indiana Jones–type, an ex-professor with his wry wit, sarcasm, and a deep knowledge of American literature who will find Tsalal and its Black inhabitants because of his purchase and authentication of the Peters manuscript. Chris enlists Garth as a second helper, Jeffree and Carlton Damon Carter as his two water treatment engineers, and his lawyer ex-girlfriend Angela Latham and her entertainment lawyer husband Nathaniel to round out the Black crew. With this task accomplished, Booker mockingly agrees to transport Chris "right down to your chasm and you can have the coldest damn book club on the planet" (74). Armed with this self-belief and the skeletal remains[18] of Dirk Peters shipped to him in a box from Mahalia Mathis in the event of her death, Chris determines to go find "the island of blackness" undisturbed by "the predations of white supremacy, colonialism, slavery, genocide, and the whole ugly story of our world" (83). Thus, the novel segues from a mockery of academic life for a Black faculty member to an Antarctic adventure story with cli-fi, apocalyptic, and utopian strands threading through a continuing racial binary.

The entirety of the plot depends on suspending disbelief, accepting the existence of the fictional Peters and Pym, allowing them to live despite the fantastic elements, and momentarily believing the veracity of Poe's novel. I previously mentioned that Pym survived, but I did not say that in Johnson's novel he has lived for two hundred years by drinking the "fermented whale piss" the Tekelians distilled for themselves as a liquor; "this is the drink of the Gods . . . the elixir of life" known as "khrud" (198–199; 201). The time-frozen Pym mistakes Chris for a white man with his companions as slaves for sale. Such things necessitate a lot of disbelief across two novels, and Johnson banks on his audience to suspend theirs in their enjoyment of ironies, while simultaneously challenging them to examine his race metaphors.

Using the planet's southernmost, least populated, least explored, and most inhospitable continent as the setting, Johnson creates two discordant white worlds upon which to offer scathing social commentary as Chris Jaynes and the Black crew members encounter them. First, he revisits a past social structure in this forbidding environment through a nostalgic return to the antebellum South as represented by the white and giant Tekelians. And second, he also envisions a white utopia, a futuristic biodome in the middle of the cold continent, built by the reclusive white artist Thomas Karvel (modeled on the deceased American painter Thomas Kinkade, self-described as a "Painter of Light"). The heat put off by the BioDome's machinery slowly melts the ice above the Tekelians' home cavern, while the crew of the *Creole* is "indefinite[ly] indenture[d]," putting the two worlds into direct conflict through this localized global warming metaphor (Fiorelli, "Against," 227). These imagined potential futures outline the poor response to climate change and the call for social justice that Johnson combines into environmental racism in his Afrofuturistic flight of fancy.

Instead of finding the Black-skinned Tsalalians, Chris and Garth first encounter the giant white beings indigenous to Antarctica that Poe tells of at the end of his novel. Attempting to recover the drill that has fallen through the ice into what appears to be a tunnel system, Chris spots one and names them the Tekelians after the excited utterances of Poe's Tsalalians ("*Tekeli-li! Tekeli-li!*") in the presence of white things like the giant birds and the shrouded titan (*Narrative*, 587). Chris takes a moment to describe the "mountainous creatures" wearing "white robes" as the rest of the mining crew arrive (*Pym*, 122). He states:

> Their size alone, their towering presence, would have been enough to provide a spectacle. . . . Their bodies were mountainous and hidden, covered in hooded capes that hung broadly from the shoulders and concealed their bulk in folds. . . . The only things that were clearly visible were their heads. And those were what froze us. What I at first glance had assumed to be horrific masks proved instead to be *their actual faces*. The color. Or lack of it, was striking. Albino, it seemed clear, but their eyes contradicted that. . . . I had never truly seen pale blue eyes before. I had seen blue but never in this shade, the lightest possible variant, which had more in common with the snow around us than with any accepted form of ocular pigment. These darting, acute, haunting orbs bobbed over noses that were so long and pointy I assume they served some sort of evolutionary purpose that was at the moment unclear. . . . Also from the holes in their noses came hair, straight and brittle, that fed into their beards, thick corn silk completely devoid of coloring, pouring out of their ponchos. (124–125, emphasis in original)

Scholar Roger Davis calls the Tekeli "yeti-like," comparing them to the ape-like creatures of Himalayan folklore ("Food," 190). And he's not wrong to think of them as abominable snowmen, but they have language, culture, and industry as evinced by their initial attempts to communicate and trade fairly. Likewise, Wilks mentions how "the Tekelians evoke the similarly attired Ku Klux Klan" with their white "'hooded capes' and menacing stature" ("'Black,'" 12). And she's not wrong in her assessment after a while. They certainly become so after

Chris and company renege on their trade agreement, brokered by Pym as a translator—Little Debbie[19] snack cakes in exchange for two Tekelians. The crew had agreed to take Pym and two Tekelians North, telling Pym that they will function as ambassadors while Booker and his colleagues hope to exploit the Tekelians for material gain. I fear that Booker Jaynes is most accurate in his branding them with the creative and pejorative slur "snow honkey" (105). And he's not wrong either, because they do enslave the newcomers and so live up to his expectations of "how all white people were . . . racist" (145). The trade deal falls apart because of the fate of the outside world, destroyed by unnamed socioeconomic difficulties caused by climate change and conflicting political systems resulting in "the familiar trauma" of violence (97). The *Creole* crew are vaguely aware of this cultural disintegration through an intermittent television signal broadcasting the bloodshed happening in Tokyo, Paris, Berlin, London, New York, LA, Sydney, and Stuttgart just before first contact with the Tekelians; the disaster is later confirmed by the "ominous," anonymous, and empty email with "the subject line: ARMAGEDDON" after the deal is struck (152). In his use of an apocalypse and slavery, Johnson draws on two well-documented themes in the Afofuturist megatext.[20]

The deal breaks down when the Tekelians arrive with their goods, Pym and the two Tekelians—Hunka and Krakeer—ready to exchange for the Little Debbies. Readers should take note of the derogatory racial connotations of the names "Hunka" (with "honkey") and "Krakeer" (with "cracker"). Blacks have used such contemptuous slurs to insult whites to no practical effect. Johnson heightens and undermines the racial tensions simultaneously in the contrast of skin colors between the two groups although the Tekelians certainly don't understand the meaning of race in relation to commerce. Unfortunately, the Black Americans, incapable of blending in with the native Antarcticans, become objects of labor for the Tekelians because of the incurred debt from the broken contract. This debt will take roughly a hundred years to work off, according to the Tekelians. With the Indigenous prevailing, Johnson causes us to look at our society more deeply with this humorous and biting moment—funny, because of the snack cakes as the medium of exchange; critical, because the *Creole* crew is just as self-serving as the Karvels and other whites portrayed in the novel; and sarcastic, in that Black people are enslaved again. The Tekelians' responses to the busted commitment merely emulate and recycle something that resembles the peculiar institution. Only Garth escapes enslavement in trading most of his Little Debbies for his own freedom without having enough to free his colleagues.

The Tekelians quickly become acquainted with whiteness and its metaphoric strength as they become slaveholders. For example, the crew is separated and taken by different Tekelians in opposite directions in their compound; Jeffree is physically abused by his owner Sausage Nose and loses his left eye because of his dissent, which tames Carlton; Nathaniel is forced to work on a sprained ankle; Angela works as a house slave cleaning the floor of her master's residence; and Booker stamps on ice to produce drinking water for a lazing female Tekelian with a lascivious gaze. As Chris drily remarks, "Turns out though that my thorough and exhaustive scholarship into the slave narratives of the African diaspora in no way prepared me to actually become a fucking slave" (161). And yet these Black folks can freely move about the Tekelian community, drink in the bars, watch martial events, and so on. It is as if Johnson seemingly removes us from time in destroying the Western world, modifying our understanding of antebellum America in his reinvention of slavery to better "mock Poe's racist fantasies of white supremacy" (Davis, "Follies," 28). Undoubtedly, Johnson offers an Afrofuturist put down of Poe and Poe's novel with this audacious and political reimaging.

The prevailing pressures of history dictate that Chris must write his own account to provide a more accurate record about the circumstances of his brief time enslaved by the Tekelians. Since the Tekelians are native to the polar region, Chris's writings end up recalling the genre of the *captivity narrative* in which white women described being taken and held as collateral by Native Americans.[21] The Tekelians hold Chris and his partners captive while Chris and company construct the Tekelians as "other" in terms of race, beliefs, and customs and find them uncivilized as they submerge into Tekelian culture. But I cannot ignore the parallels to slave narratives that Johnson makes nor the stereotypes of enslaved Blacks that he fully engages. For instance, Sausage Nose clearly represents a cruel master, who we disturbingly witness sink a bone dagger into Jeffree's eye from fifty feet. Booker's private collection of slave mementos, such as "chains . . . bills of sale, sale adverts, runaway notices, cages, neck spikes, face masks . . . cat-o'-nine-tails," regains a paradoxical significance at his own enslavement (100). There are descriptions of Tekelian cuisine such as "Krakt," a staple of the Tekelian diet made from whale blubber that "achieved a taste similar to that of unsweetened ice cream, or a mayonnaise without the vinegar" and the aforementioned whale-piss liquor (165). No wonder they desperately want the empty, processed calories of the artificially sweet Little Debbies! "Them shits is good" as Garth says (127). While the *Creole* members face continual hunger like slaves, Johnson makes a great point about how Americans in the present "starve with full bellies, starve on high-fructose corn syrup and hydrogenated oils, carbohydrates too complex for our bodies to bother deciphering. We starve and yet are fat as shit at the same time" (190). Additionally, families are divvied up and separated as is the case for Angela and Nathanial, since their marriage is not recognized. The Tekelians do not have literacy as a technology that I am aware of and so do not prevent Chris from reading or writing.

There really do not seem to be any patrols, though the Tekelians will pursue Chris and Garth. After Chris and his Tekelian master Augustus (Krakeer) visit the *Creole* in search of sweets for the Tekelian, Garth helps Chris formulate an escape plan as if he were a conductor on the underground railroad. In this sense the *Creole* gains further significance as they make their plans because an actual shipboard rebellion in 1841 occurred onboard the American slaver *Creole*. "In the case of the *Creole*," as Nihad M. Farooq describes, "U.S. slave rebels took over a ship en route from Virginia to New Orleans and demanded to be taken to a free Caribbean island," where "the rebels were taken into British custody when they arrived in Nassau [and] were released weeks later" while "the other 116 slaves aboard were granted immediate freedom" (*Undisciplined*, 15). Chris knows the value of his personhood and decides to abscond with himself in resisting his own commodification.

Three weeks beneath the ice, three weeks of slavery, prompts Chris to believe that Garth has potentially located Karvel's uncharted base in the middle of the Antarctic desert through Garth's own extensive artwork collection. Further, Chris learns of his own sale to Sausage Nose, which provokes him to escape the violent Tekelian. Chris cannot interest any of the other *Creole* members in escaping. In this moment, Pym attempts to halt their flight by destroying the snowmobiles. Pym gets knocked out for his effort to prevent Jaynes from running away and gets dragged along in the sled with limited supplies. This short journey of Chris and Garth reminds me a bit of Genly Ai and Estraven's trip over the Gobrin Ice on the planet Winter while fleeing from Orgoreyn authorities in Ursula K. Le Guin's masterful *The Left Hand of Darkness* (1969).

Garth uses his Karvel paintings as a guide and finds the general area against a mountain backdrop where Karvel could be just as a snowstorm hits, with the food supply exhausted. He walks off from their tent to find Karvel, leaving Chris and Pym. Meanwhile, Chris, in thinking of himself freezing to death, has an epiphany that whiteness is "erasure. Covering over the truth with layers of blank reality just as the snowstorm was now covering our tent"

(225). With this thought in mind, whites ignore or deny the truths of racial oppression across history, absolving themselves of guilt while celebrating their privilege in not seeing color in the twenty-first century. This epiphany answers Chris's question from the start of the novel that drives his class on the meaning of whiteness. It's why he seeks Poe. Upon waking up naked, warm, and comfortable, Chris learns that his best friend succeeded in finding "the *Dome of Light*" and in gaining admittance by pretending to be a Black Republican, of all things (234). Strictly speaking, African Americans think of Black Republicans as sellouts seeking opportunity through "shameless Uncle Tomming" despite the "sheer savagery of the Regan Revolution toward black America . . . upping the black misery index with malice aforethought" (Tate, "Ghetto," 100). Blacks have come to hold strong feelings of hostility, dislike, and fear for the party of Lincoln because of the alienation experienced under the Reagan and Bush presidencies although the Clinton presidency was certainly no better, and perhaps worse, with his "three strikes" crime bill.

Regardless, Johnson creates quite the neo-slave narrative. He describes the escape such that his recontextualized captivity narrative defamiliarizes the peculiar institution, from Chris's first moment of captivity, to his escape into the freezing cold with Garth, to his miraculous survival. Yet Chris does not experience the transformation from slave to person, having never accepted his dehumanized status. In fact, Johnson restores the memory of slavery by keeping it intact through his use of satire to lighten the taboo of discussing a topic many would like to forget.

With his employment of racial stereotypes, Johnson demonstrates how they bleed across American history into the future. For example, the militant Booker seems broken by his enslaved destiny and becomes a Mandingo of sorts in that he begins sleeping with his Tekelian master Hunka, breathing life into the hypersexual stereotype. Angela disjointedly embodies two Black female stereotypes at once. We first see her working as a kind of mammy, perhaps an Aunt Jemima, in cleaning inside her master's house, a distinct non-threat to the white Tekelians, although she is simply too beautiful for that role and there are no children in her care. Notice that Angela attempts to control Chris with her sexuality, which would disqualify her as a mammy of the antebellum era but position her as a nontraditional Jezebel in regard to her darker skin color and African features in contradistinction to European ideals of beauty. Jeffree clearly represents the Black buck in his refusal to recognize Sausage Nose's authority with his loud talk and sublimated violence until his disfigurement. Nathaniel fits the Uncle Tom stereotype in that he learns the Indigenous language to improve his station with the Tekelians in ostensibly placing their welfare over that of his Black friends in terms of negotiating for comforts. This assessment proves true in that he will eventually sell out Chris and Garth in a worse fashion than the untrusted Pym, who distained Blacks from the first instant he was introduced. Chris must be viewed as a lazy Sambo reliant on his master for direction and for motivation, therefore justifying his enslavement. And Garth exemplifies the maroon in that he avoids slavery by trading his supply of Little Debbies and establishes a free Black community of one in Antarctica, from which he will aid Chris's escape and find the BioDome.

Such stereotypes still influence white opinions of African Americans to this day and Johnson challenges his readers to reassess their own prejudices in order to begin effecting social change. Interestingly, Johnson portrays the Tekelians as Krakt addicts who become even more hooked on the processed white sugar found in the Little Debbies. The unnamed Tekelian who first bites the snack cake expresses euphoria "AAAAAAAAAAAAHHHHHHHHHHHHHHHHHHHH" in the taste (127). As Chris explains, "The sounds it made, the groans, were loud, vulgar. They were appreciative too" (127). Johnson fundamentally reveals a very different social reality in the mirror of Afrofuturism, to borrow Samuel R. Delany's expression, explaining the estranged world of the Tekelians—our white world, to be clear—where such stereotypes still imprison Black people with these racial nightmares from the past just beyond the edge of fantasy (173). Our colorblind way of not talking about race while talking about race in America justifies white dominance and supremacy in the body politic. Johnson challenges both Black and white readers to become antiracist in order to better experience the sting from his cultural barbs and to change our world for the better, to encode society differently, to liberate us.

BioDome, Invasion, and Environmental Racism

With the BioDome in mind, Johnson calls for environmental justice in mirroring the plight of the native Tekeli-li and Black people in America that have been encroached upon by white interests. Karvel sets up his Biodome beyond the jurisdiction of the American government and its institutional power, where he intentionally generates as much heat as he likes, intentionally polluting the *uninhabited* land belonging to the Tekeli-li. The Tekeli-li have no means of resistance to this disregard for their living environment beyond the will to fight. They cannot move from their land. They have neither political power nor economic power to dissuade Karvel when he learns of their existence through Chris and Garth. They are merely poor giants to him. It is in this regard that Johnson parallels the environmental racism unduly and disproportionately harming Black people in the United States, who do not have the wealth or political resources to prevent garbage dumps or chemical plants from setting up shop in their neighborhoods. What's worse is that Black people often cannot move away.

Picking up with the plot, Garth makes a calculated decision claiming to be a Black member of the Republican Party in order to save their lives upon meeting his idol. Chris and Garth awaken in the Dome of Light, a utopian white patriarchal community-for-two created by Thomas Karvel and largely maintained by his wife Mrs. Karvel, whose first name is never revealed. The "state-of-the-art 3.2 Ultra BioDome," purchased from NASA, is "Hermetically sealed, fully self-contained" with "solar panels all over the roof" and "the fauna, the exchange of CO_2 and oxygen" an "ecosystem fully self-contained," where "the exhaust system shoots the hot air right down into the ice tunnels" (239, 240). Karvel has custom-painted the interior to mirror one of his paintings, locking it in a kind of permanent twilight with too-green grass, too-blue water, and impossibly intense flower blooms with real white bunnies hopping all around as well as a "grape Kool-Aid" tasting stream (242).[22] In creating his perfect world, Karvel declares, "God created nature. I just improved on it" to which Garth emphatically agrees (241). Karvel continues, "I created this free land. First within my art, and now in life . . . A clean canvas. A place with no violence and no disease, no poverty and no crime" (241). His coded yet self-aggrandizing speech to Chris and Garth reveals his well-intended colorblindness for a place devoid of Black people and the supposed problems they bring, such as violent crime, disease, poverty, and other hardships—at least not in his technologically saturated future. Karvel's future will reproduce the mechanisms of racial inequality in short order.

Ironically, Karvel's painting of the BioDome interior prevents it from functioning properly as a self-sufficient biosphere, making it dependent on routine resupplies from the outside world. While it may look pretty on the inside and feel safe, Chris felt even before arriving at the BioDome that Karvel's paintings projected "a place where black people couldn't even exist" and found that its replication of an empty painting generates a feeling of "the fevered Caucasian dreams of Tolkien and Disney" (184). This transformation of a technological marvel meant for survival on Mars into a carefully controlled habitat in the Antarctic might have worked without Karvel's hubris disrupting its operations with needless yet addictive consumption. Other scholars have picked up on this theme. Fiorelli states, "Karvel's Dome is the perfect product of Jean Baudrillard's 'Disneyfication'" ("Against," 227). And Davis writes, "Karvel has created a utopic BioDome on Antarctica that is a detailed simulation of one of his paintings, evoking Jean Baudrillard's depiction of the 'Disneyfication' of America" ("Follies," 30). While both Fiorelli and Davis compare Karvel's dome to Jean Baudrillard's postmodern notion of Disney, neither takes the comparison far enough in that "Disneyland" is "the digest of the American way of Life, panegyric to American values, idealised transposition of a contradictory reality" (Baudrillard, *Simulations*, 24–25). Consequently, the Dome of Light is all that remains of the real America, the white America, that no longer exists, if it ever did, and Karvel remakes it from one of his own paintings into a third-order simulation with "reality-energy" and "political incantation" where his reality only exists inside the artificial barriers of the BioDome (Baurdrillard, *Simulations*, 26). Not only has Karvel stripped a real place of its original purpose in his attempt at perfection in blocking out actual sunlight with his painting, he has sanitized American history to his own liking in ignoring the manifestations of persistent discrimination.

To a large extent, Karvel's utopia starts with his discontent with the social and political chaos in his beloved America. In using his wealth, Karvel attempts to remake his own fortress of solitude based on an ideal white ethnostate of conservatism without Christianity that would exclude Black people, if not all non-whites, while protecting and preserving his own inalienable rights as a white man through all the science and technology that money can buy. My deliberate Superman parallel tracks in that Karvel locates his base away from civilization in a polar region on a frozen tundra. Likewise, he believes himself a god although he uses his artistic ability only to benefit himself and his wife while ignoring the global politics leading to planetary genocide and obviously staying blind to climate change.

A combination of right-wing talk radio and Fox News, featuring Rush Limbaugh, Glenn Beck, Bill O'Reilly, and Sean Hannity, booming across the BioDome sound-system on a repeating loop offers proof positive. This "auditory assault," as Tim Christensen calls it, "creates the effect of each voice trying to shout the others down, and provides, at the same time, a caricature of both right-wing talk radio and of the postmodern aesthetic" ("Little,"

189). This uninterrupted blaring of fundamentalist media without contact with other people for so long reinforces his radical mania. Johnson provides more evidence when Chris and Garth learn of the giant American flag painted on the roof of the BioDome. As Davis points out, "The fact that the native Tekelians view the BioDome as a destructive encroachment on their territory alludes to the U.S. takeover of Native American land" ("Follies," 31). Besides, Karvel would have established his home there even if he knew about the Tekelians. Chris and Garth will have only two weeks of sharecropping in the relative safety inside the BioDome before the Tekelians come to halt the melting of their own home from the BioDome boiler, which is set to a constant 72 degrees Fahrenheit.

This utopia serves as a warning in that Karvel's planned community for a better life in the present fails because it does not account for his social politics. Its destruction *is* inevitable because it is established on a false hope of a white ethno-state or, at the very least, a place absent of race. When Chris and Garth enter the BioDome, the perennial issues of law, economics, and race immediately arise to make these Black men less. Karvel's greed, stupidity, and arrogance undo his utopian vision. To be fair, Karvel does take these undesirables into the BioDome. But we still see his oncoming downfall in Karvel's immediate exploitation of Chris and Garth's labor. Johnson offers a truly satirical answer to the notion of a post-race civilization—there can't be one with white people because they cannot let Black people forget their color; and they demonstrate this inability through social, political, and economic means, thus revealing the patriarchal, hierarchical, and authoritarian underpinnings of their desire to maintain power. As Lyman Tower Sargent tells us, "One of the functions of most utopias is to hold the present up to ridicule" (*Utopianism*, 24). And, in so doing, Johnson also makes an environmental racism argument because the BioDome has a devastating impact on the Indigenous Tekeli-li destroying the ice caves of this uninterrupted white civilization in an approximation of global warming.

The Tekelians are at a clear technological disadvantage. Tekeli-li, situated beneath the ice, faces exposure to the heat exhaust thawing out their environment because of Karvel's decision to use a gas boiler instead of the solar paneling to heat his home. His decision undermines the functioning of the icy infrastructure critical to Tekeli-li. Karvel has turned them into something other, identifying them as "mythological creatures" in making his own whiteness superior to theirs, constructing an ethnicity for them the second he perceives their difference (260). Primarily, Karvel's environmentally racist practice makes him a scourge to the Tekelians' well-being—one that must be eliminated. Johnson's second critique of environmental racism along with the unexplained "Dayton Water Disaster," offers intelligent commentary on the precarious relationships between man, society, and their place in the environment. Karvel's practice endangers the Tekelian community he immediately ethnicizes out of fear for their size upon first seeing them up close.

Yet before this moment transpires, Karvel has to admit traditional racial others into his facility. He only decides to let his unwanted Black guests remain when Chris and Garth agree to grow crops on the bit of land he gives them—a move that mirrors sharecropping in the South after the Civil War and Reconstruction. As a result, Johnson advances his readers swiftly through a bit of Black history, a transition between systems of oppression, from chattel slavery with the Tekelians to this techno-topian moment of sharecropping since Chris and Garth have nothing to support themselves with but their hands. They enter into this agreement to stay as tenants of a sort and get seeds and tools from Mrs. Karvel from which to cultivate a vegetable garden in soil transported to the middle of the Antarctic. This farcical moment in the text serves to reestablish white power in the newly diverse BioDome, driving "home Johnson's point about the staying power of institutionalized racial inequality in the present and near-future" (Davis, "Follies," 32). Chris and Garth also stay in the "three-fifths of a house," a reminder of the compromise in the Constitution allowing Southern states more electoral power than they otherwise would have had in counting every slave as three-fifths of a person (244). This means Chris and Garth count for less, which is why they only have packing material on which to sleep. Moreover, they take to calling their spot the "plantation," where they work independently of Karvel to his benefit (249). As Fiorelli claims, "the prosperity of the ruling class continues to depend heavily upon gendered and racialized labor" ("Against," 229). While they are not enslaved, they have to labor physically to keep their place. Like Mrs. Karvel, who is responsible for cooking, cleaning, and maintenance of the BioDome machinery, they are invisible labor to the master of the domain. I agree with Tim Christensen: "the labor sustaining the fantasy of impossible, laborless abundance becomes raced, as well as gendered" ("Little," 184). Johnson merges the postbellum and post-racial eras to suggest the impossibility of ending social inequality with respect to race and gender.[23]

This temporal collapse of moments in racial history precedes the fall of both white civilizations. As Wilks accurately hypothesizes, "this provocative collapse of historical time and social progress [allows] Johnson" to redouble "his engagement with the neo-slave narrative by imagining the enslavement of his 'post-slavery' characters" while also exploring the perils of utopia in this near future through questions of power that ultimately negate the utopian vision ("'Black,'" 11). Quintuple strands—race, gender, class, pride, and greed—woven together into a self-igniting fuse by Johnson ensure the mutual destruction of the Tekelians and the Karvels in an ideological race to perpetuate white supremacy with Black participants on both sides. On one hand, the Tekelians have been successful in establishing their age-old white ethno-state and are perfectly happy living beneath the ice unbeknownst to the world. The Tekelians represent nationalism, nativism, and moral regression as the final half of the novel develops. They are preparing for war with a "fierce barking call . . . KARARUM'" and bone-sword exercises well before Chris's escape (195). Nathaniel, who is teaching himself the language to become indispensable to his Tekelian masters, translates the meaning of the word for Chris as "The melt, or the heat, or something like that . . . to describe when things start dripping" (196). The Tekelians have Nathaniel Latham as their interpreter, a de facto sellout to his Black partners, to negotiate a peace between civilizations. In terms of moral regression, the Tekelians go backward in forming an army and in enslaving the foreigners. Bigotry runs through their national experience, fed by the fear of the melting ice, demanding that they protect themselves from the foreign threat to their domicile.

On the other hand, Thomas Karvel, a technocratic visionary, uses his vast wealth to create his own utopian land in the BioDome, modeled on his painting, to replicate a vision of America that never was, right on top of the invisible southern empire that is Tekeli-li. Karvel symbolizes the abstract liberalism of colorblind racial ideology, pretending to respect difference without truly being open to new ideas that might interfere with his own rights, while further abstracting his racial concerns to seem sensible. In other words, "The pliability of the color-blind wall" that he socially constructs depends on his use of rhetorical tools to naturalize and minimize his racism (Bonilla-Silva, *Racism*, 76). For example, Karvel allows Chris and Garth to stay inside the dome but out of sight, segregated, stating, "'I can't see that from my place [but if you] Need anything, just holler, 'kay boys?'" (243). He naturalizes the separation in forcing them to live apart from him and his wife and minimizes the discrimination with a seemingly friendly "'kay boys," but by referring to adult Black men as boys, he infantilizes them in a racist fashion.

Regardless, Karvel depends on these two when the Tekelians commence their first attack and knock him out with an ice ball on the roof of the BioDome.

Shortly after he awakens, Karvel is dismayed to learn that the remainder of the Creole mining company had joined this community. He gives a look of "unhidden trepidation" that Chris recognizes as "the look [that] wasn't hatred, or racism, at least in any substantial sense" (273). This white look *is* anything but colorblind in identifying its target as Black, in its sudden awareness of its own discomfort, as self-recognition of racism becomes a moral quandary. Chris sees this look and knows his time in the BioDome is coming to an end even if Karvel does not. The presence of eight-foot-tall Tekelian Augustus, now a refugee from his own people, does not even register on Karvel, but the Black fugitives certainly do, and decidedly more so than the enraged Tekelian army noisily pounding on the roof to get inside.

When the hammering ceases, both Nathaniel and Pym show up at the rooftop door as Tekelian envoys in an attempted diplomacy to negotiate a treaty. Nathaniel declares that the Teklians will "destroy everything unless we do what they say" (276). Interestingly, Nathaniel ostensibly includes himself with his former friends in using the dictatorial "we" here in this moment, but they have already written him off as a race traitor. Yet again, Nathaniel has shown a tendency at ordering people around in an autocratic manner as an entertainment lawyer and implies with the dictatorial "we" that they should do as he commands out of fear and respect. At this point, Pym jumps into the conversation by demanding from Mrs. Karvel, his perceived near equal as a white woman, that she ceases the "great fire, and the fans to blow their heat into the corridor of heaven" (277). Nathaniel suggests that this demand to shut the power off is all the Tekelians want, but Pym interrupts with "of course we will also need the return of the human chattel" (278). With the offer—peace in return for machinery shutdown and slave recovery—on the table, Mrs. Karvel quickly determines to hold further talks with the Tekelians over supper on the rooftop, where she intends to kill all of her enemies with rat poison baked into the "Betty Crocker golden food cake" as well as the "Sara Lee easy cook and bake rolls" (282, 284). Johnson cannot help but ironically state through Chris how the prepared food "looked like it could kill you, but kill you by clogging your arteries or sending the kind of fat that sits in your gut and waits to stop you heart" (283). He implies two things: first, that many Americans prefer processed foods with their unhealthy hydrogenated fats, high amounts of sugar and salt, and carbohydrates as filler; and second, that many Americans, specifically African Americans, have limited access to affordable and nutritious food because of the food deserts they occupy and the income gap with white America. Digression aside, Wilks cheekily labels this moment "an Antarctic Thanksgiving" before more rigorously explaining how this moment of contact resembles the decimation of Native Americans by European colonists ("'Black,'" 15). Johnson makes this connection explicitly clear through Chris who feels "no less morally responsible than those that sat by while the European traders sold infected blankets to Indians" (286). Only Garth objects to the genocidal plan orchestrated by Mrs. Karvel to kill every Tekelian man, woman, and child, but his ethical disapproval is swiftly rejected since he never endured slavery under the Tekelians.

Naturally, the plan goes awry. None of the Tekelians immediately die from the intentional poisoning, not even the small children. After Mrs. Karvel sends Chris inside the BioDome to fetch more dessert, he is followed by Sausage Nose and a child. Not used to the warm environment, the child dies from the combination of mild heat and poison because of its smaller size. Sausage Nose does not immediately recognize the trap he has lead his people into, until he notices his dead child. At that point, he has already started to sicken himself, but he goes to the child before chasing and capturing the fleeing Chris. Sausage Nose nearly chokes Chris to death, but Garth kills the Tekelian leader by braining him with a garden hoe. To buy more time for the lethal ploy to work in addition to evading suspicion at Sausage Nose's disappearance and making a final escape plan, Garth attempts to pass for the Tekelian general by donning his robe, whiting up his face, arms, and hands with "teeth-whitening toothpaste" and "baking soda" and finally standing on a couple of crates near the rooftop door at some distance from the seated Tekelian army which allows Chris enough time to gather his friends and the Karvels (298–299). Johnson revisits the passing metaphor here in having Garth pass as a white Tekelian as a matter of survival. He temporarily crosses the color line to give his friends and allies a chance to slip away, in contrast to the more traditional passing of Peters who improved his social status and economic prospects. Also, Garth does not want to experience slavery firsthand with the Tekelians, on top of his everyday encounters with systemic racism.

The Tekelians eventually see through the ruse after Garth mistakenly steps outside the entryway to convince Nathaniel to come with them. He is not their general and they attack in earnest, killing Booker, Nathaniel, and Angela, who are all out on the rooftop. The Karvels die defending the rooftop entryway with their riffles while Chris, Garth, Jeffree, and Carlton leave them to turn up the heat on the broken boiler despite Mrs. Karvel's warning about blowing up the BioDome. They split up again, Jeffree and Carlton going to the boiler room and Chris and Garth going to a garage. The garage houses a sailboat that has to be towed behind two snowmobiles across the ice to escape into the chilly waters of the Southern Ocean. But they also find a drunken Pym in the sailboat, passed out along with Chris's bag of Peters's bones, and drag him along, a fortuitous moment since Pym knows the general location of Tsalal. Jeffree and Carlton do not make it outside before the BioDome explodes and the ice caves beneath it collapse, taking all of the Tekelians with them. Johnson addresses the subtlety and flexibility of contemporary racism at the novel's climax by flipping the Tekelians from white to Indigenous, in terms of how his audience perceives their identity. Similarly, he critiques the occupation and exploitation of Tekelian lands by the Karvels that results in genocide in order to express an indefinite anxiety over the continual damage that racism inflicts on Blacks and whites alike. Both civilizations fall as a result of long-running prejudices, which also reflects a fear of the changing racial and social demographics in the United States. He offers us an Afrofuturist warning about a post-racial world bound to a colorblind ideology that willfully sanitizes, if not forgets history, creates food deserts and income gaps that are so very difficult to overcome, and speeds climate change, while still endorsing racial violence to support a flagging white hegemony.

Brave New Brown World

But Johnson also conveys a smidgeon of hope too in his near-exact mirroring of Poe's *Narrative*. In Poe's novel, Dirk Peters and Pym take a Tsalalian named Nu-Nu hostage as they flee from Tsalal. The Black-skinned Nu-Nu dies suddenly in the presence of a giant white Tekelian on March 22, as they sail into some kind of chasm, consistent with hollow earth tales (214–217). Johnson inverts Poe's ending, providing two Black survivors, the white Pym, as well as the remains of Peters. Pym also drops dead upon seeing a half-naked Brown-skinned man on the shore of what is assumed to be Tsalal on March 22. The novel ends with Chris's observation, "On the shore all I could discern was a collection of brown people, and this, of course, is a planet on which such are the majority" (322). Johnson undoes Poe's absolute racism with his Black-skinned characters by indicating how the most prominent skin tone across the globe is Brown, somewhere in between white and Black. He emphasizes this point in having the remains of the mulatto Peters survive the journey, the only evidence that Chris Jaynes has of his adventure.

Scholarly opinion differs greatly on the meaning of Johnson's indefinite closing. Poe scholar Richard Kopley believes that "in both novels, then, regardless of the racial view advanced, the conclusion offers an image of transformative purity" ("The Quest," 44). Davis thinks that "the word choice for Johnson's last phrase—'a collection of brown people' who constitute the 'majority' of the planet—intentionally echoes the rhetoric of world dominance by people of color that is a standard feature of Pan-Africanism and Afrocentrism" ("Follies," 40). Wilks writes that "in sending Chris and Garth to a place where blackness and whiteness have mingled to such a degree that they have ceased to be distinct categories, Johnson suggests a need to engage with multiculturalism not as an empty ideal but as a lived reality" ("'Black,'" 16). Fiorelli states, "The focus on 'brown people' here suggests an escape within the global context from America's myopic obsession with the Black-white binary and presents the possibility of human perception and description delinked from racial categories (they are just 'brown')" ("Against," 233). But that is the wonder of an ambiguous ending: we as readers will never really know. That is to say, Johnson takes us outside of our overdetermined social reality with this new alien encounter between humans. Moreover, before the novel even starts, Johnson has already invalidated Chris Jaynes's imaginary account with the two-page preface, in which Chris tells us that he returned to the United States from his "*extraordinary series of adventures in the South Seas and elsewhere*"; he relates his story to Mr. Johnson, annulling the apocalypse and completing the trans-historic feedback loop (3, emphasis in original). Thus, Johnson's ironic Afrofuturist novel presents a future past that checks the fundamental inaccuracy of the short-lived post-racial moment, sieved through a CRT filter of counternarrative storytelling, colorblindness, and informal social rules that comprise the *noirum*.

Ultimately, Poe's novel argues for the permanence of race while Johnson's novel nullifies the ridiculousness of skin color as an identifier of being human while simultaneously calling for further emancipation from this harmful social construct. Johnson creates an Afrofuturistic masterpiece in delineating the optimisms and anxieties, dreams and nightmares, achievements and failings of his imaginary Professor Chris Jaynes. *Pym* is an effective and affective reframing of America, showing us the social fractures generated by race and racism, and a transformational counternarrative that demands the end of inequality to take us into an unfamiliar but much sought future. Yet the social engineering required to solve the race problem and its interlocking oppressions outside a work of Afrofuturism seems nigh impossible, although it is fascinating to think only Brown people exist in this future, decentering the overwhelming presence of whiteness in history and thus avoiding cultural erasure and heartbreak. Indeed, Johnson uses satire to inform us of our limitations as a divided people while blasting apart the unquestioned racial assumptions of Poe that *ghost* into our present America, resulting in the lasting inequalities of anti-Blackness. Afrofuturism provides a chance at hope and the change that comes with it.

OUTRO

Science Fiction and Racism: Decolonizing the White Problem

> We need images of tomorrow, and our people need them more than most.
>
> —Samuel R. Delany, *Starboard Wine*

The Personal

Elsewhere,[1] I have talked about my life's entanglements with science fiction and race. However, I have yet to discuss my career as a Black academic—let alone a Black academic working on SF. One concatenation of moments comes firmly to mind because it has made an indelible impression on me in terms of its frequency. Flash back eighteen years across time and space to the fall of 2008 in Conway, Arkansas, a satellite city of Little Rock, near the beginning of my professorial life. The start of that fall semester after just experiencing a rough mid-tenure review, I, once again, faced *the question*. I have faced a particularly personal question on more than one occasion for what seems my entire life and certainly across the now twentysomething years of my teaching. Most people would be offended by such a personal question outside the classroom, but it has been asked of me in Iowa City, Iowa; Conway, Arkansas; Baton Rouge, Louisiana; Athens, Georgia; and now Syracuse, New York. It has been asked by students ranging from freshman to graduate students, Black, white, Asian, Latino, First Nations, disabled students, nontraditional students, honors students, international students, students participating in Greek life, student athletes, gay and straight, men and women, and even by custodial staff, though administrators, seemingly, have functioning curiosity dampeners. In fact, I call it *the question* and use it as a learning tool. Do you want to know what *the question* is? Very well then, I will answer yet again. People always seem to have the nerve to ask me this provocative question: "Professor Lavender, what are you?"

In a classroom full of general education students, a young Black woman had the temerity to ask, "Professor Lavender, what are you?" I knew what she was getting at and I reckoned this difficult, almost science fictional, instant and its inappropriate question was a teachable moment, to which I responded:

> Maybe I am a Martian like Lil Wayne says in his song "Phone Home."[2] I must seem pretty alien to you since you apparently think I am not a human being. I don't look obviously Black since my hair is curly as opposed to kinky. I don't sound obviously Black since I have a northern accent that jangles in your ears. So how can I possibly be Black since you can't place me in a box? Well, let me tell you something: birth, experience, education, and awareness of my family's lineage as well as knowledge of American history makes me, indeed, in fact, Black. I am not Latino, Hawaiian, Mexican, Arab, Spanish, Creole, Puerto Rican, Indian, Guyanese, or Indonesian, amongst other things I've been called. I am the 1974 result of a Black man and a white woman in love and in wedlock since 1970—just three years beyond the U.S. Supreme Court's decision in *Loving v. Virginia* in 1967 striking down anti-miscegenation laws; I am a man with bronzed skin; that is who I am, mixed, biracial, mulatto, and Black by every social convention of our country. Nothing more and nothing less. And, I read science fiction. I read science fiction because it allows me to remake and remix Black identity in the past, present, and future.

In this respect, I greatly empathize with Samuel R. Delany's sense of the science fictional reality of Blacks in the United States of America as he carefully pondered Isaac Asimov's ironic quip, "we only voted you those awards because you're Negro," at the 1968 Nebula Awards banquet ("Racism," 390). Delany, thinking more self-reflectively about what Asimov said to him, states: "No one here will ever look at you, read a word you write, or consider you in any situation, no matter whether the roof is falling in or the money is pouring in, without saying to him- or herself (whether in an attempt to count it or to discount it), 'Negro . . . ' The racial situation, is nevertheless your total surround. Don't you *ever* forget it . . . ! And I never have." ("Racism," 390–391). This perfect expression of the Black (and Brown) experience, its "total surround," makes clear the pressure woke BIPOCS feel every day deep in their bones. When I think of how that student tried to imprison me into her frame of understanding, her own practice of colorism, internalized racism, because of my skin, hair, and idiolect, I confront the seeming permanence of racism in our reality. This racial surround is quite literally everywhere in the worlds we inhabit—physical, virtual, and imaginary. I grapple with my own "epidermalization," to borrow Frantz Fanon's words, where I was to be judged inferior because of skin color despite my many years of learning and ten years of teaching experience, every damn day (*Black Skin*, xv). More and more, I realize that Delany was never more right.

Even though I was the Sterling-Goodman Professor of English at the University of Georgia, the oldest state-chartered public university in the United States of America (1785), I have not forgotten for one second that I am Black. My life depends on this knowledge of the total surround. This knowledge has helped me produce seven books, one special double issue of *Extrapolation*, and a variety of articles, essays, book reviews, and encyclopedia entries on the subjects of race and racism in SF, with more to come. It matters so much and probably more than the hard work that I have put into my scholarship every single day to obtain this position. It matters to the connections, friends, and allies that I have made as I stand firm and hold the door open for the next generation of BIPOC and queer scholars. And so, I must really engage with this total racial surround as if it were a living breathing thing although it is an entirely fabricated social construction.

But I also see science fiction as the possible way out of this trap generated by pseudoscientific beliefs and capitalism. We have to first acknowledge that race matters. Of course, race matters. How could it not? To reiterate, white folks have made BIPOCs feel it every day and in every way conceivable. And the SF writing community is no different. Consider the Victorian novelist H. Rider Haggard's *She* (1887) as a lost race tale and the image of Africa it presents for a coming European hegemony; or the American SF pulp writer Edgar Rice Burroughs's *A Princess of Mars* (1912), where the former Confederate captain in the American Civil War John Carter fortuitously and mysteriously escapes to Barsoom (Mars), hiding from the Apache in an Arizona cave and setting the entire eleven-book series in motion; or the British novelist Sax Rohmer's *The Insidious Fu-Manchu* (1913) and its racist depiction of Chinese people across thirteen books at various peaks of yellow peril fear. Such vicious images are "reinforced" for the world "in the works of such geniuses of racism as a Rider Haggard" according to Ngũgĩ wa Thiong'o, not to mention Burroughs and Rohmer as well as H. P. Lovecraft (*Decolonising*, 18). These stereotypes still exist with us today more than a hundred years later. Why else would J. K. Rowling, author of the well-received Harry Potter series, support the Blacking up of the series' feminist icon Hermione Granger, whose race is never defined in the books, despite making many millions of dollars in royalties and film profits with a white actress (Emma Watson) playing the character in the films?

And the SF academic community is no different for that matter. An organization that I love and support had decided its conference theme would involve inequality—a perfectly good theme. But a mistake was made by the overseeing executive committee (all white) in terms of optics and the honored guests—both white and both good people. What does that look like to BIPOC artists and scholars? It looked like a bunch of white folks decided to have a conversation about inequality led by white folks, in all earnestness. However inadvertent this decision may have been by proven allies, it had the look and feel of an insult. The optics looked terrible because they were terrible, leaving BIPOC scholars aware of their race and ethnicity, peeved, pissed off, and largely disheartened. It's an egregious error that I feel compelled to mention since any number of BIPOC SF scholars could have spoken on this topic and waxed downright lyrical too! Indeed, it had the feel of a denied space for those who are actually in the SF sphere—the feel of a paradox, the total surround Delany mentioned in 2021?!

What solutions could there be to the white problem in SF? I am sincerely afraid that the fixity of race is too entrenched as a powerful myth to be ever overcome. Whites represent a profound threat to BIPOCs. Literally, they do not want the future to be anything but white: to reflect white supremacy and white consciousness and the pleasure they derive from their slipping dominance—monochrome! That's what makes a film like Jordan Peele's *Get Out* (2017) so science fictional and horrifying with its body-swapping white folks snatching Black bodies: white folks becoming Black, going far beyond blackface minstrelsy to reflect a white liberal elite vision of a post-race world with white minds in Black bodies. The film is the satirical opposite of the Harlem Renaissance writer George S. Schuyler's more tongue-in-cheek *Black No More* (1931), where the Black doctor Junius Crookman invents a three-day process to transform Black people into white people for fifty bucks. Contemporary Black writer Maurice Carlos Ruffin covers some of this same territory in his debut novel *We Cast a Shadow* (2019), where the desperate father of a biracial boy in a near-future Southern city decides to protect his son with the exorbitant experimental procedure known as "demelanization" that he had seen advertised in a brochure for Dr. Nzinga's clinic (149). Despite eighty-eight years passing between the publication of these two Black-authored SF novels, it doesn't seem as if much has changed with respect to the attempt to survive American racism.

Naturally, there is a white inverse to these Black works; *Soul Man* (1986), a comedy directed by Steve Miner, features the white actor C. Thomas Howell in blackface, portraying a white guy named Mark Watson admitted to Harvard Law school whose dad decides not to pay for it. Mark decides to take tanning pills and to wear a wig, pretending to be Black in order to cheat in a scholarship competition. White journalist John Howard Griffin provides a harrowing account of his trip through the Jim Crow South (Louisiana, Mississippi, Alabama, and Georgia) after transforming himself into a Black man with medication, skin paint, and UV light to experience racism firsthand in *Black Like Me* (1961). And white author Jess Row presents the idea of racial reassignment surgery in the near future in *Your Face Is Mine* (2014), where the white and Jewish Martin Lipkin undergoes racial reassignment surgery to pass as the African American Martin Wilkinson. I guess cross-racial identification is a thing if evinced by the infamous case of Rachel Dolezal.

BIPOCs cannot rely on the faulty assumption that whites truly believe in equality, that they want to grant racial justice, that they want to ease the material, social, and psychological suffering they have caused every other race and ethnicity. Inverting W. E. B. Du Bois's famous question from *The Souls of Black Folk* (1903) with respect to being a problem, let me direct the question to white folk: how does it feel to be properly identified as the true problem on a global scale, the Caucasian problem?

The Cultural

The sedition that led to the Capitol riot, worse even, the insurrection and attempted coup in Washington, DC, on January 6, 2021 during the darkest days of the COVID-19 pandemic, seems to have the proper makings of an SF novel. Except, it *ain't*.

This calamitous event happened and the world watched in horror. The Confederate battle flag, a symbol of white supremacy every bit as foul as the Nazi swastika, was marched through the halls of the US Capitol building, the apex of democracy, the seat of American power, in a brazen attempt to sustain white power in the middle of a joint session of Congress to certify President-elect Joe Biden's victory. It is really quite surreal in the sense that the Confederates never made it into the hallowed halls during the American Civil War, though the British managed to burn it during the War of 1812 in 1814. That was the last time the Capitol of the United States was breached and occupied by an enemy force. But white American supremacists, domestic terrorists, and the Christian right were spurred on by Donald Trump, the former president. Again, it sounds like science fiction, but it *ain't*! And not just the Confederate flag either, a grizzled, disheveled, bearded white man—Robert Keith Packer—also sported a "Camp Auschwitz" hoodie inside the Capitol, a sweatshirt referencing the infamous anti-Semitic Nazi death camp, among many other desecrations of my nation's Capitol. It hurt my heart immensely.

Who could believe the image of a man wearing a horned bearskin headdress, face painted red, white, and blue, bare-chested with Viking/neo-pagan tattoos on full display, while wielding a six-foot spear with the American Flag tied to the shaft, shouting "Freedom," would ever be allowed in the Capitol Building? Yet the "QAnon Shaman" and Arizona resident, Jacob Anthony Chansley did so in doing his best impression of Mel Gibson's warrior poet, the Scottish Knight William Wallace, from the Academy Award–winning *Braveheart* (1995), transporting the past into the present. Fake conspiracy-laden ancestral worship appropriated from a cross between Indigenous American heritage and Scandinavian mythology provides a way to maintain white dominance to escape the anxiety-inducing feelings of marginalization in a global workforce not centered on them—alien and alienated. The world has passed them by and they do not like being othered. No longer is the white man a "being without properties, unmarked, universal, just human" (Dyer, *White*, 30). It's truly unbelievable the extent of white American entitlement at the expense of the country's Black and Brown people! A third time, I say, it has the feel of science fictional estrangement. However, it is *not*!

Certainly, the alt-right white nationalists from the recent American insurgency effort exist within the science fiction and fantasy community as well. Proof positive—the Sad Puppies, led by Larry Correia and followed by Brad Torgersen, and the Rabid Puppies, led by Theodore Beale, and their failed racist, sexist, and homophobic voting campaigns to influence the Hugo Awards (2013–2016). Pushing this truth a little bit further, white supremacists have borrowed ideas from popular SF films such as *The Matrix* (1999), irrespective of the gender dysphoria suffered by the brother directors Andy and Larry

Wachowski before transitioning into the sisters Lily and Lana Wachowski, to push their destructive agenda to end American democracy and to rid the country of its minorities. Early in the film, Morpheus (Laurence Fishburne) offers Neo (Keanu Reeves) a choice between ingesting blue and red pills; the blue one represents his normal and unappealing way of navigating life, while the red one reveals the truth about the simulated reality of the Matrix. Of course, Neo takes the red pill and sees the truth of the world as his reality collapses—he is an energy source for machines in the real world, a de facto human battery or a "coppertop" as another character named Switch (Belinda McClory) calls him before swallowing the pill. Historian Alexandra M. Stern carefully explains how the alt-right has crafted a social meme out of this moment in that "To be red pilled is to accept the cold, hard truth about the foundations of individual and collective existence" (*Proud Boys*, 16). Stern reasonably implies that this new fabrication of reality leads "to an epiphany about the rightness of white nationalism and/or the repudiation of feminism, multiculturalism, leftism, liberalism, and globalism, followed by the embrace of traditionalism, hierarchy, and inequality" (16). That is, for the alt-right, "to be red pilled" is to wake up and see through the politically correct world and all its liberal propaganda, espousing equality for all and social justice, and to secure the future for white people alone.

In fact, the alt-right in SF fandom champion novels such as *Victoria: A Novel of 4th Generation War* (2014) by Thomas Hobbes (a pseudonym for William S. Lind), in which America collapses and Christian marines rise up to carve out a new white civilization among the ruins. Ostensibly, Lind chose the English Enlightenment philosopher as his nom de plume because he likes Hobbes's political philosophies espoused in *Leviathan* (1651) with respect to social contract theory, where, as it were, might makes right in the state of nature. But who knows? Public consciousness of a pervasive white nationalism and its fascist ideologies at this moment must not fade into the background. We must heed the warnings now before it's too late and begin the hard work of assiduously taking apart the corrosive messaging of racism, xenophobia, misogyny, and homophobia. But these warnings have been made by American authors before concerning the deep-seated fear of a looming white genocide harbored by white supremacists.

If anything, the Capitol Hill riot should remind us that fascism can arise anywhere. Sinclair Lewis warned us long ago in his science fictional novel *It Can't Happen Here* (1935), where he demonstrates how fragile democracy is during the Great Depression and imagines the defeat of President Roosevelt from within his own Democratic party by the imaginary Senator Buzz Windrip, promising to return the country to greatness and prosperity. In turn, Windrip defeats the Republican nominee in the 1936 election. President Windrip adapts authoritarian measures for his corporatist regime to thrive, puts men to work with his own paramilitary force known as the Minute Men, and jails political dissenters in concentration camps. Octavia E. Butler provides a second cautionary notice with *Parable of the Sower* (1993) and *Parable of the Talents* (1998). She explores the convergence of political, environmental, and economic crises across the two novels, which culminates in the election of Andrew Steele Jarret, an imaginary Christian fundamentalist senator from Texas, to the presidency, with his promise of "making America great again" (*Parable of the Talents*, 21). And Philip Roth offers a third timely reminder with his alternate history *The Plot Against America* (2004), imagining the aviator Charles Lindbergh, a real-life advocate for the isolationist group the America First Committee, defeating Franklin Roosevelt in the 1940 presidential election and then promptly signing a treaty with Adolf Hitler promising no interference from the United States in the German European expansion and a second treaty with Japan and its expansion in Asia, contracts known as "the Iceland Understanding" and "the Hawaii Understanding" respectively (54). These past literary musings vividly outline the caustic nature of white supremacy eating away at the heart of America.

The Analytical

Why are *these* white people so afraid? These white folks have truly lost their damn minds! Absurdly, they must have seen too many Marvel films and fear a backlash of epic proportions led by a Killmonger-type[3] with the training, skill, desire, charisma, determination, and commitment to "kill-the-white-folks" (Tal, "'That,'" 67). And I mean all of them. Sam Greenlee's *The Spook Who Sat by the Door* (1969) remains the quintessential example of an attempted Black revenge. But it is simply preposterous in this day and age and has always been preposterous. And yet some white people can only envision a reversal of circumstances, largely two in particular: one where the Confederacy wins the Civil War as in Ward Moore's *Bring the Jubilee* (1953), Harry Turtledove's *The Guns of the South* (1992), and Andrew J. Heller's *If the North Had Won the Civil War: An Alternate History* (2015); and one where the Axis powers win World War II like in Philip K. Dick's well-known *The*

Man in the High Castle (1962), Robert Harris's *Fatherland* (1992), or Daniel Quinn's *After Dachau* (2001). Of course, the novel I think about most in this respect is the little-known nineteenth-century near-future antebellum novel *The Partisan Leader: A Tale of the Future* (1836), written by the eminent law professor Nathaniel Beverley Tucker of Virginia. Tucker imagines a secession war in 1849, where Virginia secedes and joins the Southern Confederacy of states that had already left the Union to continue their slaveholding ways. I often wonder if secessionist thought of yesteryear would align with white supremacist thought of the current time, and I think yes, decidedly so. Science fiction *is* complicit in this belief as evinced by John Rieder's important *Colonialism and the Emergence of Science Fiction* (2008), where he tracks the genre's history and its ideological underpinnings of colonialism, imperialism, and racism in the Euro-American imagination as early SF vacillates between adventure stories on the African continent involving lost races and alien invasions, among many other scenarios.

I haven't really seen too many BIPOC novels where Native Americans successfully defend their land, or Africans successfully resist enslavement, or Jews revoke the Holocaust, or Indians repel British colonization. I'm sure they exist, though. One exception that quickly comes to mind is P. Djèlí Clark's phenomenal novella *Ring Shout* (2020), wherein a trio of Black women literally take on a demon-infested Ku Klux Klan in the Deep South setting of Macon, Georgia in 1922 to prevent Hell on Earth. With the assistance of the Gullah folk from the Sea Islands and their ring shout tradition, a transcendental Black ritual where the participants move in a circle, shuffling their feet, clapping their hands, and shouting praise to their ancestors to memorialize their own history, they triumph. In confronting one of the demon Ku Kluxes, Butcher Clyde, the main character Maryse Boudreaux gives voice to how Black people have trans-historically felt for a long time: "'You see, the hate they give is senseless. They already got power. Yet they hate those over who they got control, who don't really pose a threat to them. Their fears aren't real—just insecurities and inadequacies. Deep down they know that. Makes their hate like . . . watered-down whiskey.'" (148) This speech brings together the Jim Crow and Trump eras in an ahistorical moment creating a feedback loop to help a vital sense of Blackness survive and speak truth to power and it is astonishing, inspirational, and heart-stopping all at once.

Come to think of it, the Canadian Métis author Cherie Dimaline's beautifully written novel *The Marrow Thieves* (2017) provides a second example. Dimaline describes an apocalyptic near-future Earth destroyed by global warming, natural disasters, and disappeared coastlines, where most of the surviving human population has lost the ability to dream, the sole exception being the Indigenous peoples of North America. Driven mad by the loss and dying as a result, white people figure out a way to harvest Indigenous bone marrow to survive, at first asking for Native volunteers before fully commodifying their bones. But the white folks deliberately revisit history and determine to reestablish Indian Residential Schools in which to extract the bone marrow. Such schools existed in Canada and the USA for more than a hundred years and were putatively established by Christian organizations that forcibly colonized child residents, a direct application of the white man's burden meant to destroy their heritages and cultures and identities. Many Indigenous children died at these boarding schools. Make no mistake, in this dystopian projection these schools are deathcamps and the nebulous government recruiters are their agents hunting the teenaged protagonist Frenchie and his patchwork Indigenous family as they run, hide, and survive on their way farther north over the course of the novel. Dimaline helps her audience to understand the devastation and trauma inflicted on her people by confronting it in full color.

And what is there in place to prevent such a recurrence of genocide against Indigenous peoples? The storytelling that the group's Cree elder Miigwans teaches to preserve painful memories and safeguard their cultures, sustainable ways, and sacred knowledges—voicing the un-voiceable tragedies—becomes the key. He relates the story of the first schools:

> "We suffered there. We almost lost our languages. Many lost their innocence, their laughter, their lives. But we got through it, and the schools were shut down. We returned to our home places and rebuilt, relearned, regrouped. We picked up and carried on. There were a lot of years where we were lost, too much pain drowned in forgetting that came in convenient packages: bottles, pills, cubicles where we settled to move around papers. But we sang our songs and brought them to the streets and into the classrooms—classrooms we built on our own lands and with our own words and books. And once we remembered we were warriors, once we honored the pain and left it on the side of the road, we moved ahead. We were back." (23–24)

Ultimately, the novel concerns the survival of a people with their cultures intact, what Anishinaabe writer and scholar Gerald Vizenor terms "native survivance," or "an active sense of presence over absence, deracination, and oblivion" via "the continuance of stories" ("Aesthetics," 1). Dimaline creates a powerful "*miinidiwag*" with *The Marrow Thieves*, whereby her storytelling, "an ironic Native giveaway . . . challenges readers to recognize their positions with regard to the diasporic condition of contemporary Native peoples" (Dillon, "Imagining," 6). Telling this story in this way at this time promotes healing. I call this novel a purposeful undoing of colonialism and a simultaneous demand for unequivocal restorative justice—a complete unravelling of the white problem. Quite simply decolonization.

Let me switch racial registers a third time to the author Ling Ma, a naturalized American citizen of Chinese descent. Ma writes a pandemic survival narrative in *Severance* (2018), where the pregnant narrator Candace Chen relates an alienating tale of traveling through the decaying infrastructure of the United States after the world succumbs to the fungal infection Shen Fever, originating in Shenzen, China, which makes benign zombies out of the Fevered. The narrator, Candace, is a millennial Chinese immigrant from the city of Fuzhou, in the southeastern Fujian province of China, whose parents relocated to Salt Lake City, Utah when she was six years old. A naturalized American citizen, she experiences a kind of millennial conditioning, which I think of as being pampered by parents afraid to make the mistakes of boomers, yet conditioned to be confident, oriented toward achievement, intuitive with technology, and questioning of authority while adaptive to change—except her parents are not of the American baby-boomer generation. Instead, they seem to reflect a stereotypical Asian immigrant experience in valuing emotional restraint and hard work to be successful. Combining this millennial conditioning with the identity issues caused by her gently warring parents who want Candace to lead a useful life—Dad sees Candace as an American woman free of the vestiges of the Cultural Revolution, Mom sees Candace as a Chinese woman connected to her heritage—she, consequently, experiences alienation.

Ostensibly, Candace works in a Times Square office building at Spectra, a publishing production firm as the head of the Bibles Division, but in her time off she takes photos of the city and blogs about NYC life on her anonymous webpage NY Ghost. And she continues posting pictures of an abandoned and dead city as the pandemic overwhelms its human resources. My favorite example of a Fevered zombie from the novel has to be the saleslady at the Fifth Avenue "Juicy Couture flagship shop" that Candace spies, who, even in death, kept the store immaculate through the apocalypse, "folding and refolding pastel polo shirts" while also maintaining "the wall of handbags, artfully arranged, by model and color" with half a jaw missing (258). Candace posts a thirty-second video of this zombie maintaining the store on her webpage; a post that becomes her most popular and controversial since survivors visit her blog seeking news before the power grid fails and knocks out the internet. In any case, Candace's job directly involves outsourcing the production of Bibles to China, where she visits Shenzen to oversee the work nearly every quarter at the Chinese partner business Phoenix Sun and Moon. Let's momentarily recall that the fever originates in Shenzen. These multilayered meanings come together to depict Candace's bifurcated relationship to China and America since she does not express many concrete thoughts on her country of birth, loses much of her native fluency in Mandarin Chinese, and gets caught up in being a functional worker as everything collapses. Ma's novel explores how Asian Americans can often be conflated with their Asian counterparts in the sense that Candace struggles with her displaced identity in early adulthood. While the premise of Ma's novel feels all too real against the backdrop of the COVID-19 pandemic, *Severance* investigates late-stage capitalism, nostalgia, immigration, and a continued, if subliminal, fixation with race.

As the novel progresses, Bob, a religious infotech worker, believes that the ragtag group of survivors have been divinely selected and so he leads them west from NYC to a place he partly owns called the Facility, which turns out, to everyone's bewilderment, to be a shopping mall in suburban Chicago. He operates from a position of an assumed white male privilege in taking charge of the survivors. In this regard, Ma also offers ironic commentary on white male religious dominance by demonstrating his fascist tendencies, intolerance, and hatred for those who disobey his rule. In short, Bob is a vengeful dick who imprisons Candace in the L'Occitane store—think high-end skincare products—that she chose as her living space to see out the pregnancy she tried to keep secret from Bob. He may have expelled her from the group after a clandestine live "stalking" orchestrated by the younger members goes tragically awry until another member betrays knowledge of Candace's pregnancy to Bob, resulting in her imprisonment to care for the unborn babe. A "stalking," live or dead, is basically a supply run through stores or homes where the Fevered, slow decaying husks, are unconsciously doing a repetitive task over and over ad infinitum, or are dead already. At the novel's end, an enraged, panicked Candace stomps to death a recently zombified Bob, endlessly walking his mall, in making good on her escape from the group in the pre-dawn hours.

Severance is a very different kind of science fiction novel with its dark humor in that it does not engage with yellow peril or techno-Orientalism. Why should it? Instead, it concerns a lost connection to family and critiques globalization and profit-driven American consumerism. It reflects Stephen H. Sohn's binary notion of the "Alien/Asian . . . how the connection between the Asian American and the alien other still remains a force to draw upon to allegorize racial tension and exclusion" ("Introduction," 6). This racial tension and exclusion become most visible when Candace is locked away in the mall shop by Bob, where she experiences the separation and loneliness of "the migrant subject excluded from legislative enfranchisement" (Sohn, "Introduction," 6). She exists to the group as a metaphoric extraterrestrial at Bob's behest, which paradoxically mirrors the Japanese American internment camp experience in World War II. This deliberate echo of internment experience affords the novel's audience an opportunity to witness racial politics at work in terms of the anxiety Candace has caused in the group with her presence and with her pregnancy. As Sohn indicates, "such anxieties concerning the Alien/Asian do not appear out of a sociohistoric vacuum" ("Introduction," 11). Candace's marginalized position as an Asian American woman transforms into a racialized alien experience largely because of Bob's messiah complex.

Amid the perceived whiteness of popular imagination, the American writer of Mexican and Guatemalan descent Sabrina Vourvoulias's near-future novel *Ink* (2012) also stands out for its biting social critique of US immigration policies concerning Latinx peoples. The basic plot concerns how totalitarian immigration laws come into existence within the United States of America over the span of ten years that provide the mirage of border security for American citizens who paradoxically depend on immigrant labor. As the title suggests, "aliens" residing within US borders get biometrically tattooed on the wrist, instead of documentation, with colors directly corresponding to their immigrant status—permanently marking them "other" as the government passes "identity law" into being (16). A black tattoo denotes a temporary status, and the unfortunate bearers of this mark are fitted with tracking devices; a green tattoo represents a work visa and permanent residency; a blue one designates a naturalized citizen. As Sherryl Vint remarks, "The use of tattoos to mark immigrant status is multiply evocative, from the connection to the visual difference of skin color, through the Nazis' use of tattoos to track Jewish inmates, to the increasing prevalence of biometric data (such as iris scans) used in passports, driver's licenses and other kinds of identification protocols" ("Don't"). Consequently, this law targets Latinx immigrants; try as they might to pass as white with "instaskin" to cover their tattoos, skin color, language, or accent will always give them away (Vourvoulias, *Ink*, 123). Again, as Vint mentions, *Ink* "makes chillingly clear how close beneath the surface of a liberal civil order lies a more oppressive regime willing to quickly narrow the category of the fully human to a smaller subset of those who have traditionally held power in Western societies (masculine, white)" ("Don't"). In this respect, here we are talking lost identity, stripped citizenship, and material dehumanization, perhaps even social death.

This first repressive step against non-white people leads to an English-only decree, curfews for the Inked, segregated bus lines, and false allegations of a communicable disease only infecting immigrants, leading to the nationally legislated creation of Inkatoriums, where the detained are confined for treatment and fitted with GPS trackers, while facing eventual sterilization without consent and mass deportation. That's an awful lot to process in the age of US Immigration and Customs Enforcement detention facilities. The collapsing science fictional boundaries between the created world (Inkatoriums) and our reality (ICE detention centers) uncannily and terrifyingly recall the concentration camps of Nazi Germany as well the Japanese Internment Camps of World War II America. Nothing feels far-fetched in Vourvoulias's novel; it is an entirely recognizable world that we experience with daily headlines outlining the xenophobic response to illegal immigration, Trump's expensive, inept, and idiotic border wall construction project, and technological surveillance. Cathyrn Josefina Merla-Watson claims that a "general discursive excision of Latin@s from the future signals a deep-seated and even genocidal desire of white America to disappear Latinos altogether" as evinced by Trump's border wall and threat to "deport millions of Mexican immigrants" ("The Altermundos"). And she's not wrong!

While Vourvoulias's world feels imminent in its becoming, she does provide hope as the main characters work together to build a sense of community despite race, class, and cultural differences. Vourvoulias oscillates between four main characters to tell her story: Finn, an American journalist; Mari, a US citizen from Guatemala, who works for a local Population Control Office, responsible for tracking all immigrants, and who becomes Finn's source and baby's mama; Del, Finn's brother-in-law, who works with Latinx laborers at a carpet company; and Abbie, a teenage hacker of a mixed white and unidentified Native American heritage (Wolf Clan, which could be Cherokee), whose white mother directs an Inkatorium. As the characters intermingle, form alliances and romantic attachments, it is their relationships—inked and citizens—that survive as they confront the unfolding dystopia and resist it together. Likewise, Vourvoulias also mixes to brilliant effect the near future technology on display with the Indigenous beliefs of Mari, who has a spirit animal protector, by suggesting how a supernatural dimension serves as a useful reminder of understanding human subjectivity, with religion included as a natural part of things. "Already," as Latinx scholar Catherine S. Ramírez notes, "people of color have been erased from the future," but BIPOCS like Vourvoulias, Clark, Dimaline, and Ma, and so many others, are writing themselves into our own futures as they become visible "in the barrios, ghettoes, reservations, and prisons of the present" ("Afrofuturism," 188). These wonderful writers become part of a global cofuturisms canon curated by people like Sheree Rénee Thomas and Bill Campbell.

SF, at its most vital, at least for me, has always depended on its short stories to allow authors to find their own voices and their own audiences before moving on to longer-form writing. Thomas holds an important place for BIPOCs in this colored science fiction wave because she edited the groundbreaking first anthology to focus on Black speculative fiction twenty-five years ago. *Dark Matter: A Century of Speculative Fiction from the African Diaspora*, published in 2000, remains the definitive collection of stories and essays representing a rich tradition of speculative writing and it won the 2001 World Fantasy Award for the Best Anthology. A veritable explosion of speculative anthologies featuring BIPOCs, edited by BIPOCS, has occurred since this moment: *Whispers from the Cotton Tree Root: Caribbean Fabulist Fiction* (2000), *Cosmos Latinos: An Anthology of Science Fiction from Latin America* (2003), *Mojo: Conjure Stories* (2003), *Dark Matter: Reading the Bones* (2004), *So Long Been Dreaming: Postcolonial Science Fiction & Fantasy* (2004), *Walking the Clouds: An Anthology of Indigenous Science Fiction* (2012), *AfroSF: Science Fiction by African Writers* (2012), *We See a Different Frontier: A Postcolonial Speculative Fiction Anthology* (2013), *Long Hidden: Speculative Fiction from the Margins of History* (2014), *AfroSFv2: 5 Novellas* (2014), *The Sea Is Ours: Tales of Steampunk Southeast Asia* (2015), *Terra Incognita: New Short Speculative Stories from Africa* (2015), *The City: A Cyberfunk Anthology* (2015), *Octavia's Brood: Science Fiction Stories from Social Justice Movements* (2015), *Invisible Planets: An Anthology of Contemporary Chinese Science Fiction in Translation* (2016), *AfroSFv3* (2018), *New Suns: Original Speculative Fiction by People of Color* (2019), *Black from the Future: A Collection of Black Speculative Writing* (2019), *Sunspot Jungle: The Ever Expanding Universe of*

Fantasy and Science Fiction, volumes 1 and 2 (2019), *Broken Stars: Contemporary Chinese Science Fiction in Translation* (2019), *The Gollancz Book of South Asian Science Fiction* (2019), *Readymade Bodhisattva: The Kaya Anthology of South Korean Science Fiction* (2019), *A People's Future History of the United States: Speculative Fiction from 25 Extraordinary Writers* (2019), *Latinx Rising: An Anthology of Latinx Science Fiction and Fantasy* (2020), *A Phoenix First Must Burn: Sixteen Stories of Black Girl Magic, Resistance, and Hope* (2020), *Africa Risen: A New Era of Speculative Fiction* (2022), and *New Suns 2: Original Speculative Fiction by People of Color* (2023). These are the twenty-eight anthologies that I know about and own in my personal collection. More importantly, Sheree Rénee Thomas recently became the tenth editor, and the first Black woman, to edit *The Magazine of Fantasy and Science Fiction*, a magazine continuously published since 1949, the end of the American Golden Age, and the third oldest surviving magazine behind the early pulp origins of *Amazing Stories* and *Analog*. I can hardly wait to see what Thomas does with this magazine! She's a big effing deal!

Bill Campbell is also a big effing deal in that he founded Rosarium Publishing in 2013. Campbell simply wanted to see speculative fiction and comics through a multicultural lens irrespective of identity issues such as race, gender, religion, or nationality and put together a group of like-minded people and got the publishing house off the ground with an IndieGoGo crowdsourcing campaign to fund the publication of the first book, the coedited anthology, *Mothership: Tales from Afrofuturism and Beyond* (2013). I have it on good authority that Campbell worked a variety of day jobs to realize this ambition and grow it from a solo operation to a collective of fifty artists and writers with the desire to tell good stories. I respect the grind and the grit of Campbell et al. who have so far produced and published nineteen novels, seven anthologies, sixteen graphic novels, and seven ongoing comics, such as *Super Sikh* and *Box of Bones*, as well as an art book. Campbell's publishing house advocates for social change through stories that reflect the globe's diversity. My favorite Rosarium publication has to be Campbell's own *Koontown Killing Kaper* (2012), which I discussed in the third chapter.

I would find this outro supremely troubling if I failed to say something about the 37th Damon Knight Grand Master of Science Fiction—Nalo Hopkinson. Hopkinson is the first Black woman so honored by her creative peers and only the second Black person following living legend Samuel R. Delany. I could easily talk about the tremendous impact of Hopkinson's fiction as a multiple-award winning, groundbreaking Black Caribbean speculative fiction writer, editor, and teacher who fully engages issues of race, gender, queerness, technology, science, and the occult in her body of work. I could do so quite effortlessly. Instead, I will talk about Hopkinson's celebrated, at least among BIPOCs, Guest of Honor lecture at the 31st International Conference of the Fantastic in the Arts in 2010, entitled "A Reluctant Ambassador from the Planet of Midnight." But first, here's a little-known fact: I cowrote the proposal for that year's conference theme "Race and the Fantastic" along with Patrica Melzer and Kim Surkan.

With her forty-five-minute ICFA address in a largely white banquet hall in Orlando, Florida, Nalo Hopkinson tackled the difficult subject of translation, about what people mean when they say "I'm not racist," by performing her talk as an alien ambassador. I will never forget the power of her performance, her chin hitting her collar bone, her head lifting and the alien ambassador emerging channeled through her body, possessing her mind as a translator grappling with the concepts of race and racism. I found it to be riveting and instructive as well as one of the bravest actions I have ever witnessed. I watched Hopkinson demand an understanding of how erasure feels from that largely white audience; challenge how science fiction and fantasy often present a monochrome vision of the future where white people are the only ones that matter; and insist upon people of color writing themselves into the future to countermand the long-term effects of colonialism, such as alienation, victimization, and trauma. Writers and educators like Nalo Hopkinson create better worlds with their words when they question the normality of master narratives such as colorblindness, which heavily influences popular culture and our social lives. She helped to launch SF's current colored wave with its critique of inequality and difference in general and its appreciation for diversity. Her talk still represents a powerful teaching moment and generated a standing ovation from that particular audience.

Her bravery was later echoed by N. K. Jemisin in her acceptance speech for the 2018 Hugo Award for Best Novel for *The Stone Sky* (2017). Winning for an unprecedented third time in a row, Jemisin, in standing up to the Sad/Rabid Puppies, declared: "But this is the year in which I get to smile at all of those naysayers—every single mediocre insecure wannabe who fixes their mouth to suggest that I do not belong on this stage, that people like me cannot possibly have earned such an honor, that when they win it it's meritocracy but when we win it it's 'identity politics'—I get to smile at those people, and lift a massive, shining, rocket-shaped middle finger in their direction" ("The Stars"). Welcome to FULL COLOR science fiction and fantasy. Written about by people like me—a Black academic who reads science fiction, researches science fiction, and teaches science fiction. I am delving into one of a billion "Black Anthropocenes," where "the proximity of black and brown bodies to harm in this intimacy with the inhuman . . . is repurposed for survival and formed into a praxis for remaking other selves that were built in the harshest of conditions" (Yusoff, *A Billion*, xii). Science fiction can, it has, and it will solve the white problem again and again and again.

To conclude: the personal involves my time as a professor; the cultural concerns the Capitol riot, and the analytical displays my scholarly look at multiple examples of cofuturisms. The Black, the Red, the Brown, the Yellow analyses represent BIPOC authors disrupting a perceived monochrome future, writing themselves into it, creating alternatives where they see themselves in all their own glories and with all their own flaws representing humanity itself—decolonizing whiteness, decentering whiteness, and finally, dismissing it. White people need to start understanding that they ain't runnin' shit no mo.' Ya dig?

NOTES

Introduction

1. See my "Mapping the Blackground," in *Race in American Science Fiction* (2011) for more information.

2. For further information, see Paul Youngquist's *A Pure Solar World: Sun Ra and the Birth of Afrofuturism* (2016); and Erik Steinskog's *Afrofuturism and Black Sound Studies: Culture, Technology, and Things to Come* (2018).

3. The Black Lives Matter movement began as a hashtag on twitter in 2013 in response to the acquittal of George Zimmerman for the murder of Black teenager Trayvon Martin in 2012. Alicia Garza, Patrisse Cullors, and Opal Tometi, three Black women activists used the social media platform to express their fury and frustration with the world at this continuing injustice and for this enduring plight that Blacks in the United States face every day.

Chapter 1

1. See John A. Williams's *Sons of Darkness, Sons of Light: A Novel of Some Probability* (1969). The basic plot involves Eugene Browning of the imaginary civil rights organization Institute for Racial Justice hiring a professional hitman to assassinate Sergeant Carrigan of the NYPD in revenge for his killing of an unarmed Black teenager. This single act of payback sets off a race war across the country as the novel ends.

2. See Sam Greenlee's *The Spook Who Sat by the Door* (1969). The novel involves Dan Freeman, a Black man, who uses his CIA training to teach Chicago gang members how to fight a guerilla war against the government while maintaining his cover as a social worker at the beginning of this freedom fight.

3. See William M. Kelley's *A Different Drummer* (1962). Kelley describes a bloodless revolution, where the Black Tucker Caliban decides to burn down his house, salt his fields, kill his livestock, and then walk away from his land with his family causing a Black exodus, economically crippling the imaginary Southern state.

4. See vol. 18, no. 2 of *Black American Literature Forum*.

5. See vol. 48, no. 3 of *African American Review*.

6. Robert A. Heinlein presents a postapocalyptic far future world where the white middle-aged Hugh Farnham and his family survive in a fallout shelter along with their Black servant Joe after being nuked into the future only to be captured and enslaved by French-speaking Africans with advanced technology in *Farnham's Freehold* (1964). Ultimately, Hugh creates an alternate timeline when he volunteers to test an experimental time machine rather than live as a castrated slave.

7. John M. Faucette Jr.'s debut novel *Crown of Infinity* (1968) is a space opera detailing the rise and fall of a superhuman race known as the Star Kings. Originating on Earth, the Star Kings defeat the Masters of the Universe and become protectors of the universe. Its follow-up, *The Age of Ruin* (1968) is a postapocalyptic tale that combines sword and sorcery as the purple-skinned hero Jahalazar undertakes a quest to avenge his mother's killing and to defeat the Vish empire.

8. See Mark Bould's essay "Space/Race: Recovering John M. Faucette," in Isiah Lavender III and Lisa Yaszek's collection *Literary Afrofuturism in the Twenty-First Century* (2020).

9. Päivi Väätänen notes the possibility of how Delany likely references A. E. van Vogt's well-known short story "Black Destroyer" (1939) in naming his character Destroyer as well as offers conjecture for the irony of doing so (45).

10. Delany himself is in an interracial marriage to the Jewish American poet Marilyn Hacker; they married in Detroit, Michigan, one of two states where interracial marriage, combined with age of consent laws, was legal in 1961 (*Motion*, 22). Certainly, interracial marriage was controversial in much of the United States at this time, but I remain unsure of how alert Delany was to the *Loving v. Virginia* case slowly winding its way through the judicial system since 1963 with a plethora of other major court decisions and civil rights battles occurring in the 1960s. Ultimately, the US Supreme Court struck down interracial marriage restrictions in 1967. I found myself pondering if the relationship between Leela and the Destroyer somehow strangely mirrored that of Delany and Hacker since *The Ballad of Beta-2* was published in 1965. But I found no evidence for it beyond the mention of miscegenation laws in his autobiography *The Motion of Light in Water: Sex and Science Fiction Writing in the East Village* (1988).

11. North Carolina A&T College students Ezell Blair Jr., David Richmond, Franklin McCain, and Joseph McNeil became known as the Greensboro Four for their bravery.

12. For more information, see B. J. Hollars's *The Road South: Personal Stories of the Freedom Riders* (2018).

13. See Frank Lambert's *The Battle of Ole Miss: Civil Rights v. States' Rights* (2009) for more information.

14. See Dan T. Carter's *The Politics of Rage: George Wallace, the Origins of the New Conservatism, and the Transformation of American Politics* (2000) for further information.

15. See Julie Buckner Armstrong's *Learning from Birmingham: A Journey into History and Home* (2023) for more information.

16. Dhonielle Clayton describes the citizens of Orléans as gray-skinned until they receive beauty treatments from magically gifted beauticians controlled by the monarchy in her debut novel *The Belles* (2018).

17. In *Bug Jack Barron*, Norman Spinrad features Mississippi as a Black separatist state lead by its Black governor Lukas Greene as a side plot to the story of TV talk show host Jack Barron. Jack wants immortality through cryogenic stasis, but finds out the freezing process offered by the Foundation for Human Immortality is segregated and will not offer contracts to Black Americans. Jack learns this information during his show upon receiving a live call from Black Mississippian Rufus Johnson.

18. The trilogy—*North and South* (1982), *Love and War* (1984), and *Heaven and Hell* (1987)—details the saga of two families on opposite sides of the Civil War bound in enduring friendship when the two eldest sons first meet at West Point in the 1840s: Orry Main of South Carolina and George Hazard of Pennsylvania.

19. As Joan D. Hedrick notes, "*Uncle Tom's Cabin* sold 10,000 copies within the week and 300,000 by the end of the first year" (*Harriet Beecher Stowe*, 223). Likewise, Kenneth DiMaggio

writes that Stowe's novel "also earned the distinction of being the best-selling book in its day after the Bible" ("*Uncle Tom's Cabin*," 15).

Chapter 2

1. For further information, see Ojibwe historian Brenda J. Child's *Boarding Seasons: American Indian Families, 1900–1940* (2000).

2. See Anishinaabe author and theorist Gerald Vizenor's *Manifest Manners: Narratives on Postindian Survivance* (1999).

3. In *The Souls of Black Folk*, W. E. B. Du Bois writes: "It is a peculiar sensation, this double-consciousness, this sense of always looking at one's self through the eyes of others, of measuring one's soul by the tape of a world that looks on in amused contempt and pity. One ever feels his twoness,—an American, a Negro; two souls, two thoughts, two unreconciled strivings; two warring ideals in one dark body, whose dogged strength alone keeps it from being torn asunder" (45).

4. According to Gina Marchetti, "the yellow peril [narrative] combines racist terrors of alien cultures, sexual anxieties, and the belief that the West will be overpowered and enveloped by the irresistible, dark, occult forces of the East" (*Romance*, 2).

5. With Japan in mind, David Morley and Kevin Robins first formulated techno-Orientalism to mean racist images of Asians as "unfeeling aliens . . . cyborgs and replicants" within "the political and cultural unconscious of the West" resulting from "the dystopian image of capitalist progress" ("Techno-Orientalism," 170).

6. Vincent Chin was a Chinese American engineer mistaken for a Japanese who was beaten to death outside a Detroit McDonalds with a baseball bat in 1982. Two white men, autoworker Ronald Ebens and his laid-off stepson Michael Nitz, who blamed the encroaching Japanese auto industry for their plight, got away with murder and three years of probation, prompting Asian Americans to get more deeply involved in the fight for Civil Rights. For more information, see page 22 in Robert S. Chang's *Disoriented* (1999) in addition to Alethea Yip's article "Remembering Vincent Chin" (1997).

7. See Langston Hughes's essay "The Negro Artist and the Racial Mountain" (1926).

8. See Martin Luther King Jr.'s "I've Been to the Mountaintop" (1968).

9. See Andrew Gyory's *Closing the Gate: Race, Politics and the Chinese Exclusion Act* (1998), Erika Lee's *At America's Gates: Chinese Immigration During the Exclusion Era, 1882–1943* (2003), and Beth Lew-Williams's *The Chinese Must Go: Violence, Exclusion, and the Making of the Alien in America* (2021) for relevant information.

10. For more information, see the September 23, 2014 article "Ice Opens Its First-Ever Designed-and-Built Civil Detention Center."

11. See Silvia Martínez-Falquina's "Louise Erdrich's *Future Home of the Living God*: Uncertainty, Proleptic Mourning and Relationality in Native Dystopia" (2019), Anna Kemball's "Biocolonial Pregnancies: Louise Erdrich's *Future Home of the Living God* (2017)" (2022), and Kaylee J. Mootz's "The Body and the Archive in Louise Erdrich's *Future Home of the Living God*" (2020).

12. Interestingly, Eddy will later organize and lead the Indigenous effort to "take back the land" by capturing a weapon depot, creating a "new unbreakable code" based on the howl of wolves, and training a militia to resist, but that is a tangential point at best (Erdrich, *Future Home of the Living God*, 111, 274).

13. Anna Kemball notes how "Erdrich herself has described both the novel and policy in terms of reversal and regression" with respect to both George W. Bush and Donald Trump's presidencies ("Biocolonial Pregnancies," 61).

14. For more information on the data-thief concept, see John Akomfrah's documentary *The Last Angel of History* (1996).

15. I learned this information from Smith because of my nontraditional student Jane Travis, a retired librarian, who took it upon herself to find out why Mississippi was not included in the quarantine declaration after an exciting class discussion in my 2021 UGA summer class.

16. For further information, see African American medical ethicist Harriet A. Washington's *Medical Apartheid: The Dark History of Medical Experimentation on Black Americans from Colonial Times to the Present* (2007).

17. Butler states, "I'm a pessimist if I'm not careful, a feminist, a black, a former Baptist, an oil-and-water combination of ambition, laziness, insecurity, certainty, and drive" (quoted in Canavan, *Octavia E. Butler*, 1).

Chapter 3

1. See Jean Baudrillard's *Simulacra and Simulation* (1981).

2. See Isiah Lavender III's *Afrofuturism Rising: The Literary Prehistory of a Movement* (2019).

3. See Langston Hughes's poem "Harlem" (1951).

4. I cannot help but laugh at what seems a reference to the Black comedy classic film *Coming to America* (1988), starring Eddie Murphy as Prince Akeem, with Ruffin's reference to Prince Akeem's home country of Zamunda. While this moment is funny, both whites and Blacks have seriously pondered back-to-Africa plans across the centuries as a solution to the race problem. For example, Thomas Jefferson advocated freeing and sending Blacks back to Africa later in his life. Black abolitionist Martin R. Delany wanted to establish a Black American colony in west Africa in the nineteenth century as did Black nationalist Marcus Garvey in the twentieth century; in fact, Garvey incorporated the shipping company Black Star Line for that purpose.

5. See Erum Salam's 2021 article "Black US High School Student Forced to Cut Hair During Softball Game" as well as Roman Stubbs's 2019 article "A Wrestler Was Forced to Cut His Dreadlocks Before a Match."

6. See Janelle Griffith's 2020 article "Black Teen Told to Cut His Locs by Texas School Wins Court Ruling."

7. Thurman's novel concerns the cross-country journey of a dark-skinned woman, Emma Lou Morgan, born to a light-skinned Black family who ends up in Harlem and faces constant rejection because of her skin color.

8. Schuyler's social satire involves the invention of a skin-lightening process and the social mayhem it unleashes in a newly color-conscious United States as Black people become white.

9. For further information, see Audrey E. Kerr's incisive study *The Paper Bag Principle: Class, Colorism, and Rumor and the Case of Black Washington, D.C.* (2006).

10. Daniel Patrick Moynihan's infamous 1965 report "The Negro Family: The Case for National Action," caused tremendous social harm in reinforcing stereotypes of absentee Black fathers, Black single mother households, and violent ghetto culture leading to the deterioration of Black communities as opposed to the loss of good paying industrial jobs.

11. "BBQ Becky" is the name of the social meme acquired by Jennifer Schulte, the white woman who called the police on a Black family grilling out at an Oakland, California park back in the spring of 2018.

12. "Central Park Karen" threatened police violence on Christian Cooper, a birdwatcher who happened to be Black, in the form of a phone call because he dared to call the white Amy Cooper out for violating the leash law for her dog in the spring of 2020.

Chapter 4

1. The steampunk subgenre emerges in the 1980s and describes an alternate nineteenth century dominated by steam-power inventions with stories typically set in Victorian England or the Wild West of the United States. Splatterpunk also begins in the 1980s and refers to graphic gore and violence in the horror genre. Biopunk originates in the 1990s and features the shady side of biotechnology and genetic engineering, such as gene-hackers, in an otherwise cyberpunk setting. Solarpunk arrives in the aughts and represents the synchronicity of nature and technology in ecocritical utopias. Silkpunk provides an East Asian blend of culture, myth, and technology to go along with rebellion as it develops in the 2010s.

2. See my 2019 essay "Critical Race Theory" in *The Routledge Companion to Cyberpunk Culture.*

3. I purposely invert Bruce Sterling's formulation of cyberpunk as a "combination of lowlife and high tech" to better express the social feel of cyberpunk in our world today (Sterling, "Preface," in *Burning Chrome*, xiv).

4. See Frances Bonner's 1992 essay "Separate Development: Cyberpunk in Film and TV" in support of the "the four C's of cyberpunk" identified as a "concentration on computers, corporations, crime, and corporeality" (191).

5. See Chapter 6, entitled "Technologically Derived Ethnicities," in my *Race in American Science Fiction* (2011), 186–210, for a full explanation of technicity.

6. In *How We Became Posthuman: Virtual Bodies in Cybernetics, Literature, and Informatics* (1999), N. Katherine Hayles explains how her definition of "virtuality . . . seeks to connect virtual technologies with the sense, pervasive in the late twentieth century that all material objects are interpenetrated by flows of information, from DNA code to the global reach of the World Wide Web" (14).

7. See Bruce Sterling's depiction of the twenty-first century in *Islands in the Net* (1988), where "Africa" symbolizes a "desperate exceptionalism, that it is the benchmark against which to measure the extent to which you have escaped disaster, barbarism, backwardness everywhere in the novel" (Bould, "Afrocyberpunk 2"). Sterling exhibits a near future world where multinational companies matter far more than sovereign political entities and the Net's interconnectivity reinforces baser human impulses.

8. To a degree, Gibson's *Neuromancer*, Stephenson's *Snow Crash*, Sterling's *Islands in the Net*, and Cadigan's *Mindplayers* (1987) all concern the intersections of technology and the mind.

9. Philip E. Baruth makes a similar argument in "The Excesses of Cyberpunk: Why No One Mentions Race in Cyberspace" (1997).

10. Cline uncannily forecasts the gamergate controversy of 2014/2015, where women in the video game industry were targeted online and subjected to misogynistic harassment.

11. In a likely nod to Don DeLillo's novel *White Noise* (1985), an exemplar of postmodernism, like cyberpunk itself, Mosley experiments with this (new-to-him) subgenre by challenging the authorities of cyberpunk per se with storylines featuring political issues germane to Black culture like the judicial system and the prison industrial complex.

12. See the third edition of Manning Marable's classic study *Race, Reform, and Rebellion: The Second Reconstruction and Beyond in Black America, 1945–2006* (2007).

13. For a sustained comparison between Delany's *Stars in My Pocket Like Grains of Sand* and Gibson's *Neuromancer*, see Thomas Foster's essay "'Innocent by Contamination': Ethnicity and Technicity in Delany's *Stars in My Pocket Like Grains of Sand*" (2015).

14. See *Narrative of the Life of Frederick Douglass* (1845).

15. Carl Van Vechten was severely and rightly criticized for writing his novel *Nigger Heaven* (1926) and claiming that it celebrated Black Life in Harlem, thus undermining the good will he received from the Black community for his philanthropy and photography in his willful exercise of white privilege.

16. See Eric Lott's classic study *Love & Theft: Blackface Minstrelsy and the American Working Class* (1993) for further information.

17. Five novels make up the series: *Patternmaster* (1976), *Mind of My Mind* (1977), *Survivor* (1978), *Wild Seed* (1980), and *Clay's Ark* (1984)—though Butler disowned *Survivor*. The publishing order of the novels does not follow the chronological order of the entire story.

18. Okorafor cleverly puns on the surveillance capabilities of totalitarian regimes in science fiction perhaps best represented by the all-seeing gaze of Big Brother in George Orwell's *1984* (1949).

Chapter 5

1. It's worth mentioning that the *Creole* was the name of a slave ship sailing from Richmond to New Orleans in 1841 on which a mutiny occurred led by Madison Washington, a revolt that inspired fictional accounts by Frederick Douglass, Lydia Maria Child, William Wells Brown, and Pauline Hopkins.

2. See my introduction to *Race in American Science Fiction* (2011) for further information on "blackground" (6).

3. See the monumental collection, Nikole Hannah-Jones et al., eds., *The 1619 Project: A New Origin Story* (2021).

4. Little scholarship actually exists on Poe as an SF writer.

5. This novel imagines a future United States of 1849, where most of the South has already seceded to continue the practice of slavery. Hoping to join the Confederacy, Douglas Trevor, the main character, leads secessionist Virginians in a guerrilla war against the federal government and President Martin Van Buren.

6. See page 235 in J. Gerald Kennedy's "'Trust No Man.'"

7. For more information, see Ralph Clayton's "E. A. Poe, Dealer in Slaves."

8. For example, Richard J. Herrnstein and Charles Murray claim in *The Bell Curve* (1994) that "the difference in test scores between African-Americans and European-Americans as measured in dozens of reputable studies has converged on approximately a one standard deviation difference for several decades . . . this means that the average white person tests higher than about 84 percent of the population of blacks" (269). It may be a different century, but the racism remains unchanged. Much like Herrnstein and Murray's controversial renown, "Morton's fame as a scientist rested upon his collection of skulls and their role in racial ranking," according to the famed Harvard scientist Stephen Jay Gould (*Mismeasure*, 85).

9. See the picture on page 275 in Robert McCracken Peck and Patricia Tyson Stroud's *A Glorious Enterprise: The Academy of Natural Sciences of Philadelphia and the Making of American Science* (2012).

10. For example, J. Gerald Kennedy writes, "Pym here expresses a white racial fear common in the South after the Nat Turner insurrection (and the earlier, abortive uprising led by

Denmark Vesey)" ("'Trust,'" 248). John C. Rowe sees the novel as an "allegory of white Southern fears regarding slave insurrections" spurred by Nat Turner's rebellion in 1831 ("Antebellum," 912). And Betsy Erkkila states, "*The Narrative of Arthur Gordon Pym* (1838) makes explicit the phobia about the dark other, the fear of black insurrection, and the flight into an otherworldly space of pure whiteness" ("The Poetics," 57).

11. For more information on cognitive estrangement, see Darko Suvin's *Metamorphosis of Science Fiction* (1979).

12. See W. E. B. Du Bois's *The Souls of Black Folk* (1903) for more information on double consciousness.

13. See Lisa Yaszek's "The Bannekerade: Genius, Madness, and Magic in Black Science Fiction" (2014) for deeper reflection on the Black scientist.

14. See chapter 6 ("Technologically Derived Ethnicities"), in my own *Race in American Science Fiction* (2011), for more consideration on racialized androids.

15. See *The History of Mary Prince, a West Indian Slave. Related by Herself* (1831), *Twelve Years a Slave* (1853) by Solomon Northup, and *Incidents in the Life of a Slave Girl* (1861) by Harriet Jacobs.

16. Three of the other paragraphs concern the attempt of Peters to track down Poe while the fifth describes "a big pale guy in a white robe," a "Tekeleli," which strangely broadcasts the image of Klansman to my own imagination (*Pym*, 67).

17. Many scholars make note of the Morrison and Poe connection that Johnson makes in his novel as indicated by the title of this imaginary course. For example, Richard Kopley remarks that "The college course that Chris Jaynes offers, 'Dancing with the Darkies: Whiteness in the Literary Mind' (7), suggests Toni Morrison's book, *Playing in the Dark: Whiteness and the Literary Imagination*" ("The Quest," 43).

18. In *Fugitive Science* (2017), Britt Rusert explores how digging up bones represents "haunting reanimations of racial science under the rule of Jim Crow" and "illuminates the science of segregation while exposing the sheer absurdity and groundlessness of race science" (222–223). I think it safe to say that Mathis was afraid of the specter of her Blackness and also that Johnson comically, perhaps horrifically, implies that the United States of America is still haunted by the lingering presence of racial science in the twenty-first century.

19. Tim Christensen offers a scintillating reading of consumerism and race through Garth's obsession with Little Debbie snack cakes in his essay "Little Debbie, or the Logic of late Capitalism: Consumerism, Whiteness, and Addiction in Mat Johnson's *Pym*" (2017). For instance, Christensen notes how "Garth has literally consumed tons of Little Debbie snack cakes—and both figuratively and literally consumed whiteness in the process—in his dedication to the sugary treats and their corporate icon" (173).

20. See Samuel R. Delany's *Stars in My Pockets Like Grains of Sand* (1984), Octavia E. Butler's *Dawn* (1987), and N. K. Jemisin's *The Fifth Season* (2015).

21. Think along the lines of the quintessential model of this genre, *A Narrative of the Captivity and Restoration of Mrs. Mary Rowlandson* (1682). It is also known as *The Sovereignty and Goodness of God.*

22. This moment reminds me of Mike Judge's cult classic *Idiocracy* (2006), wherein the moron populace of the twenty-sixth century United States is facing a food shortage because they are watering crops with Mountain Dew soda.

23. Unfortunately, this essay doesn't cover gender since Johnson follows Poe in exploring race in the traditionally masculine world of adventure.

Outro

1. See my introductions to both *Black and Brown Planets: The Politics of Race in Science Fiction* (2014) and *Dis-Orienting Planets: Racial Representations of Asia in Science Fiction* (2017), as well as my essay "Black Grit: or, Why I Study Race and Racism in Science Fiction" (2014).

2. See Lil Wayne's sixth studio album *Tha Carter III* (2008).

3. Erik "Killmonger" Stevens (Michael B. Jordan) is a lost prince who nearly overthrows his cousin T'Challa, the King of Wakanda and proverbial *Black Panther* in the 2018 film.

WORKS CITED

Adams, Bluford. *E Pluribus Barnum: The Great Showman and the Making of U.S. Popular Culture.* U of Minnesota P, 1997.

Adams, John Joseph, and Victor LaValle, eds. *A People's Future of the United States: Speculative Fiction from 25 Extraordinary Writers.* One World, 2019.

Agamben, Giorgio. *Homo Sacer: Sovereign Power and Bare Life.* Translated by Daniel Heller-Roazen. Stanford UP, 1998.

Ahmed, Samira. *Internment.* Little, Brown, 2019.

Akomfrah, John, dir. *The Last Angel of History.* First Run/Icarus Films, 1996.

Al-Ayad, Djibril, and Fabio Fernandes, eds. *We See a Different Frontier: A Postcolnial Speculative Fiction Anthology.* Futurefire.net, 2013.

Alexander, Michelle. *The New Jim Crow: Mass Incarceration in the Age of Colorblindness.* The New Press, 2010.

Allen, Stephanie A. and Lauren Cherelle, eds. *Black from the Future: A Collection of Black Speculative Writing.* BLF Press, 2019.

Allen, Violet. "The Venus Effect." [2016.] In *Resist: Tales from a Future Worth Fighting Against,* edited by Gary Whitta, Christie Yant, Hugh Howey, 341–365. Independently published, 2018.

Apter, Emily. *Continental Drift: From National Characters to Virtual Subjects.* U of Chicago P, 1999.

Archambauld, Paul. "An Hour of Last Things: An Interview with George P. Elliott." *Syracuse Scholar* 1, no. 2 (1980): 35–43.

Armstrong, Julie B. *Learning from Birmingham: A Journey into History and Home.* U of Alabama P, 2023.

Atwood, Margaret. *The Handmaid's Tale.* Houghton Mifflin, 1985.

Barnes, Steven. *Firedance.* Tor, 1994.

———. *Gorgon Child.* Tor, 1989.

———. *Great Sky Woman.* One World Books, 2006.

———. *Shadow Valley.* Del Rey, 2009.

———. *Streetlethal.* Ace, 1983.

Barnett, Randy E. *Restoring the Lost Constitution: The Presumption of Liberty.* Revised ed. Princeton UP, 2014.

Barnum, Phineas T. *The Life of P. T. Barnum, Written by Himself.* [1855.] U of Illinois P, 2000.

Baruth, Philip E. "The Excesses of Cyberpunk: Why No One Mentions Race in Cyberspace." In *Into Darkness Peering: Race and Color in Fantastic Fiction,* edited by Elisabeth Leonard, 105–118. Greenwood Press, 1997.

Baudemann, Kristina. "Removed to the Signifier: Utopia in Stephen Graham Jones's *The Bird Is Gone: A Manifesto* (2003)." *Open Library of Humanities* 4, no.1 (2018): 1–31. https://doi.org/10.16995/olh.232.

Baudrillard, Jean. *Simulacra and Simulation*. [1981.] Translated by Sheila F. Glaser. U of Michigan P, 1994.

———. *Simulations*. Translated by Paull Foss, Paul Patton, and Philip Beitchman. Semiotext(e), 1983.

Beck, John. *Dirty Wars: Landscape, Power, and Waste in Western American Literature*. U of Nebraska P, 2009.

Bell, Andrea L., and Yoland Molina Gavilán, eds. *Cosmos Latinos: An Anthology of Science Fiction from Latin America*. Wesleyan UP, 2003.

Bell, Bernard W. *The Afro-American Novel and Its Tradition*. U of Massachusetts P, 1987.

Bell, Derrick A., Jr. "*Brown v. Board of Education* and the Interest Convergence Dilemma." In *Critical Race Theory: The Key Writings That Formed the Movement*, edited by Kimberlé Crenshaw et al., 20–29. The New Press, 1995.

———. *Faces at the Bottom of the Well: The Permanence of Racism*. Basic, 1992.

———. "Serving Two Masters: Integration Ideals and Client Interests in School Desegregation Litigation." In *Critical Race Theory: The Key Writings That Formed the Movement*, edited by Kimberlé Crenshaw et al., 5–19. The New Press, 1995.

———. "The Space Traders." In *Faces at the Bottom of the Well: The Permanence of Racism*, 158–194. Basic, 1992.

Bellamy, Brent R. *Remainders of the American Century: Post-Apocalyptic Novels in the Age of U.S. Decline*. Wesleyan UP, 2021.

Bertamini, Marco, et al. "The Venus Effect in Real Life and in Photographs." *Attention, Perception, and Psychophysics* 72, no. 7 (2010): 1948–1964. https://doi:10.3758/APP.72.7.1948.

Bertamini, Marco, Richard Latto, and Alice Spooner. "The Venus Effect: People's Understanding of Mirror Reflections in Paintings." *Perception* 32, no. 5 (2003): 593–599. https://doi:10.1068/p3418.

The Bible: The New Living Translation. 2nd ed. Tyndale House Publishers, 1988.

Blum, Hester. "Archipelagic Pym." *Poe Studies: History, Theory, Interpretation* 54 (2021): 49–66.

Bonilla-Silva, Eduardo. *Racism Without Racists: Color-Blind Racism and the Persistence of Racial Inequality in America*. 5th ed. Roman & Littlefield, 2018.

Bonner, Frances. "Separate Development: Cyberpunk in Film and TV." In *Fiction 2000: Cyberpunk and the Future of Narrative*, edited by George Slusser and Tom Shippey, 191–207. U of Georgia P, 1992.

Bould, Mark. "Afrocyberpunk 1: The Enervated Ghosts of Zion." *Mark Bould* (blog), October 1, 2015, https://markbould.com/2015/10/01/the-enervated-ghosts-of-zion-afrocyberpunk-1/.

———. "Afrocyberpunk 2: Bruce Sterling, Islands in the Net (1988), Part One." *Mark Bould* (blog), November 16, 2015, markbould.com/2015/11/16/afrocyberpunk-2-bruce-sterling-islands-in-the-net-1988-part-one/.

———. "Afrocyberpunk Cinema: The Postcolony Finds Its Own Use for Things." In *Cyberpunk and Visual Culture*, edited by Graham J. Murphy and Lars Schmeink, 213–234. Routledge, 2018.

———. "Space/Race: Recovering John M. Faucette." In *Literary Afrofuturism in the Twenty-First Century*, edited by Isiah Lavender III and Lisa Yaszek, 109–127. Ohio State UP, 2020.

Bradbury, Ray. *Fahrenheit 451*. [1953.] Simon & Shuster, 2012.

Brickler, Alexander Dumas J., IV. "Soul in the Shell: Steven Barnes's Aubry Knight Trilogy, Black Cyborgs, and Cyberpunk Investigations of Technological Black Bodies." In *Black Bodies and Transhuman Realities: Scientifically Modifying the Black Body in Posthuman Literature and Culture*, edited by Melvin G. Hill, 151–176. Lexington Books, 2019.

brown, adrienne m., and Walidah Imarisha. *Octavia's Brood: Science Fiction Stories from Social Justice Movements*. AK Press, 2015.

Burroughs, Edgar R. *The Land That Time Forgot*. [1918.] Penguin, 1979.

———. *A Princess of Mars*. [1912.] Project Gutenberg, 2008.

Butler, Octavia E. *Dawn*. [1987.] Grand Central, 2021.

———. *Kindred*. [1979.] Beacon, 1988.

———. *Mind of my Mind*. [1977.] Warner, 1994.

———. *Parable of the Sower*. [1993.] Grand Central, 2000.

———. *Parable of the Talents*. [1998.] Grand Central, 2019.

———. "Positive Obsession." In *Bloodchild and Other Stories*, by Octavia E. Butler, 123–136. 2nd ed. Seven Stories Press, 2005.

———. *Seed to Harvest*. Grand Central, 2007.

Cadigan, Pat. *Mindplayers*. Bantam Spectra, 1987.

Caldwell, Patrice, ed. *A Phoenix First Must Burn: Sixteen Stories of Black Girl Magic, Resistance, and Hope*. Viking, 2020.

Campbell, Bill. *Koontown Killing Kaper*. Rosarium Publishing, 2012.

———, ed. *Sunspot Jungle: The Ever Expanding Universe of Fantasy and Science Fiction*. 2 vols. Rosarium, 2019.

Campbell, Bill, and Edward Austin Hall, eds. *Mothership: Tales from Afrofuturism and Beyond*. Rosarium, 2013.

Canavan, Gerry. *Octavia E. Butler*. U of Illinois P, 2016.

Carter, Dan T. *The Politics of Rage: George Wallace, the Origins of the New Conservatism, and the Transformation of American Politics*. 2nd ed. Louisiana State UP, 2000.

Chang, Robert S. *Disoriented: Asian Americans, Law and the Nation-State*. NYU P, 1999.

Child, Brenda J. *Boarding Seasons: American Indian Families, 1900–1940*. U of Nebraska P, 2000.

Child, Lydia Maria. "The Quadroons." [1842.] In *Fact and Fiction: A Collection of Stories*, 61–76. New York, 1846.

Chiles, Katy L. *Transformable Race: Surprising Metamorphoses in the Literature of Early America*. Oxford UP, 2014.

Chng, Joyce, and Jaymee Goh, eds. *The Sea Is Ours: Tales of Steampunk Southeast Asia*. Rosarium, 2015.

Chow-White, Peter A. and Lisa Nakamura. Introduction. In *Race After the Internet*, edited by Chow-White and Nakamura, 1–18. Routledge, 2012.

Christensen, Tim. "Little Debbie, or the Logic of Late Capitalism: Consumerism, Whiteness, and Addiction in Mat Johnson's *Pym*." *College Literature* 44, no. 2 (2017): 166–199.

Chude-Sokei, Louis. *The Sound of Culture: Diaspora and Black Technopoetics*. Wesleyan UP, 2016.

Chun, Wendy H. K. *Control and Freedom: Power and Paranoia in the Age of Fiber Optics*. MIT Press, 2005.

Clark, P. Djèlí. *Ring Shout*. Tordotcom, 2020.

Clayton, Dhonielle. *The Beauty Trials*. Disney Hyperion, 2023.

———. *The Belles*. Freeform Books, 2018.

———. *The Everlasting Rose*. Freeform Books, 2019.

Clayton, Ralph. "E. A. Poe, Dealer in Slaves." *Baltimore Sun*, October 1, 1993, www.baltimoresun.com/news/bs-xpm-1993-10-01-1993274244-story.html.

Clute, John, David Langford, David Pringle, and Brian M. Stableford. "Lost Races." *The Encyclopedia of Science Fiction*, May 11, 2016, https://sf-encyclopedia.com/entry/lost_races.

Coleman, Christian A. "Interview: Louise Erdrich." *Lightspeed: Science Fiction and Fantasy*, December 2017, www.lightspeedmagazine.com/nonfiction/interview-louise-erdrich/.

Condis, Megan A. "Playing the Game of Literature: *Ready Player One*, the Ludic Novel, and the Geeky 'Canon' of White Masculinity." *Journal of Modern Literature* 39, no. 2 (2016): 1–19.

Connors, Sean P., and Roberta S. Trites. "Neoliberalism's Erasure of Race in Young Adult Fiction: Sherri L. Smith's *Orleans* as Counterexample." In *Race in Young Adult Speculative Fiction*, edited by Meghan Gilbert-Hickey and Miranda A. Green-Barteet, 75–92. UP of Mississippi, 2021.

The Constitution of the United States. National Archives, September 21, 2022, www.archives.gov/founding-docs/constitution.

Coogler, Ryan, dir. *Black Panther*. Marvel Studios, 2018.

Cook, Daniella A., and Adrienne D. Dixson. "Writing Critical Theory and Method: A Composite Counterstory on the Experiences of Black Teachers in New Orleans Post-Katrina." *International Journal of Qualitative Studies in Education* 26, no. 10 (2013): 1238–1258.

Crane, David. "In Medias Race: Filmic Representation, Networked Communication, and Racial Intermediation." In *Race in Cyberspace*, edited by Beth E. Kolko et al., 87–115. Routledge, 2000.

Crenshaw, Kimberlé. "Mapping the Margins: Intersectionality, Identity Politics, and Violence Against Women of Color." In *Critical Race Theory: The Key Writings That Formed the Movement*, edited by Kimberlé Crenshaw, et al., 257–383. The New Press, 1995.

Crenshaw, Kimberlé, Neil Gotanda, Gary Peller, and Kendall Thomas, eds. *Critical Race Theory: The Key Writings That Formed the Movement*. The New Press, 1995.

Csicsery-Ronay, Istvan, Jr. "Empire." In *The Routledge Companion to Science Fiction*, edited by Mark Bould et al., 362–372. Routledge, 2009.

———. *Seven Beauties of Science Fiction*. Wesleyan UP, 2008.

Cutter, Martha J. "Why Passing Is (Still) Not Passé After More Than 250 Years: Sources from the Past and Present." In *Neo-Passing: Performing Identity After Jim Crow*, edited by Mollie Godfrey and Vershawn Ashanti Young, 49–67. U of Illinois P, 2018.

Davis, Kimberly C. "The Follies of Racial Tribalism: Mat Johnson and Anti-Utopian Satire." *Contemporary Literature* 58, no. 1 (2017): 18–52.

Davis, Milton J. "Welcome to the City." In *The City: A Cyberfunk Anthology*, edited by Davis, 5–8. MVmedia Publishing, 2015.

Davis, Roger. "Food for Thoughts: Thinking Through Cannibals and Plagiarists." *University of Toronto Quarterly* 87, no. 1 (2018): 176–195.

Davis, Thulani. "The Future May Be Bleak, But It's Not Black." *Village Voice*, February 1, 1983, 17–19.

Dawkins, Marcia Alesan. *Clearly Invisible: Racial Passing and the Color of Cultural Identity*. Baylor UP, 2012.

———. "Passing at the Intersections." In *Neo-Passing: Performing Identity After Jim Crow*, edited by Mollie Godfrey and Vershawn Ashanti Young, 135–141. U of Illinois P, 2018.

DeGraw, Sharon. *The Subject of Race in American Science Fiction*. Routledge, 2007.

Delany, Samuel R. *The Ballad of Beta-2*. [1965.] In *a, b, c: three short novels*, 177–262. Vintage, 2015.
———. *Dhalgren*. Bantam Books, 1975.
———. "Introduction: Reading and the Written Interview." In *Silent Interviews: On Language, Race, Sex, Science Fiction, and Some Comics*, 1–17. Wesleyan UP, 1994.
———. "The Mirror of Afrofuturism." *Extrapolation* 61, no. 1/2 (2020): 173–184.
———. *The Motion of Light in Water: Sex and Science Fiction Writing in the East Village*. [1988.] U of Minnesota P, 2004.
———. *Nova*. Doubleday, 1968.
———. "Racism and Science Fiction." [1998.] In *Dark Matter: A Century of Speculative Fiction from the African Diaspora*, edited by Sheree R. Thomas, 383–397. Warner, 2000.
———. "Science Fiction and Criticism: The *Diacritics* Interview." In *Silent Interviews: On Language, Race, Sex, Science Fiction, and Some Comics*, 186–215. Wesleyan UP, 1994.
———. "The Semiology of Silence: The *Science Fiction Studies* Interview." In *Silent Interviews: On Language, Race, Sex, Science Fiction, and Some Comics*, 21–58. Wesleyan UP, 1994.
———. *Starboard Wine: More Notes on the Language of Science Fiction*. Revised ed. Wesleyan UP, 2012.
———. *Stars in My Pockets Like Grains of Sand*. Bantam, 1984.
———. "Toto, We're Back!: The *Cottonwood Review* Interview." In *Silent Interviews: On Language, Race, Sex, Science Fiction, and Some Comics*, 59–82. Wesleyan UP, 1994.
———. *Trouble on Triton*. [1976.] Wesleyan Up, 1996.
Delgado, Richard. "Introduction." In *Critical Race Theory: The Cutting Edge*, edited by Delgado, xii-xvi. Temple UP, 1995.
———. "Storytelling for Oppositionists and Others; A Plea for Narrative." [1989.] In *Critical Race Theory: The Cutting Edge*, edited by Richard Delgado and Jean Stefancic, 71–80. 3rd ed. Temple UP, 2013.
Delgado, Richard, and Jean Stefancic. *Critical Race Theory: An Introduction*. 3rd ed. NYU P, 2017.
DeLillo, Don. *White Noise*. Viking, 1985.
DeMille, James. *A Strange Manuscript Found in a Copper Cylinder*. [1888.] New Canadian Library, 1969.
DeMonaco, James, dir. *The Purge*. Universal Pictures, 2013.
Deonn, Tracy. *Bloodmarked*. Simon & Schuster, 2022.
———. *Legendborn*. Margaret K. McElderry Books, 2020.
Dery, Mark. "Black to the Future: Interviews with Samuel R. Delany, Greg Tate, and Tricia Rose." [1993.] In "Flame Wars: The Discourse of Cyberculture," edited by Mark Dery, special issue, *South Atlantic Quarterly* (1994): 179–222.
Dick, Philip K. *The Crack in Space*. Ace, 1966.
———. *The Man in the High Castle*. [1962.] Vintage, 1992.
Dickerson, James L. *Inside America's Concentration Camps: Two Centuries of Internment and Torture*. Lawrence Hill Books, 2010.
Dillon, Grace. "Imagining Indigenous Futurisms." In *Walking the Clouds: An Anthology of Indigenous Science Fiction*, edited by Grace L. Dillon, 1–12. U of Arizona P, 2012.
———. "Native Slipstream: Blackfeet Physics in *The Fast Red Road*." In *The Fictions of Stephen Graham Jones: A Critical Companion*, edited by Billy J. Stratton, 343–355. U of New Mexico P, 2016.

DiMaggio, Kenneth. "*Uncle Tom's Cabin*: Global Best Seller, Anti-slave Narrative, Imperialist Agenda." *Global Studies Journal* 7, no. 1 (2014): 15–23.

Dimaline, Cherie. *The Marrow Thieves*. DCB, 2017.

Dorman, Nerine, ed. *Terra Incognita: New Short Speculative Stories from Africa*. Modjaji Books, 2015.

Douglass, Frederick. *Narrative of the Life of Frederick Douglass*. [1845.] Signet Classic, 1997.

Du Bois, W. E. B. *The Souls of Black Folk*. 1903. Signet Classic, 1995.

Dubey, Madhu. *Signs and Cities: Black Literary Postmodernism*. U of Chicago P, 2003.

duCille, Ann. "Black Barbie and the Deep Play of Difference." In *The Feminism and Visual Culture Reader*, edited by Amelia Jones, 337–348. Routledge, 2003.

Dyer, Richard. *White*. Routledge, 1997.

Edwards, Justin D. *Gothic Passages: Racial Ambiguity in the American Gothic*. U of Iowa P, 2003.

Ekpeki, Oghenechovwe Donald, Zelda Knight, and Sheree R. Thomas, eds. *Africa Risen: A New Era of Speculative Fiction*. Tordotcom, 2022.

Elam, Michele. *The Souls of Mixed Folk: Race, Politics, and Aesthetics in the New Millennium*. Stanford UP, 2011.

Elliott, George P. "The NRACP." [1949.] In *Social Problems Through Science Fiction*, edited by Martin H. Greenberg et al., 55–83. St. Martin's Press, 1975.

Ellison, Ralph. *Invisible Man*. [1952.] Vintage, 1990.

Equiano, Olaudah. *The Interesting Narrative of the Life of Olaudah Equiano, or Gustavas Vassa, the African, Written by Himself*. [1789.] In *The Classic Slave Narratives*, edited by Henry Louis Gates Jr., 10–182. Signet, 2002.

Erdrich, Louise. *Future Home of the Living God*. [2017.] Harper Perennial, 2020.

Erkkila, Betsy. "The Poetics of Whiteness: Poe and the Racial Imaginary." In *Romancing the Shadow: Poe and Race*, edited by J. Gerald Kennedy and Lilian Weissberg, 41–74. Oxford UP, 2001.

Eshun, Kodwo. "Further Considerations of Afrofuturism." *CR: The New Centennial Review* 3, no. 2 (2003): 287–302.

———. *More Brilliant than the Sun: Adventures in Sonic Fiction*. Quartet, 1998.

"Executive Order 9981." *National Archives and Records Administration, Harry S. Truman Library & Museum*, accessed September 27, 2022, https://www.trumanlibrary.gov/library/executive-orders/9981/executive-order-9981.

Faflik, David. "South of the 'Border,' or Poe's *Pym*: A Case Study in Region, Race, and American Literary History." *Mississippi Quarterly* 57, no. 2 (2004): 265–288.

Fanon, Frantz. *Black Skin, White Masks*. [1952.] Translated by Richard Philcox. Grove Press, 2008.

Farooq, Nihad M. *Undisciplined: Science, Ethnography, and Personhood in the Americas, 1830–1940*. NYU P, 2016.

Faucette, John M., Jr. *The Age of Ruin*. Ace, 1968.

———. *Black Science Fiction*. Infinity Publishing, 2002.

———. *Crown of Infinity*. Ace, 1968.

Fiorelli, Julie A. "Against 'a Place Without History': Contemporary Racism and Utopian Dynamism in Mat Johnson's *Pym*." In *Race and Utopian Desire in American Literature and Society*, edited by Edward K. Chan and Patricia Ventura, 221–240. Palgrave Macmillan, 2019.

Foster, Thomas. "'Innocent by Contamination': Ethnicity and Technicity in Delany's *Stars in My Pocket Like Grains of Sand*." In "Delany Lately," special issue, *African American Review* 48, no. 3 (2015): 239–256.

Foucault, Michel. *"Society Must Be Defended": Lectures at the College de France, 1975–1976.* Translated by David Macey. Picador, 2003.
Fox, Rose, and Daniel José Older, eds. *Long Hidden: Speculative Fiction from the Margins of History.* Crossed Genre Publications, 2014.
Franklin, H. Bruce. *Future Perfect: American Science Fiction of the Nineteenth Century.* [1966.] Rutgers UP, 1995.
Freedman, Carl. *Critical Theory and Science Fiction.* Wesleyan UP, 2000.
Gaines, Ernest J. *The Autobiography of Miss Jane Pittman.* [1971.] Bantam, 1982.
Gardner, Jared. *Master Plots: Race and the Founding of an American Literature, 1787–1845.* Johns Hopkins UP, 1998.
Gernsback, Hugo. "A New Sort of Magazine." *Amazing Stories* 1, no. 1 (April 1926): 3.
Gibson, Mel, dir. *Braveheart.* Paramount, 1995.
Gibson, William. *Mona Lisa Overdrive.* Bantam, 1988.
———. *Neuromancer.* Ace, 1984.
Giddings, Megan. *Lakewood.* Amistad, 2020.
Gilroy, Paul. *Against Race: Imagining Political Culture Beyond the Color Line.* Harvard UP, 2000.
Goddu, Teresa. "Rethinking Race and Slavery in Poe Studies." In "Dark Romanticism," special issue, *Poe Studies* 33, no. 1/2 (2000): 15–18.
Goeman, Mishuana. *Mark My Words: Native Women Mapping Our Nations.* U of Minnesota P, 2013.
Goodwin, Mathew D., ed. *Latinx Rising: An Anthology of Latinx Science Fiction and Fantasy.* Mad Creek Books, 2020.
Gordon, Andrew, and Hernan Vera. *Screen Saviors: Hollywood Fictions of Whiteness.* Roman & Littlefield, 2003.
Gotanda, Neil. "A Critique of 'Our Constiution is Color-blind.'" In *Critical Race Theory: The Key Writings That Formed the Movement*, edited by Kimberlé Crenshaw et al., 257–275. The New Press, 1995.
Gould, Stephen Jay. *The Mismeasure of Man.* Norton, 1996.
Govan, Sandra Y. "The Insistent Presence of Black Folk in the Novels of Samuel Delany." *Black American Literature Forum* 18, no. 2 (1984): 43–48.
Greenlee, Sam. *The Spook Who Sat by the Door.* Bantam, 1969.
Griffin, John H. *Black Like Me.* [1961.] Signet, 2010.
Griffith, Janelle. "Black Teen Told to Cut His Locs by Texas School Wins Court Ruling." *NBC News*, 18 Aug. 2020. Accessed 24 Oct. 2022.
Grimstad, Paul. "Poe and Science Fiction." In *The Oxford Handbook of Edgar Allan Poe*, edited by J. Gerald Kennedy and Scott Peeples, 735–751. Oxford UP, 2019.
Gyory, Andrew. *Closing the Gate: Race, Politics and the Chinese Exclusion Act.* U of North Carolina P, 1998.
Haggard, H. R. *King Solomon's Mines.* [1885.] Modern Library, 1957.
———. *She.* [1887.] Modern Library, 1957.
Haney López, Ian F. "The Social Construction of Race: Some Observations in Illusion, Fabrication, and Choice." *Harvard Civil Rights–Civil Liberties Law Review* 29, no. 1 (1994): 1–62.
Hannah-Jones, Nikole, et al., eds. *The 1619 Project: A New Origin Story.* One World, 2021.
Haraway, Donna. "A Cyborg Manifesto: Science, Technology and Socialist-Feminism in the Late Twentieth Century." In *The Cybercultures Reader*, edited by David Bell and Barbara M. Kennedy, 291–324. Routledge, 2000.

Harley, Alexis. "The Slavery of the Machine." In *Afterimages of Slavery; Essays on Appearances in Recent American Films, Literature, Television and Other Media*, edited by Marlene D. Allen and Seretha D. Williams, 218–231. McFarland, 2012.

Harris, Robert. *Fatherland*. [1992.] Random House, 2006.

Hartmann, Ivor W., ed. *AfroSF: Science Fiction by African Writers*. StoryTime, 2012.

———. *AfroSFv2: 5 Novellas*. StoryTime, 2014.

———. *AfroSFv3*. StoryTime, 2018.

Hattenhauer, Darryl. "The Politics of Kurt Vonnegut's 'Harrison Bergeron.'" *Studies in Short Fiction* 35, no. 4 (1998): 387–392.

Havard, John C. "'Trust to the Shrewdness and Common Sense of the Public': *The Narrative of Arthur Gordon Pym* as a Hoaxical Satire of Racist Epistemologies." In *Deciphering Poe: Subtexts, Contexts, Subversive Meanings*, edited by Alexandra Urakova, 107–120. Lehigh UP, 2013.

Hayles, N. Katherine. *How We Became Posthuman: Virtual Bodies in Cybernetics, Literature, and Informatics*. U of Chicago P, 1999.

Hedrick, Joan D. *Harriet Beecher Stowe: A Life*. Oxford UP, 1995.

Heinlein, Robert A. *Farnham's Freehold*. [1964.] Baen, 1994.

Heller, Andrew J. *If the North Had Won the Civil War: An Alternate History*. Wordwooze, 2015.

Henning, Kristin. "Boys to Men: The Role of Policing in the Socialization of Black Boys." In *Policing the Black Man: Arrest, Prosecution, and Imprisonment*, edited by Angela J. Davis, 57–94. Vintage, 2017.

Herrnstein, Richard J., and Charles Murray. *The Bell Curve: Intelligence and Class Structure in American Life*. Free Press, 1994.

Higgins, David M. *Reverse Colonization: Science Fiction, Imperial Fantasy, and Alt-Victimhood*. Iowa UP, 2021.

Hines, Alicia H., Alondra Nelson, and Thuy Linh N. Tu, eds. "Introduction: Hidden Circuits." In *Technicolor: Race, Technology, and Everyday Life*, 1–12. NYU P, 2001.

Hobbes, Thomas [William S. Lind]. *Victoria: A Novel of 4th Generation War*. Castalia House, 2014.

Hobbs, Allyson. "Passing at the Turn of the Twenty-First Century." In *Neo-Passing: Performing Identity After Jim Crow*, edited by Mollie Godfrey and Vershawn Ashanti Young, 43–48. U of Illinois P, 2018.

Hollars, B. J. *The Road South: Personal Stories of the Freedom Riders*. U of Alabama P, 2018.

Hollinger, Veronica. "Cybernetic Deconstructions: Cyberpunk and Postmodernism." In *Storming the Reality Studio: A Casebook of Cyberpunk and Postmodern Science Fiction*, edited by Larry McCaffery, 203–218. Duke UP, 1991.

Hopkins, Pauline. *Of One Blood; Or, The Hidden Self*. [1903.] Washington Square, 2004.

Hopkinson, Nalo . *Midnight Robber*. Warner, 2000.

———, ed. *Mojo: Conjure Stories*. Warner/Aspect, 2003.

———. "A Reluctant Ambassador from the Planet of Midnight." *Journal of the Fantastic in the Arts* 21, no. 3 (2010): 339–350.

———, ed. *Whispers from the Cotton Tree Root: Caribbean Fabulist Fiction*. Invisible Cities Press, 2000.

Hopkinson, Nalo, and Uppinder Mehan. *So Long Been Dreaming: Postcolonial Science Fiction & Fantasy*. Arsenal Pulp Press, 2004.

Howe, LeAnne. *Choctalking on Other Realities*. Aunt Lute Books, 2013.

Hughes, Langston. "Harlem." [1951.] In *The Collected Poems of Langston Hughes*, edited by Arnold Rampersad, 426. Vintage, 1994.

———. "The Negro Artist and the Racial Mountain." *Nation*, June 23, 1926, 692–694.

———. "The Negro Speaks of Rivers." [1921.] In *The Norton Anthology of African American Literature*, vol. 1, edited by Henry Louis Gates Jr. and Valerie Smith, 1304–1305. 3rd ed. Norton, 2014.

Hurston, Zora N. *Their Eyes Were Watching God*. [1937.] Perennial Library, 1990.

"Ice Opens Its First-Ever Designed-and-Built Civil Detention Center." *U.S. Immigration and Customs Enforcement*, September 23, 2014, www.ice.gov/news/releases/ice-opens-its-first-ever-designed-and-built-civil-detention-center.

Ireland, Justina. *Deathless Divide*. Balzer + Bray, 2020.

———. *Dread Nation*. Balzer + Bray, 2018.

Iyer, Nalini. "Digital Subaltern Counterpublics and Muslim Women's Resistance in Kamil Shamsie's *Home Fire* and Samira Ahmed's *Internment*." *Tulsa Studies in Women's Literature* 41, no. 1 (Spring 2022): 135–154.

Jacobs, Harriet. *Incidents in the Life of a Slave Girl*. [1861.] Dover, 2001.

Jakes, John. *Black in Time*. Bart Books, 1970.

———. *Heaven and Hell*. Harcourt Brace Jovanovich, 1987.

———. *Love and War*. Harcourt Brace Jovanovich, 1984.

———. *North and South*. Harcourt Brace Jovanovich, 1982.

Jefferson, Thomas. *Notes on the State of Virginia*. [1785.] Penguin Classics, 1998.

Jemisin, N. K. *The City We Became*. Orbit, 2020.

———. *The Fifth Season*. Orbit, 2015.

———. "The Ones Who Stayed and Fought." In *How Long 'Til Black Future Month*, 1–13. Orbit, 2018.

———. "The Stars are Ours." Speech at the 76th World Science Fiction Convention, San Jose McEnery Convention Center, San Jose, KA, August 20, 2018.

———. *The Stone Sky*. Orbit, 2017.

———. "Valedictorian." In *How Long 'til Black Future Month*, 150–169. Orbit, 2018.

Jerng, Mark C. *Racial Worldmaking: The Power of Popular Fiction*. Fordham UP, 2018.

Johnson, Mat. *Pym*. Spiegel & Grau, 2011.

Jones, Stephen Graham. *The Bird Is Gone: A Manifesto*. Fiction Collective 2, 2003.

Judge, Mike, dir. *Idiocracy*. Twentieth Century Fox, 2006.

Kelley, William M. *A Different Drummer*. [1962.] Anchor, 1990.

Kemball, Anna. "Biocolonial Pregnancies: Louise Erdrich's *Future Home of the Living God* (2017)." *Medical Humanities* 48, no. 2 (2022): 159–168.

Kendall, Francis E. *Diversity in the Classroom and Understanding White Privilege: Creating Pathways to Authentic Relationships Across Race*. 2nd ed. Routledge, 2013.

Kendi, Ibram X. *How to Be an Antiracist*. One World, 2019.

Kennedy, J. Gerald. *Strange Nation: Literary Nationalism and Cultural Conflict in the Age of Poe*. Oxford UP, 2016.

———. "'Trust No Man': Poe, Douglass, and the Culture of Slavery." In *Romancing the Shadow: Poe and Race*, edited by J. Gerald Kennedy and Lilian Weissberg, 225–257. Oxford UP, 2001.

Kerr, Audrey E. *The Paper Bag Principle: Class, Colorism, and Rumor and the Case of Black Washington, D.C.* U of Tennessee Press, 2006.

Kevorkian, Martin. *Color Monitors: The Black Face of Technology in America*. Cornell UP, 2006.

Kim, Myungsung. "The Grapevine Telegraph 'Jes Grew': Sonic Materialism, Afrofuturism and Information Theory in Ishmael Reed's *Mumbo Jumbo*." *TOPIA: Canadian Journal of Cultural Studies* 39 (2018): 89–109.

Kincaid, Paul. "On the Origins of Genre." *Extrapolation* 44, no. 4 (2003): 409–419.

King, Martin L., Jr. "I've Been to the Mountaintop." [1968.] In *The Norton Anthology of African American Literature*, edited by Henry L. Gates Jr. and Nellie Y. McKay, 110–16. 2nd ed. Norton, 2007.

Kopley, Richard. "The Quest for Tsalal: Mat Johnson's *Pym: A Novel*." *Edgar Allen Poe Review* 13, no. 1 (2012): 41–45.

Lambert, Frank. *The Battle of Ole Miss: Civil Rights v. States' Rights*. Oxford UP, 2009.

Landis, John, dir. *Coming to America*. Paramount Pictures, 1988.

Lang, Cady. "'Karen' and the Violence of White Womanhood." *Time*, July 20, 2020, 30–31.

Langford, David. "Jonbar Point." *Encyclopedia of Science Fiction*, August 12, 2018, https://sf-encyclopedia.com/entry/jonbar_point.

Lavender, Isiah, III. *Afrofuturism Rising: The Literary Prehistory of a Movement*. Ohio State UP, 2019.

———. "Black Grit: or, Why I Study Race and Racism in Science Fiction." *Deletion: The Open Access Online Forum in Science Fiction Studies* 7 (2014). http://www.deletionscifi.org/episodes/black-grit-study-race-racism-science-fiction.

———. "Critical Race Theory." In *The Routledge Companion to Cyberpunk Culture*, edited by Anna McFarlane, Graham J. Murphy, and Lars Schmeink, 308–316. Routledge, 2019.

———. "Critical Race Theory." In *The Routledge Companion to Science Fiction*, edited by Mark Bould et al., 185–193. Routledge, 2009.

———. "Incendiary Dramas: Black Theatre Classics and Afrofuturism." In "Afrofuturism," special issue, *Black Theatre Review* 2, no. 1 (July 2023): 12–22. https://doi.org/10.2458/tbtr.5674.

———. "Introduction: Coloring Outside Science Fiction's Lines." In *Dis-Orienting Planets: Racial Representations of Asia in Science Fiction*, edited by Isiah Lavender III, 3–10. UP of Mississippi, 2017.

———. "Introduction: Coloring Science Fiction." In *Black and Brown Planets: The Politics of Race in Science Fiction*, edited by Isiah Lavender III, 3–11. UP of Mississippi, 2014.

———. *Race in American Science Fiction*. Indiana UP, 2011.

———. "Reframing *Heart of Darkness* as Science Fiction." *Extrapolation* 56, no. 1 (2015): 15–39.

———. "Technicity: AI and Cyborg Ethnicity in *The Matrix*." *Extrapolation* 45, no. 4 (2004): 436–457.

Lavender, Isiah, III, and Graham J. Murphy. "Afrofuturism." In *The Routledge Companion to Cyberpunk Culture*, edited by Anna McFarlane, Graham J. Murphy, and Lars Schmeink, 353–361. Routledge, 2020.

Lavender, Isiah, III, and Lisa Yaszek. "The *First* Death of Afrofuturism." In "Beyond Afrofuturism," special [double] issue, *Extrapolation* 61, nos. 1–2 (2020): 1–5.

Le Guin, Ursula K. *The Lathe of Heaven*. [1971.] Scribner, 2008.

———. *The Left Hand of Darkness*. Ace, 1969.

———. "The Ones Who Walk Away from Omelas." [1973.] In *The Real and the Unreal: The Selected Short Stories of Ursula K. Le Guin*, 329–336. Saga Press, 2017.

Lee, Erika. *At America's Gates: Chinese Immigration During the Exclusion Era, 1882–1943*. U of North Carolina P, 2003.

Lew-Williams, Beth. *The Chinese Must Go: Violence, Exclusion, and the Making of the Alien in America*. Harvard UP, 2021.
Lewis, Sinclair. *It Can't Happen Here*. [1935.] New American Library, 2005.
Lil Wayne. *Tha Carter III*. Cash Money/Universal Motown, 2008.
Lillvis, Kristen. *Posthuman Blackness and the Black Female Imagination*. U of Georgia P, 2017.
Liu, Ken, ed. and trans. *Broken Stars: Contemporary Chinese Science Fiction in Translation*. Tor, 2019.
———. *Invisible Planets: An Anthology of Contemporary Chinese Science Fiction in Translation*. Tor, 2016.
Lott, Eric. *Love & Theft: Blackface Minstrelsy and the American Working Class*. Oxford UP, 1993.
Lovecraft, H. P. *At the Mountains of Madness*. [1936.] Ballantine, 1973.
Ma, Ling. *Severance*. Farrar, Straus and Giroux, 2018.
Marable, Manning. *Race, Reform, and Rebellion: The Second Reconstruction and Beyond in Black America, 1945–2006*. 3rd ed. UP of Mississippi, 2007.
Marchetti, Gina. *Romance and the 'Yellow Peril': Race, Sex, and Discursive Strategies in Hollywood Fiction*. U of California P, 1993.
Marotta, Melanie. "Sherri L. Smith's *Orleans* and Karen Sandler's *Tankborn*: The Female Leader, the Neo-Slave Narrative, and Twenty-first Century Young Adult Afrofuturism." *MOSF: Journal of Science Fiction* 1, no. 2 (2016): 56–70.
Martínez-Falquina, Silvia. "Louise Erdrich's *Future Home of the Living God*: Uncertainty, Proleptic Mourning and Relationality in Native Dystopia." *Atlantis: Journal of the Spanish Association of Anglo-American Studies* 41, no. 2 (2019): 161–178.
Matias, Cherryl E., et al. "Exposing the White Avatar: Projections, Justifications, and the Ever-Evolving American Racism." *Social Identities* 21, no. 5 (2015): 459–473.
Matsuda, Mari J. "Voices of America: Accent, Antidiscrimination Law, and a Jurisprudence for the Last Reconstruction." *Yale Law Journal* 100, no. 5 (1991): 1329–1407.
———. "When the First Quail Calls; Multiple Consciousness as Jurisprudential Method." [1989.] In *Critical Race Theory: The Cutting Edge*, edited by Richard Delgado and Jean Stefancic, 31–34. 3rd ed. Temple UP, 2013.
Maus, Derek C. "Cyberfunk: Walter Mosley Takes Black to the Future." In *Finding a Way Home: A Critical Assessment of Walter Mosley's Fiction*, edited by Owen E. Brady and Derek C. Maus, 148– 160. UP of Mississippi, 2008.
McEvoy, Seth. *Samuel R. Delany*. Frederick Ungar Publishing, 1984.
McIntosh, Peggy. "White Privilege: Unpacking the Invisible Knapsack." *Peace & Freedom Magazine*, July/Aug 1989, 10–12.
Merla-Watson, Cathyrn Josefina. "The Altermundos of Latin@futurism." *Alluvium*, March 15, 2017, https://www.alluvium-journal.org/2017/03/15/the-altermundos-of-latinfuturism/.
Minch-de Leon, Mark. "Race and the Limitations of 'the Human.'" In *After the Human: Culture, Theory and Criticism in the 21st Century*, edited by Sherryl Vint, 206–219. Cambridge UP, 2020.
Miner, Steve, dir. *Soul Man*. New World Pictures, 1986.
Mishra, Sangay. "Religion and Race: South Asians in Post 9/11 United States." In *Faith and Race in American Political Life*, edited by Robin D. Jacobson and Nancy D. Wadsworth, 231–248. U of Virginia P, 2012.
"Mississippi River Facts." National Park Service, September 28, 2021, www.nps.gov/miss/riverfacts.htm.

Miyake, Perry. *21st Century Manzanar*. Really Great Books, 2002.
Moore, Ward. *Bring the Jubilee*. [1953.] Avon, 1972.
Mootz, Kaylee J. "The Body and the Archive in Louise Erdrich's *Future Home of the Living God*." *Journal of the Fantastic in the Arts* 31, no. 2 (2020): 263–276.
Morley, David, and Kevin Robins. "Techno-Orientalism: Japan Panic." In *Spaces of Identity: Global Media, Electronic Landscapes and Cultural Boundaries*, edited by David Morley and Kevin Robins, 147–173. Routledge, 1995.
Morris, Sam. "'Anything Be Better than This': Utopian Impulses in *The Hunger Games* Series and *Orleans*." *The Lion and the Unicorn* 44, no. 3 (2020): 262–280.
Morrison, Toni. *Beloved*. [1987.] Plume, 1998.
———. *The Bluest Eye*. [1970.] Vintage International, 2007.
———. *Playing in the Dark: Whiteness and the Literary Imagination*. Vintage, 1992.
———. *Recitatif: A Story*. [1983.] Knopf, 2022.
Morton, Samuel George. *Crania Americana*. J. Dobson, 1839.
Mosley, Walter. "Black to the Future." In *Dark Matter: A Century of Speculative Fiction from the African Diaspora*, edited by Sheree R. Thomas, 405–406. Warner, 2000.
———. *Futureland: Nine Stories of an Imminent Future*. Warner, 2001.
———. *Workin' on the Chain Gang: Shaking Off the Dead Hand of History*. Ballantine, 2000.
Murphy, Graham J. "The *Mirrorshades* Collective." In *The Routledge Companion to Cyberpunk Culture*, edited by Anna McFarlane, Graham J. Murphy, and Lars Schmeink, 15–23. Routledge, 2020.
Nelson, Alondra. "Introduction: Future Texts." In "Afrofuturism," special issue, *Social Text* 20, no. 2 (2002): 1–15.
Nelson, Dana D. *The Word in Black and White: Reading Race in American Literature, 1638–1867*. Oxford UP, 1992.
Nishime, LeiLani. "The Mulatto Cyborg: Imagining a Multiracial Future." *Cinema Journal* 44, no. 2 (2005): 34–49.
Northup, Solomon. *Twelve Years a Slave*. [1853.] Dover, 1970.
Obama, Barack. "Eulogy for Rep. John Lewis." *Washington Post*, July 30, 2020, YouTube video, https://www.youtube.com/watch?v=V1pKoCq1bn0.
Okorafor, Nnedi. "Africanfuturism Defined." *Nnedi's Wahala Zone Blog*, October 19, 2019. http://nnedi.blogspot.com/2019/10/africanfuturism-defined.html.
———. *The Book of Phoenix*. DAW, 2015.
———. *Who Fears Death*. DAW, 2010.
Olney, Clarke. "Edgar Allan Poe—Science-Fiction Pioneer." *Georgia Review* 12, no. 4 (1958): 416–421.
Olney, James. "'I Was Born': Slave Narratives, Their Status as Autobiography and as Literature." *Callaloo* 7, no. 1 (1984): 46–73.
Omi, Michael, and Howard Winant. *Racial Formation in the United States: From the 1960s to the 1990s*. 2nd ed. Routledge, 1994.
Onyebuchi, Tochi. *Riot Baby*. Tor, 2019.
Orwell, George, *1984*. [1949.] Signet Classics, 1961.
Park, Sang Joon, and Sunyoung Park, eds. *Readymade Bodhisattva: The Kaya Anthology of South Korean Science Fiction*. Kaya Press, 2019.
Parks, Gordon, dir. *Shaft*. Metro-Goldwyn-Mayer, 1971.

Peck, Robert McCracken, and Patricia Tyson Stroud. *A Glorious Enterprise: The Academy of Natural Sciences of Philadelphia and the Making of American Science.* U of Pennsylvania P, 2012.

Peele, Jordan, dir. *Get Out.* Universal Pictures, 2017.

Poe, Edgar A. "The Gold-Bug." [1843.] In *The Essential Tales and Poems of Edgar Allan Poe*, edited by Benjamin F. Fisher, 286–318. Barnes & Noble, 2004.

———. "Hop-Frog." [1849.] In *The Essential Tales and Poems of Edgar Allan Poe*, edited by Benjamin F. Fisher, 433–441. Barnes & Noble, 2004.

———. "The Man That Was Used Up." [1839.] In *The Complete Tales and Poems of Edgar Allen Poe*, edited by Milton Creek Editorial Services, 360–366. Rock Point, 2020.

———. "The Murders in the Rue Morgue." [1841.] In *The Essential Tales and Poems of Edgar Allan Poe*, edited by Benjamin F. Fisher, 196–228. Barnes & Noble, 2004.

———. *The Narrative of Arthur Gordon Pym.* [1838.] In *The Essential Tales and Poems of Edgar Allan Poe*, edited by Benjamin F. Fisher, 443–606. Barnes & Noble, 2004.

———. "A Predicament." [1838.] In *The Essential Tales and Poems of Edgar Allan Poe*, edited by Benjamin F. Fisher, 150–158. Barnes & Noble, 2004.

Prince, Mary. *The History of Mary Prince, A West Indian Slave, Related by Herself.* [1831.] Edited by Moira Ferguson. Revised ed. U of Michigan P, 1997.

Quinn, Daniel. *After Dachau.* Context Books, 2001.

Ramírez, Catherine S. "Afrofuturism/Chicanafuturism." *Aztlán: A Journal of Chicano Studies* 33, no. 1 (2008): 185–194.

Reed, Ishmael. *Mumbo Jumbo.* Scribner, 1972.

Rieder, John. *Colonialism and the Emergence of Science Fiction.* Wesleyan UP, 2008.

———. "On Defining SF, or Not: Genre Theory, SF, and History." *Science Fiction Studies* 37, no. 2 (2010): 191–209.

Rifkin, Mark. *Fictions of Land and Flesh: Blackness, Indigeneity, Speculation.* Duke UP, 2019.

Robinson, Jill. "BLACKout." [2004.] In *Dark Matter: Reading the Bones*, edited by Sheree R. Thomas, 232–242. Warner, 2004.

Rohmer, Sax. *The Insidious Fu-Manchu.* [1913.] Project Gutenberg, 2008.

Rosenthal, Bernard. "Poe, Slavery, and the *Southern Literary Messenger*: A Reexamination." *Poe Studies* 7, no. 2 (1974): 29–38.

Roth, Philip. *The Plot Against America.* Vintage, 2004.

Rothstein, Richard. *The Color of Law: A Forgotten History of How Our Government Segregated America.* Liveright, 2017.

Row, Jess. *Your Face Is Mine.* Riverhead Books, 2014.

Rowe, John C. "Antebellum Slavery and Modern Criticism: Edgar Allan Poe's *Pym* and 'The Purloined Letter.'" In *The Selected Writings of Edgar Allan Poe: A Norton Critical Edition*, edited by G. R. Thompson, 904–920. Norton, 2004.

———. "Edgar Allan Poe's Imperial Fantasy and the American Frontier." In *Romancing the Shadow: Poe and Race*, edited by J. Gerald Kennedy and Lilian Weissberg, 75–105. Oxford UP, 2001.

———. "Poe, Antebellum Slavery, and Modern Criticism." In *Poe's Pym: Critical Explorations*, edited by Richard Kopley, 117–138. Duke UP, 1992.

Rowlandson, Mary. *A Narrative of the Captivity and Restoration of Mrs. Mary Rowlandson.* [1682.] In *The Norton Anthology of American Literature*, vol. A, *Beginnings to 1820*, edited by Robert S. Levine, 269–300. 9th ed. Norton, 2017.

Rubens, Peter Paul. *Venus in Front of the Mirror*. 1614–1615. Private collection, Liechtenstein Garden Palace, Vienna.

Ruffin, Maurice C. *We Cast a Shadow*. One World, 2019.

Rusert, Britt. *Fugitive Science: Empiricism and Freedom in Early African American Culture*. NYU P, 2017.

Rushdy, Ashraf H. A. *Neo-Slave Narratives: Studies in the Social Logic of a Literary Form*. Oxford UP, 1999.

Saint, Tarun K., ed. *The Gollancz Book of South Asian Science Fiction*. Hachette India, 2019.

Salam, Erum. "Black US High School Student Forced to Cut Hair During Softball Game." *Guardian*, May 15, 2021.

Sanchez-Taylor, Joy. *Diverse Futures: Science Fiction and Authors of Color*. Ohio State UP, 2021.

Sargent, Lyman Tower. *Utopianism: A Very Short Introduction*. Oxford UP, 2010.

Scalzi, John. *Lock In*. Tor, 2014.

Schuyler, George S. *Black No More*. [1931.] Northeastern UP, 1989.

Seed, David. "Breaking the Bounds: The Rhetoric of Limits in the Works of Edgar Allan Poe, His Contemporaries and Adaptors." In *Anticipations: Essays on Early Science Fiction & Its Precursors*, 75–97. Liverpool UP, 1995.

Shawl, Nisi. "Expanded Course in the History of Black Science Fiction: Walter Mosley's *Futureland*." *Reactor*, September 6, 2017, www.tor.com/2017/09/06/expanded-course-in-the-history-of-black-science-fiction-walter-mosleys-futureland/.

———, ed. *New Suns: Original Speculative Fiction by People of Color*. Solaris, 2019.

———, ed. *New Suns 2: Original Speculative Fiction by People of Color*. Solaris, 2023.

Shockley, Evie. "Separation Anxiety." In *Dark Matter: A Century of Speculative Fiction from the African Diaspora*, edited by Sheree R. Thomas, 51–68. Warner/Aspect, 2000.

Siepak, Julia. "Dimensions of Decolonial Future in Contemporary Indigenous Speculative Fiction: Louise Erdrich's *Future Home of the Living God* and Rebecca Roanhorse's *Trail of Lightning*." *Anglica: An International Journal of English Studies* 29, no.1 (2020): 57–74.

Simal González, Begoña. "Revisiting the Campo: A Biopolitical Reading of Perry Miyake's *21st Century Manzanar*." *Revista de estudios Norteamericanos* 20 (2016): 159–180.

Smith, Sherri L. *Orleans*. Speak, 2013.

———. "Re: Form Submission—Contact Sherri—Why Is Mississippi Not Included in the 'Declaration of Separation' in your book 'Orleans.'" Received by Jane Travis, May 28, 2021.

Sohn, Stephen H. "Introduction: Alien/Asian: Imagining the Racialized Future." *MELUS* 33, no. 4 (2008): 5–22.

Sorg, Arley. "Author Spotlight: Violet Allen." *Lightspeed*, December 2016, https://www.lightspeedmagazine.com/nonfiction/author-spotlight-violet-allen-2/.

Spillers, Hortense J. "Mama's Baby, Papa's Maybe: An American Grammar Book." [1987.] In *Within the Circle: An Anthology of African American Literary Criticism from the Harlem Renaissance to the Present*, edited by Angelyn Mitchell, 454–481. Duke UP, 1994.

Spinrad, Norman. *Bug Jack Barron*. Avon Books, 1969.

Sponsler, Claire. "Beyond the Ruins: The Geopolitics of Urban Decay and Cybernetic Play." *Science Fiction Studies* 20, no. 2 (1993): 251–265.

Steinskog, Erik. *Afrofuturism and Black Sound Studies: Culture, Technology, and Things to Come*. Palgrave Macmillan, 2018.

Stephenson, Neal. *Snow Crash*. Bantam Spectra, 1992.

Sterling, Bruce. *Islands in the Net*. Arbor House, 1988.

———. "Preface." In *Burning Chrome* by William Gibson, xi-xiv. Arbor House, 1986.

———. "Preface." In *Mirrorshades: The Cyberpunk Anthology*, edited by Bruce Sterling, ix–xvi. Ace, 1986.

Stern, Alexandra M. *Proud Boys and the White Ethnostate: How the Alt-Right Is Warping the American Imagination*. Beacon, 2019.

Stowe, Harriet B. *Uncle Tom's Cabin*. [1852.] Bantam Classics, 2003.

Stubbs, Roman. "A Wrestler Was Forced to Cut His Dreadlocks Before a Match." *Washington Post*, April 17, 2019.

Suvin, Darko. *Metamorphosis of Science Fiction: On the Poetics and History of a Literary Genre*. Yale UP, 1979.

Tal, Kali. "'That Just Kills Me': Black Militant Near-Future Fiction." *Social Text* 20, no. 2 (2002): 65–91.

Tate, Greg. "Ghetto in the Sky: Samuel Delany's Black Whole." In *Flyboy in the Buttermilk: Essays on Contemporary America*, 159–167. Simon & Schuster, 1992.

Thiong'o, Ngũgĩ wa. *Decolonising the Mind: The Politics of Language in African Literature*. Heinemann, 1986.

Thomas, Ebony E. *The Dark Fantastic: Race and the Imagination from Harry Potter to the Hunger Games*. NYU P, 2019.

———. "Notes Toward a Black Fantastic: Black Atlantic Flights Beyond Afrofuturism in Young Adult Literature." *The Lion and the Unicorn* 43, no. 2 (2019): 282–301.

Thomas, Sheree R., ed. *Dark Matter: A Century of Speculative Fiction from the African Diaspora*. Warner, 2000.

———. *Dark Matter: Reading the Bones*. Warner, 2004.

——— (@blackpotmojo). "The outrage over faux 'critical race theory' is not about white children's 'hurt' feelings. It's about the very real fear some parents have that if their children learn the darker truths about America, they may not choose to perpetuate the racial apartheid that's built upon lies." *Twitter*, November 16, 2021, 8:57 a.m., twitter.com/blackpotmojo/status/1460607838892535812.

Thurman, Wallace. *The Blacker the Berry*. [1929.] Penguin, 2018.

Titian. *Venus with a Mirror*. 1555. 124.5 x 105.5 cm (49 x 41.56 in). National Gallery of Art, Washington, DC.

Toliver, S. R. "Afrocarnival: Celebrating Black Bodies and Critiquing Oppressive Bodies in Afrofuturist Literature." *Children's Literature in Education* 52, no. 1 (2021): 132–148.

Tucker, Jeffrey A. *A Sense of Wonder: Samuel R. Delany, Race, Identity, and Difference*. Wesleyan UP, 2004.

Tucker, Nathaniel Beverley. *The Partisan Leader: A Tale of the Future*. [1836.] U of North Carolina P, 1971.

Turtledove, Harry. *The Guns of the South*. Ballantine, 1992.

Väätänen, Päivi. "Narrating Alien Encounters: Race, Identity, and Generic Change in Science Fiction." PhD diss., University of Helsinki, 2021.

Van Vechten, Carl. *Nigger Heaven*. [1926.] U of Illinois P, 2000.

Velázquez, Diego. *The Toilet of Venus ("Rokeby Venus")*. 1647. 122.5 x 177 cm (48.2 x 69.6 in). National Gallery, London.

Verne, Jules. *Journey to the Center of the Earth*. [1864.] Sterling, 2007.

Vint, Sherryl. "Don't Let the Future Be Written for You: Sabrina Vourvoulias's 'Ink.'" *Los Angeles Review of Books*, December 27, 2012, https://lareviewofbooks.org/article/dont-let-the-future-be-written-for-you-sabrina-vourvouliass-ink/.

———. *Science Fiction: A Guide for the Perplexed.* Bloomsbury, 2014.

"Violet Allen, Pocket Interview No. 5." *Storyological: A Podcast About Stories*, November 27, 2017, https://www.storyological.com/interviews/violet-allen.

Vizenor, Gerald. "Aesthetics of Survivance: Literary Theory and Practice." In *Survivance: Narratives of Native Presence*, edited by Gerald Vizenor, 1–23. U of Nebraska P, 2008.

———. *Manifest Manners: Narratives on Postindian Survivance.* U of Nebraska P, 1999.

Vonnegut, Kurt, Jr. "Harrison Bergeron." [1961.] In *The Story and Its Writer: An Introduction to Short Fiction*, edited by Ann Charters, 846–850. Compact 8th ed. Bedford/St. Martin's, 2011.

———. "What I'd Say If They Asked Me." *Nation*, July 16/23, 1988, 53–54.

Vourvoulias, Sabrina. *Ink.* [2012.] Rosarium Publishing, 2018.

Wachowski, Lana, and Lily Wachowski, dirs. *The Matrix.* Warner Brothers, 1999.

Wacquant, Loïc. "Class, Race & Hyperincarceration in Revanchist America." *Daedalus* 139, no. 3 (Summer 2010): 74–90.

Washington, Booker T. "From *Up from Slavery.*" In *The Norton Anthology of African American Literature*, vol. 1, edited by Henry Louis Gates Jr. and Valerie A. Smith, 550–579. 3rd ed. Norton, 2014.

Washington, Harriet A. *Medical Apartheid: The Dark History of Medical Experimentation on Black Americans from Colonial Times to the Present.* Anchor, 2008.

Weheliye, Alexander G. "Feenin' Posthuman Voices in Contemporary Black Popular Music." *Social Text* 20, no. 2 (2002): 21–47.

———. *Habeas Viscus: Racializing Assemblages, Biopolitics, and Black Feminist Theories of the Human.* Duke UP, 2014.

Weinstock, Jeffrey A. "Tekeli-li!: Poe, Lovecraft, and the Suspicion of Sameness." In *The Lovecraftian Poe: Essays on Influence, Reception, Interpretation and Transformation*, edited by Sean Moreland, 51–67. Lehigh UP, 2017.

Westfahl, Gary. "Who Governs Science Fiction?" *Extrapolation* 41, no.1 (2000}: 63–72.

Whalen, Terence. "Average Racism: Poe, Slavery, and the Wages of Literary Nationalism." In *Romancing the Shadow: Poe and Race*, edited by J. Gerald Kennedy and Lilian Weissberg, 3–40. Oxford UP, 2001.

———. *Edgar Allan Poe and the Masses: The Political Economy of Literature in Antebellum America.* Princeton UP, 1999.

Wheeler, Elizabeth A. "Runoff: Afroaquanauts in Landscapes of Sacrifice." In *Literary Afrofuturism in the Twenty-First Century*, edited by Isiah Lavender III and Lisa Yaszek, 128–148. Ohio State UP, 2020.

Wiegman, Robyn. *American Anatomies: Theorizing Race and Gender.* Duke UP, 1995.

Wilderson, Frank B., III. *Afropessimism.* Liveright, 2020.

Wilks, Jennifer M. "'Black Matters': Race and Literary History in Mat Johnson's *Pym.*" *European Journal of American Studies* 11, no. 1 (2016): 1–20. https://doi.org./10.4000/ejas.11523.

Williams, Apryl. "Black Memes Matter: #LivingWhileBlack with Becky and Karen." *Social Media + Society* 6, no. 4 (October 2020): 1–14. https://doi.org/10.1177/2056305120981047.

Williams, John A. *Sons of Darkness, Sons of Light: A Novel of Some Probability.* [1969.] Northeastern UP, 1999.

Williams, Robert A., Jr. "Documents of Barbarism: The Contemporary Legacy of European Racism and Colonialism in the Narrative Traditions of Federal Indian Law." [1989.] In *Critical Race Theory: The Cutting Edge*, edited by Richard Delgado and Jean Stefancic, 125–135. 3rd ed. Temple UP, 2013.

Wilson, Daniel H. *Amped*. Vintage, 2012.

Winters, Ben H. *Underground Airlines*. Mulholland Books, 2016.

Wright, Tom F. "Edgar Allan Poe and the Southern Gothic." In *The Palgrave Handbook of the Sothern Gothic*, edited by Susan Castillo Crow and Charles L. Crow, 9–20. Palgrave Macmillan, 2016.

Yaszek, Lisa. "An Afrofuturist Reading of Ralph Ellison's *Invisible Man*." *Rethinking History: The Journal of Theory and Practice* 9, no. 2/3 (2005): 297–313.

———. "The Bannekerade: Genius, Madness, and Magic in Black Science Fiction." In *Black and Brown Planets: The Politics of Race in Science Fiction*, edited by Isiah Lavender III, 15–30. UP of Mississippi, 2014.

Yip, Alethea. "Remembering Vincent Chin." *AsianWeek*, June 13, 1997, https://web.archive.org/web/20070318184237/http://www.asianweek.com/061397/feature.html.

Youngquist, Paul. *A Pure Solar World: Sun Ra and the Birth of Afrofuturism*. U of Texas P, 2016.

Yusoff, Kathryn. *A Billion Black Anthropocenes or None*. U of Minnesota P, 2018.

INDEX

ableism, 112–17
abolitionism, 45–46
affirmative action, 115, 141; reversal of 40, 72
Africa, 126–29, 149, 152–54, 158
Afrofuturism, 5, 9–13, 19, 27, 60, 84, 87–108, 117–20, 145, 152–63, 169–70, 174–84, 188, 191, 199–201
Afrofuturist megatext, 175–78, 184, 187
Afropunk, 125–26, 141
After Dachau (Quinn), 211
Agamben, Georgio, 61–62, 64
Age of Ruin, The (Faucette), 26, 222n7
Ahmed, Samira, 65–70
Alexander, Michelle, 53
alienation, racial, 5–6, 60, 141, 177, 213
alien contact trope, 1–3, 28–36, 39, 95, 160, 168, 174–75
Allen, Violet, 10, 95–98
alternate history, 2, 42–57, 116–17, 208–11
alt-right science fiction, 109–16, 209
Amazing Stories, 161, 218
American Indigenes, 49–64, 73, 171; stereotypes of, 57–58
Amped (Wilson), 57–59
Analog magazine, 26, 146, 218
androids, 144–45, 176–77
"Angel's Island" (Mosley), 137–38
Antarctica, 156–58, 161–62, 168, 175, 180–98
anti-miscegenation laws, 7, 204
anti-racism, 13, 121–220
Arbery, Ahmaud, 86–87
artificial insemination, 74–75
artificial intelligences, 124–25, 128, 130–31, 135–37, 152–54
Asian-Americans, 59–64
Asimov, Isaac, 204
assimilation, 10, 25, 50, 101
"Atlanta Compromise" ("Atlanta Exposition Address") (Washington), 45, 111
At the Mountains of Madness (Lovecraft), 161
Atwood, Margaret, 74
Aubry Knight trilogy (Barnes), 51–53, 125, 147–50
Autobiography of Miss Jane Pittman, The (Gaines), 178
authoritarianism, 208–9

Babel-17 (Delany), 32
Ballad of Beta-2, The (Delany), 27–36, 42, 222n10
Barnes, Steven, 14, 51–53, 59, 125–36, 145, 147, 149–50
Baudemann, Kristina, 54–55
Baudrillard, Jean, 193
beauty, Eurocentric concepts of, 30, 100–102, 169–70, 183, 204–5, 224n5; antiracist critiques of, 106–8
Beauty Trials, The (Clayton), 106–8
Bell, Bernard W., 178
Bell, Derrick, 3–5, 8, 13–14, 19, 115, 178
Belles, The (Clayton), 106–8, 222n16
Beloved (Morrison), 178
Beverly Tucker, Nathaniel, 164–65, 211
biodome, 191–99
biopower, 83, 134–40
Bird Is Gone, The (Jones), 53–54, 69
Blacker the Berry, The (Thurman), 104, 224n7
blackface minstrelsy, 144–45, 176–77
Black hair discrimination, 30, 102, 107, 169, 172, 224nn5–6
Black in Time (Jakes), 42–47
Black Like Me (Griffin), 207

Black Lives Matter (BLM) movement, 10, 88–100, 221n3
Blackness, 13–14, 25–27, 35, 38–44, 48, 84, 88–101, 130, 140, 149, 157–59. *See also* science-fictional blackness
Black No More (Schuyler), 104, 176–77, 206, 224n8
"BLACKout" (Robinson), 88–90
Black Power movement, 24–25, 27
Black progress, radicalized reactions to, 93–100
Black social death, 84, 95
Black stereotypes, 41–42, 98,117, 165–67, 171, 190–91
"Black to the Future" (Dery), 6, 128–29
Black uprising, white fears of, 167–68, 174–75
blood magic, 100, 106
Bloodmarked (Deonn), 98–100
Bluest Eye, The (Morrison), 100
Bonilla-Silva, Eduardo, 14, 40
Book of Phoenix, The (Okorafor), 126, 151–52
Bould, Mark, 26, 126, 222n8
Bradbury, Ray, 66
brain implants, 58–59. *See also* cybernetic implants
Bring the Jubilee (Moore), 210
Browder v. Gayle, 7
Brown Girl in the Ring (Hopkinson), 150
Brown v. Board of Education, 7–8, 19, 58
"*Brown v. Board of Education* and the Interest Convergence Dilemma" (Bell), 8
Bug Jack Barron (Spinrad), 42, 222n17
Burroughs, Edgar Rice, 161, 205
Butler, Octavia E., 1, 13, 16, 23, 25, 85, 125–26, 145–47, 178, 210, 224n17

Cadigan, Pat, 131, 225n8
Campbell, Bill, 104–6, 217–18
Campbell, John W. Jr., 26, 35, 142
capitalism, discontent with, 126–28, 134–41, 149, 151
Chang, Robert S., 60
Charleston, South Carolina church shooting, 94
Chinese Exclusion Act of 1882, 66
Christian nationalism, 105, 109–16
Chude-Sokei, Louis, 124
Chun, Wendy Hui Kyong, 134
citizenship, 73: suspension of, 59–70, 134–38, 216
City We Became, The (Jemisin), 117–20
Civil Rights Act of 1964, 32, 141
Civil Rights Act of 1968, 141
civil rights movement, 5, 7, 13, 23–24, 27–36; cooption of by whites, 94
Civil War, American 44–47, 49–50, 205, 210–11
Clark, P. Djèlí, 10, 211, 217
Clayton, Dhonielle, 106–8, 222n17
climate change, 2, 13, 38, 74, 81, 83, 184–87, 193, 199
Cline, Ernest, 133–34, 225n10
clones, 148–49
Clute, John, 160
cognitive estrangement, 2, 177, 227n11
Collins, Addie May, 32
colonialism, 156, 160, 174–75, 211; settler, 53–57; trauma of, 219
Colonialism and the Emergence of Science Fiction (Rieder), 211
colonization, 36–37; narratives of failed colonization, 174–75
colorblindness, 8–9, 12, 15, 35, 38–43, 47, 89, 95, 97, 111, 124, 127–29, 131–32, 136–38, 155, 159, 163, 166, 170, 181, 192, 190, 200, 219; counteraction of, 93
colorism, 30–31, 87, 100–108, 176, 182–83, 205. *See also* internalized racism and skin color
color line. *See* segregation
concentration camps, 20–22, 56, 59, 62, 64–70, 72, 216
confinement narratives, 49–85
contagion, 79–83
corporeality, 128, 130–34
counternarratives, 2, 9–10, 54, 57, 68, 83, 90, 96–100, 118, 138, 154, 176–201
Crack in Space, A (Dick), 26, 36–38
Crenshaw, Kimberlé, 7, 14
Creole rebellion (1841), 189, 226n1
crime, 14, 71, 101, 135, 145
criminality, 3, 53, 96, 128
criminal justice system, 136–38. *See also* mass incarceration
Critical Race Theory (Crenshaw, et. al.), 7
Crown of Infinity (Faucette), 26, 222n7
cryogenics, 36–37
cultural fugue, 143

culture wars, 109–16
cyberfunk, 13, 140–55
cybernetic implants, 125–26, 134, 142–43, 146, 148–49
cyberpunk, 13, 51, 123–55, 225nn3–4; white and male, 130–34, 147
cyberspace, 128–34, 146, 148–49
"Cyborg Manifesto" (Haraway), 146
cyborgs, 123–25, 128, 145–56, 147–49, 151–52; as representations of mixed-race people, 131; terminology, 140–42

Dark Matter (Thomas), 217
Davis, Kimberly C., 193–94, 200
Davis, Milton J., 126–27
Davis, Thulani, 25–26, 39
Deathless Divide (Ireland), 49–51
DeGraw, Sharon, 26, 30
dehumanization, 61–70, 79–85, 116–20, 123–40, 152–54, 166–67, 172, 215–16
Delany, Samuel, 9, 12–13, 19–20, 24–36, 47, 87, 125–26, 128–29, 142–43, 145, 147, 152, 157–59, 191, 203–6, 222nn9–10, 226n13
Delgado, Richard, 2, 14
DeMille, James, 161
Deonn, Tracy, 98–100
deportation, 102, 216
Dery, Mark, 6, 128–29, 158
detention. *See* internment
Dhalgren (Delany), 19
Dick, Philip K., 19, 26, 36–38, 47, 210–11
digital divide, 128, 154
Dillon, Grace L., 57
Dimaline, Cherie, 211–13, 217
disability, 58, 113–16; manufactured, 23
disenfranchisement, 66, 102
diversity, 10–11; illusion of, 19; lack of, 147; intolerance of, 35, 41, 109–17
Dobbs v. Jackson Women's Health Organization, 73
double consciousness, 151, 222n3
Douglass, Fredrick, 44, 46, 142–43, 163, 179–80
Dread Nation (Ireland), 49–51
drugs, 71, 150; war on, 52
Du Bois, W. E. B., 6, 59, 69, 111, 207, 223n3
Due Process Clause, 73
Due, Tananarive, 14
dystopia, 10–11, 20–24, 38, 49–85, 90–94, 101–2, 125–27, 133–40, 148, 150, 160, 210–17

education, 49–50; segregation, of, 19, 32, 58
Elliott, George P., 19–23, 47
Ellison, Ralph, 140–41, 143–45, 152
Emancipation Proclamation, 44–46, 49, 88–89, 124
embodiment, 148–49, 153
Encyclopedia of Science Fiction, The (Clute et. al.), 160
"En Masse" (Mosley), 138–40
environmental catastrophe, 79–83, 184–87
environmental racism, 184–86, 191–99
epidermalization, 151
Equiano, Olaudah, 174, 179–80
Erdrich, Louise, 51, 73–78, 223nn12–13
Erkkila, Betsy, 164–65, 226–27n10
Eshun, Kodwo, 155, 175
estrangement, 2, 5, 159, 208. *See also* cognitive estrangement
ethnic cleansing. *See* genocide
eugenics, 63, 139–40, 153
Everlasting Rose, The (Clayton), 106–8
Executive Order 9066, 59–60

fabricated African presence, 129–30
Fahrenheit 451 (Bradbury), 66
Fanon, Franz, 130, 205
Farnham's Freehold (Heinlein), 26, 221n6
Farooq, Nihad N., 189
Fatherland (Harris), 211
Faucette, John M. Jr., 26, 222n7
fertility crisis, 73–74
Fifteenth Amendment, 49, 141
Fiorelli, Julie A., 184, 193, 195, 200
Firedance (Barnes), 147–49
First Amendment, 73–74
first contact trope. *See* alien contact trope
Floyd, George, 86–87
Folsom, Bob, 32
forced removal, 53–58
Foster, Thomas, 142–43, 226n13
Foucault, Michel, 83
Fourteenth Amendment, 49, 58, 73
Freedman, Carl, 25
freedom riders, 31–32
Fugitive Slave Act of 1850, 46
fugitivity, 184–91

Future Home of the Living God (Erdrich), 73–79, 223n12
Futureland (Mosley) 125–26, 134–40

Gaines, Ernest J., 178
gaming, 133–34
Gardner, Jared, 165, 171
gender, 117–20, 133–34
genetic engineering, 148, 151–52
genetic research on BIPOC, 13, 51, 116, 151
genocide, 21–22, 28, 34–36, 54, 57, 59–64, 79–85, 136–40, 199, 212
Gernsback, Hugo, 161
Get Out (Peele), 206
ghetto, 70–72
Gibson, William, 125, 128–31, 142–43, 145–49, 148, 153, 158, 225n8, 226n13
Giddings, Megan, 100–101
Gilroy, Paul, 131
Goddu, Teresa, 163–64, 171–72
Goeman, Mishuana, 55
"Gold-bug, The" (Poe), 166
Gorgon Child (Barnes), 147–49
Gotanda, Neil, 7, 181
Govan, Sandra, 35
Great Sky Woman (Barnes), 149
Greenlee, Sam, 25, 210, 221n2
Greensboro, North Carolina sit-ins of 1960, 31, 222n11
Griffin, John Howard, 207
Guns of the South (Turtledove), 210

hackers/hacking, 128, 139
Haggard, H. Rider, 156, 178, 205–6
Handmaid's Tale, The (Atwood), 74
Hannah-Jones, Nikole, 159
Harris, Robert, 211
"Harrison Bergeron" (Vonnegut), 22–24
Havard, John C., 163, 171
Hayles, N. Katherine, 130, 225n6
Heinlein, Robert A., 26, 221n6
Heller, Andrew J., 210
Henning, Kristin, 87
Heth, Joice, 123–24
Hines, Alicia, 154
Hollinger, Veronica, 128
Holmesburg Prison, 52
Holocaust, references to, 29, 61–63, 67
homo sacer, 61–64
Hood, James, 32
hoodoo, 144–45
"Hop-Frog" (Poe), 167
Hopkinson, Nalo, 9, 145, 150, 218–19
Hopkins, Pauline E., 178
Hughes, Langston, 42–43, 64

identity politics, 24–27, 35, 88–90, 115, 153–54
If the North Had Won the War (Heller), 210
"I Have a Dream" (King), 32
immigration, 63–65, 68–70, 214–16
Immigration Act of 1924, 66
Immigration and Customs Enforcement (ICE), 63, 69, 216
Incidents in the Life of a Slave Girl (Jacobs), 125, 227n15
Indian boarding schools, 13, 50, 62, 212
Indian Removal Act, 56
indigeneity, 55–57
Ink (Vourvoulias), 69–70, 215–16
integration, social, 19, 32, 131–32, 180
interest convergence, 4, 8–9, 50, 55, 90, 105
Interesting Narrative of the Life of Olaudah Equiano, or Gustavus Vassa, the African, Written by Himself, The (Equiano), 179–80
internalized racism, 21, 102–4, 106–7, 152, 174, 181–83. *See also* colorism and skin color
internment, 13, 55–72, 102, 215–16; women's medical, 73–79
Internment (Ahmed), 65–69
interracial relationships, 28, 33, 37, 41–42, 45
invasion, 191–99
Invisible Man (Ellison), 140–42
Ireland, Justina, 10, 49–51
Islam, 44–45
Islamophobia, 65–69, 110
Islands in the Net (Sterling), 149, 225nn7–8
It Can't Happen Here (Lewis), 208–9

Jacobs, Harriet, 125, 152, 180
Jakes, John 19, 42–47
January 6, 2021 failed coup, 16, 63–64, 73, 109, 207–8
Japanese-Americans, internment of 59–64, 66
Jefferson, Thomas, 123, 155, 166–67, 169
Jemisin, N. K., 10–12, 117–20, 145, 152–54, 219–20

Jerng, Mark C., 48
Jim Crow era, 21–22, 49, 89–90, 159
Johnson, Lyndon B., 32, 141
Johnson, Mat, 13, 156–57, 176–201
Jones, Stephen Graham, 51, 53–59, 69
Journey to the Center of the Earth (Verne), 177

Karens, 117–20, 224n11, 225n12
Kelley, William Melvin, 25, 221n3
Kendi, Ibram X., 101
Kennedy, J. Gerald, 165–66, 169–70, 174, 226–27n10
Kennedy, John F., 31–32, 141
Kilgore, DeWitt, 135
Kim, Myungsung, 144
Kindred (Butler), 178
King, Martin Luther Jr., 32, 64, 89
King, Rodney, 64, 91–93
King Solomon's Mines (Haggard), 178
Koontown Killing Kaper (Campbell), 104–6, 218
Korematsu v. United States, 65–66

Lacks, Henrietta, 101
Lakewood (Giddings), 100–101
Land That Time Forget, The (Burroughs) 161
Lang, Cady, 117
LA Riots of 1992, 90–92
Lathe of Heaven, The (Le Guin), 38–42
Left Hand of Darkness, The (Le Guin), 189
Legendborn (Deon), 98–100
Le Guin, Ursula K., 10–11, 20, 38–42, 47, 189
Lewis, John, 31, 68, 93
Lewis, Sinclair, 16, 208–9
Life and Times of Frederick Douglass, The (Douglass), 46
Lillvis, Kristen, 149
Lincoln, Abraham, 44–45, 49, 116, 124
Lind, William F., 109–12, 116, 209
literacy, 142–43
literary canon, white and male, 133, 157, 162
"Little Brother" (Mosley), 136–37
Lock In (Scalzi), 112–15, 117
lost race tales, 13, 156–201, 205
lost world narratives, 160–61, 177–78
Lott, Eric, 123
Lovecraft, H. P., 156, 161, 206
Loving v. Virginia, 7, 222n10

Ma, Ling, 213–17
Malone, Vivian, 32
Man in the High Castle, The (Dick), 210–11
"Man That Was Used Up, The" (Poe), 166
Manzanar War Relocation Center (California), 59, 61–63, 65–66
March on Washington for Jobs and Freedom (1963), 32
Marotta, Melanie, 82
Marrow Thieves, The (Dimaline), 211–13
Martin, Trayvon, 87, 98, 221n3
mass incarceration, 3, 12–13, 37–38, 51–53, 59, 63, 67–68, 91, 93–94, 102–3, 106, 134–40, 167
Matsuda, Mari J., 60
Maus, Derek C., 137
McEvoy, Seth, 25
McIntosh, Peggy, 4
McNair, Denise, 32
medical experimentation, 9, 13, 15, 51–53, 72, 81–83, 100–101, 105–6, 116, 138, 142–43, 151
megatexts, 176–84
memes, 117–18
Meredith, James, 32
Merla-Watson, Cathryn Josefina, 216
microchipping, 92. *See also* cybernetic implants
Midnight Robber (Hopkinson), 150
Minch-de Leon, Mark, 177
Mind of My Mind (Butler), 125, 146
Mirrorshades (Sterling), 150
mixed-race people/characters. *See* multiracial people/characters
Miyake, Perry, 59–61, 64, 69
model minority myth, 60–61
Mohammad, 44–45
Mona Lisa Overdrive (Gibson), 145
Moore, Ward, 210
Morrison, Toni, 5–6, 100, 129, 158, 162–63, 169, 175, 178, 227n17
Morton, Samuel George, 170, 173
Mosley, Walter, 125–26, 134–40, 225n11
motherhood, 73–79
Mothership (Campbell and Hall), 218
Moynihan Report (1965), 106
multiracial people/characters, 28, 30, 32, 38–42, 131–32, 146, 156–57, 167, 170–72, 175–85, 198–99, 227n16
Mumbo Jumbo (Reed), 143–45, 176–77

"Murders in the Rue Morgue, The" (Poe), 166–67
Muslim ban, 66–67. *See also* Islamophobia
My Bondage and My Freedom (Douglass), 46

Narrative of Arthur Gordon Pym of Nantucket, The (Poe), 13, 156–201
Narrative of the Life of Frederick Douglass, The (Douglass), 46, 179
National Association for the Advancement of Colored People (NAACP), 7, 19–20
native survivance, 57, 79, 212–13
Nat Turner rebellion, 45, 167–68, 226–27n10
Nazis/neo-Nazis, 65
near future, 2, 13–14, 43, 58–59, 65, 69–70, 73, 104, 109, 133, 162, 207, 211–17
Nebula Awards, 19, 27
"Negro Speaks of Rivers, The" (Hughes), 42–43
Nelson, Alondra, 128, 145, 154
Nelson, Dana D., 164–65, 173
Neo-slave narrative genre, 157, 159, 178–91
Neuromancer (Gibson), 125, 128–30, 142, 146–49, 158, 225n8, 226n13
New Orleans, Louisiana, 79–83, 101–2, 106–8
"Nig in Me, The" (Mosley), 138–40
9/11, 64–65, 76
Nishime, LeiLani, 131
North and South trilogy (Jakes), 42, 222n18
Northup, Solomon, 180
Notes on the State of Virginia (Jefferson), 123, 155, 167, 169
Nott, Josiah, 172
Nova (Delany), 26, 142
"NRACP, The" (Elliott), 20–22
nuclear war, 139–40, 143

Obama, Barack, 93–94, 159
Of One Blood (Hopkins) 178
Okorafor, Nnedi, 126, 145, 150–52, 226n18
Olney, James, 179
one-drop rule, 100, 140, 172, 176
"Ones Who Stayed and Fought, The" (Jemisin), 10–11
"Ones Who Walk Away from Omelas, The" (Le Guin), 10–11
Onyebuchi, Tochi, 10, 90–94
Orleans (Smith), 79–83
Otherness, racial, 124–25, 133
overpopulation, 36–39

Page Act of 1875, 66
pandemics, 79–83, 112–16, 148
Parable of the Sower (Butler), 209
Parable of the Talents (Butler), 209
parallel earth, 36–38
Partisan Leader, The (Tucker), 165, 211
passing, racial, 31, 100, 104, 130–31, 139, 157, 176–84, 198
Patriot Act of 2001, 75–77
"Paulding-Drayton Review," 164–65
Peele, Jordan, 206
Playing in the Dark (Morrison), 162, 227n17
Plessy v. Ferguson, 7, 140
Plot Against America, The (Roth), 209
Poe, Edgar Allan, 13, 156–201, 227n17; racism of, 163–76
police brutality, 77–78, 86–87, 91–95, 99, 101–3
policing, 13, 51, 77–78, 86–87, 91–95, 99, 103, 106, 117–18
"Positive Obsession" (Butler), 1
post-apocalyptic world, 79–83, 139–40, 152–52, 191–99
post-humanism/post-human, 112–17, 124–25, 131–32, 144–149
post-racial future, 128, 130–32, 136–37, 191–99
poverty, 37, 71, 83, 125, 134–40, 154
"Predicament, A" (Poe), 166
pregnancy, coerced, 74–79
Prince, Mary, 180
Princess of Mars, A (Burroughs), 205
prison. *See* mass incarceration
pseudoscience, 123, 160, 170–71
Pym (Johnson), 156–201

quarantine, 79–83

Rabid Puppies. *See* Sad/Rabid Puppies
race-less future, 22–24, 127, 193–94. *See also* post-racial future
race, social construction of, 130–32, 170, 177, 181–84
race war, 42–47, 142
racial history, inclusion of, 134–38; disavowal of, 132

racialization, 4–6, 8, 12, 35, 38–48, 56–57, 60, 65, 120, 130, 134–40, 171–74
racial profiling, 13, 86, 90–94, 102, 118
racial science, 170–71, 176, 227n18. *See also* pseudoscience
racism, institutional, 21, 31, 115–16, 124, 127; structural, 16, 21, 93, 103, 108, 140, 164
"Racism and Science Fiction" (Delany), 26, 87, 159
racism in science fiction, 24–27, 130–34
Ramírez, Catherine S., 217
Ready Player One (Cline), 133–34, 225n10
"Recitatif" (Morrison), 5–6
Reed, Ishmael, 143–45, 176–77
"Reluctant Ambassador from the Planet of Midnight, A" (Hopkinson), 219
removal and relocation, 54–69
reparations for slavery, 88–90
replacement theory, 209
resistance, 67–68, 74–79, 90–100, 136–40
revenge, 90–94
Rieder, John, 161, 211
Ring Shout (Clark), 211
Riot Baby (Onyebuchi), 90–94
Robertson, Carole, 32
Robinson, Jill, 88–90
Roe v. Wade, 63–64, 67, 73
Rokeby Venus (Velázquez), 96
Roof, Dylan, 94
Roosevelt, Franklin D., 59, 209–10
Rosarium Publishing, 218
Rosenthal, Bernard, 164–65
Roth, Philip, 16, 210
Rothstein, Richard, 20
Rowe, John C., 164, 168, 171, 226–27n10
Rubens, Peter Paul, 96
Ruffin, Maurice Carlos, 101–4, 206–7
Rushdy, Ashraf H. A., 178

Sad/Rabid Puppies, 109, 208, 218
Sanchez-Taylor, Joy, 69, 177
satire, 20–22, 104, 145, 157–59, 176–201
Saunders, Charles, 25
Scalzi, John, 112–15, 117
school-to-prison pipeline, 94, 106
Schuyler, George S., 104, 176–77, 206, 224n8
science-fictional Blackness, 5, 87, 101, 158, 169
scientific racism, 13, 51, 83–84, 173
Scottsboro Boys, 167
Second Amendment, 110
Seed, David, 161
Seed to Harvest (Butler), 146
segregation, 5–7, 20–22, 31–33, 37, 40, 47–49, 55–72, 80, 82, 104, 111, 140–41, 154, 198, 227nn17–18. *See also* Jim Crow era
separate-but-equal doctrine, 7, 21, 72
"Separation Anxiety" (Shockley), 70–71
"Serving Two Masters" (Bell), 19
Severance (Ma), 213–16
SF megatext, 158, 160–63, 177
Shadow Valley (Barnes), 149
Shawl, Nisi, 14, 134
She (Haggard), 178, 205
Shelley v. Kramer, 7
Shockley, Evie, 70–72
Siepak, Julia, 74–75
Simal González, Begoña, 61
Sims, J. Marion, 72
16th Street Baptist Church bombing (1963), 32
skin color, 149–51, 157, 159, 169–72, 177, 182–84, 190, 200, 224n8. *See also* colorism and internalized racism
slave narratives, 46, 125, 142, 178–79
slavery, 44–47, 49, 52–53, 82, 84, 88–90, 116, 123–25, 136, 138, 141–43, 148, 159, 165–67, 175, 184–91; and race, 171–72
slaves as machines, 123–25, 141
Smith, Sherri L., 79–83
Smith v. Allwright, 7
Snow Crash (Stephenson), 131–32, 147, 225n8
social death, 84, 95, 159, 216
social justice, 13, 88–94, 134–40
Sohn, Stephen Hong, 60, 215
Solomon, Rivers, 10
Souls of Black Folk, The (Du Bois), 207, 223n3
Southern Literary Messenger, 164–65
"Space Traders, The" (Bell), 3–5
Spillers, Hortense J., 85
Spinrad, Norman, 42, 222n17
Sponsler, Claire, 148
Spook Who Sat by the Door, The (Greenlee), 210
Stars in My Pocket Like Grains of Sand (Delany), 142–43, 226n13

Stefancic, Jean, 14
Stephenson, Neal, 131–32, 147, 225n8
sterilization, 63, 69, 216
Sterling, Bruce, 131, 150, 225nn7–8
Stone Sky, The (Jemisin), 219
Stowe, Harriet Beecher, 44, 46, 182, 222–23n19
Strange Manuscript Found in a Copper Cylinder, A (DeMille), 161
Streetlethal (Barnes), 51, 125, 147–48
Supreme Court, U.S., 5, 7, 27–36, 66, 73
surveillance, 13, 51, 66, 71–72, 74–79, 92, 117–20, 216, 226n18
Suvin, Darko, 3, 177
Symzonia (Seaborn), 161

Tate, Greg, 5–6, 25–26
Taylor, Breonna, 86–87, 98
technoculture, 15, 126–41, 145, 152–54
techno-Orientalism, 60, 215, 223n5
terrorism, white, 31–32, 109–16
Thiong'o, Ngũgĩ wa, 206
Thirteenth Amendment, 47, 49
Thomas, Ebony Elizabeth, 2, 80
Thomas, Sheree Renée, 10, 217–18
Thurman, Wallace, 104, 224n7
Till, Emmett, 87, 98, 167
time travel trope, 2–3, 42–47
Titian, 96
Toliver, S. R., 81
total surround, 87, 159, 205–6
transatlantic slave trade, 44–47
transhistorical feedback loop, 158, 170, 175, 178
Truman, Harry S., 21
Trump, Donald J., 66–67, 73, 87, 208, 216
Tucker, Jeffrey A., 25, 27, 31
Turing test, 130
Turtledove, Harry, 210
Tuskegee Study of Untreated Syphilis in the Negro Male (Tuskegee Experiment), 81–83, 101
Tu, Thuy Linh N., 154
21st Century Manzanar (Miyake), 59, 63–64, 69

Uncle Tom's Cabin (Stowe), 44, 46, 182, 222–23n19
Underground Airlines (Winters), 116–17
University of Alabama, desegregation of, 32
U.S. armed forces, integration of, 21, 131–32
utopia, 10–12, 159–60, 180, 193–96

Väätänen, Päivi, 30, 96, 222n9
"Valedictorian" (Jemisin), 152–54
Velázquez, Diego, 96
"Venus Effect, The" (Allen), 94–98
Venus in front of the Mirror (Rubens), 96
Venus with a Mirror (Titian), 96
Verne, Jules, 156, 161–62, 177
victimhood, weaponization of, 117–20
Victoria (Lind), 109–12, 116, 209
Vint, Sherryl, 215–16
violence, hyperreal, 93–94
virtual reality, 125, 133–34, 225n6
viruses, 136, 139, 143–44, 148
Vizenor, Gerald, 79, 213–14
Vonnegut, Kurt Jr., 19, 22–24, 47
voting rights, 7, 32, 141
Voting Rights Act of 1965, 32, 141
Vourvoulias, Sabrina, 14, 69–70, 215–17

Wallace, George, 32, 99
Washington, Booker T., 45, 111
Washington, Harriet A., 171
wealth inequality, 134–41
We Cast a Shadow (Ruffin), 101–3, 206–7
Weheliye, Alexander G., 9–10
Weinstock, Jeffrey A., 171–74
Wesley, Cynthia, 32
Whalen, Terence, 163–64
Wheeler, Elizabeth A., 80, 184
white gaze, 130–34, 149
white nationalism, 16, 43, 54–69, 208–9
whiteness, 3–5, 14–15, 30, 42, 47, 79, 101, 104, 107, 124, 128–31, 158, 162–90, 194, 200–201, 220, 226–27n10
white privilege, 3–4, 12, 41, 93, 102, 104, 117–20, 124, 126, 131–32, 144, 155, 159, 163–64, 166, 170, 177, 181, 190, 214
white supremacy, 13–15, 32, 35, 42–47, 51, 68, 90–96, 109–17, 124, 131–40, 143, 155, 157–67, 173, 175, 188, 196, 206–8, 210
Who Fears Death (Okorafor), 151
Wiegman, Robin, 172
Wilderson, Frank B. III, 84
Wild Seed (Butler), 146
Wilks, Jennifer M., 180, 182, 186, 195–98, 200

Williams, Apryl, 117
Williams, John A., 25, 221n1
Williams, Robert A. Jr., 55
Wilson, Daniel H., 14, 51, 57–59
Winters, Ben H., 116–17
women's rights, curtailment of, 73–79
workers as machines, 123–25, 141
workers' rights, 134–38
World War II, 59, 63

Yaszek, Lisa, 141
yellow peril fears, 60, 205, 215, 223n4

zombies/zombie apocalypse, 49–50, 213–14

ACKNOWLEDGMENTS

God has seen fit to bless me a third time in my vocation as both a knowledge seeker and creator with this latest effort. I am so incredibly thankful. I recognize the power of words. I also appreciate these are hard words that I have written for some, but necessary words that not everyone has the ears to hear. And so, I will leave it at that.

Only one person sees me on this planet named Earth and I love her above all other human beings, although our sons Kingsley and Frazier are a close second. Our golden-doodle Beignet also gets some love for spending many a night at my feet while I wrote, revised, and revised some more. My sister and brother had a small role to play too in terms of phone conversations. Additionally, my godchildren Zoë and Eli and their parents Toby and Nicole Jenkins helped me through conversation, rest, play, and relaxation.

I have Sherryl Vint and Mark Bould to thank for initially sparking my interest in Critical Race Theory in the aughts when they invited me to write a chapter on Afrofuturism for the *Routledge Companion to Science Fiction* that spun into critical race theory. I don't believe I consciously started to write this book until I knew I was leaving Baton Rouge for Athens when my writing exchange partner, the incomparable Sharon Weltman read and critiqued the earliest version of what became the cyberfunk chapter during the spring of 2019. I had lots of beneficial conversations with my friends and colleagues Mari Kornhauser, Pallavi Rastogi, Michael Bibler, Irina Shport, Bill Demastes, Carl Freedman, and Brannon Costello. I must also thank Lori Leavell of the University of Central Arkansas for reading that early chapter.

When I arrived at the University of Georgia, I found a new writing exchange partner in Becky Hallman Martini and got to work on what I think of as my UGA book. I also have incredibly supportive colleagues who have specifically listened to me talk about the pleasures and challenges of writing this book: Barbara McCaskill, Esra Santesso, Channette Romero, Nate Kreuter, LeAnne Howe, Ro Martini, Lesley Feracho, and David Diamond, as well as Christina Carter, Laurie Norris, and Claire Reed Baeckeroot, in addition to my graduate students Ruth Beard, Chanara Andrews-Bickers, Julia Lindsay, and Hannah Warren. I also want to thank Nicholas Allen and the Willson Center for having the courage to support a CRT book manuscript in the Deep South with a Willson Center Research Fellowship, which gave me an essential teaching break to finish and revise the initial book draft in 2023. Most importantly, I must not forget John Lowe, mentor, friend, and suite mate, who I would often see in the building on Saturdays and Sundays just like myself, where we would discuss everything and anything about life, academia, sports, etc. My wife and I miss that man!

I've had the honor of being invited to places all over the world to give keynote addresses, lectures from this book before, during, and after the pandemic, as well as to participate on panels. I have Mark Hines to thank at the University of Kentucky, Chuck and Paulette Bane at Harding University, Derek Lee at Wake Forest University, Salma Mochtari, Juliette Kernin, and Martin Guinard at LUMA Arles, Daniel Novak at the University of Alabama, Bodhisattva Chattopadhyay at the University of Oslo, Päivi H. Väätänen and Merja Polvinen at the University of Helsinki, GerShun Avilez at the University of Maryland, Lysa Rivera at Western Washington University, M. B. Fernandes of St. Andrew's College of Arts, Science, & Commerce in Mumbai, and Aisha Matthews at the Museum of Science Fiction in Washington, DC. Of special significance to my heart, I'd like to thank the organizers of the 44th International Conference of the Fantastic in the Arts for inviting me as the Distinguished Scholar to provide the keynote address for the conference. I've been a long time IAFA member from my graduate student days and it was a tremendous experience. While I do not attend the Science Fiction Research Association Conference as frequently, this organization and its membership also support my work and I respect it just as much.

Once again, I also owe my thanks to Lisa Yaszek for being a sounding board for a lot of my ideas; to Taryne Jade Taylor for our many zoom conversations; to Graham Murphy my constant ICFA roommate, not to mention friend; to Gerry Canavan for our email conversations regarding administrative duties and SF; to Joy Sanchez-Taylor, now a leading light in her own right; to the wonderful Grace Dillon who encourages us all; to Andrew Butler, Rachel Haywood, and John Rieder, my other editing colleagues at *Extrapolation* not yet mentioned, and the work we put in together; to Bodhi Chattopadhyay who walks the walk; and to my dissertation director Brooks Landon for helping to light the fire. Likewise, my longtime indexer June Pulliam of

LSU needs to be singled out for praise. Further, I feel compelled to thank my two favorite living writers, Chip Delany and Nalo Hopkinson, generous human beings both! Likewise, thanks to the blind reviewers for making this a better book. Finally, Walter Biggins and his team at Penn deserve a shout out for helping to get this book out in the world.

Scholarship doesn't happen in a vacuum, and my audience might notice that roughly a quarter of this book already exists in other guises as book chapters and peer reviewed articles, albeit as early versions or shorter takes. "The *Noirum* in Science Fiction," is a 2,500-word essay on Delany's *The Ballad of Beta-2*, commissioned by LUMA Arles for inclusion in *Realities of Science Fiction* that's forthcoming sometime in 2025 and that represents a small part of the first chapter. An earlier version of a portion of Chapter 3 was published as "Tochi Onyebuchi, *Riot Baby* (2020) / The Hyperreal Violence Loop's Impact on Black Lives Matter," published in *UNEVEN FUTURES: Strategies for Community Survival from Speculative Fiction*, edited by Gerry Canavan, Sean Guynes, and Ida Yoshinaga (MIT Press, 2022, 265–274). Likewise, my book chapter, "Steven Barnes: Black Cyberpunk," first appeared in a modified form in *50 Key Figures in Cyberpunk*, edited by Anna McFarlane, Graham J. Murphy, and Lars Schmeink (Routledge, 2022, 14–19), and represents a tiny section of Chapter 4 as does my chapter "Critical Race Theory," first published in *The Routledge Companion to Cyberpunk Culture*, edited by Anna McFarlane, Graham J. Murphy, and Lars Schmeink (Routledge, 2019, 308–316). Copyright © 2023 Johns Hopkins University Press and Washington State University, the significantly shorter article "'It Was All So White': Mat Johnson's Afrofuturist Retelling of Poe," first appeared in *Poe Studies: History, Theory, Interpretation* 56 (2023): 83–101. A vastly expanded and revised version now exists as Chapter 5. Likewise, an earlier version of the conclusion, "Science Fiction and Racism: Decolonizing the White Problem," was previously published in *Foundation: The International Review of Science Fiction*, no. 139 (2021): 106–120. My thanks to all the editors, publishers, and presses for permission to reprint the content accordingly.

FSC
www.fsc.org
MIX
Papier | Fördert gute Waldnutzung
FSC® C083411

Kolibri 360 GmbH
Ferdinand-Jühlke-Straße 7
99095 Erfurt, Deutschland
produktsicherheit@kolibri360.de